# STOP!

## You may be reading the wrong way!

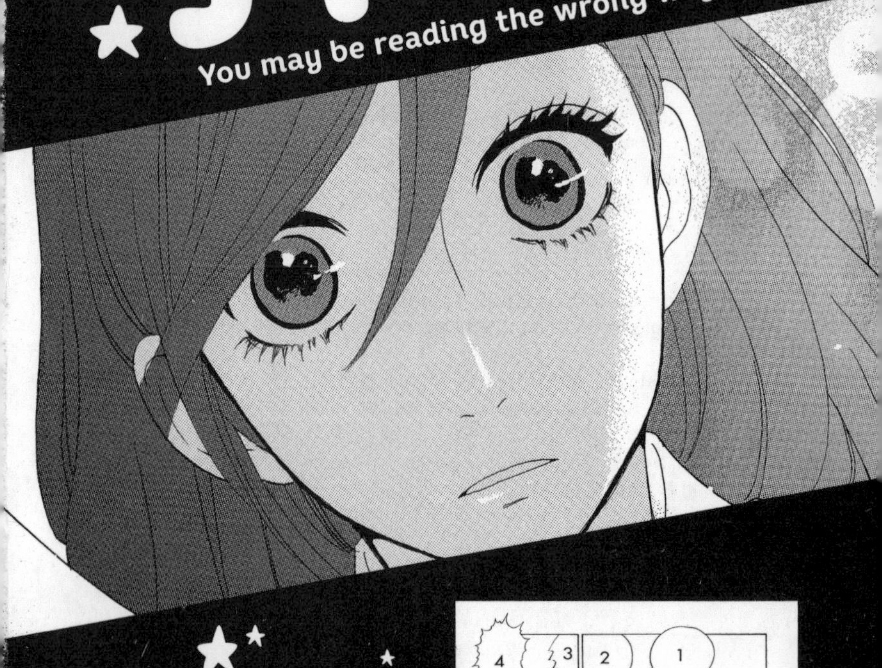

In keeping with the original Japanese comic format, this book reads from right to left—so action, sound effects and word balloons are completely reversed to preserve the orientation of the original artwork.

Check out the diagram shown here to get the hang of things, and then turn to the other side of the book to get started!

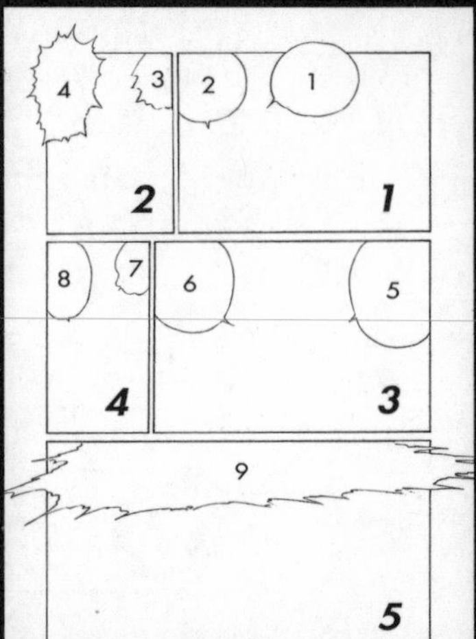
1
2
3
4
1
2
5
6
7
8
3
4
9
5
142

# ★DAYTIME★SHOOTING★STAR★ *11*

## SHOJO BEAT EDITION

Story & Art by
### Mika Yamamori

Translation ★ **JN Productions**
Touch-Up Art & Lettering ★ **Inori Fukuda Trant**
Design ★ **Alice Lewis**
Editor ★ **Karla Clark**

HIRUNAKA NO RYUSEI © 2011 by Mika Yamamori
All rights reserved.
First published in Japan in 2011 by SHUEISHA Inc., Tokyo.
English translation rights arranged by SHUEISHA Inc.

The stories, characters and incidents mentioned in this
publication are entirely fictional.

Printed in the U.S.A.

Published by VIZ Media, LLC
P.O. Box 77010
San Francisco, CA 94107

10 9 8 7 6 5 4 3 2 1
First printing, March 2021

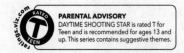

**PARENTAL ADVISORY**
DAYTIME SHOOTING STAR is rated T for
Teen and is recommended for ages 13 and
up. This series contains suggestive themes.

viz.com

shojobeat.com

Shojo Beat

# DAYTIME SHOOTING STAR

Story & Art by
**Mika Yamamori**

**11**

# CONTENTS

## STORY THUS FAR

Suzume Yosano is a second-year in high school. Born in the country, she grew up living a free and easy life. Due to family circumstances, she was forced to transfer to a school in Tokyo. Lost on her first day in the city, she is found by a man who later turns out to be her homeroom teacher, Mr. Shishio. Suzume gradually develops feelings for him, but he ends up breaking her heart—twice.

After Mamura confesses his feelings to Suzume a second time, she loses sleep agonizing over how to respond, but comes to the conclusion that it's best to be honest with him. Throughout their entire friendship, Mamura has always been there for her, so she decides to focus her attention on him.

However, the day before Sports Day, Suzume finds herself alone with Mr. Shishio after volunteering to make pom-poms and headbands. She tries to act nonchalant, but Mr. Shishio embraces her out of the blue. She breaks free and rushes home, but that's not the end of it. The next day, Mr. Shisho tells her he hugged her because he loves her.

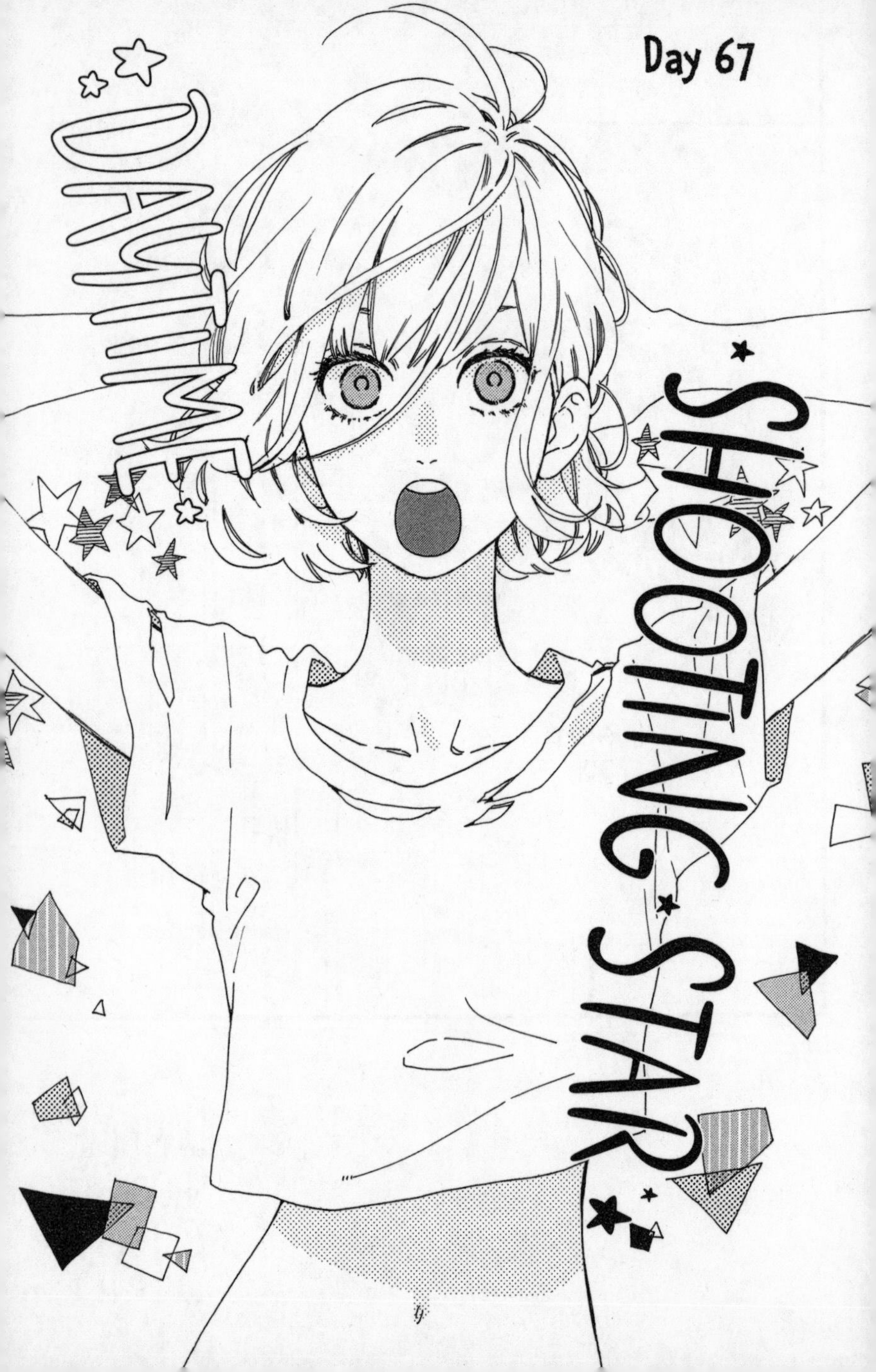
Day 67
DAYTIME
SHOOTING STAR

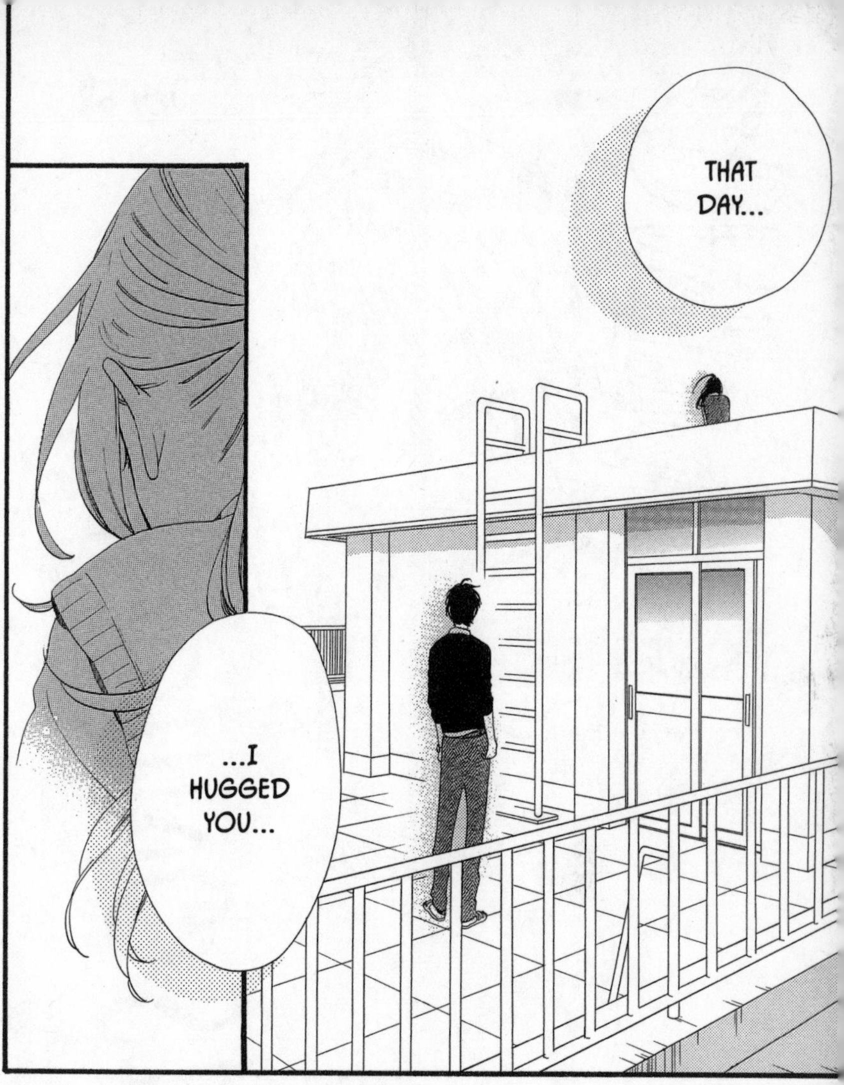
THAT DAY...
...I HUGGED YOU...

DAYTIME SHOOTING STAR

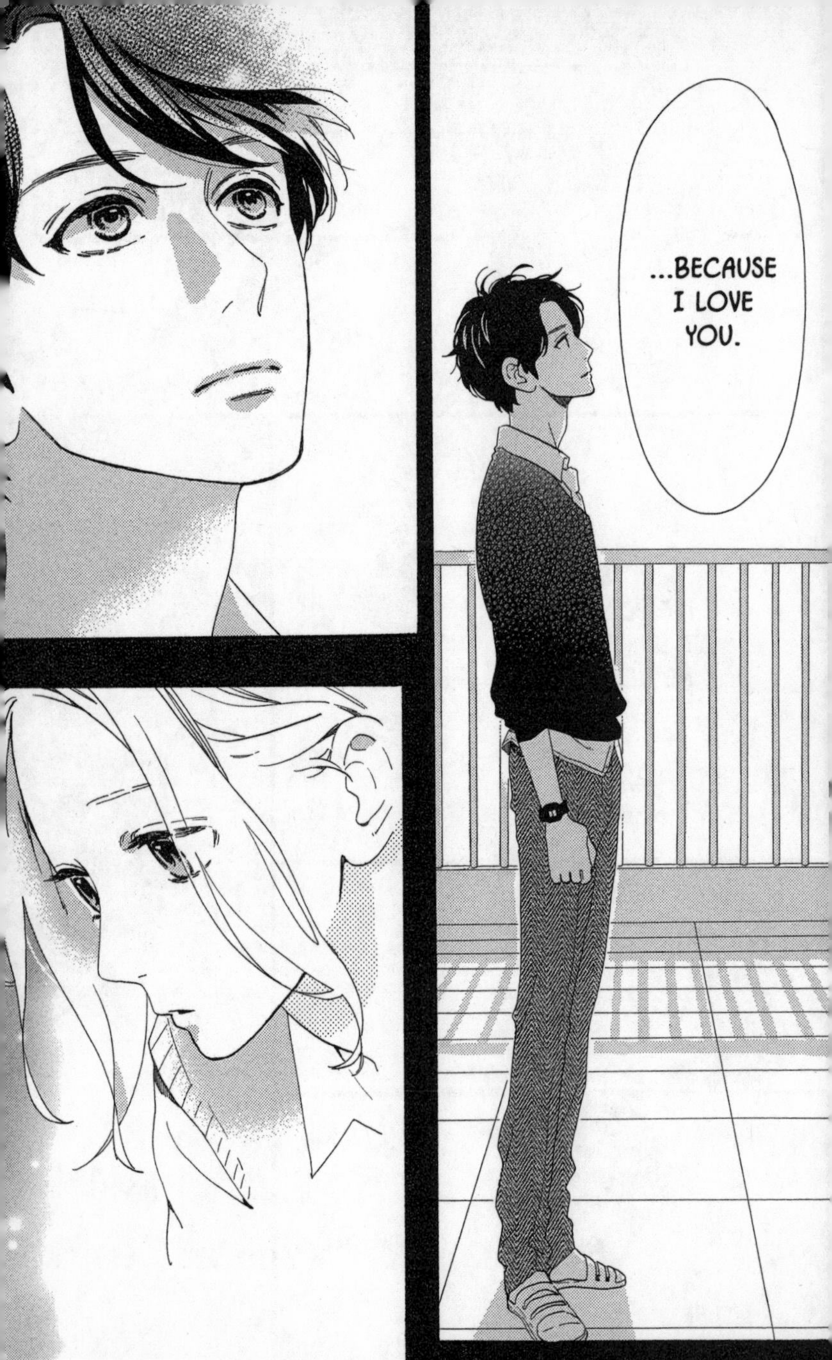
...BECAUSE I LOVE YOU.

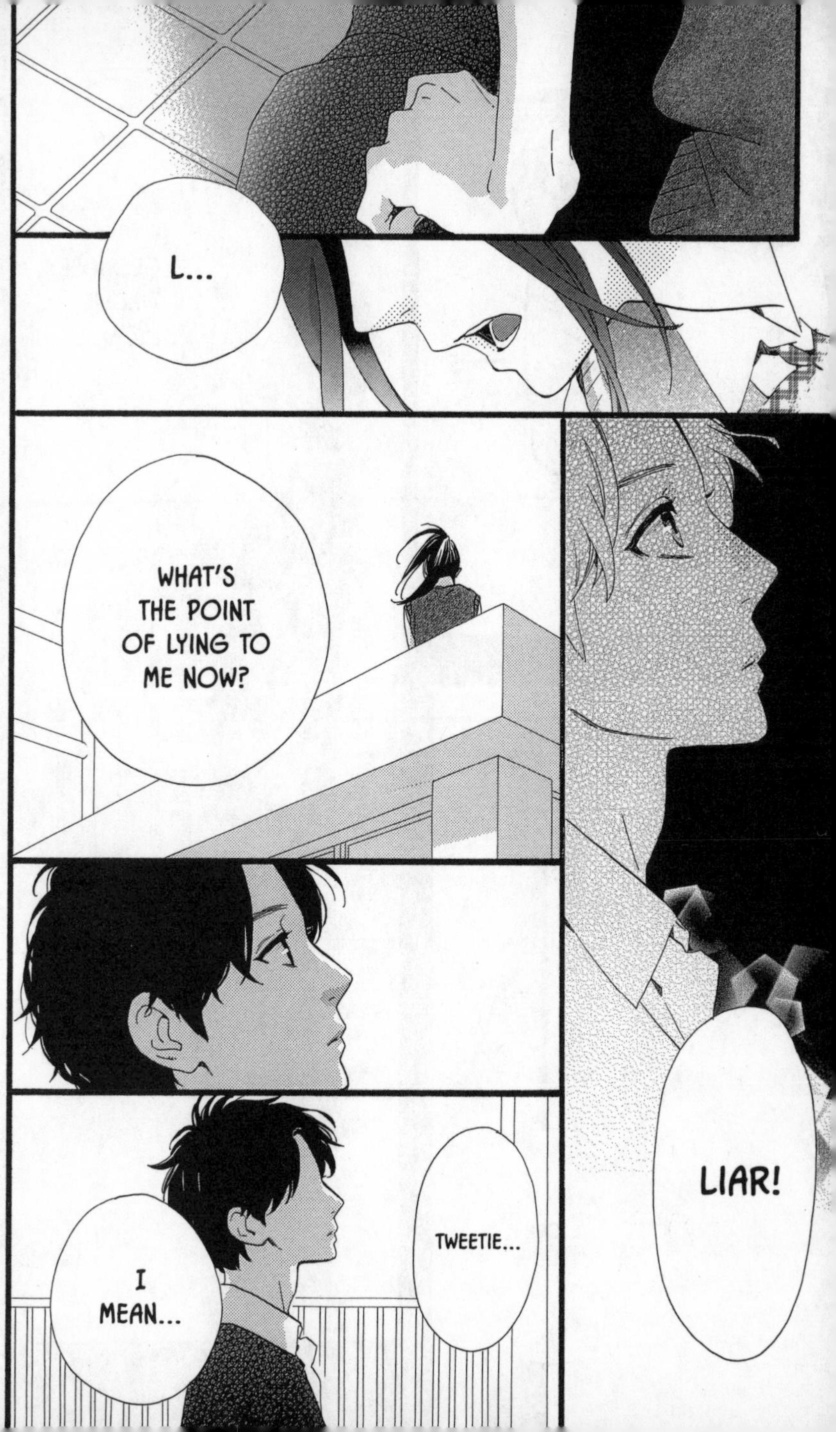

L...
LIAR!
WHAT'S THE POINT OF LYING TO ME NOW?
TWEETIE...
I MEAN...

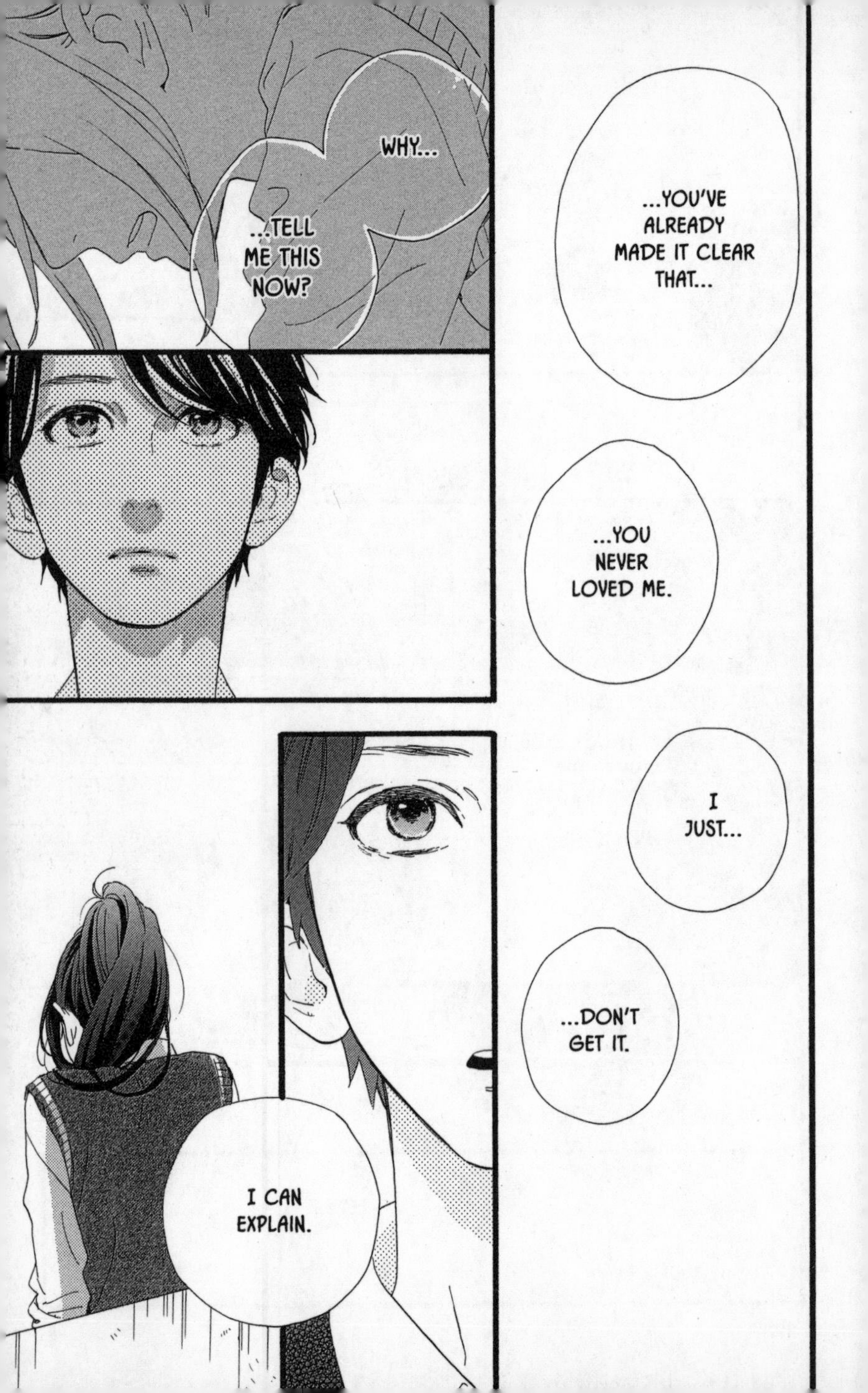
...YOU'VE ALREADY MADE IT CLEAR THAT...
...YOU NEVER LOVED ME.
I JUST...
...DON'T GET IT.
WHY...
...TELL ME THIS NOW?
I CAN EXPLAIN.

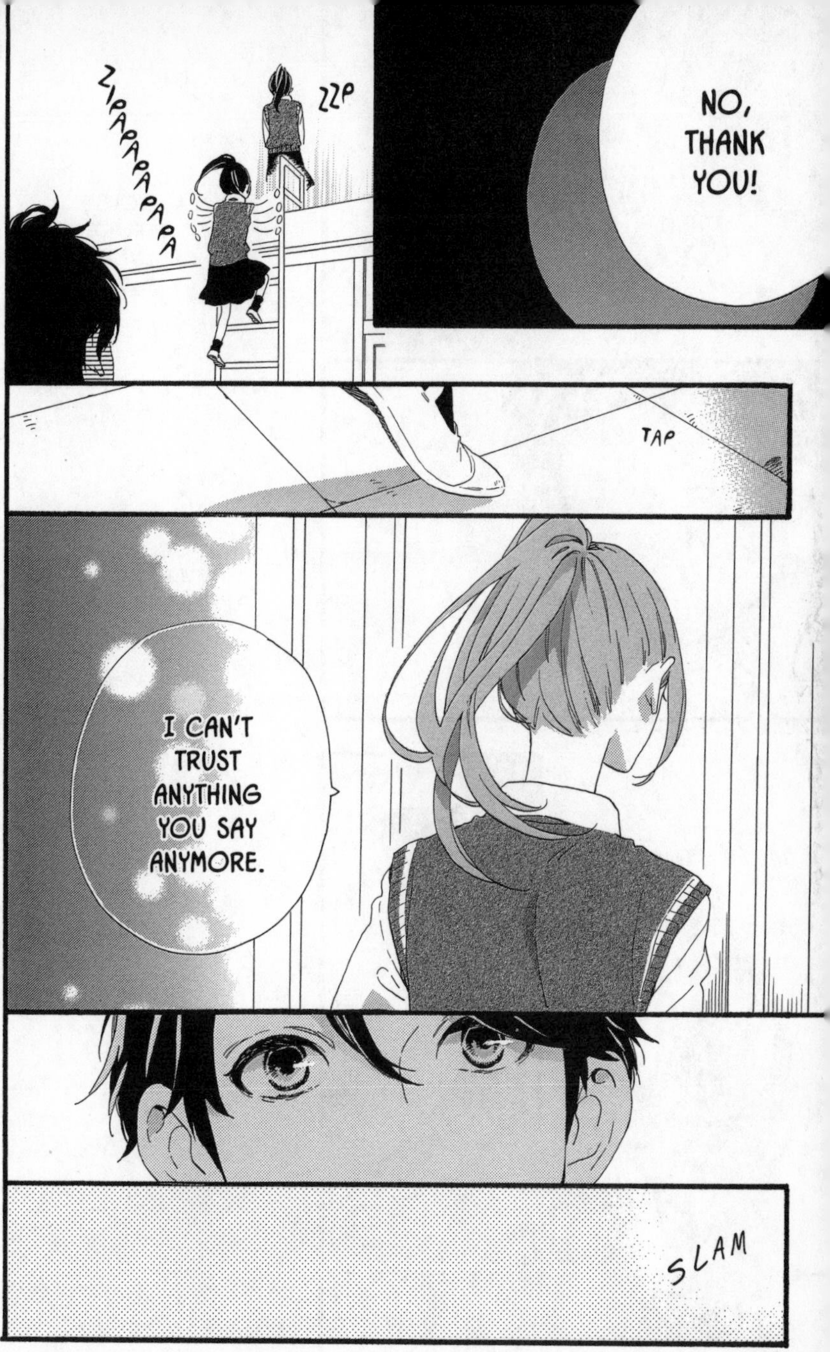
NO, THANK YOU!
ZZP
ZIPAPAPAPAPA
TAP
I CAN'T TRUST ANYTHING YOU SAY ANYMORE.
SLAM

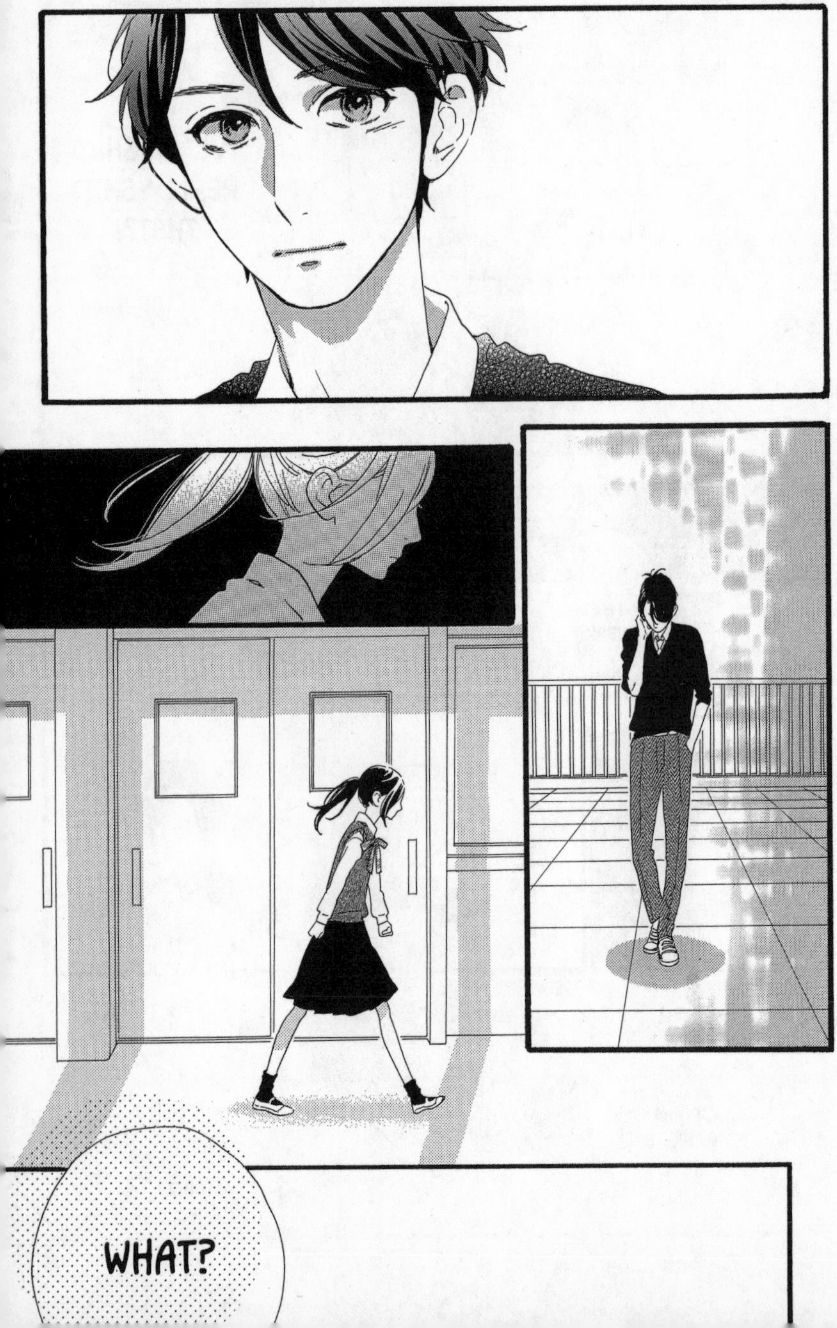
WHAT?

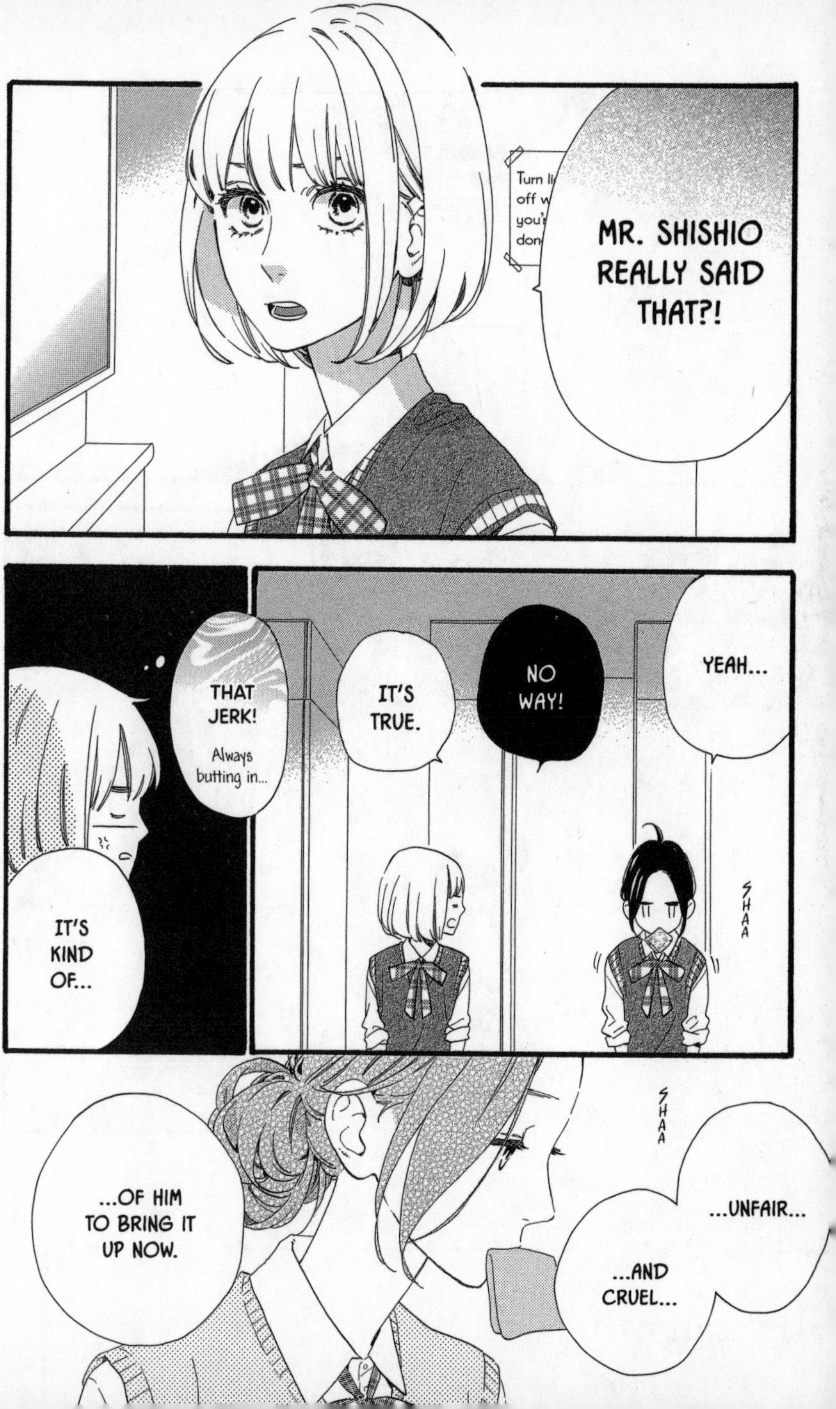
MR. SHISHIO REALLY SAID THAT?!
YEAH...
SHAA
NO WAY!
IT'S TRUE.
THAT JERK!
Always butting in...
IT'S KIND OF...
...UNFAIR...
...AND CRUEL...
SHAA
...OF HIM TO BRING IT UP NOW.

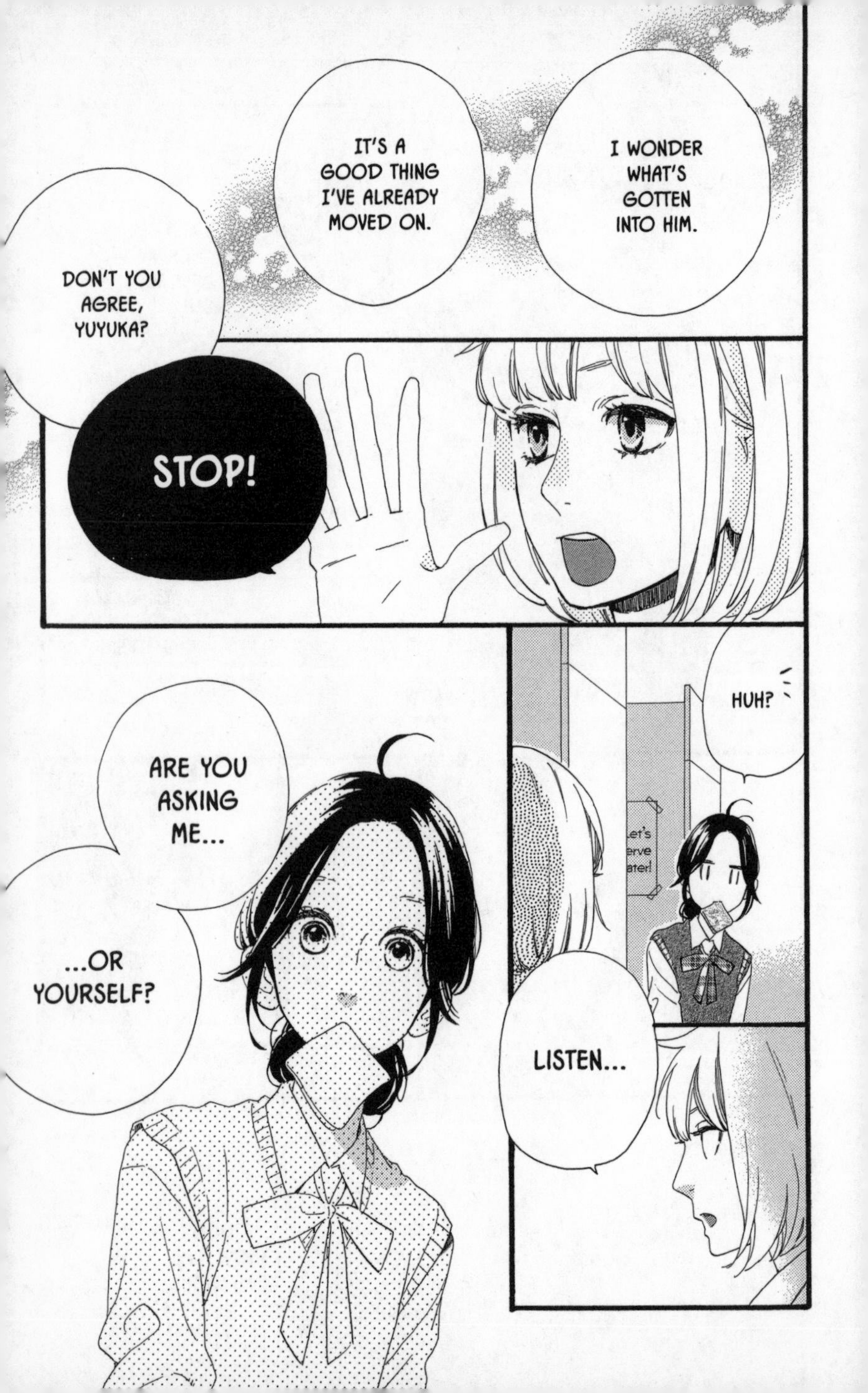
I WONDER WHAT'S GOTTEN INTO HIM.
IT'S A GOOD THING I'VE ALREADY MOVED ON.
DON'T YOU AGREE, YUYUKA?
STOP!
HUH?
LISTEN...
ARE YOU ASKING ME...
...OR YOURSELF?

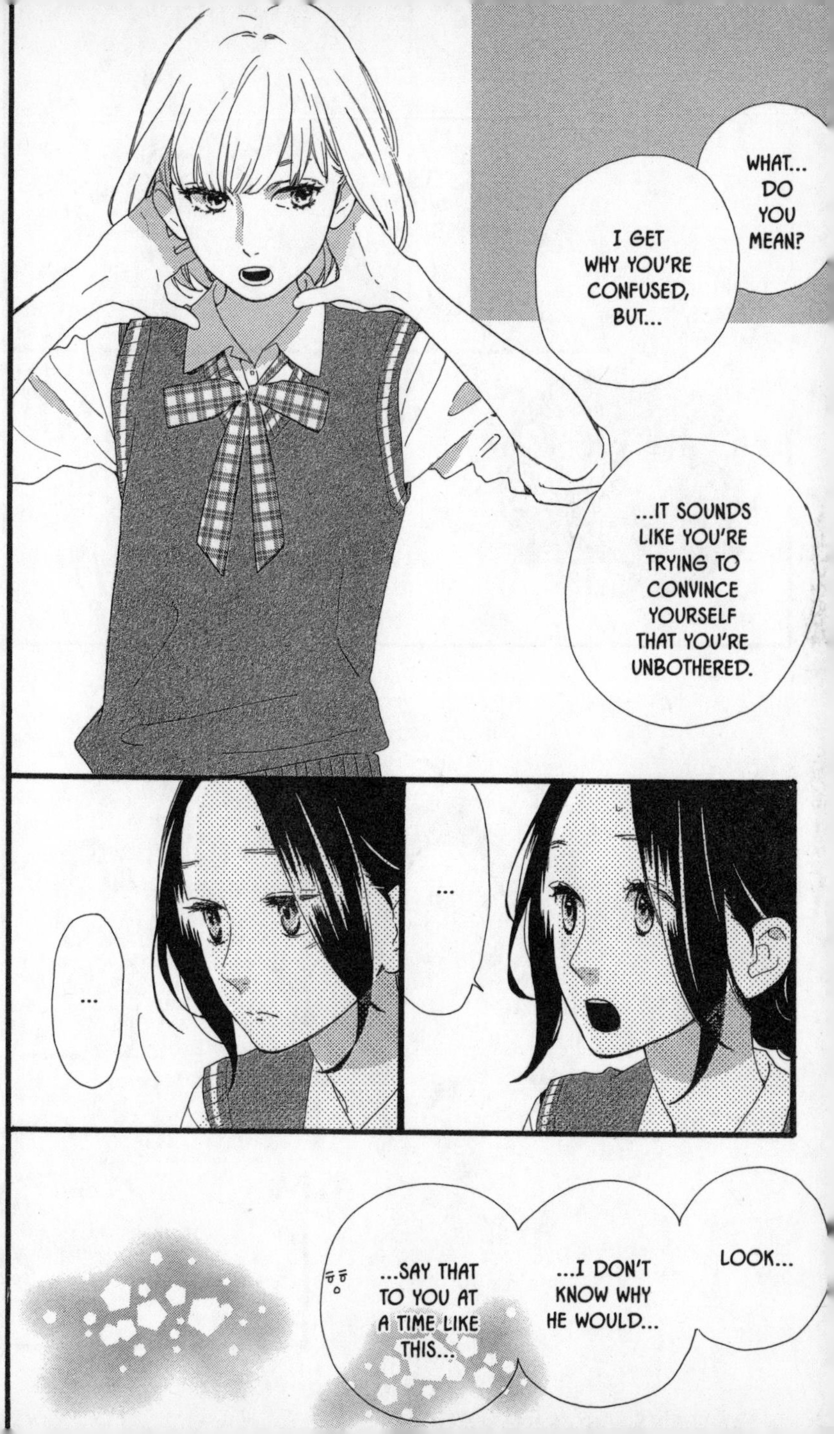
WHAT... DO YOU MEAN?
I GET WHY YOU'RE CONFUSED, BUT...
...IT SOUNDS LIKE YOU'RE TRYING TO CONVINCE YOURSELF THAT YOU'RE UNBOTHERED.
...
...
LOOK...
...I DON'T KNOW WHY HE WOULD...
...SAY THAT TO YOU AT A TIME LIKE THIS...

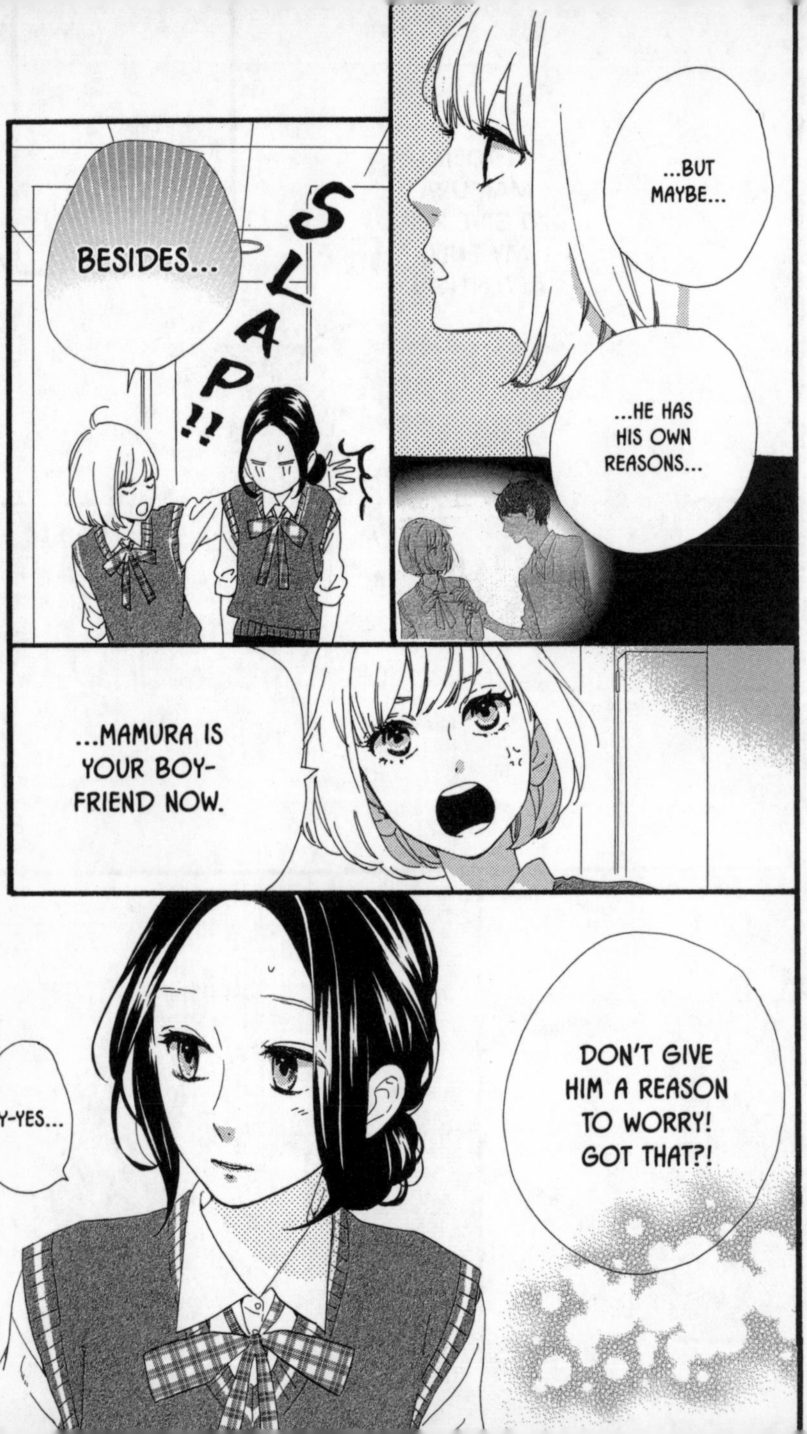
...BUT MAYBE...
...HE HAS HIS OWN REASONS...
BESIDES...
SLAP!!
...MAMURA IS YOUR BOY-FRIEND NOW.
DON'T GIVE HIM A REASON TO WORRY! GOT THAT?!
Y-YES...

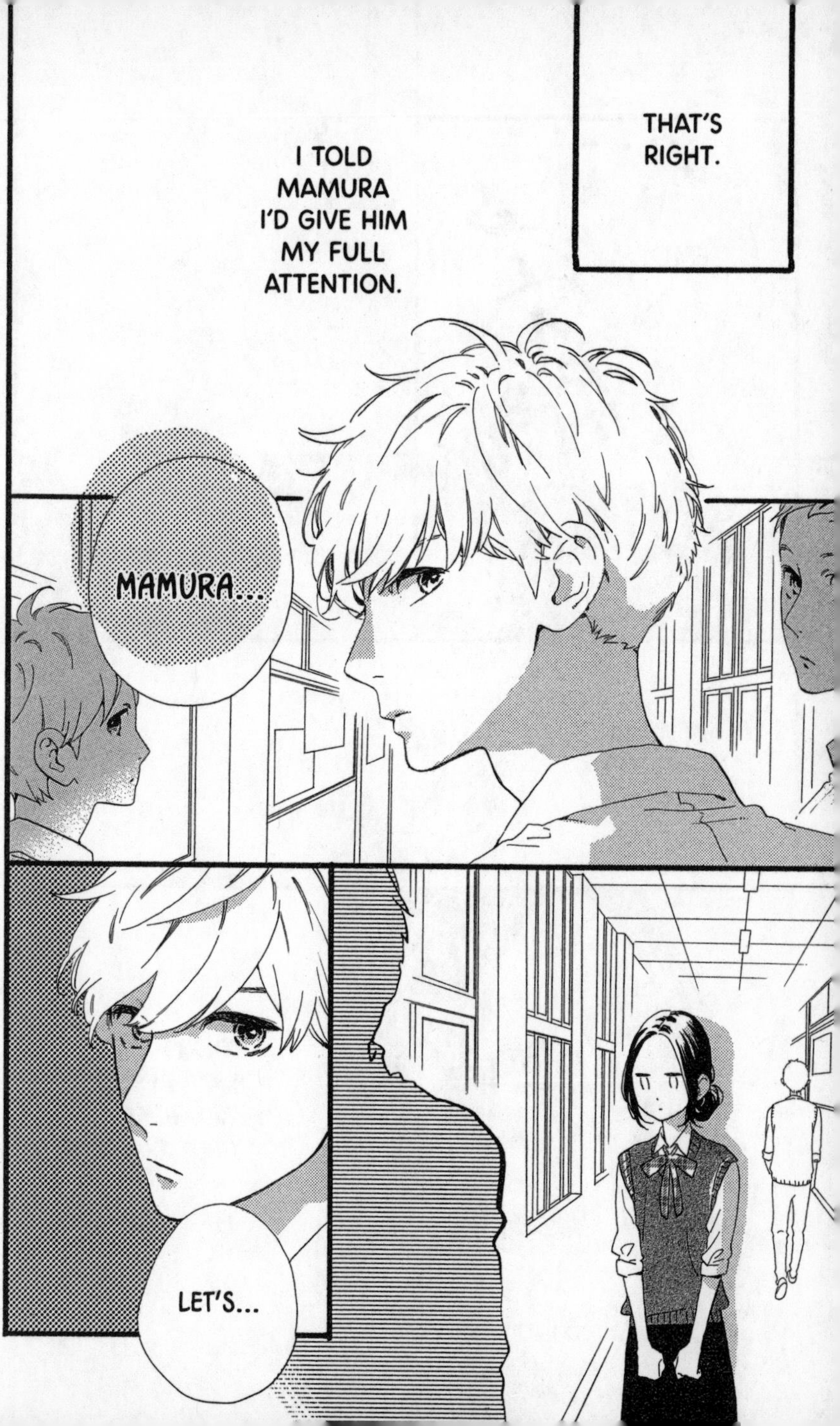
THAT'S RIGHT.
I TOLD MAMURA I'D GIVE HIM MY FULL ATTENTION.
MAMURA...
LET'S...

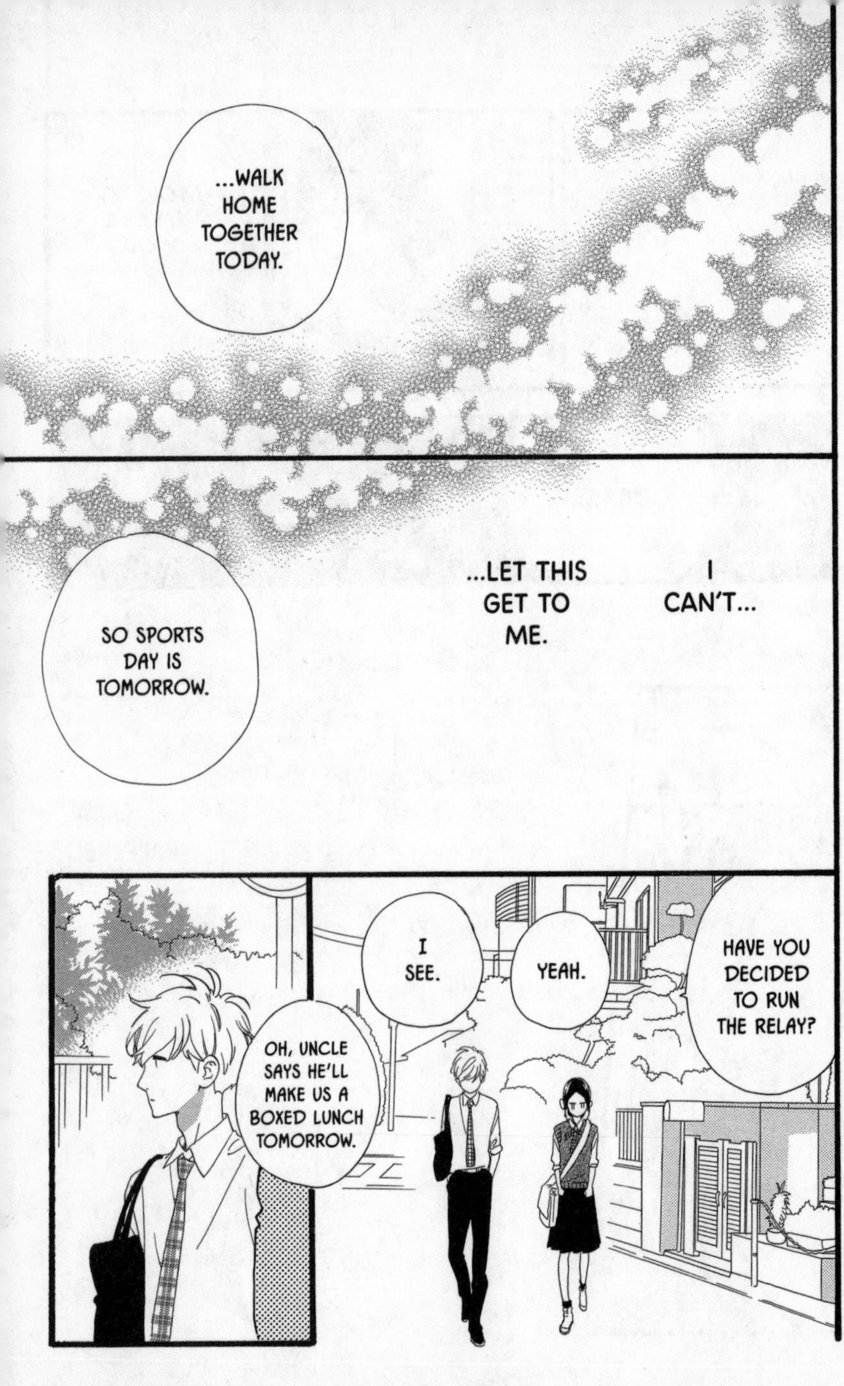
...WALK HOME TOGETHER TODAY.
I CAN'T...
...LET THIS GET TO ME.
SO SPORTS DAY IS TOMORROW.
HAVE YOU DECIDED TO RUN THE RELAY?
YEAH.
I SEE.
OH, UNCLE SAYS HE'LL MAKE US A BOXED LUNCH TOMORROW.

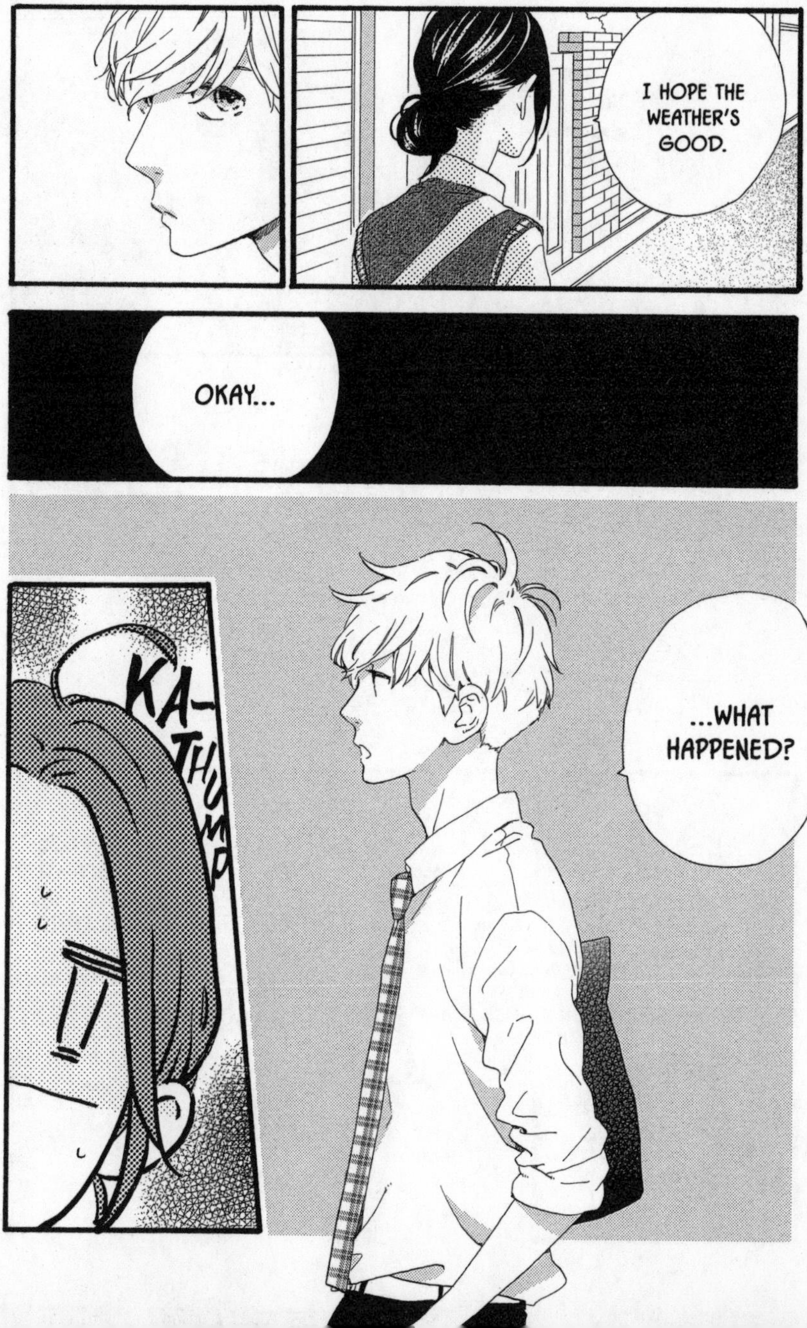
I HOPE THE WEATHER'S GOOD.
OKAY...
...WHAT HAPPENED?
KA-THUMP
!!

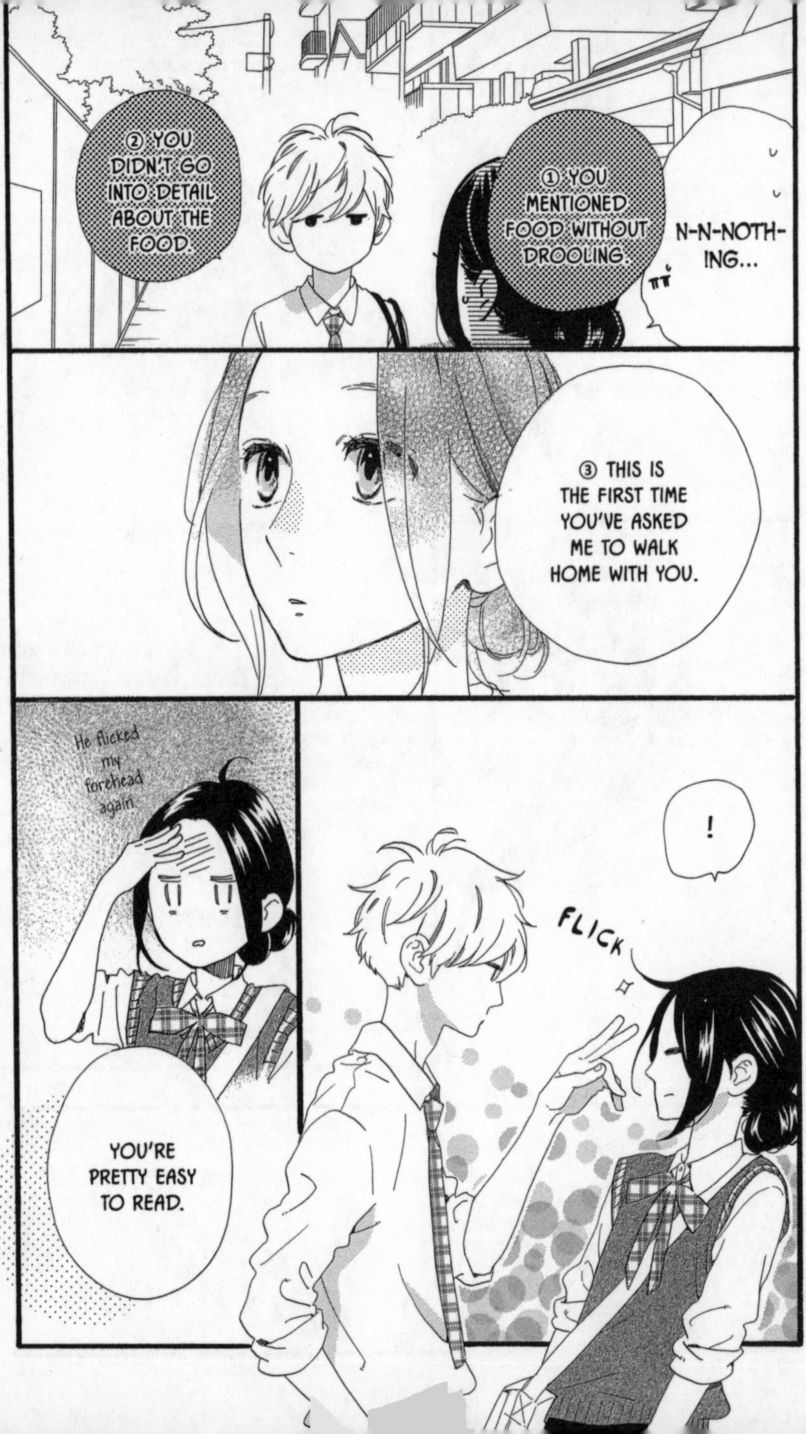
N-N-NOTH-ING...
① YOU MENTIONED FOOD WITHOUT DROOLING.
② YOU DIDN'T GO INTO DETAIL ABOUT THE FOOD.
③ THIS IS THE FIRST TIME YOU'VE ASKED ME TO WALK HOME WITH YOU.
!
FLICK
YOU'RE PRETTY EASY TO READ.
He flicked my forehead again.

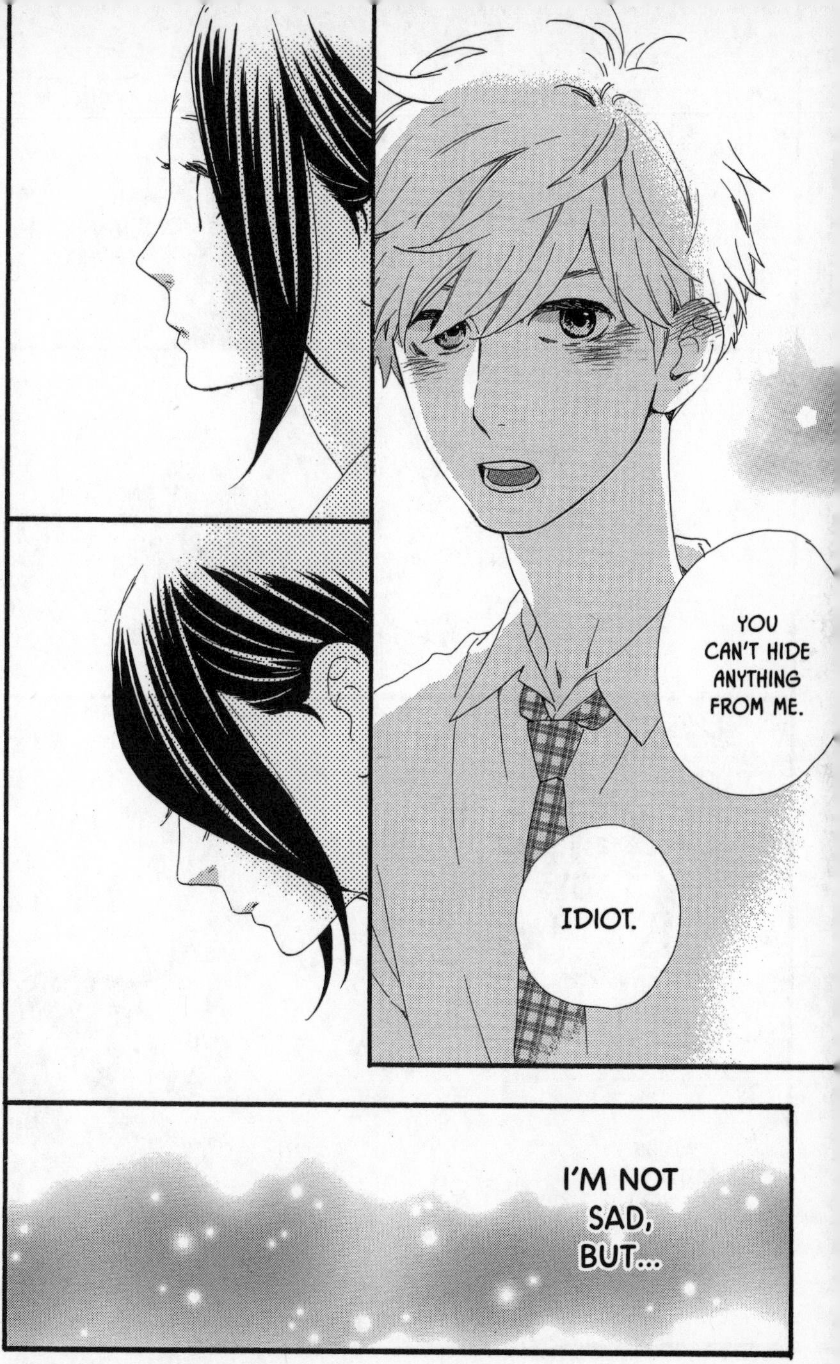
YOU CAN'T HIDE ANYTHING FROM ME.
IDIOT.
I'M NOT SAD, BUT...

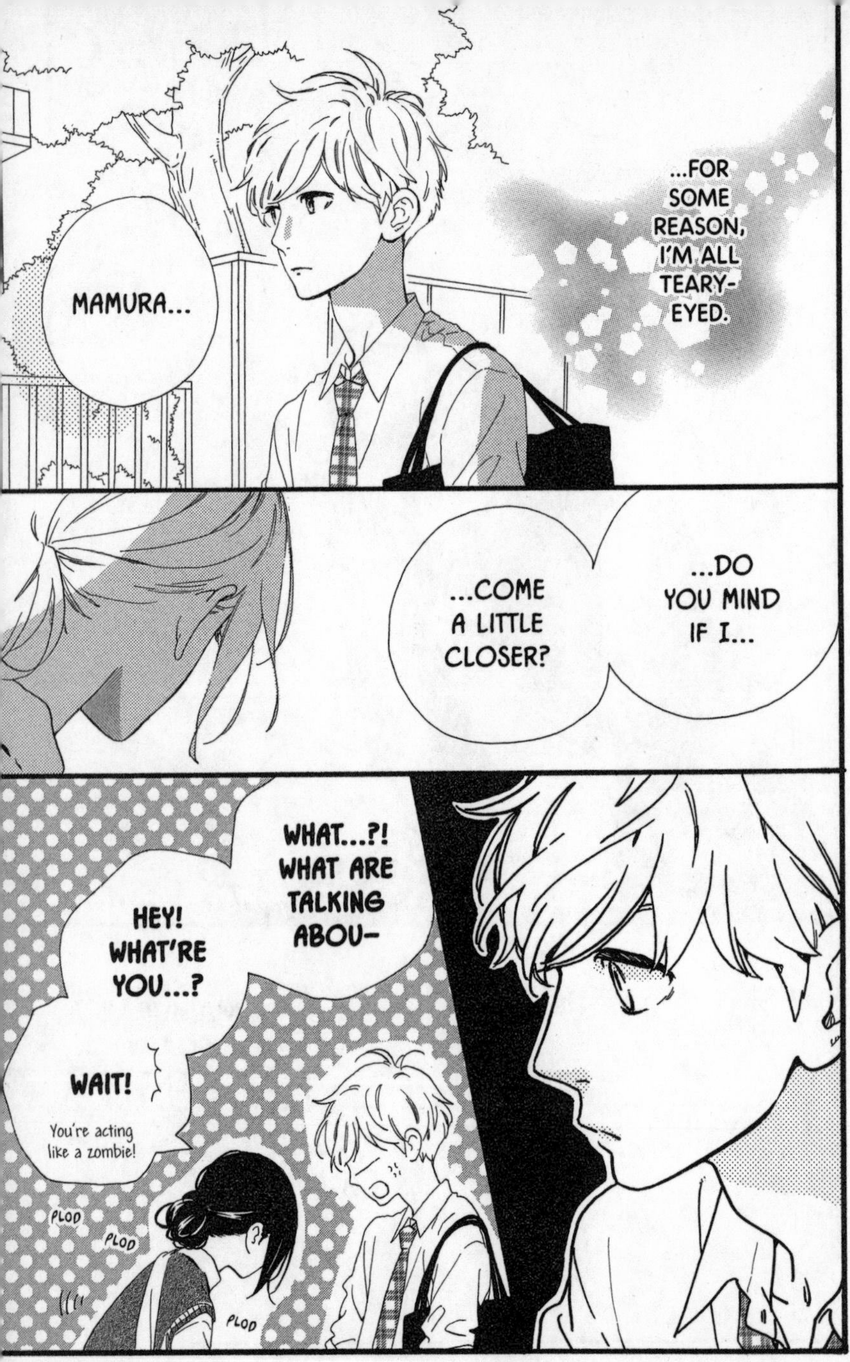
...FOR SOME REASON, I'M ALL TEARY-EYED.
MAMURA...
...DO YOU MIND IF I...
...COME A LITTLE CLOSER?
WHAT...?! WHAT ARE TALKING ABOU-
HEY! WHAT'RE YOU...?
WAIT!
You're acting like a zombie!
PLOD
PLOD
PLOD

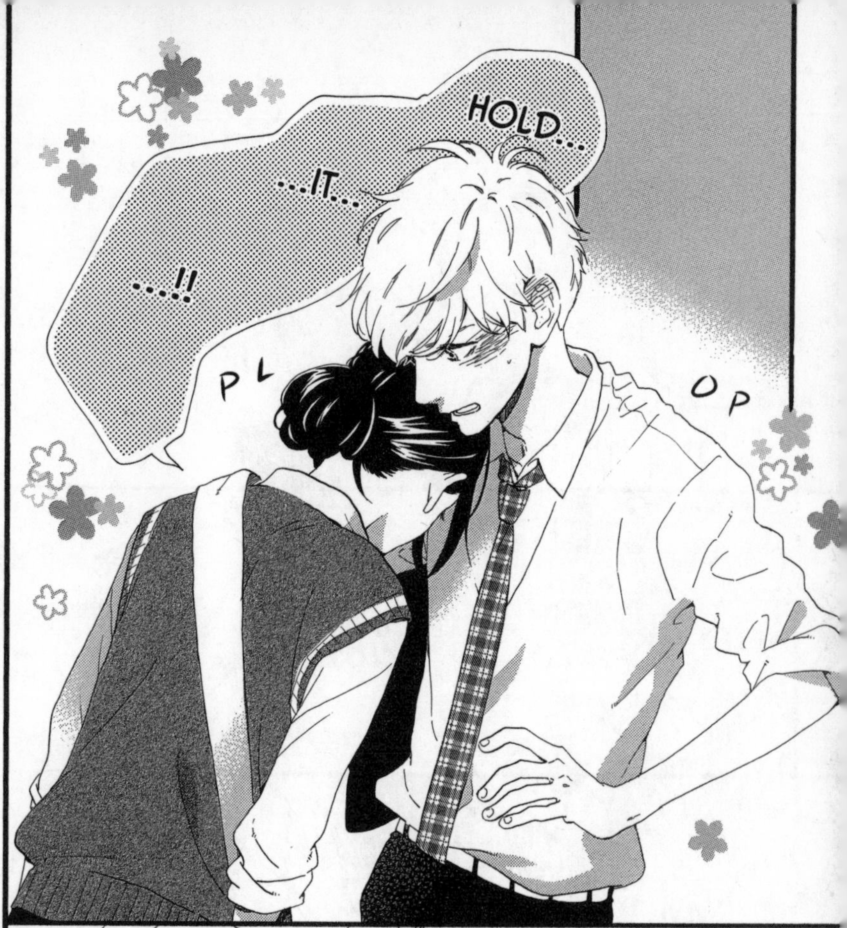
HOLD...
...IT...
...!!
PL OP
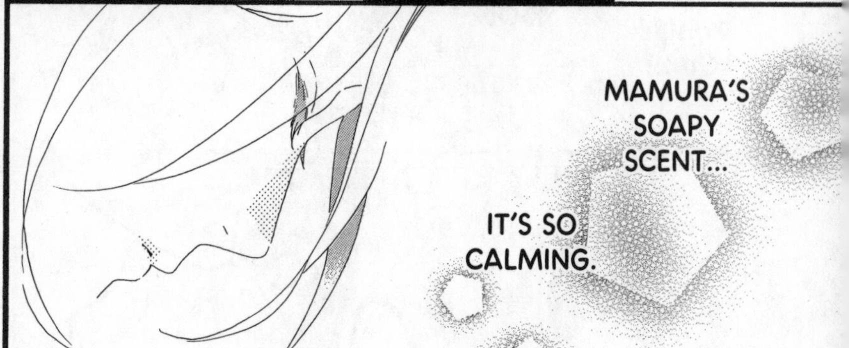
MAMURA'S SOAPY SCENT...
IT'S SO CALMING.

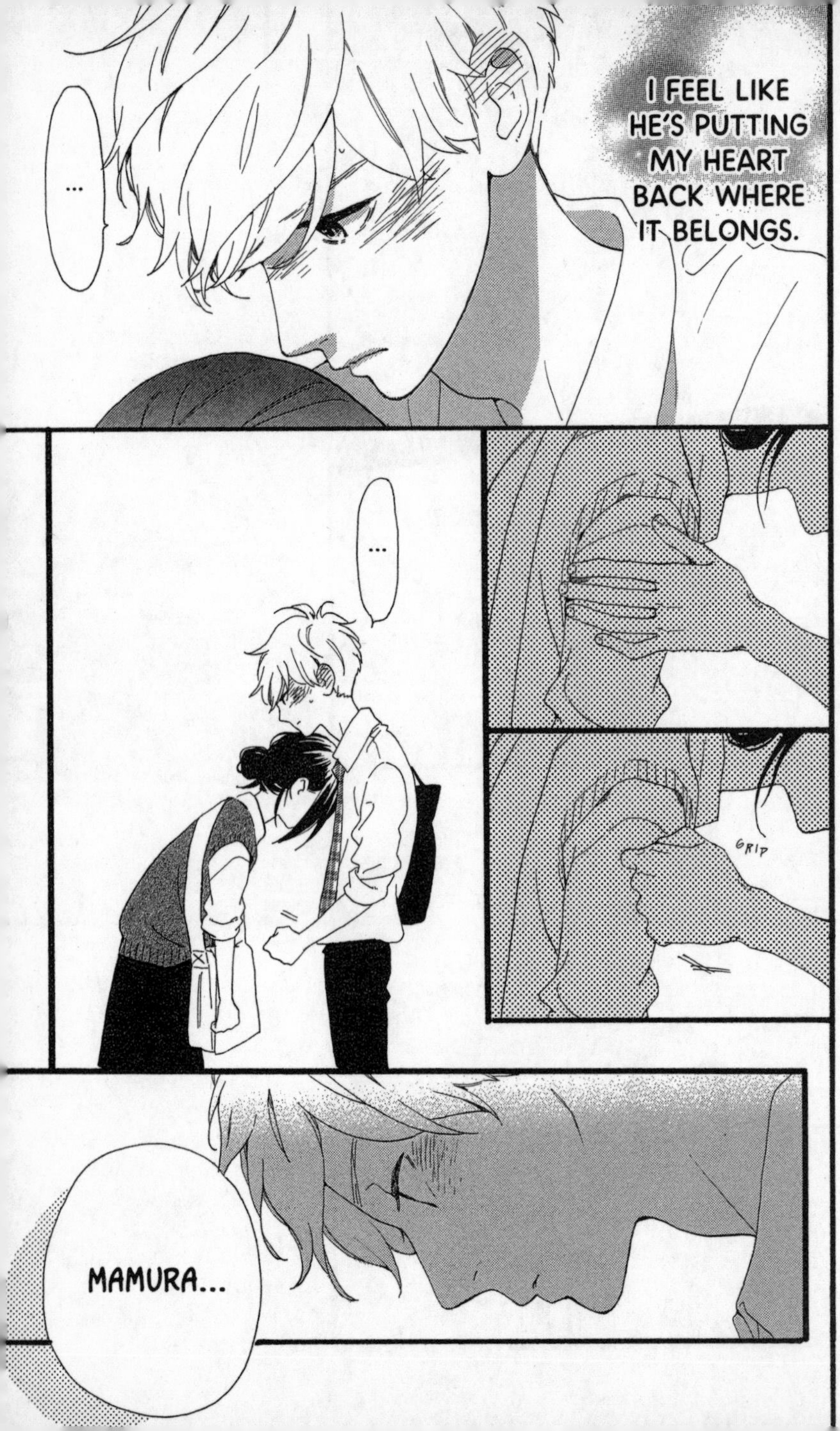
I FEEL LIKE HE'S PUTTING MY HEART BACK WHERE IT BELONGS.
...
GRIP
...
MAMURA...

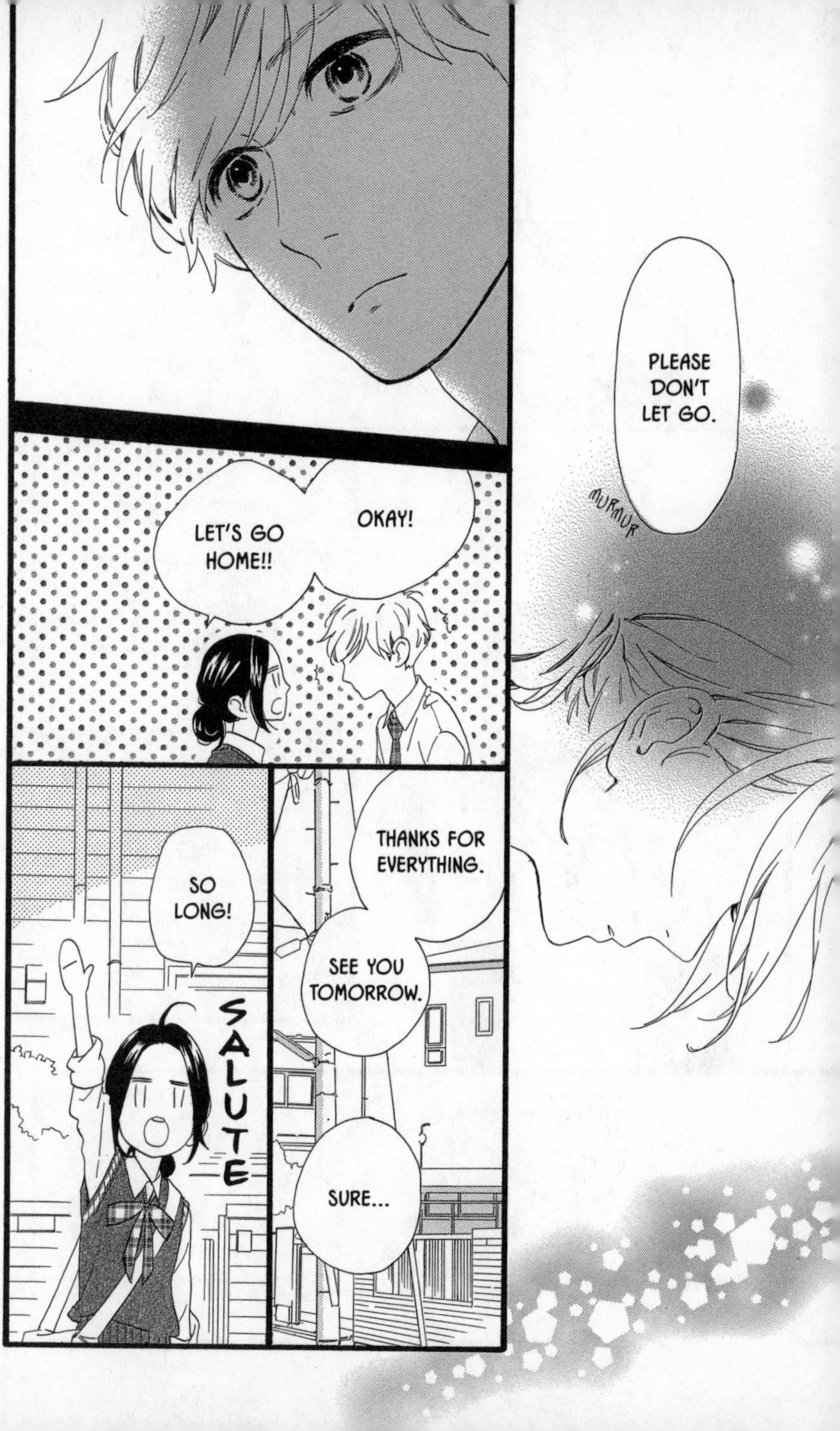
PLEASE DON'T LET GO.
MURMUR
OKAY!
LET'S GO HOME!!
THANKS FOR EVERYTHING.
SEE YOU TOMORROW.
SURE...
SO LONG!
SALUTE

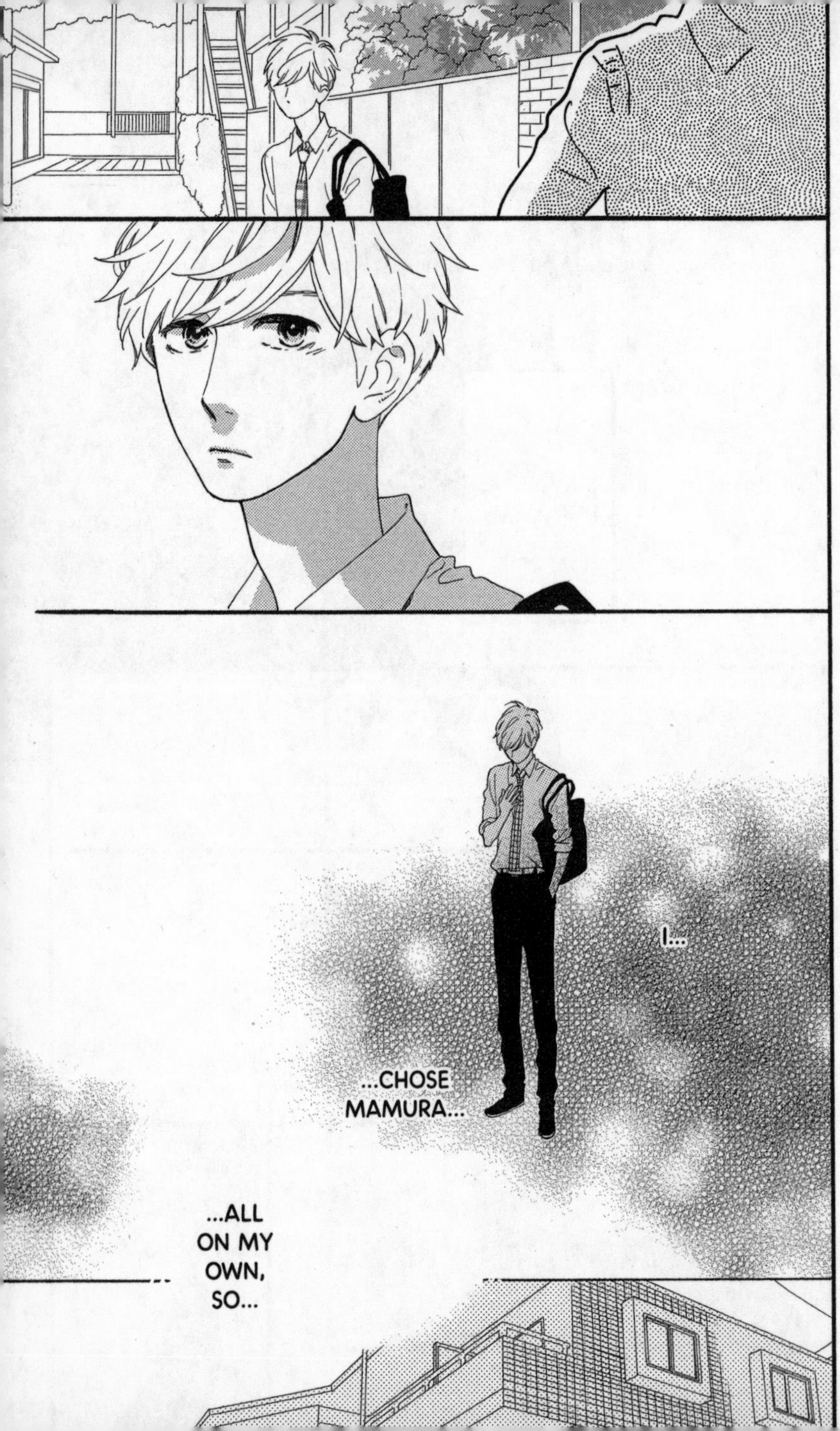
I...
...CHOSE MAMURA...
...ALL ON MY OWN, SO...

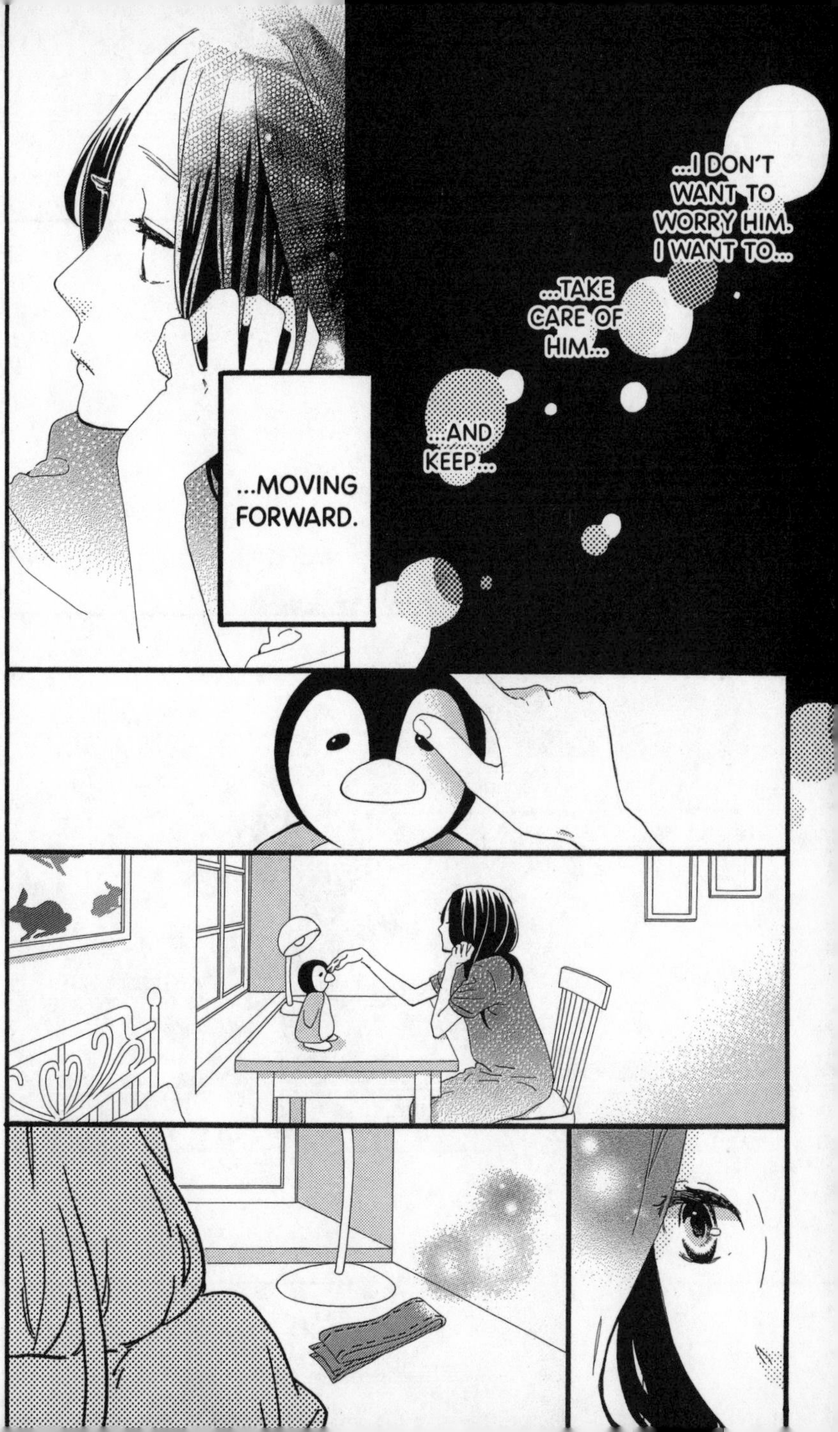
...I DON'T WANT TO WORRY HIM. I WANT TO...
...TAKE CARE OF HIM...
...AND KEEP...
...MOVING FORWARD.

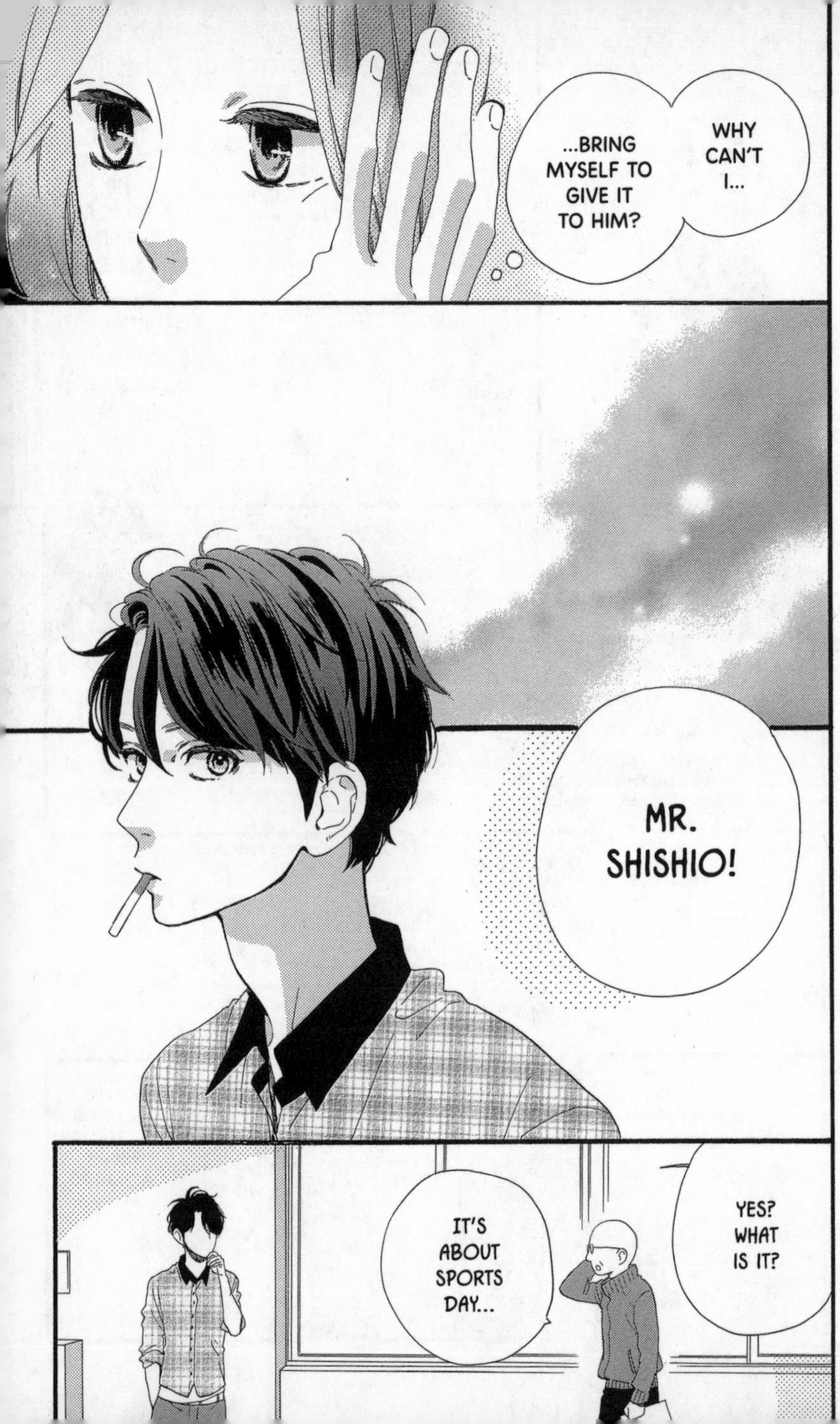
WHY CAN'T I...
...BRING MYSELF TO GIVE IT TO HIM?
MR. SHISHIO!
YES? WHAT IS IT?
IT'S ABOUT SPORTS DAY...

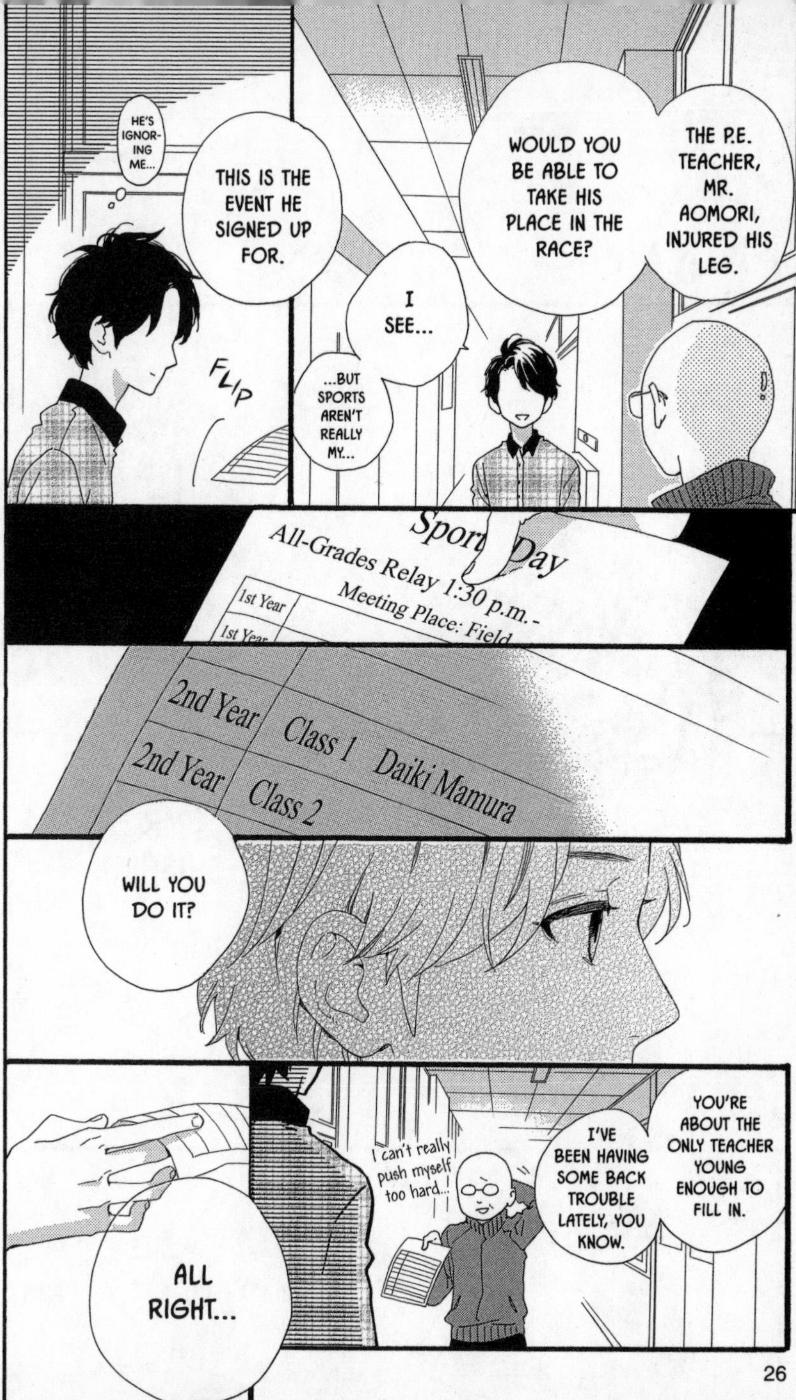
THE P.E. TEACHER, MR. AOMORI, INJURED HIS LEG.
WOULD YOU BE ABLE TO TAKE HIS PLACE IN THE RACE?
I SEE...
...BUT SPORTS AREN'T REALLY MY...
HE'S IGNORING ME...
THIS IS THE EVENT HE SIGNED UP FOR.
FLIP
Sports Day
All-Grades Relay 1:30 p.m.-
Meeting Place: Field
1st Year
1st Year
2nd Year Class 1 Daiki Mamura
2nd Year Class 2
WILL YOU DO IT?
YOU'RE ABOUT THE ONLY TEACHER YOUNG ENOUGH TO FILL IN.
I'VE BEEN HAVING SOME BACK TROUBLE LATELY, YOU KNOW.
I can't really push myself too hard...
ALL RIGHT...

I'LL
DO IT.

Sports Day

All-Grades Relay 1:30 p.m.-

Meeting Place: Field

| | | |
|---|---|---|
| 1st Year | Class 1 | Shunsoku Hayami |
| 1st Year | Class 2 | Taro Tanaka |
| 1st Year | Class 3 | Ichiro Yamada |
| 1st Year | Class 4 | Takuya Suzuki |
| 1st Year | Class 1 | Daiki Mamura |

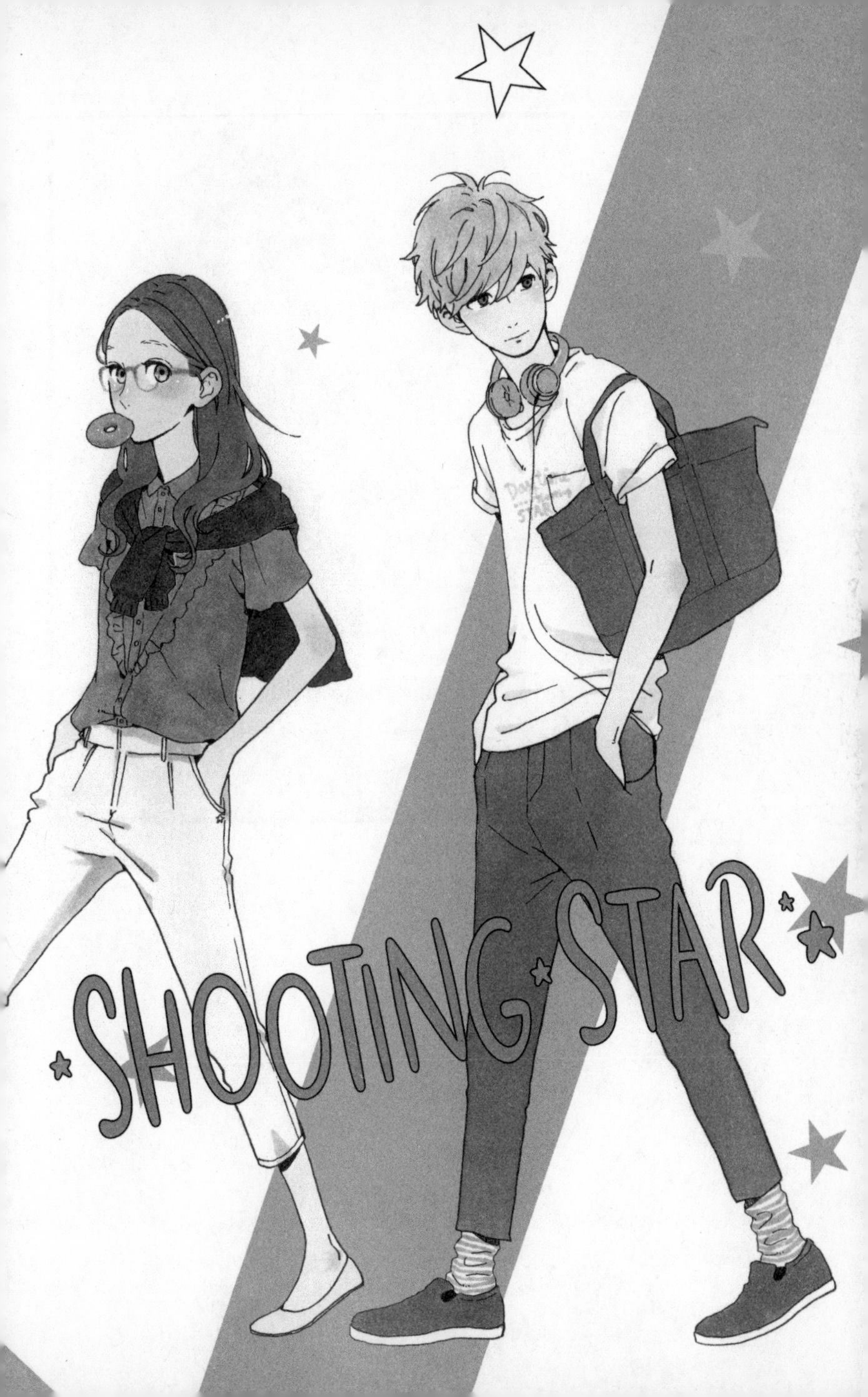
SHOOTING STAR

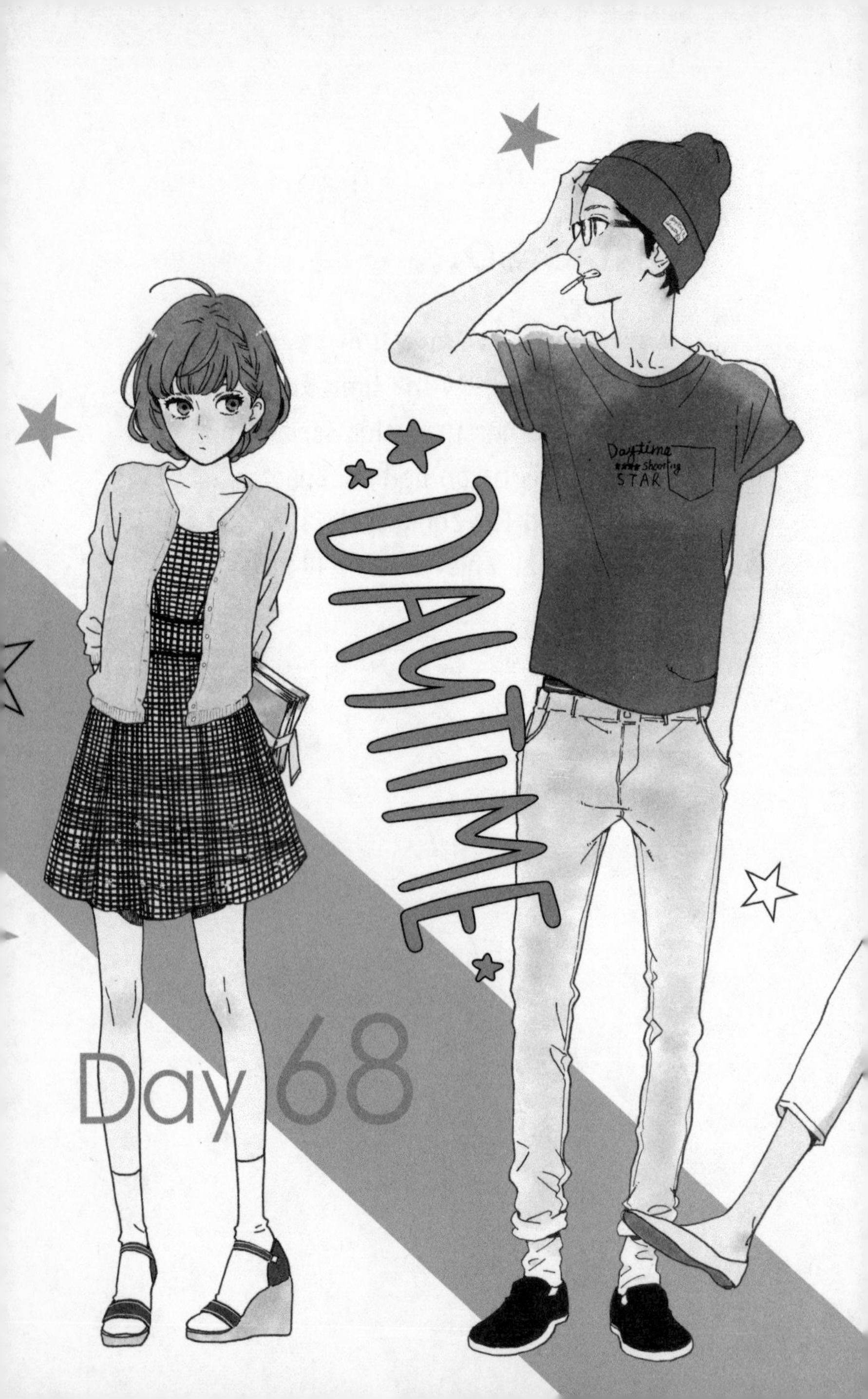
DAYTIME
Day 68
Daytime Shooting STAR

# And so...

We've reached volume 11 of *Daytime Shooting Star*!! By the time this volume is published, the magazine serialization will probably be on its final chapter. I just realized I've come quite a long way. I hope you all enjoy volume 11!

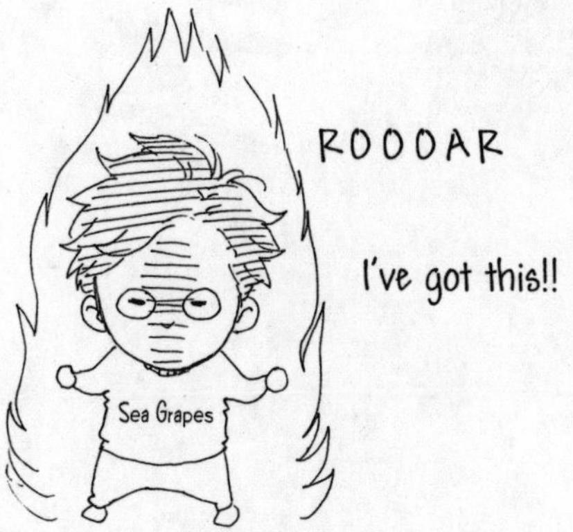
ROOOAR
I've got this!!
Sea Grapes

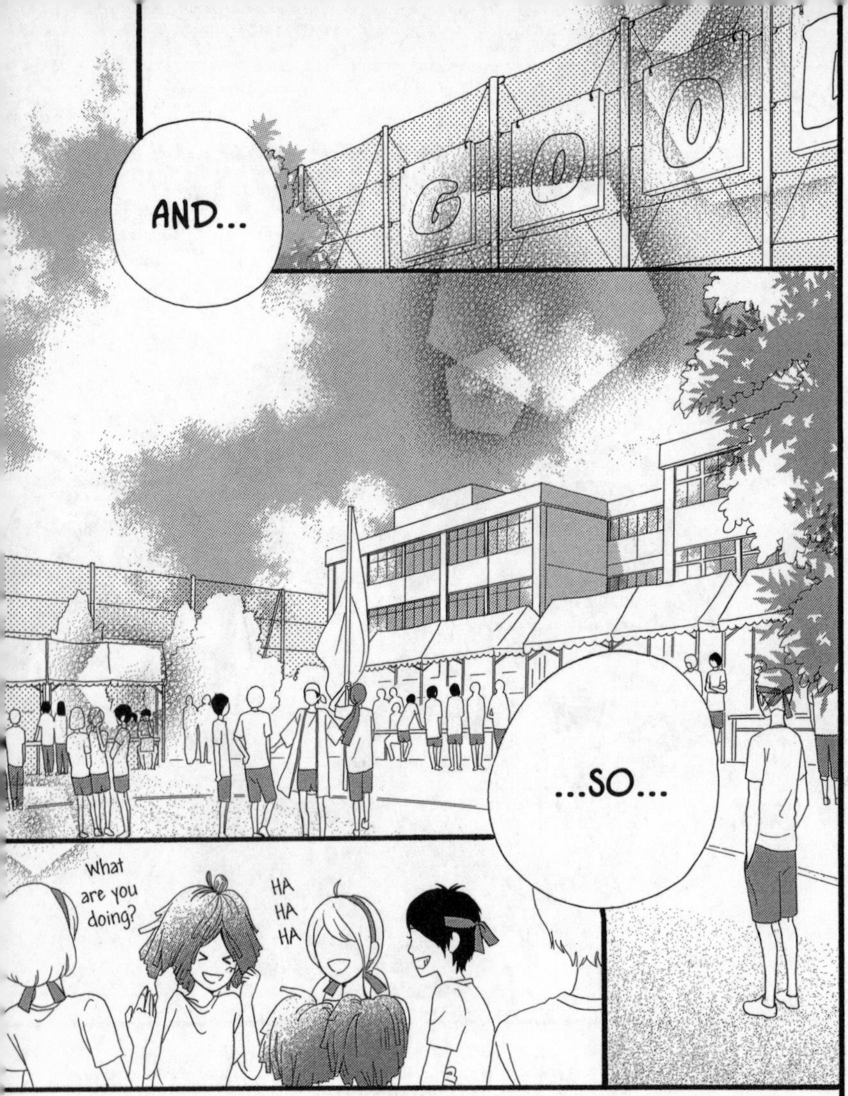
AND...
...SO...
HA HA HA
What are you doing?

DAYTIME SHOOTING STAR

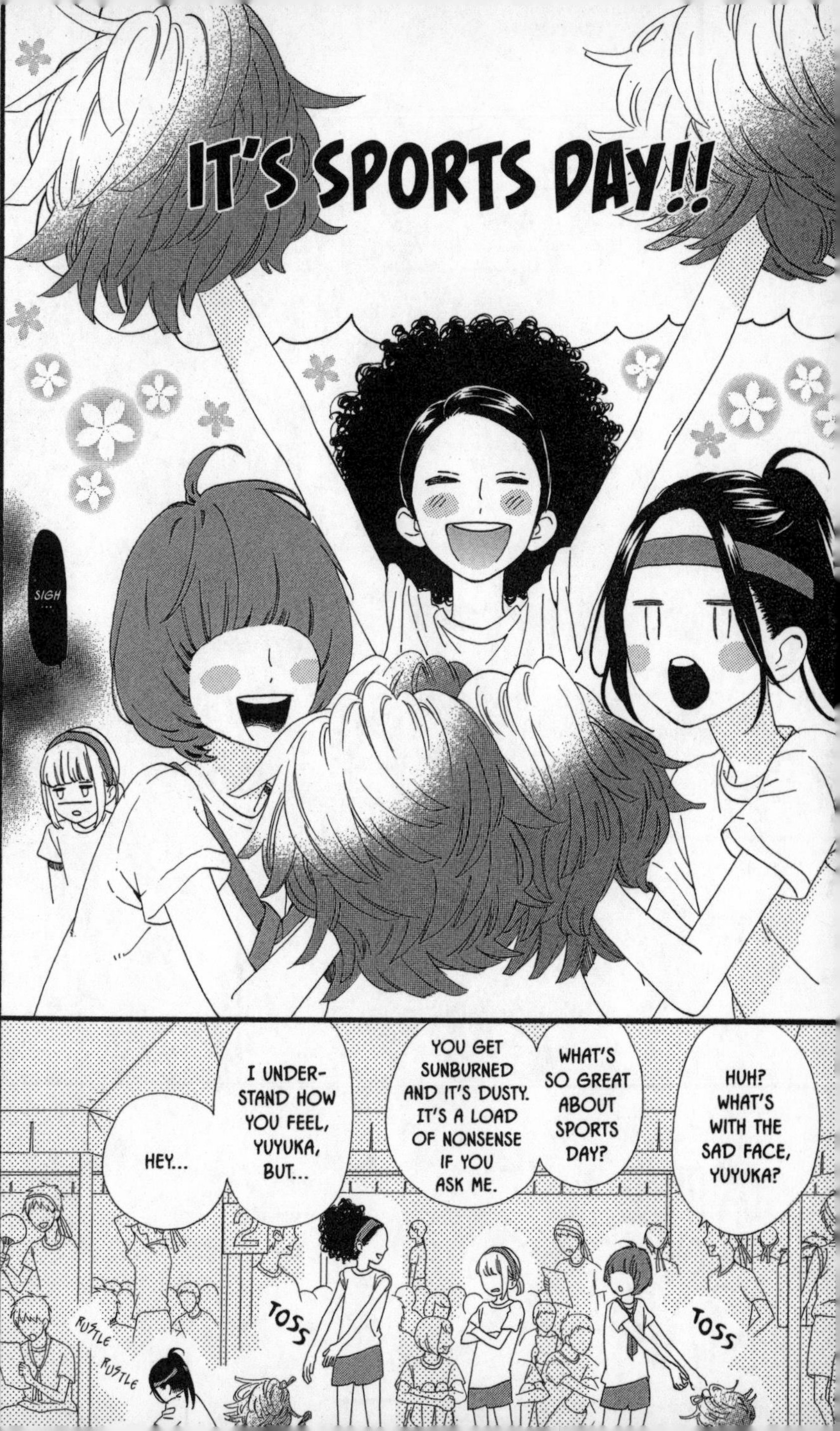
IT'S SPORTS DAY!!
SIGH...
HUH? WHAT'S WITH THE SAD FACE, YUYUKA?
WHAT'S SO GREAT ABOUT SPORTS DAY?
YOU GET SUNBURNED AND IT'S DUSTY. IT'S A LOAD OF NONSENSE IF YOU ASK ME.
I UNDER-STAND HOW YOU FEEL, YUYUKA, BUT...
HEY...
TOSS
TOSS
RUSTLE RUSTLE

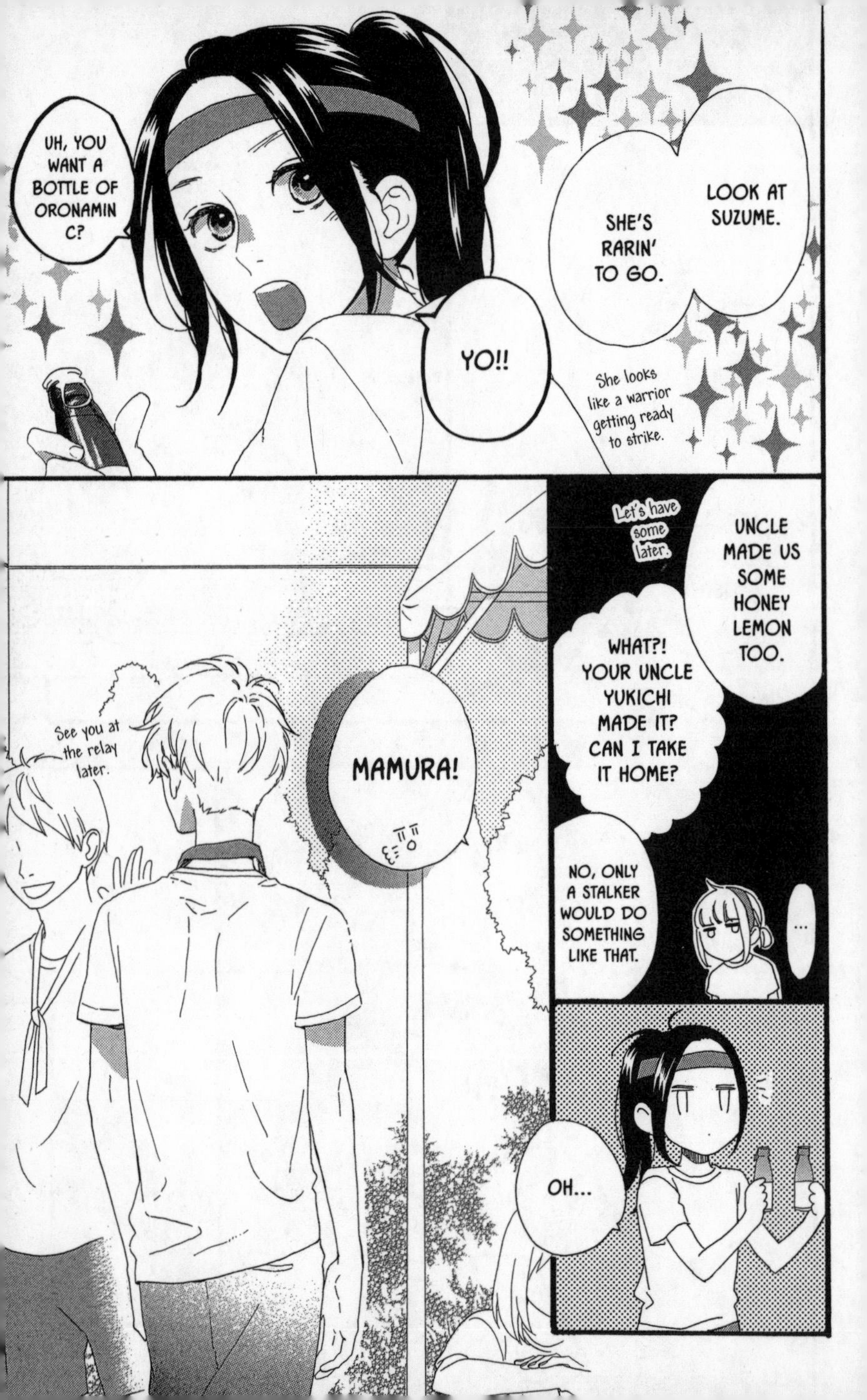
LOOK AT SUZUME.
SHE'S RARIN' TO GO.
She looks like a warrior getting ready to strike.
YO!!
UH, YOU WANT A BOTTLE OF ORONAMIN C?
UNCLE MADE US SOME HONEY LEMON TOO.
Let's have some later.
WHAT?! YOUR UNCLE YUKICHI MADE IT? CAN I TAKE IT HOME?
NO, ONLY A STALKER WOULD DO SOMETHING LIKE THAT.
...
OH...
MAMURA!
See you at the relay later.

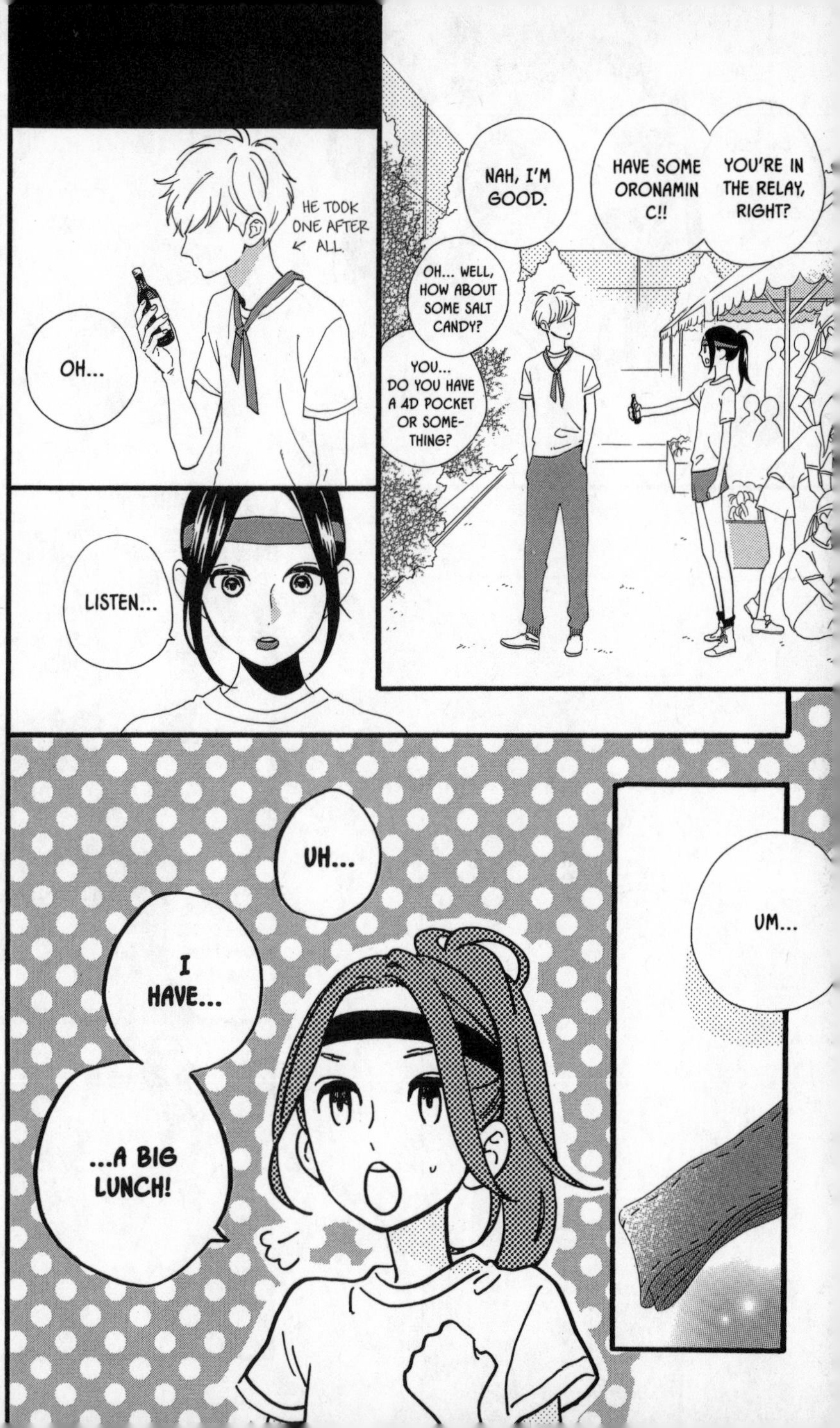
YOU'RE IN THE RELAY, RIGHT?
HAVE SOME ORONAMIN C!!
NAH, I'M GOOD.
OH... WELL, HOW ABOUT SOME SALT CANDY?
YOU... DO YOU HAVE A 4D POCKET OR SOMETHING?
HE TOOK ONE AFTER ALL.
OH...
LISTEN...
UM...
UH...
I HAVE...
...A BIG LUNCH!

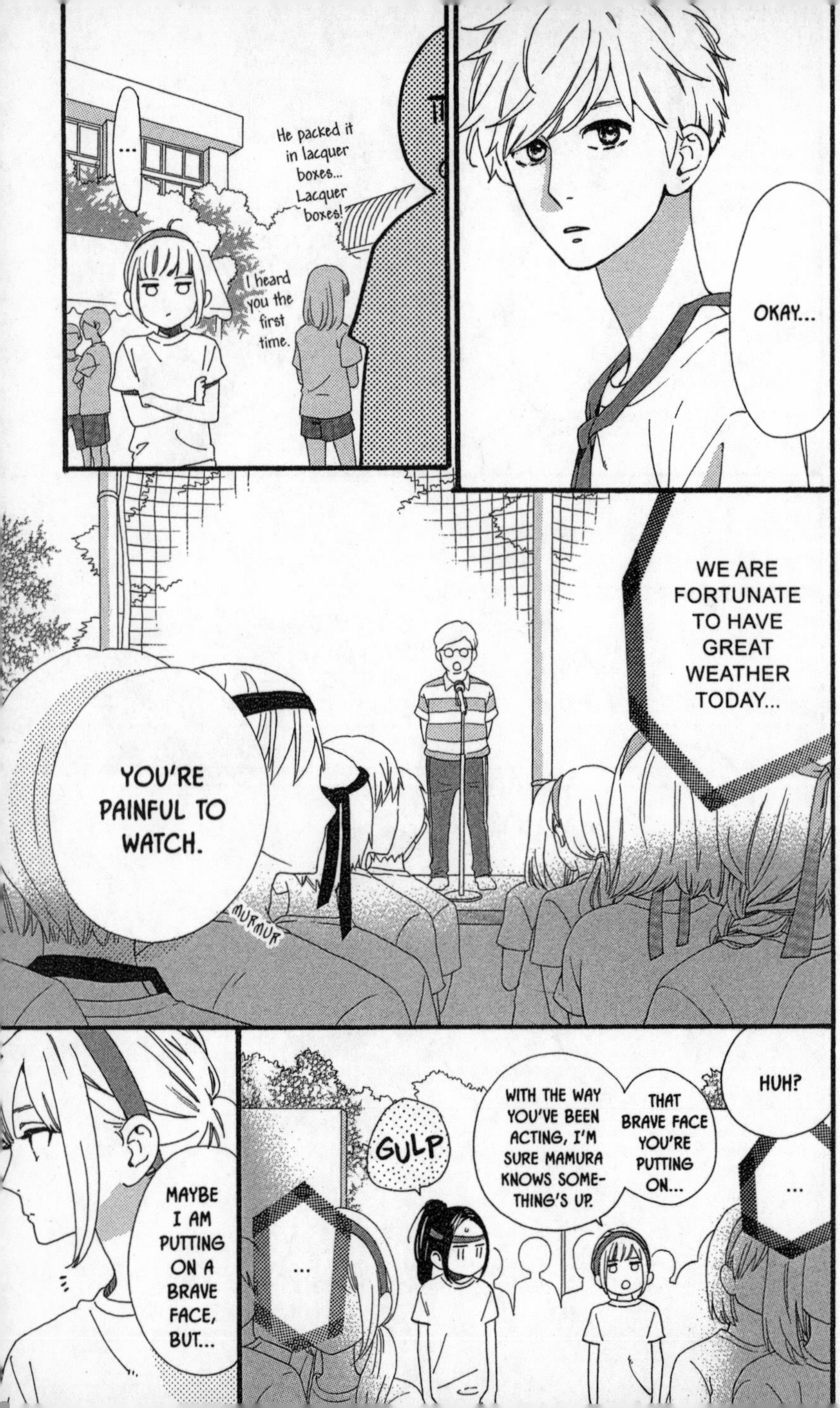
OKAY...
He packed it in lacquer boxes... Lacquer boxes!
...
I heard you the first time.
WE ARE FORTUNATE TO HAVE GREAT WEATHER TODAY...
YOU'RE PAINFUL TO WATCH.
MURMUR
HUH?
...
THAT BRAVE FACE YOU'RE PUTTING ON...
WITH THE WAY YOU'VE BEEN ACTING, I'M SURE MAMURA KNOWS SOME-THING'S UP.
GULP
...
MAYBE I AM PUTTING ON A BRAVE FACE, BUT...

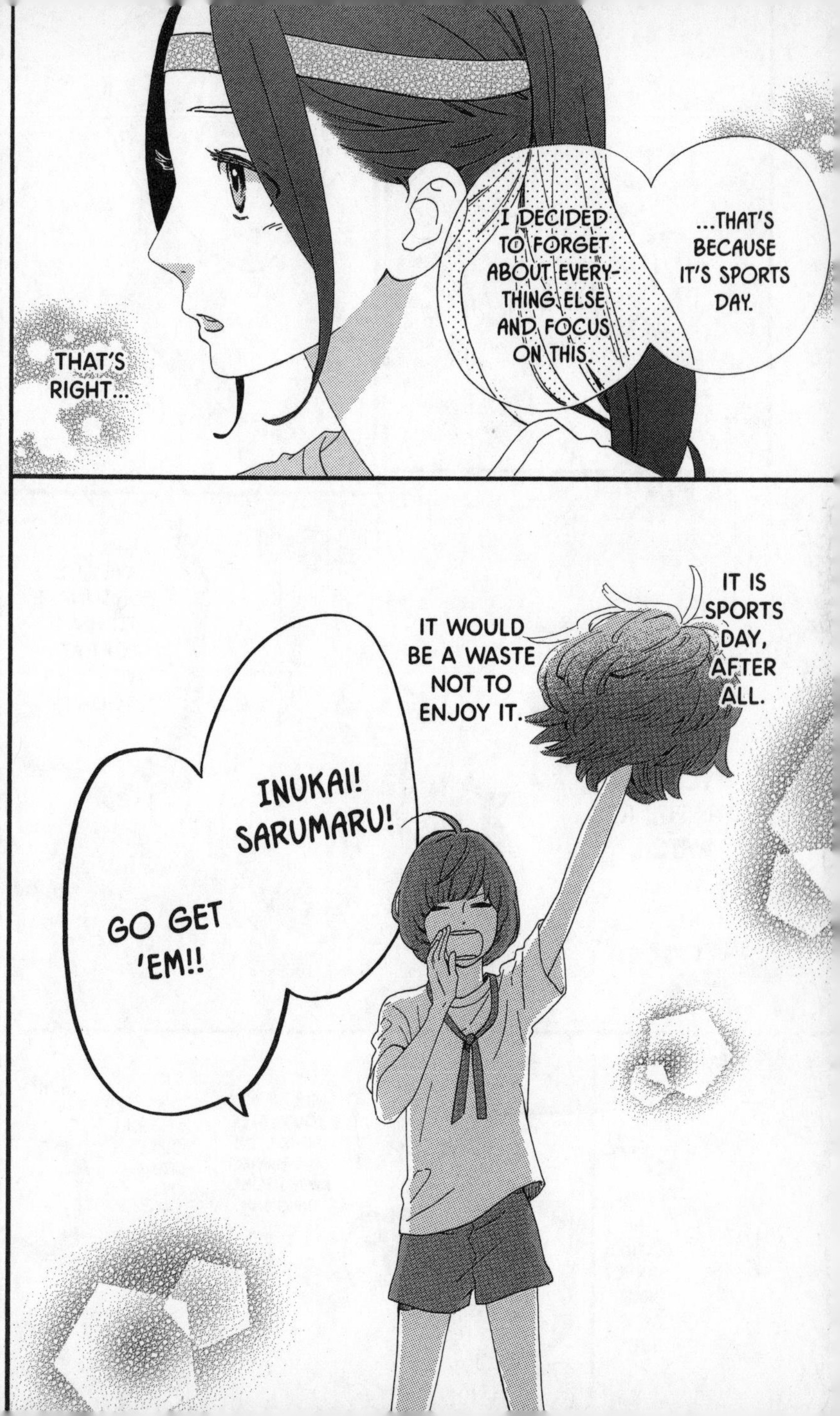
...THAT'S BECAUSE IT'S SPORTS DAY.
I DECIDED TO FORGET ABOUT EVERY-THING ELSE AND FOCUS ON THIS.
THAT'S RIGHT...
IT IS SPORTS DAY, AFTER ALL.
IT WOULD BE A WASTE NOT TO ENJOY IT.
INUKAI! SARUMARU!
GO GET 'EM!!

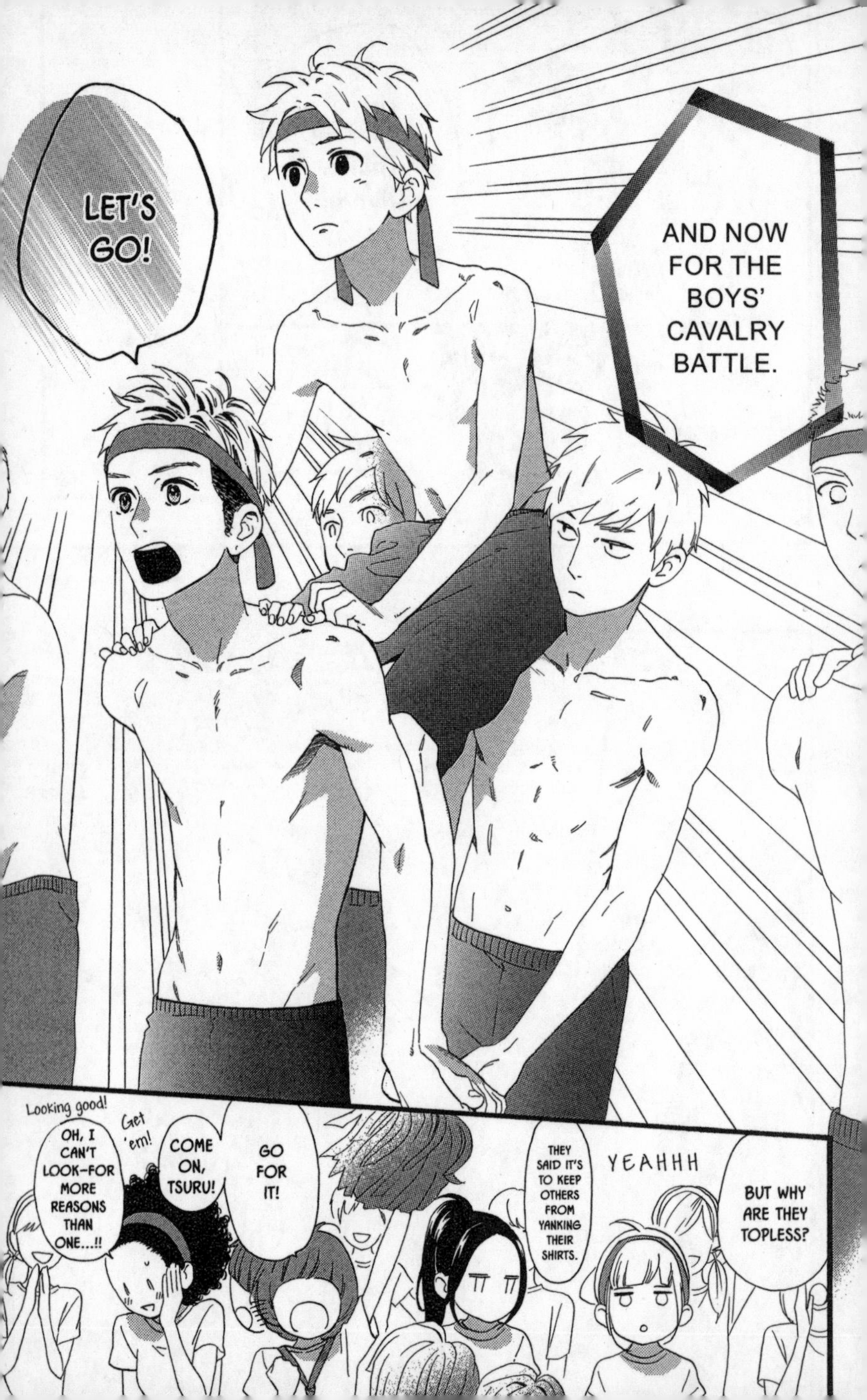
AND NOW FOR THE BOYS' CAVALRY BATTLE.
LET'S GO!
BUT WHY ARE THEY TOPLESS?
YEAHHH
THEY SAID IT'S TO KEEP OTHERS FROM YANKING THEIR SHIRTS.
GO FOR IT!
COME ON, TSURU!
Get 'em!
OH, I CAN'T LOOK—FOR MORE REASONS THAN ONE...!!
Looking good!

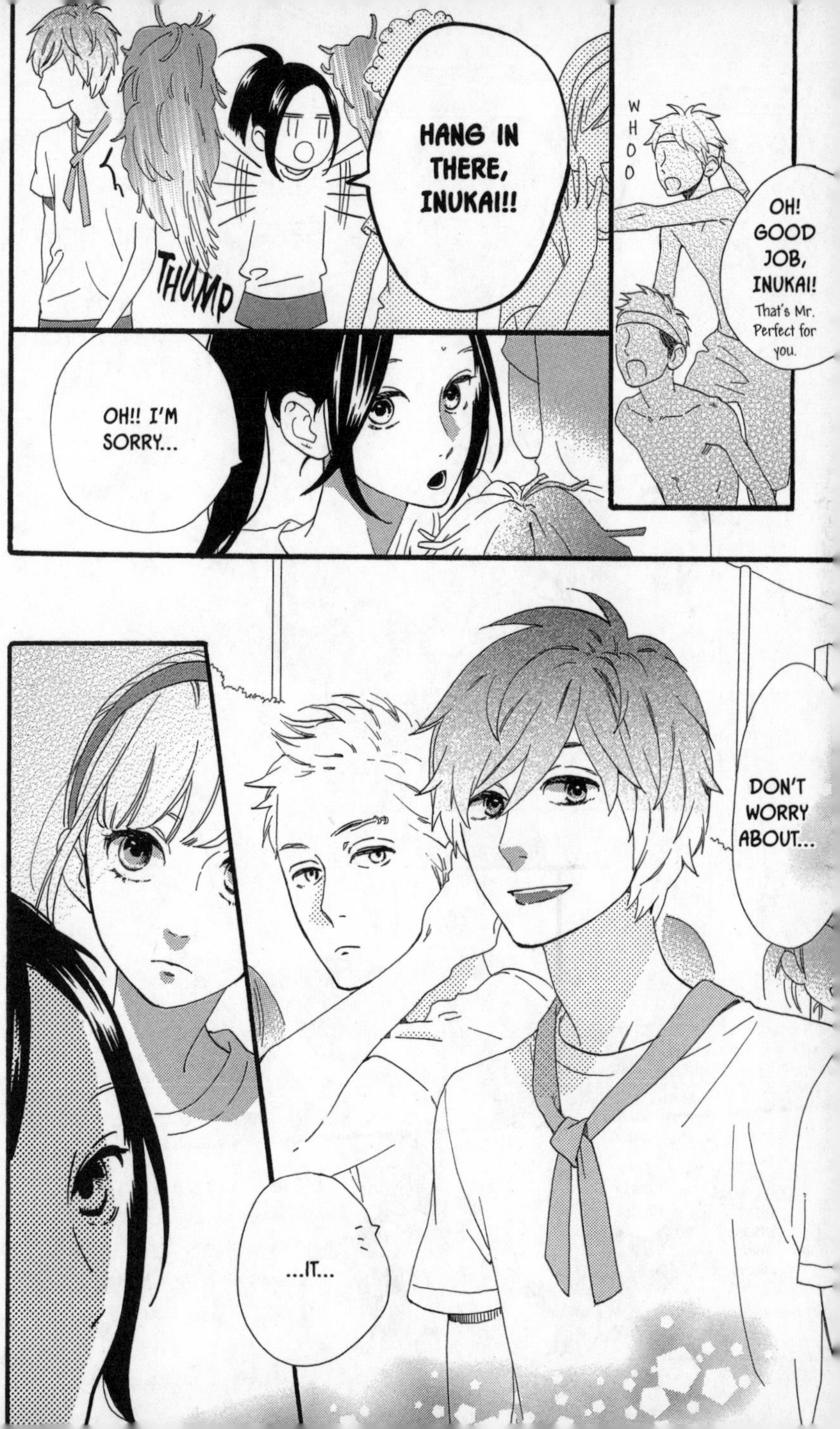
WHOO
OH! GOOD JOB, INUKAI! That's Mr. Perfect for you.
HANG IN THERE, INUKAI!!
THUMP
OH!! I'M SORRY...
DON'T WORRY ABOUT...
...IT...

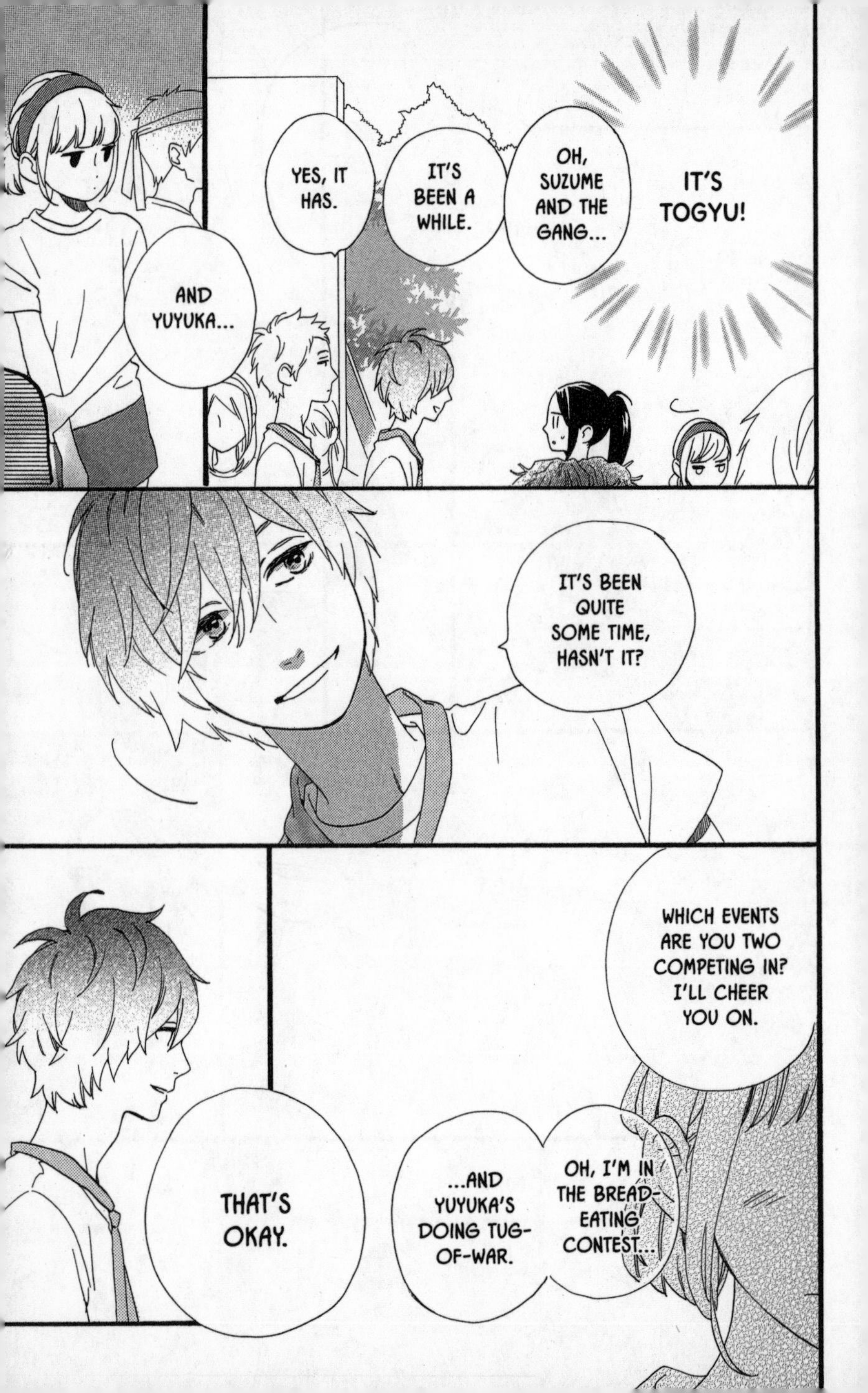
IT'S TOGYU!
OH, SUZUME AND THE GANG...
IT'S BEEN A WHILE.
YES, IT HAS.
AND YUYUKA...
IT'S BEEN QUITE SOME TIME, HASN'T IT?
WHICH EVENTS ARE YOU TWO COMPETING IN? I'LL CHEER YOU ON.
OH, I'M IN THE BREAD-EATING CONTEST...
...AND YUYUKA'S DOING TUG-OF-WAR.
THAT'S OKAY.

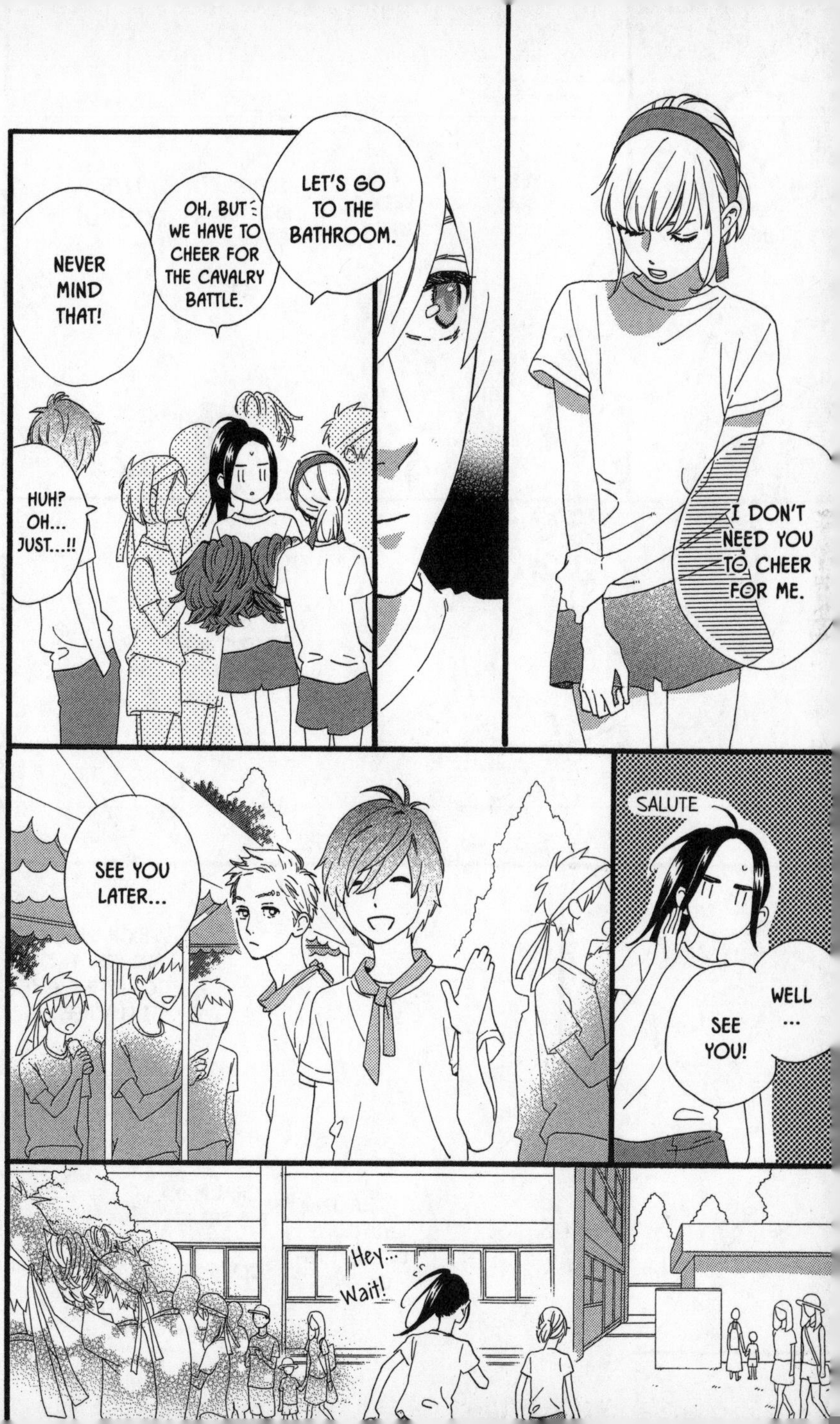
I DON'T NEED YOU TO CHEER FOR ME.
LET'S GO TO THE BATHROOM.
OH, BUT WE HAVE TO CHEER FOR THE CAVALRY BATTLE.
NEVER MIND THAT!
HUH? OH... JUST...!!
SALUTE
WELL... SEE YOU!
SEE YOU LATER...
Hey... Wait!

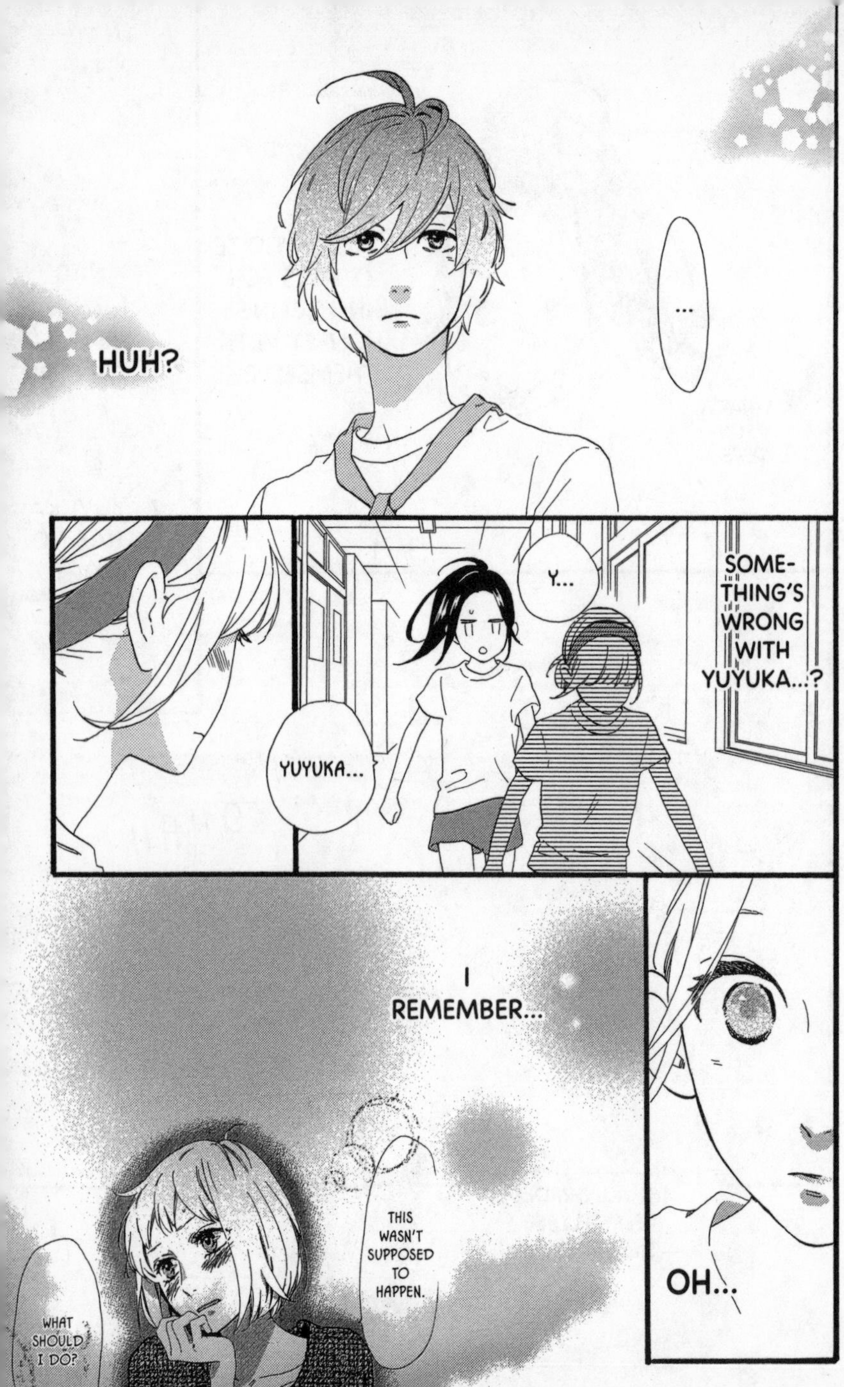
...
HUH?
SOMETHING'S WRONG WITH YUYUKA...?
Y...
YUYUKA...
OH...
I REMEMBER...
THIS WASN'T SUPPOSED TO HAPPEN.
WHAT SHOULD I DO?

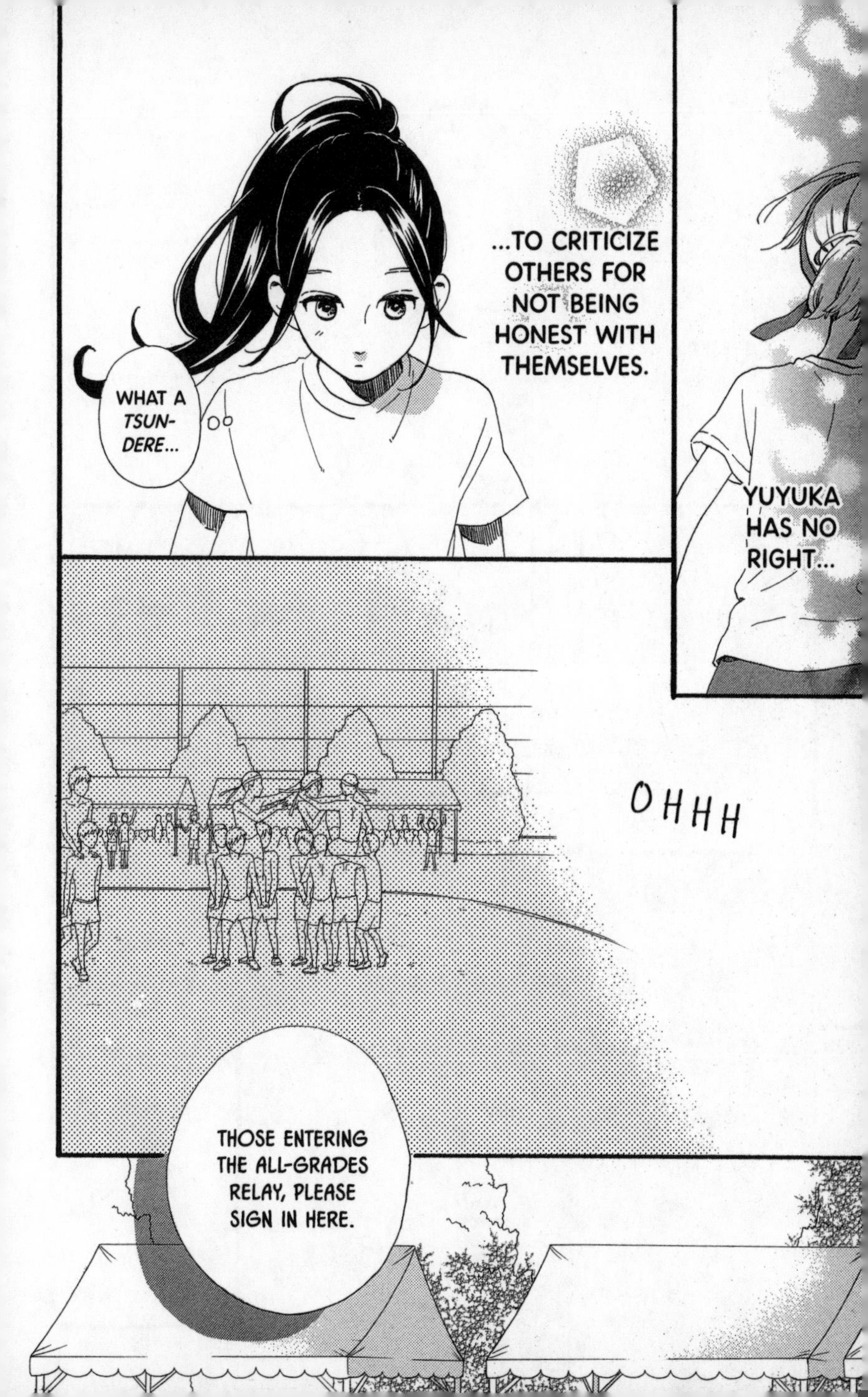
YUYUKA HAS NO RIGHT...
...TO CRITICIZE OTHERS FOR NOT BEING HONEST WITH THEMSELVES.
WHAT A *TSUNDERE*...
OHHH
THOSE ENTERING THE ALL-GRADES RELAY, PLEASE SIGN IN HERE.

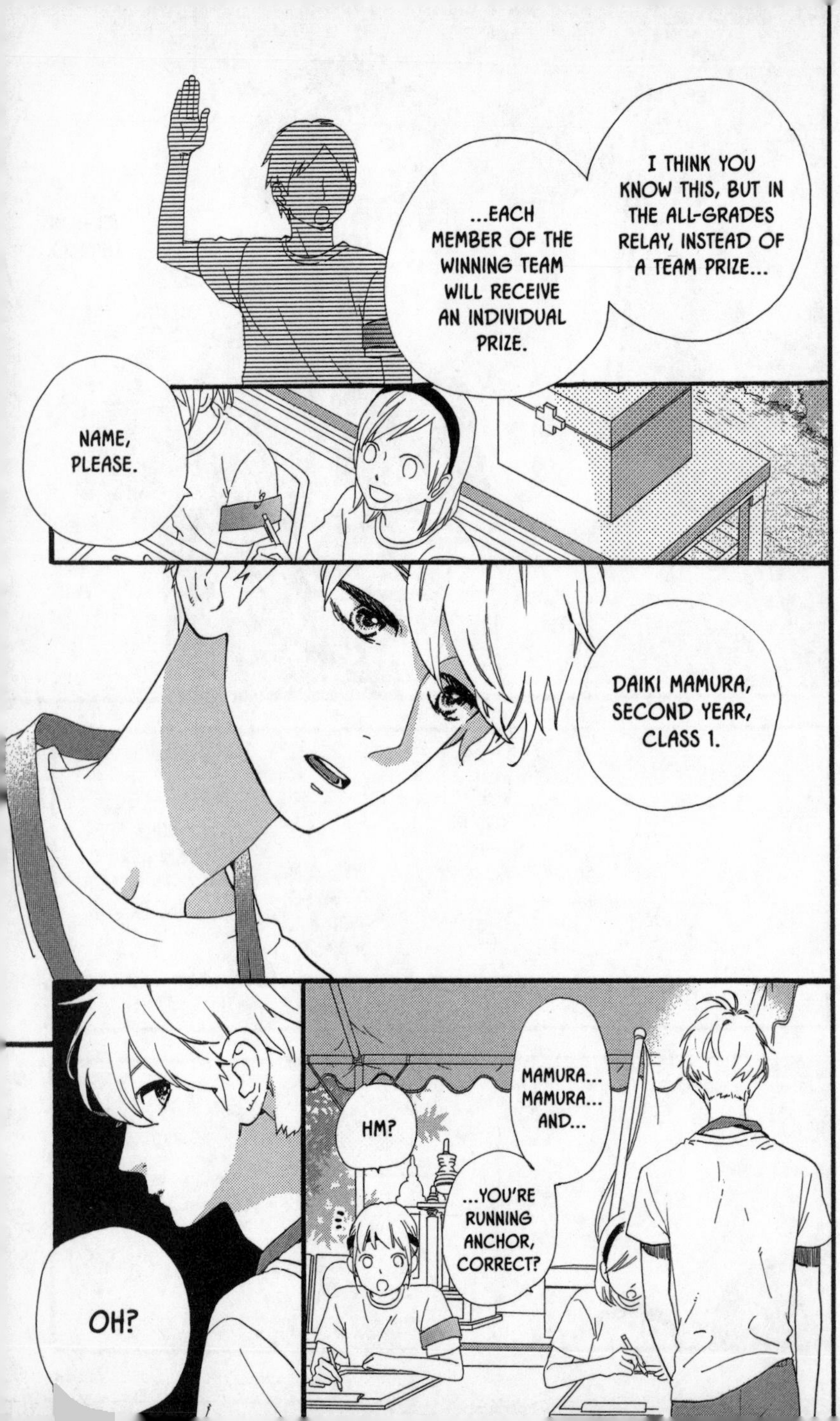
I THINK YOU KNOW THIS, BUT IN THE ALL-GRADES RELAY, INSTEAD OF A TEAM PRIZE...
...EACH MEMBER OF THE WINNING TEAM WILL RECEIVE AN INDIVIDUAL PRIZE.
NAME, PLEASE.
DAIKI MAMURA, SECOND YEAR, CLASS 1.
MAMURA... MAMURA... AND...
HM?
...YOU'RE RUNNING ANCHOR, CORRECT?
OH?

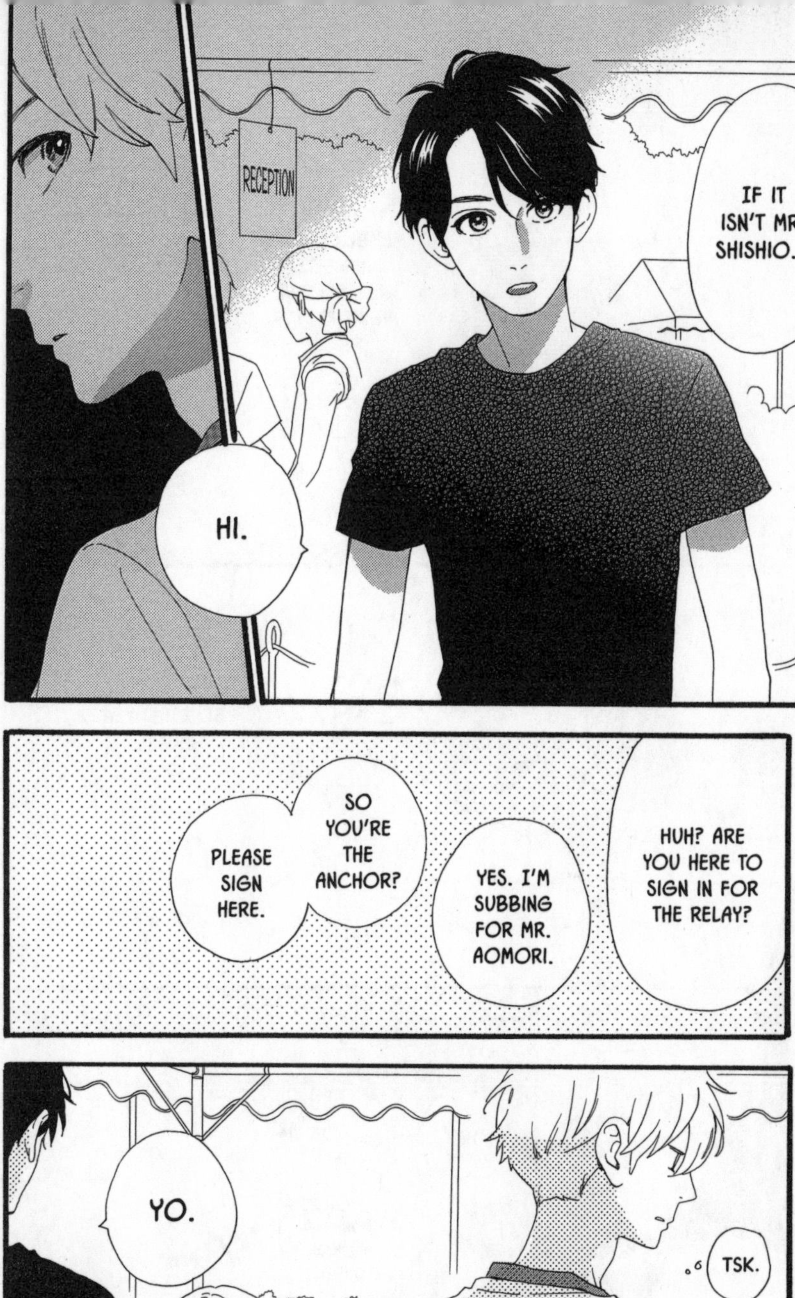
RECEPTION
IF IT ISN'T MR. SHISHIO...
HI.
HUH? ARE YOU HERE TO SIGN IN FOR THE RELAY?
YES. I'M SUBBING FOR MR. AOMORI.
SO YOU'RE THE ANCHOR?
PLEASE SIGN HERE.
YO.
TSK.

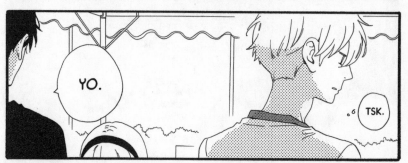

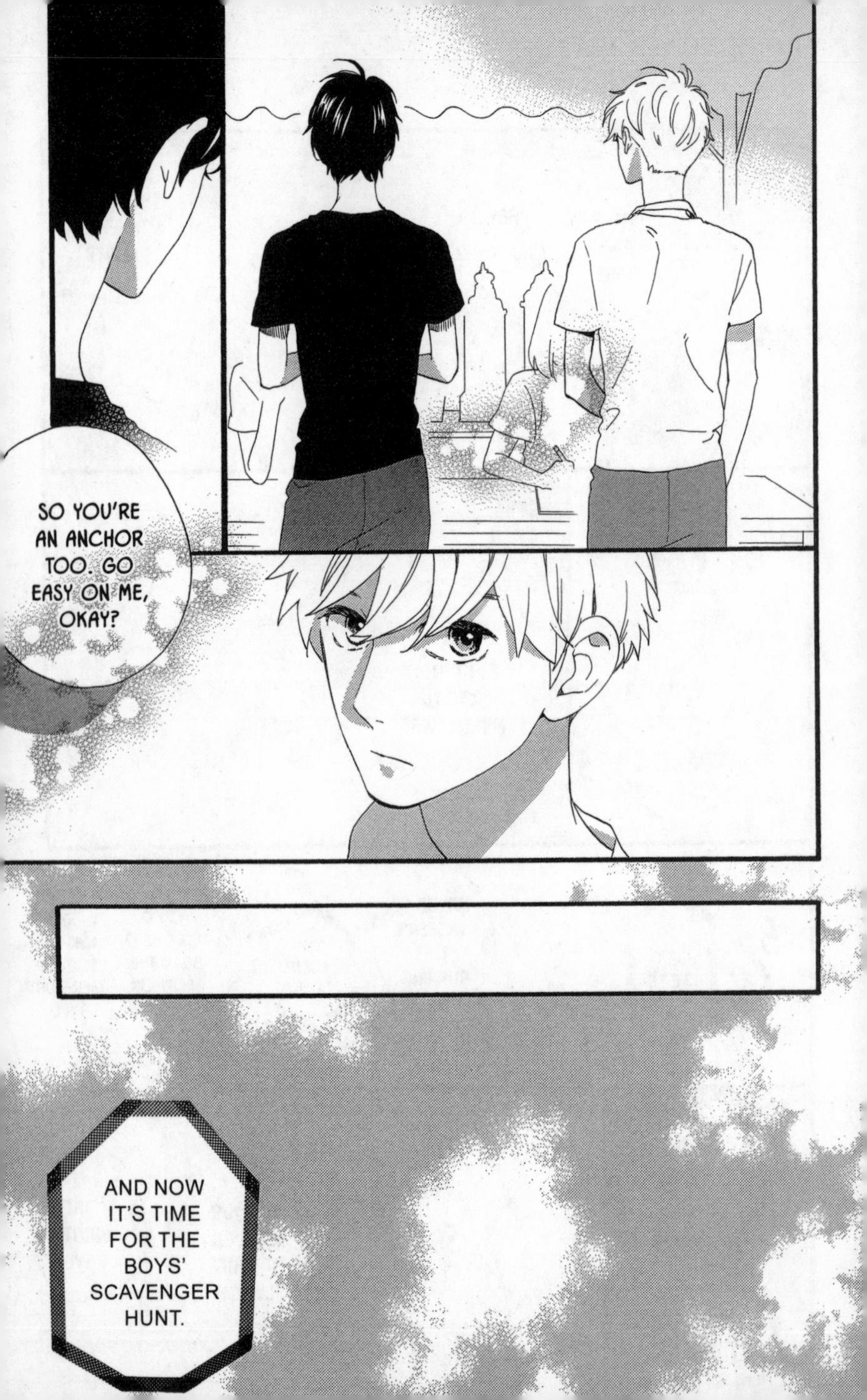
SO YOU'RE AN ANCHOR TOO. GO EASY ON ME, OKAY?
AND NOW IT'S TIME FOR THE BOYS' SCAVENGER HUNT.

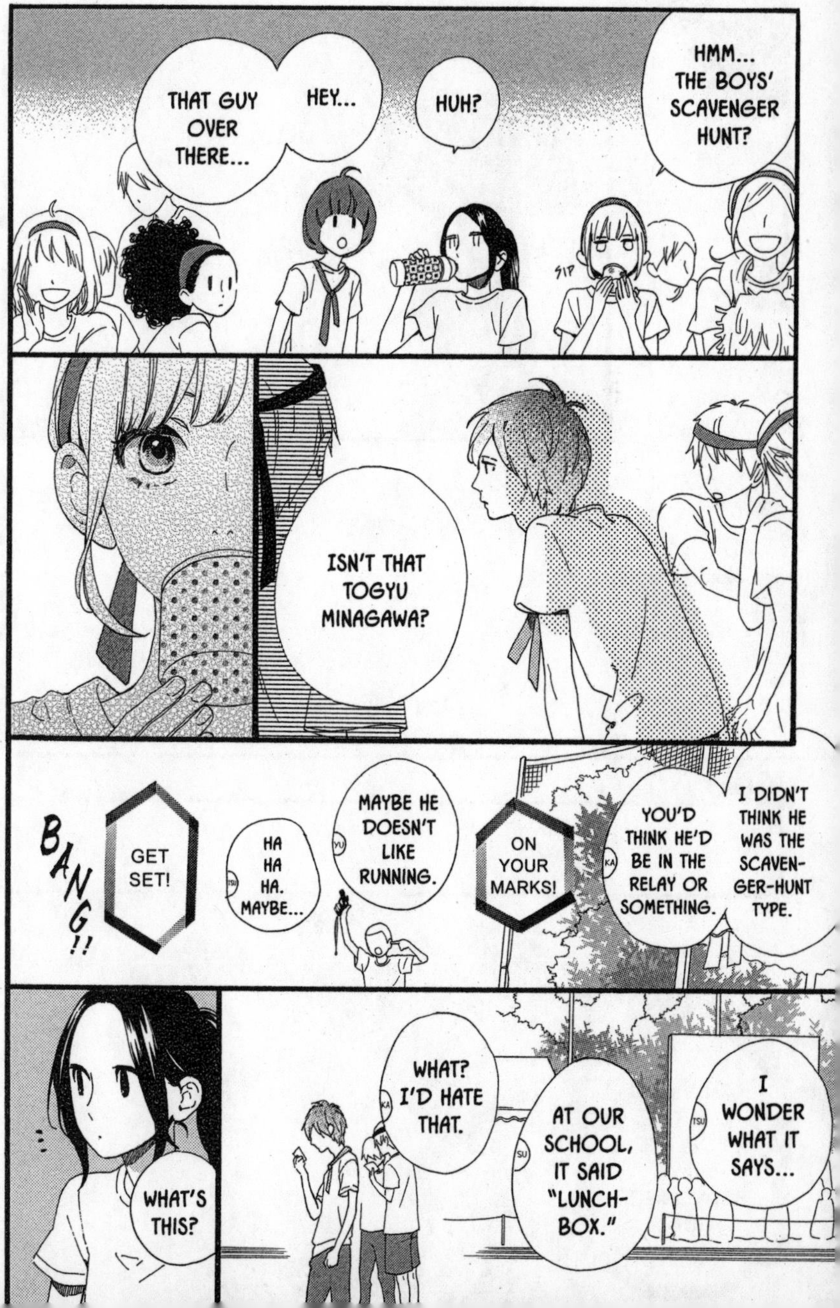
HMM... THE BOYS' SCAVENGER HUNT?
HUH?
HEY...
THAT GUY OVER THERE...
SIP
ISN'T THAT TOGYU MINAGAWA?
I DIDN'T THINK HE WAS THE SCAVEN-GER-HUNT TYPE.
YOU'D THINK HE'D BE IN THE RELAY OR SOMETHING.
ON YOUR MARKS!
MAYBE HE DOESN'T LIKE RUNNING.
HA HA HA. MAYBE...
GET SET!
BANG!!
I WONDER WHAT IT SAYS...
AT OUR SCHOOL, IT SAID "LUNCH-BOX."
WHAT? I'D HATE THAT.
WHAT'S THIS?

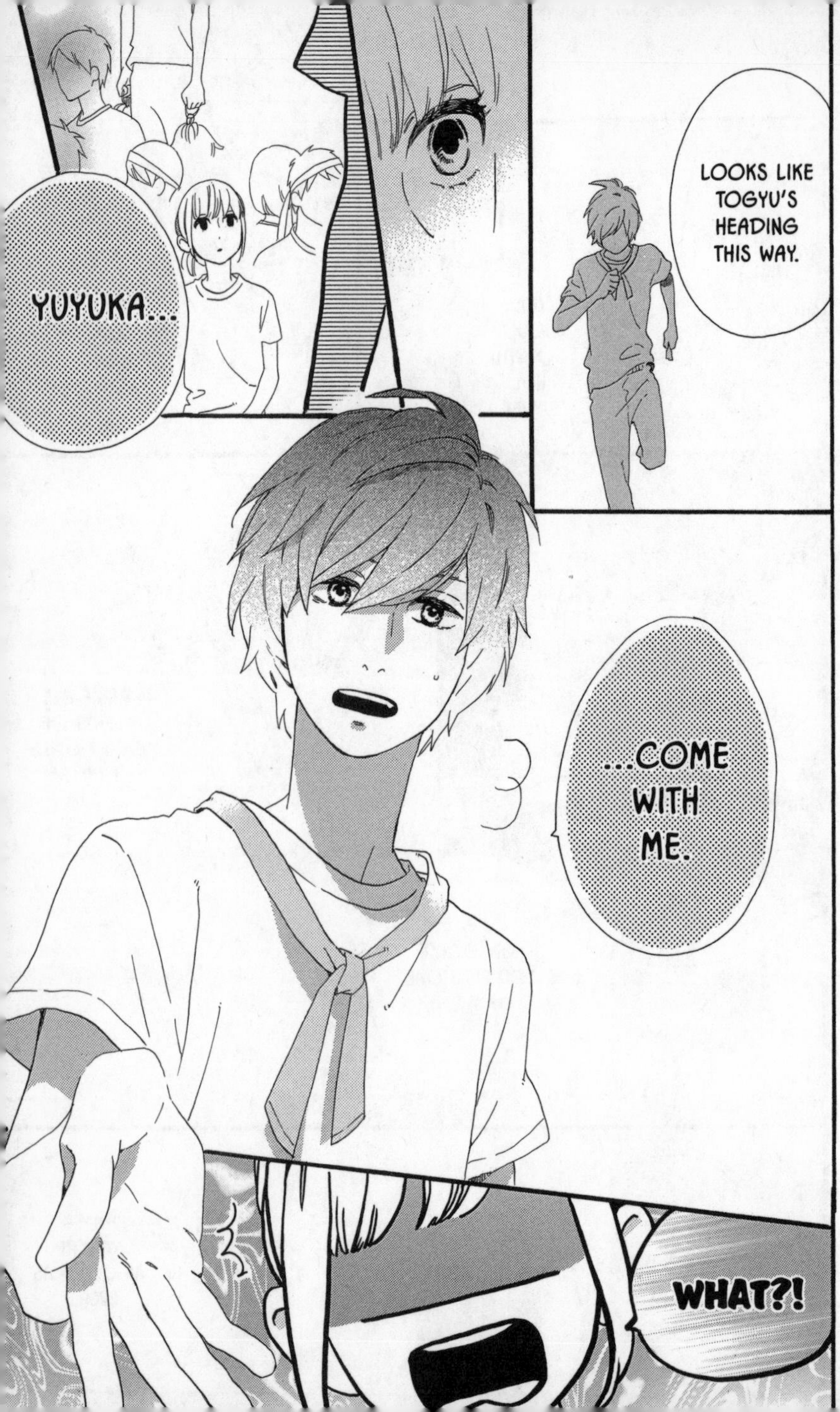
LOOKS LIKE TOGYU'S HEADING THIS WAY.
YUYUKA...
...COME WITH ME.
WHAT?!

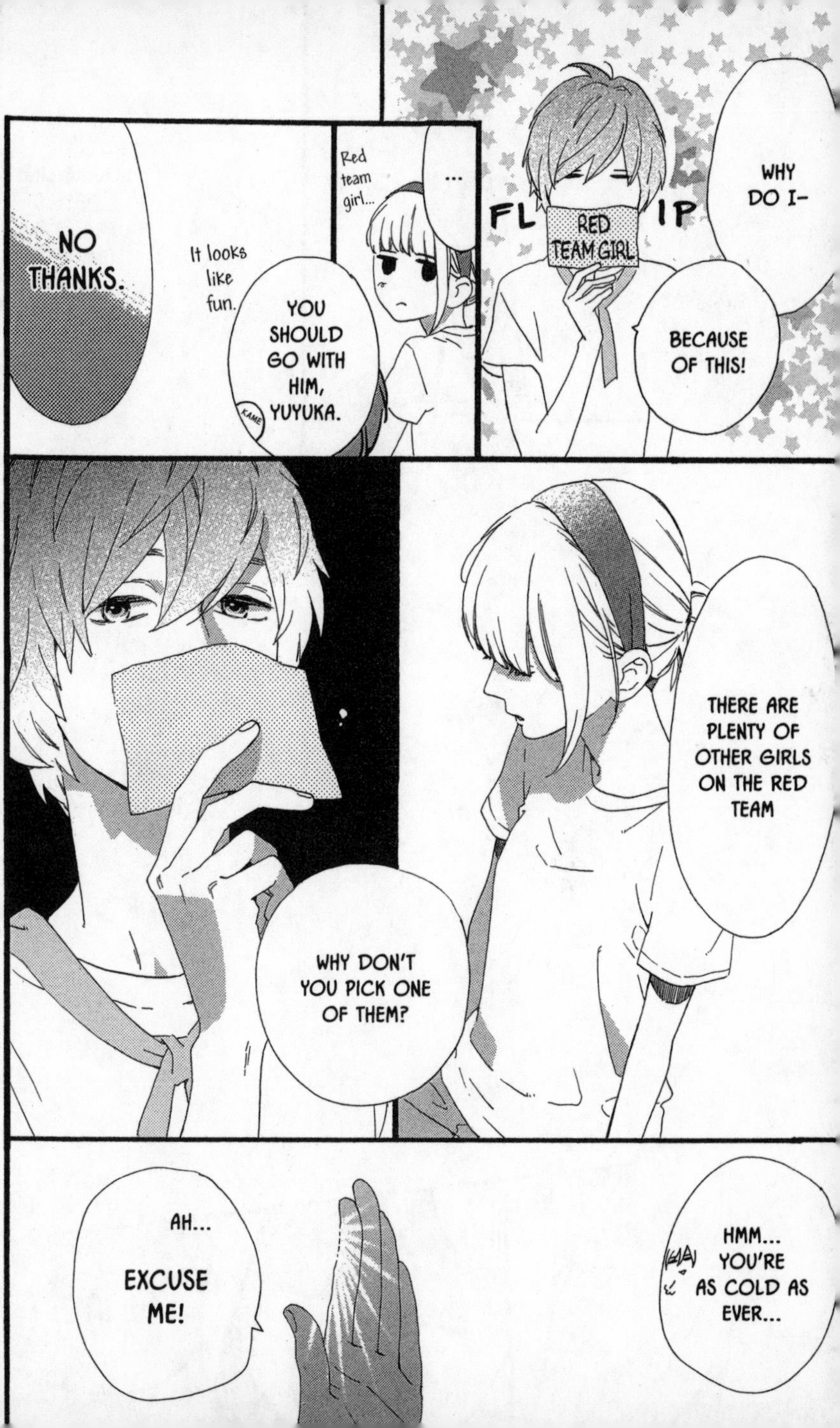
WHY DO I-
FL IP
RED TEAM GIRL
BECAUSE OF THIS!
...
Red team girl...
It looks like fun.
YOU SHOULD GO WITH HIM, YUYUKA.
KAME
NO THANKS.
THERE ARE PLENTY OF OTHER GIRLS ON THE RED TEAM
WHY DON'T YOU PICK ONE OF THEM?
HMM... YOU'RE AS COLD AS EVER...
AH...
EXCUSE ME!

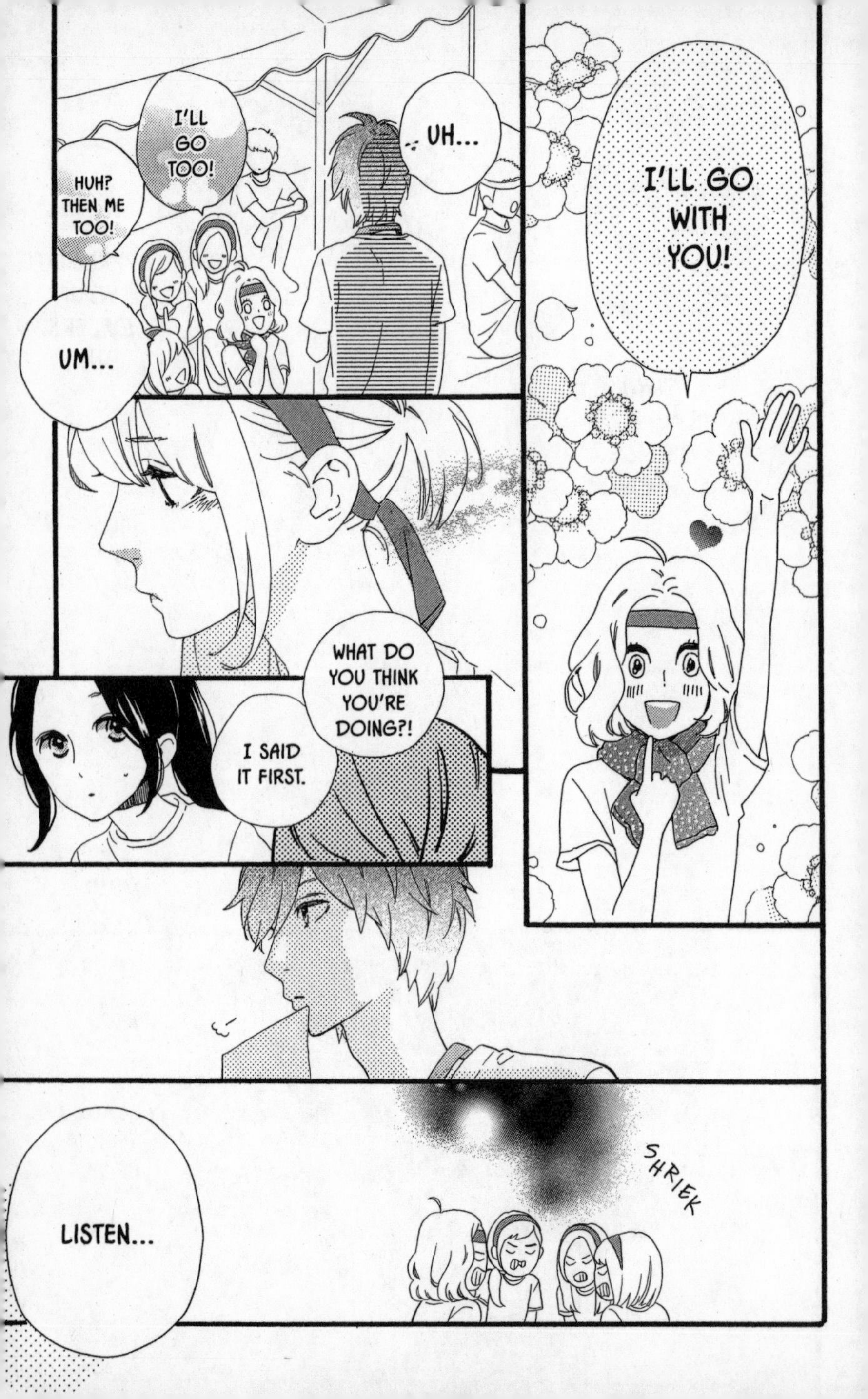
I'LL GO WITH YOU!
UH...
I'LL GO TOO!
HUH? THEN ME TOO!
UM...
WHAT DO YOU THINK YOU'RE DOING?!
I SAID IT FIRST.
SHRIEK
LISTEN...

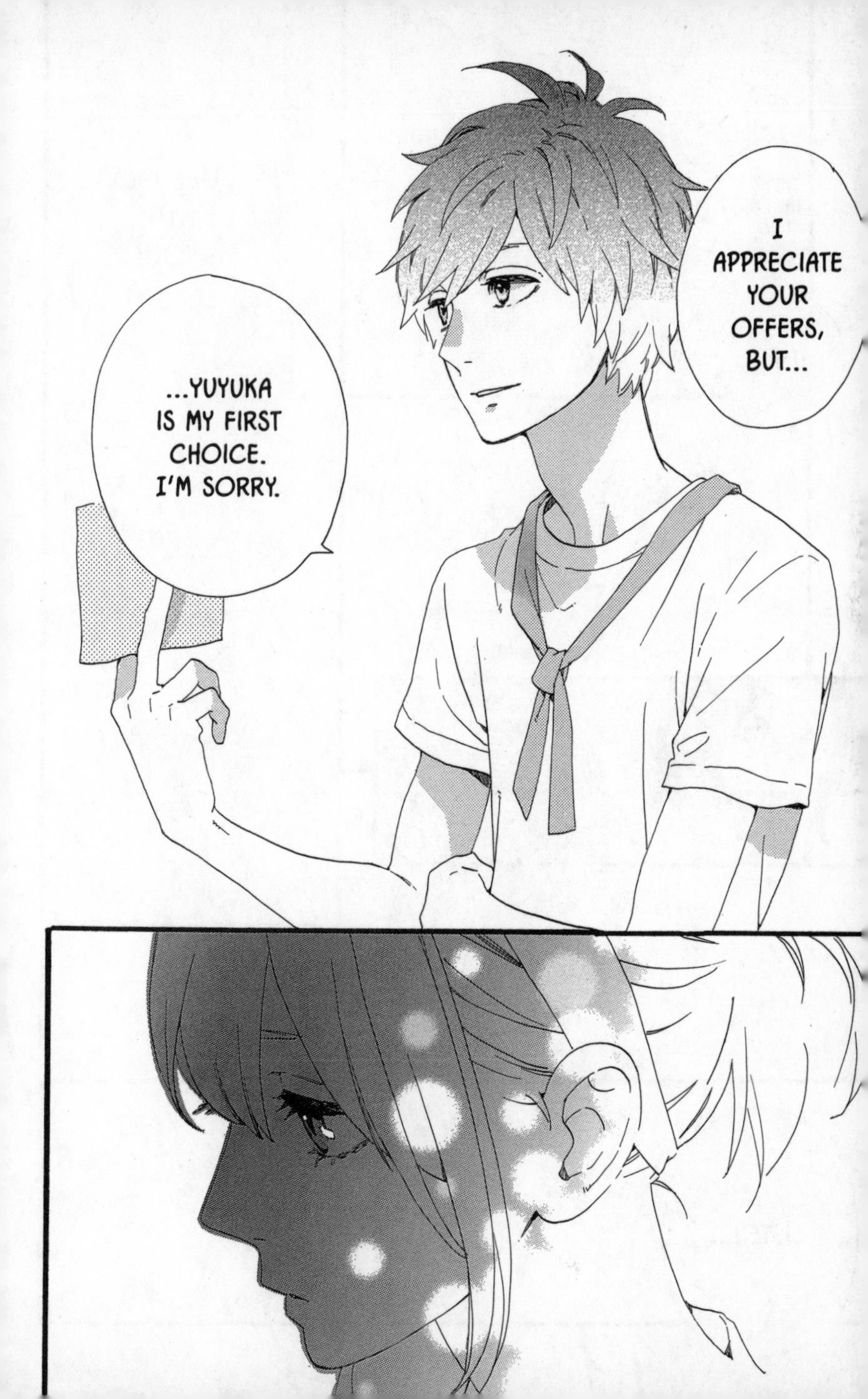
I APPRECIATE YOUR OFFERS, BUT...
...YUYUKA IS MY FIRST CHOICE. I'M SORRY.

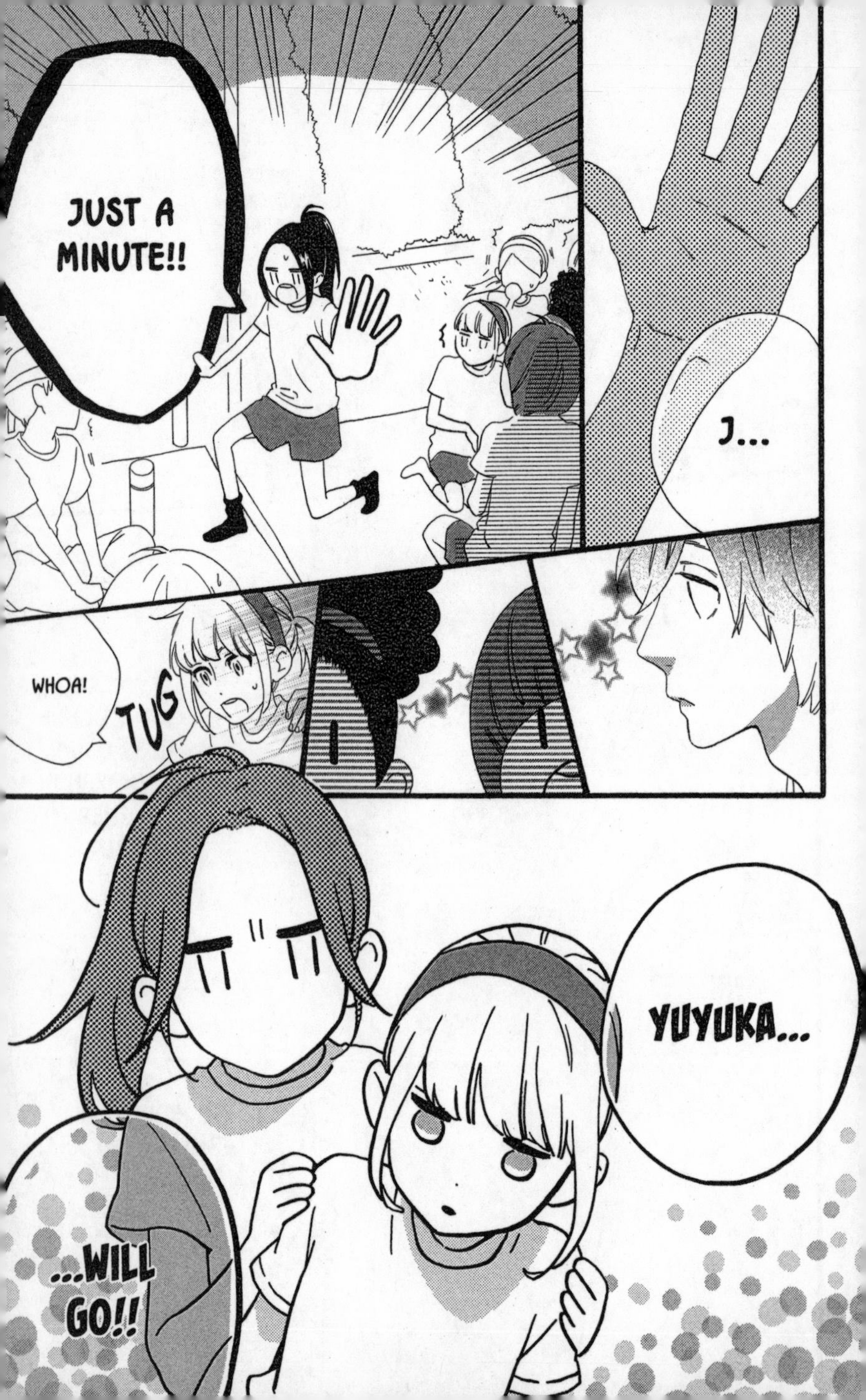
J...
JUST A MINUTE!!
WHOA!
TUG
YUYUKA...
...WILL GO!!

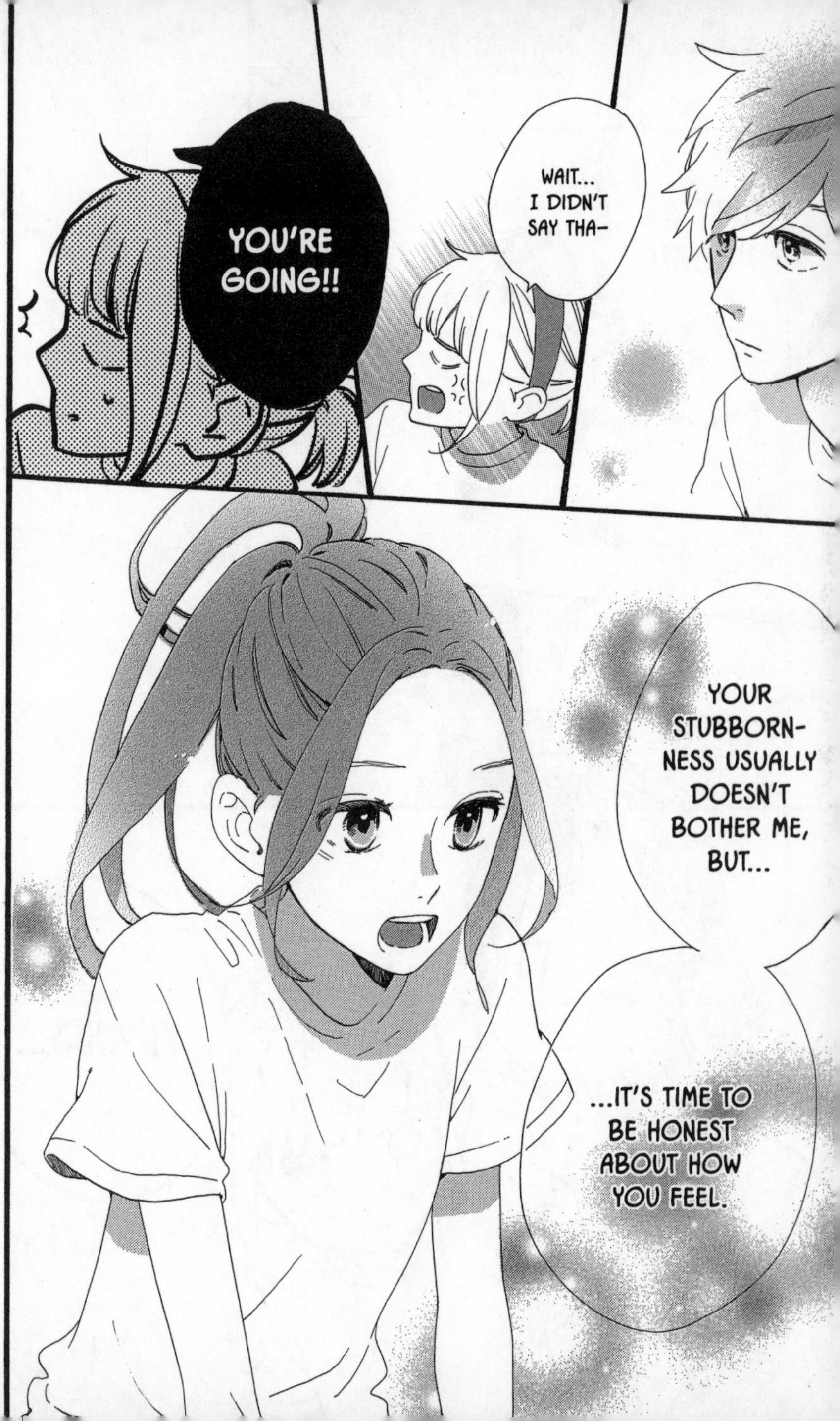
WAIT... I DIDN'T SAY THA-
YOU'RE GOING!!
YOUR STUBBORN-NESS USUALLY DOESN'T BOTHER ME, BUT...
...IT'S TIME TO BE HONEST ABOUT HOW YOU FEEL.

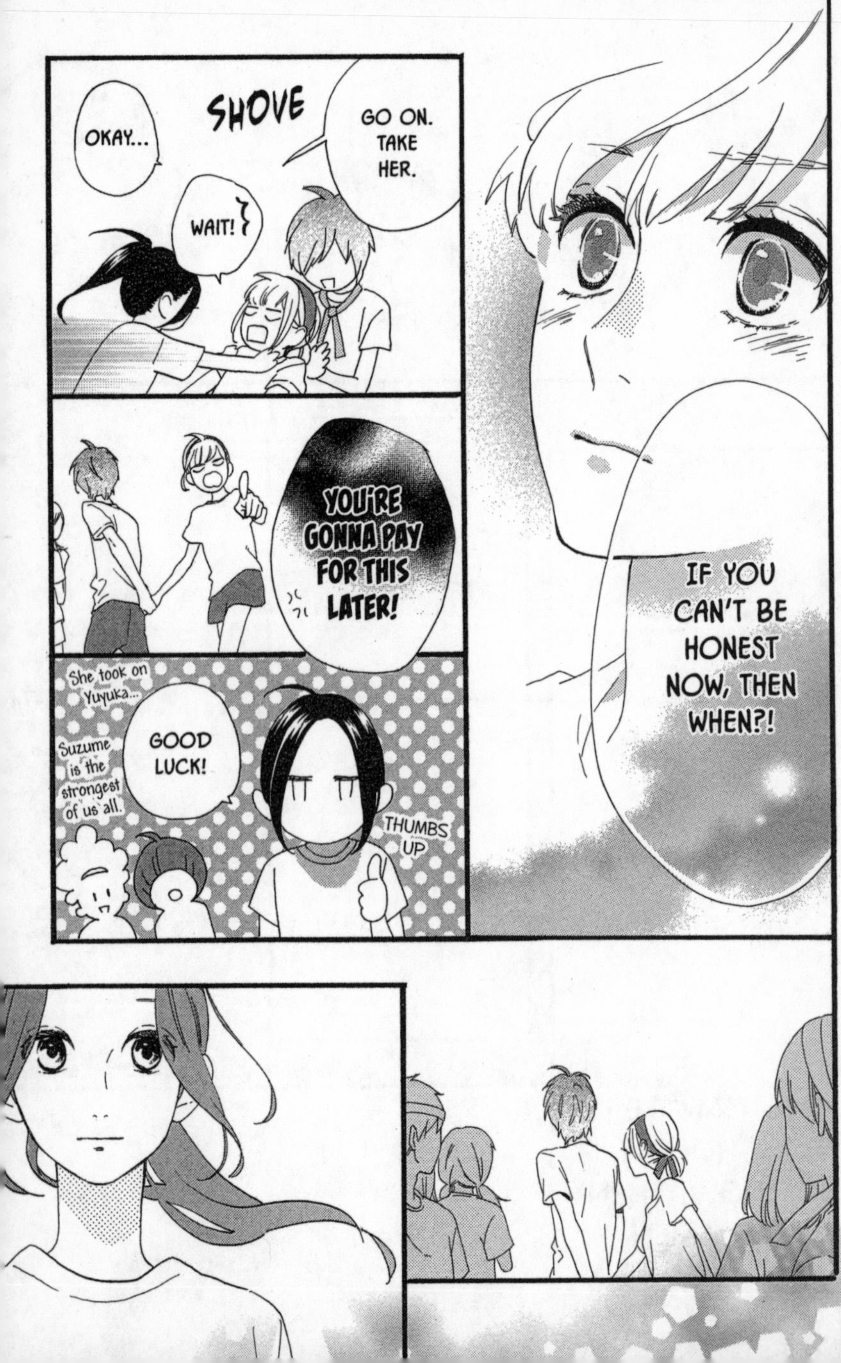
IF YOU CAN'T BE HONEST NOW, THEN WHEN?!
GO ON. TAKE HER.
SHOVE
OKAY...
WAIT!
YOU'RE GONNA PAY FOR THIS LATER!
GOOD LUCK!
She took on Yuyuka...
Suzume is the strongest of us all.
THUMBS UP

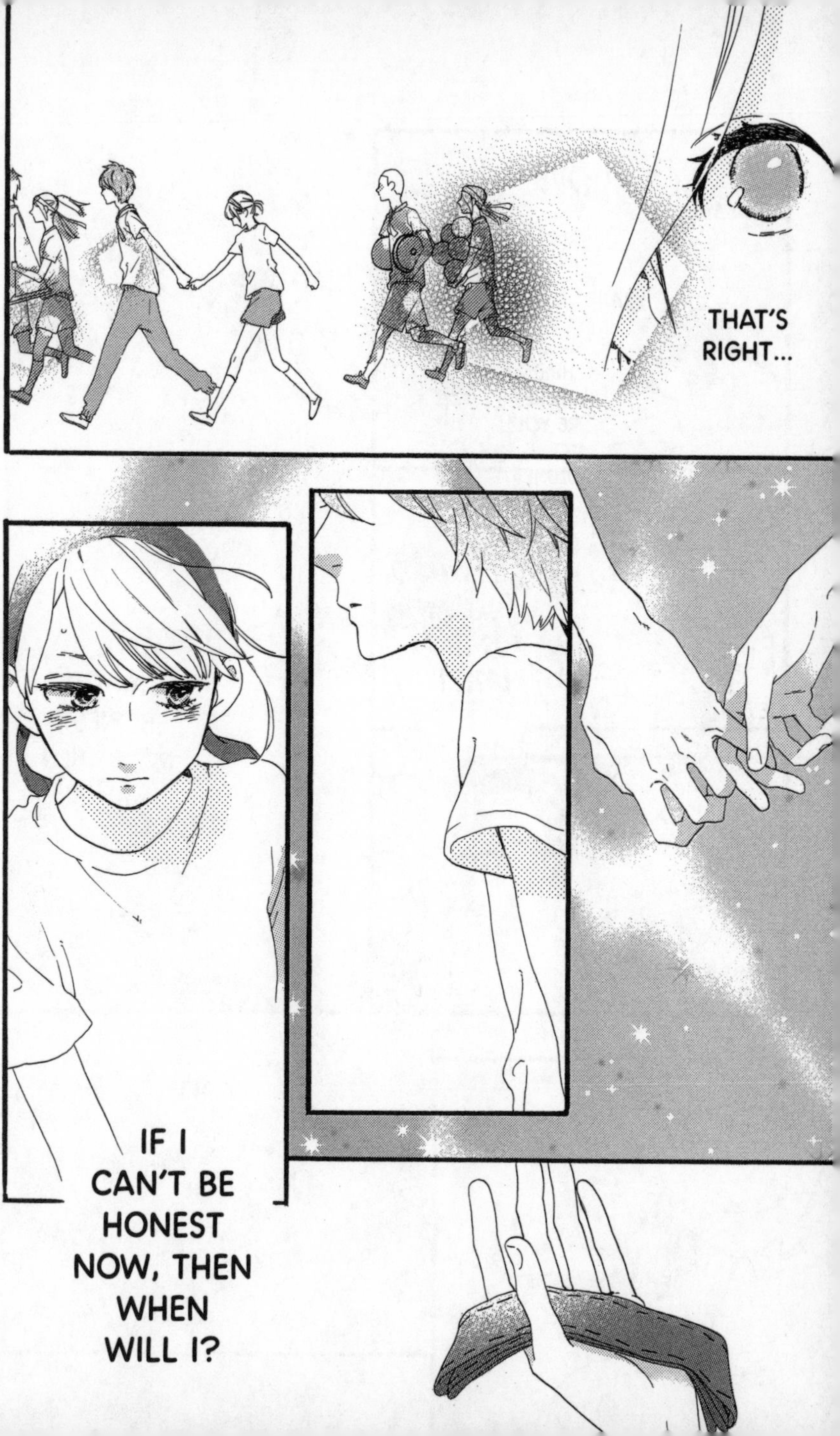
THAT'S RIGHT...
IF I CAN'T BE HONEST NOW, THEN WHEN WILL I?

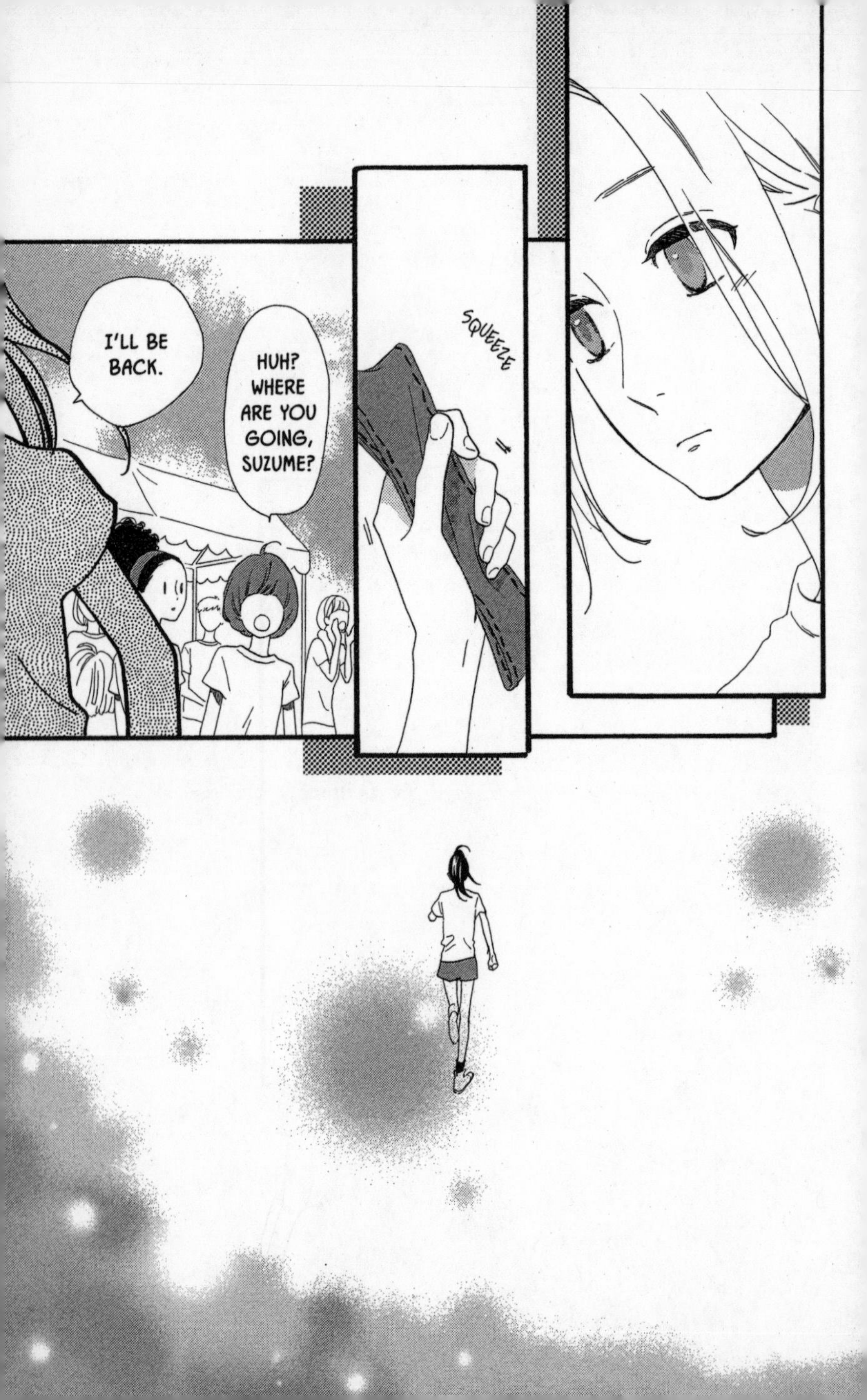
SQUEEZE
HUH? WHERE ARE YOU GOING, SUZUME?
I'LL BE BACK.

The guy standing next to Togyu is his
friend Koshin Samejima.

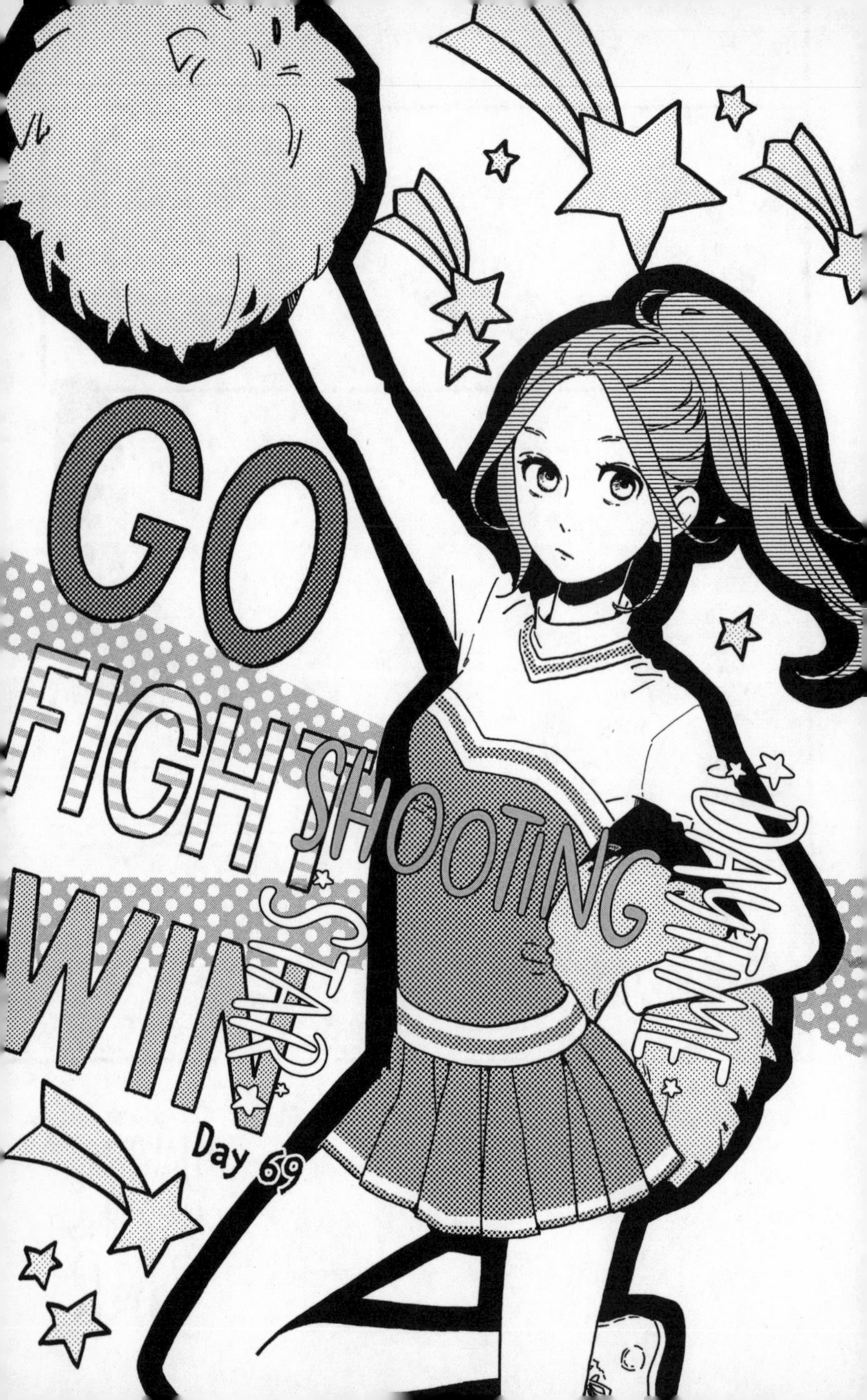
GO
FIGHT
WIN
SHOOTING STAR
DAYTIME
Day 69

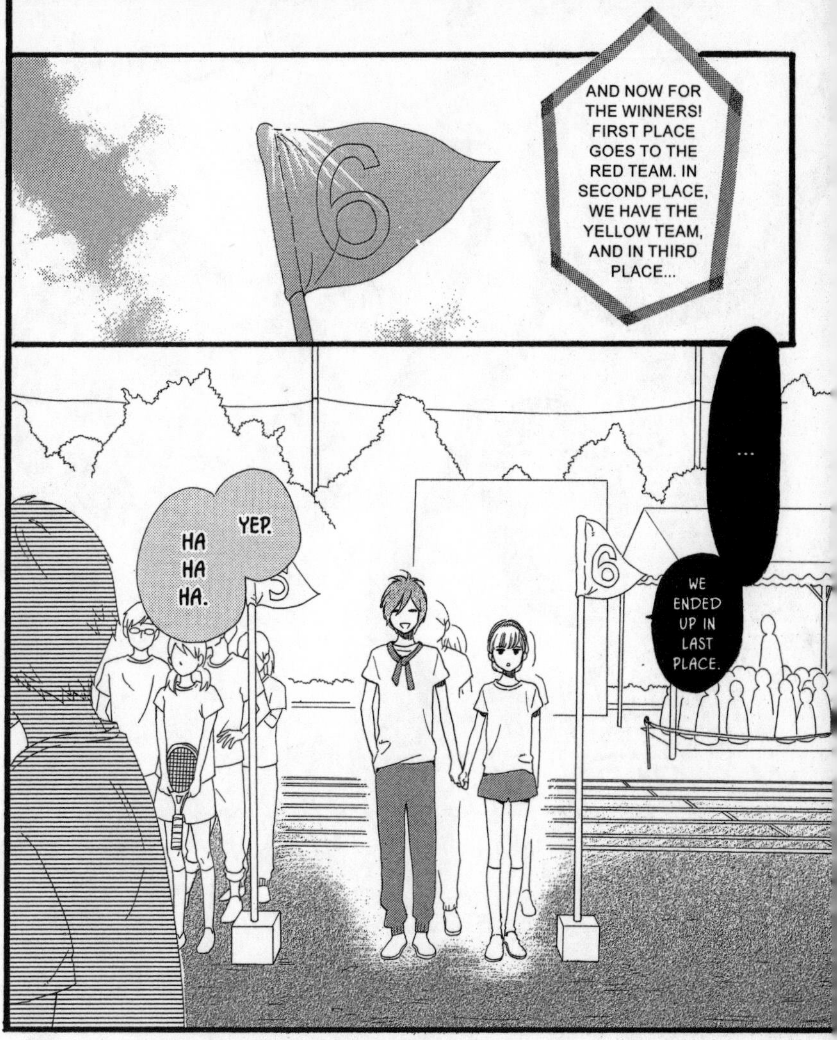
AND NOW FOR THE WINNERS! FIRST PLACE GOES TO THE RED TEAM. IN SECOND PLACE, WE HAVE THE YELLOW TEAM, AND IN THIRD PLACE...
...
WE ENDED UP IN LAST PLACE.
YEP.
HA HA HA.

DAYTIME SHOOTING STAR

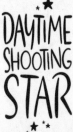

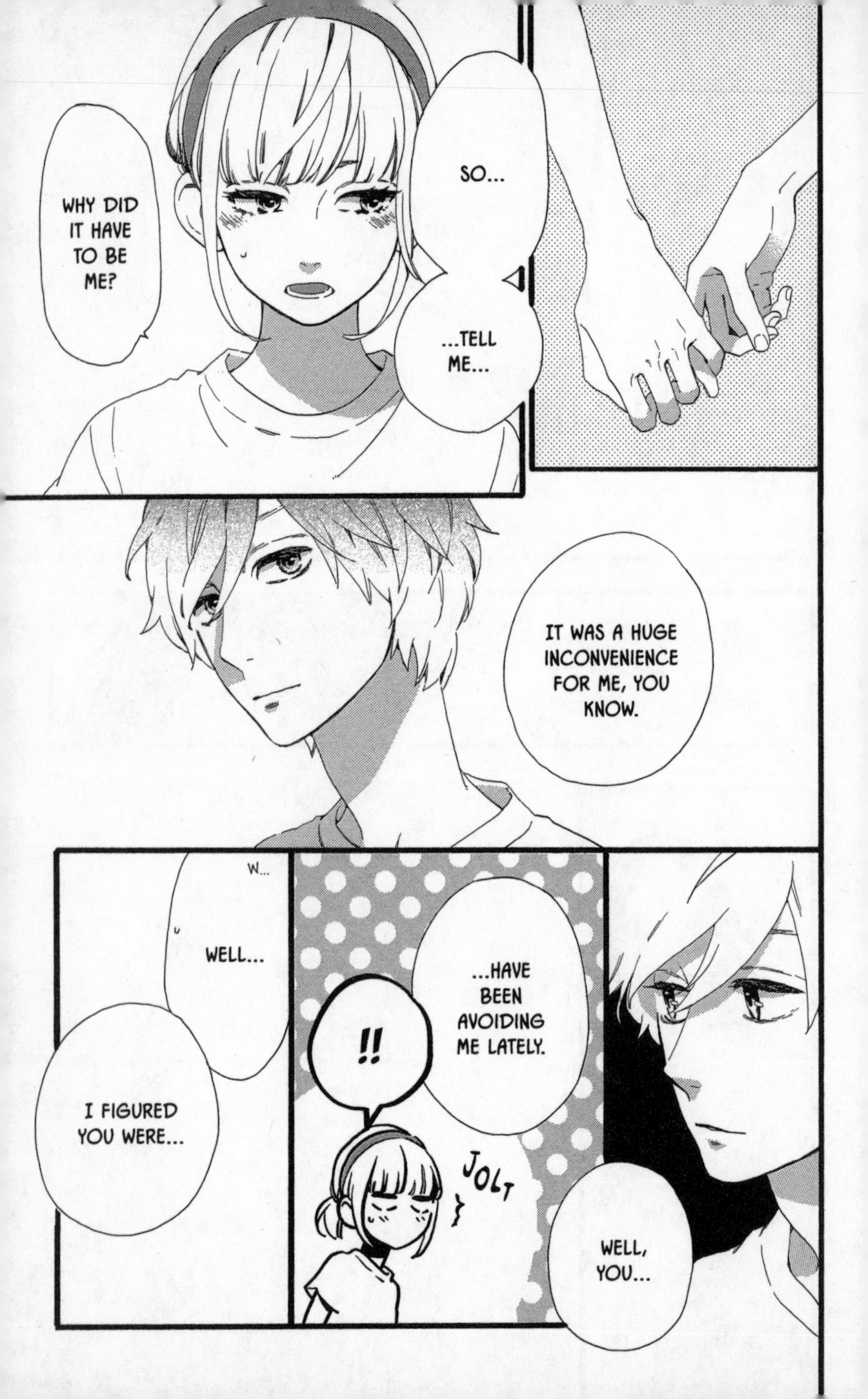
SO...
...TELL ME...
WHY DID IT HAVE TO BE ME?
IT WAS A HUGE INCONVENIENCE FOR ME, YOU KNOW.
WELL, YOU...
...HAVE BEEN AVOIDING ME LATELY.
!!
JOLT
W... WELL...
I FIGURED YOU WERE...

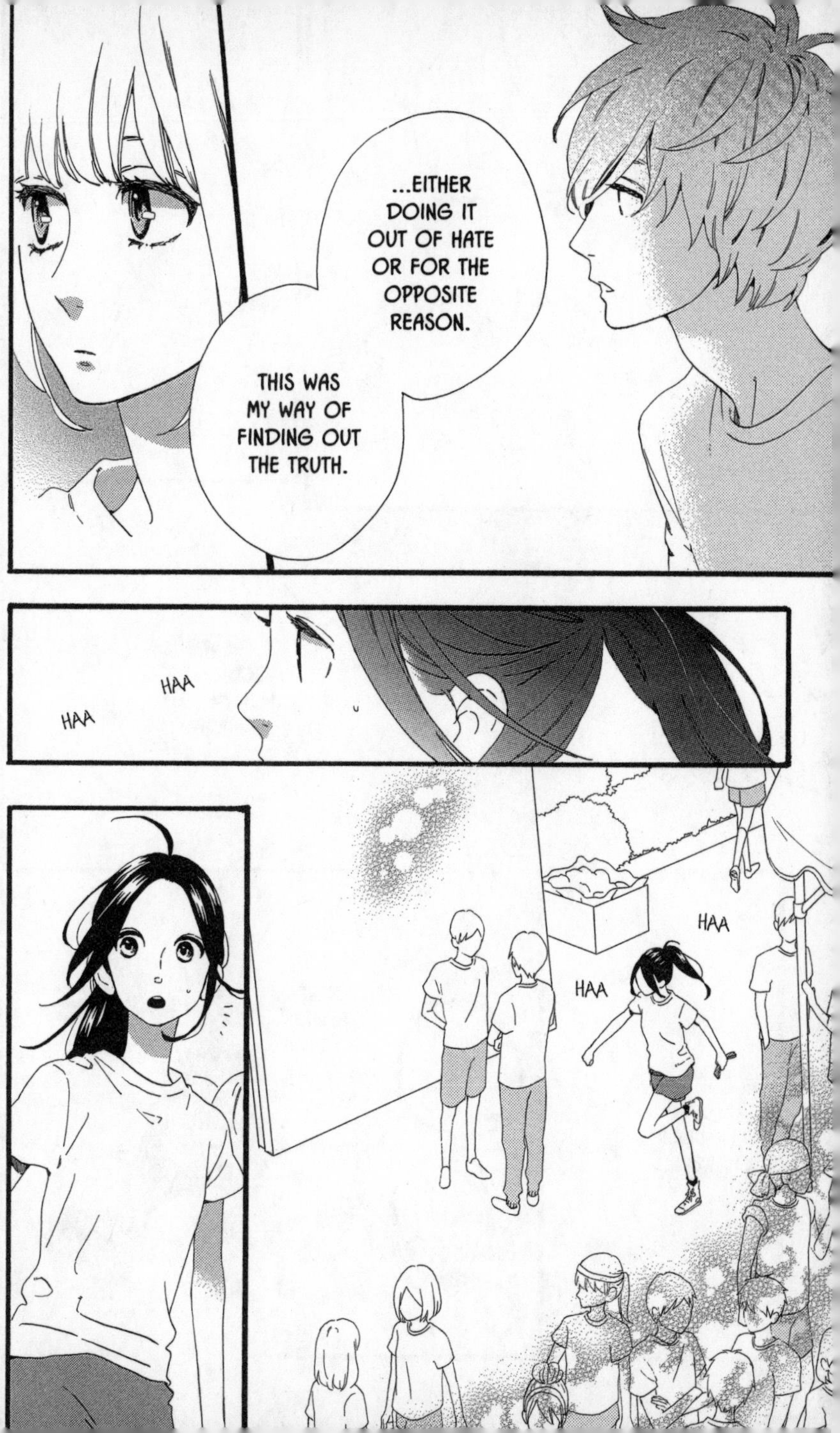
...EITHER DOING IT OUT OF HATE OR FOR THE OPPOSITE REASON.
THIS WAS MY WAY OF FINDING OUT THE TRUTH.
HAA
HAA
HAA
HAA

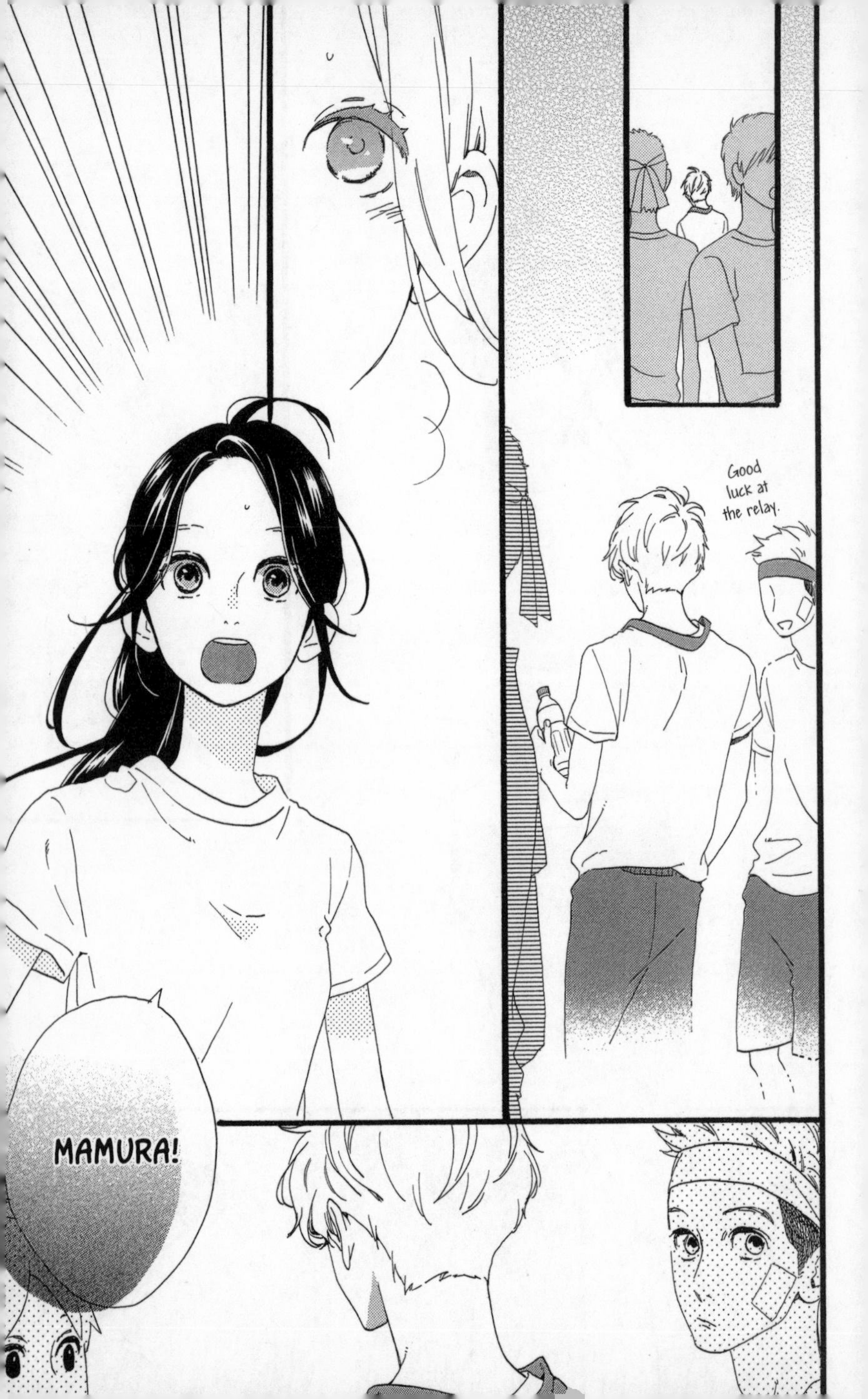
Good luck at the relay.
MAMURA!

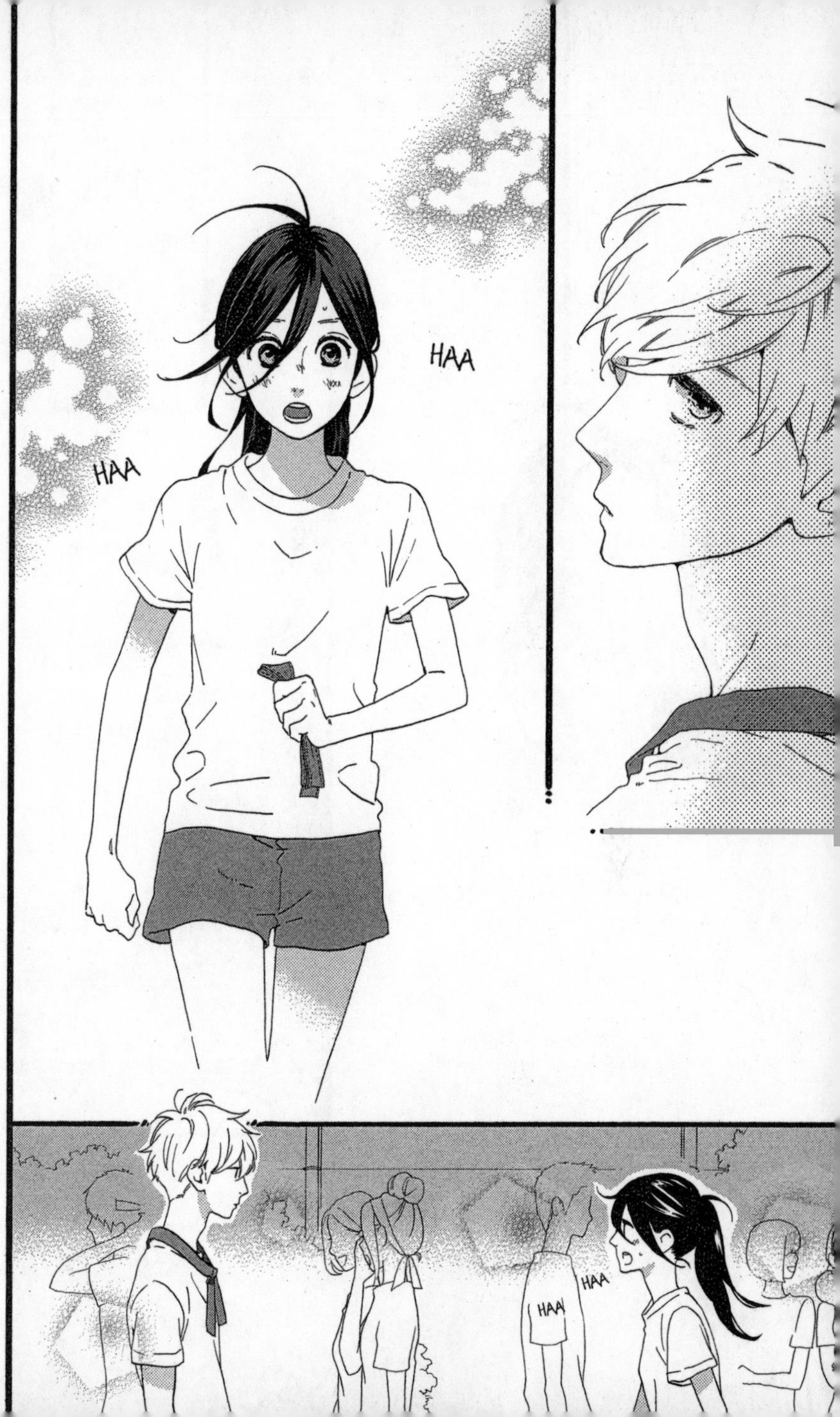
HAA
HAA
HAA
HAA

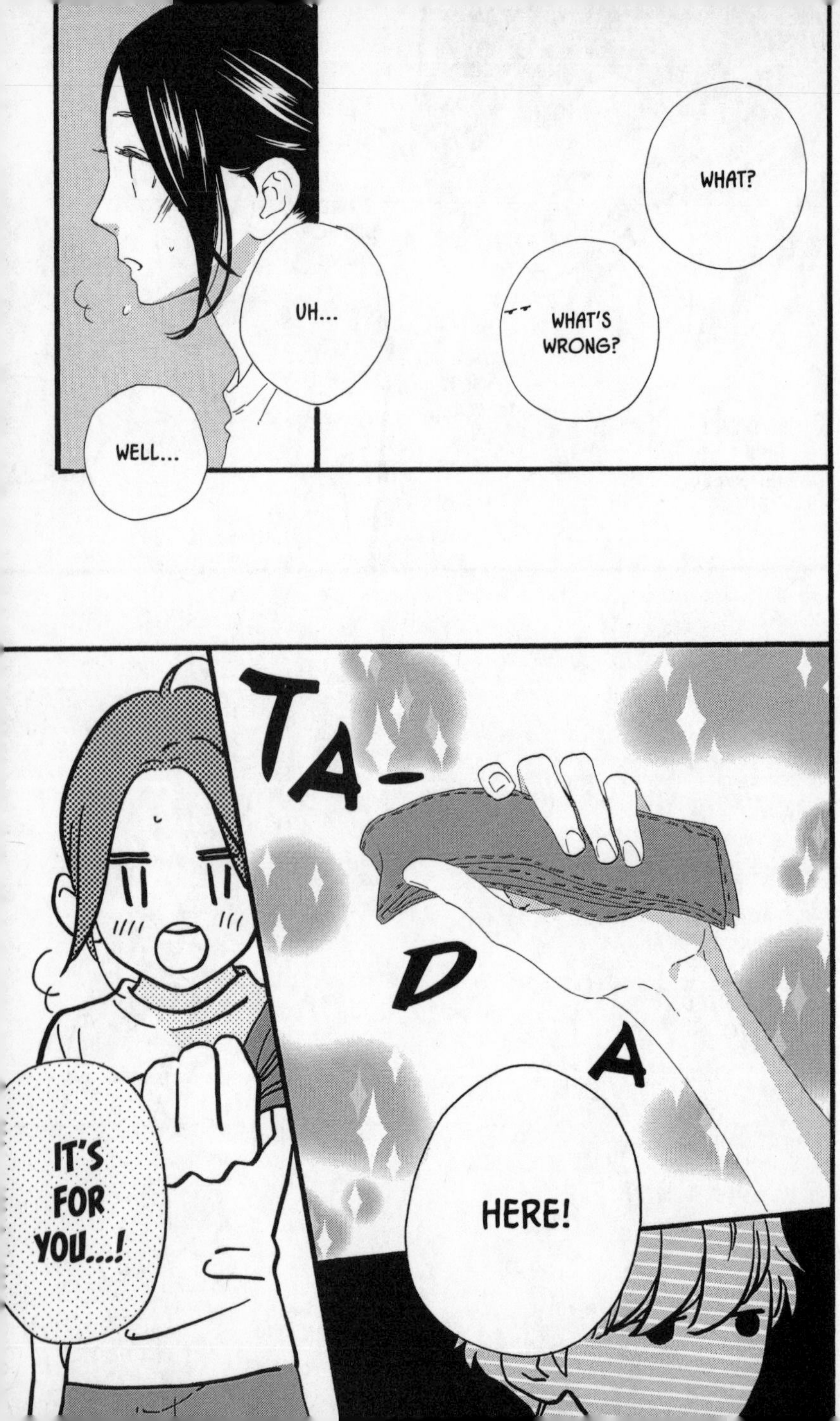
WHAT?
WHAT'S WRONG?
UH...
WELL...
TA-DA
HERE!
IT'S FOR YOU...!

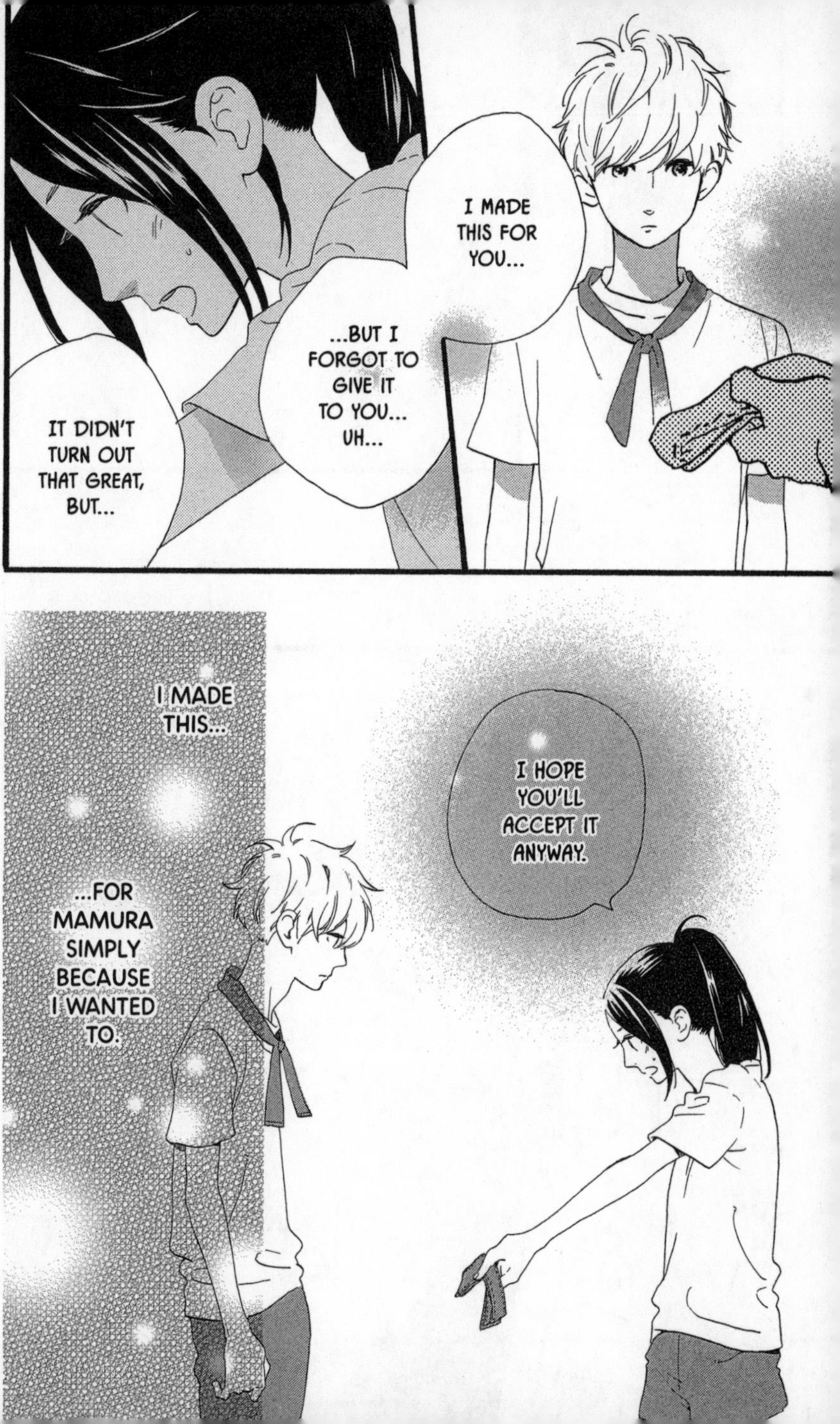
I MADE THIS FOR YOU...
...BUT I FORGOT TO GIVE IT TO YOU... UH...
IT DIDN'T TURN OUT THAT GREAT, BUT...
I HOPE YOU'LL ACCEPT IT ANYWAY.
I MADE THIS...
...FOR MAMURA SIMPLY BECAUSE I WANTED TO.

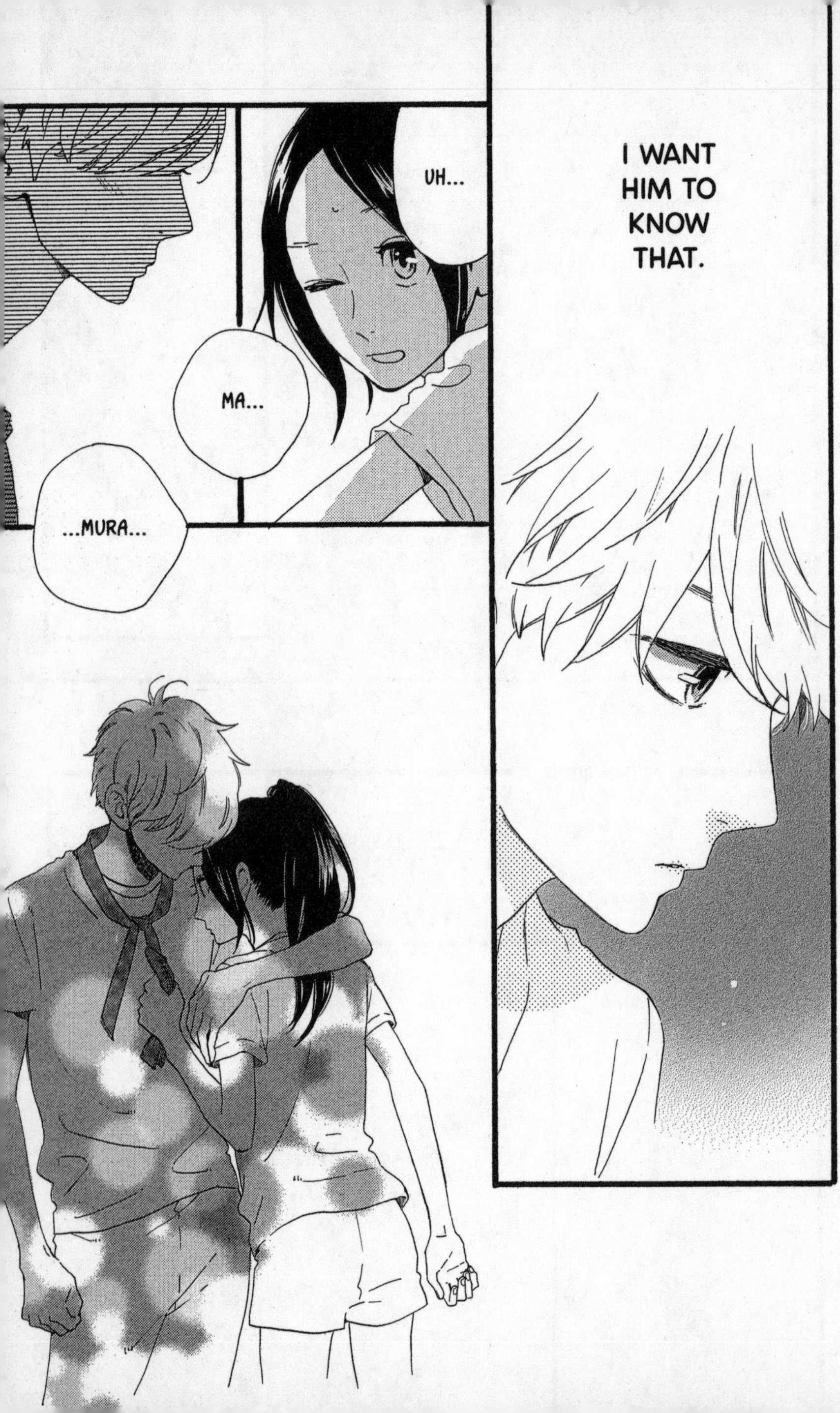

I WANT HIM TO KNOW THAT.
UH...
MA...
...MURA...

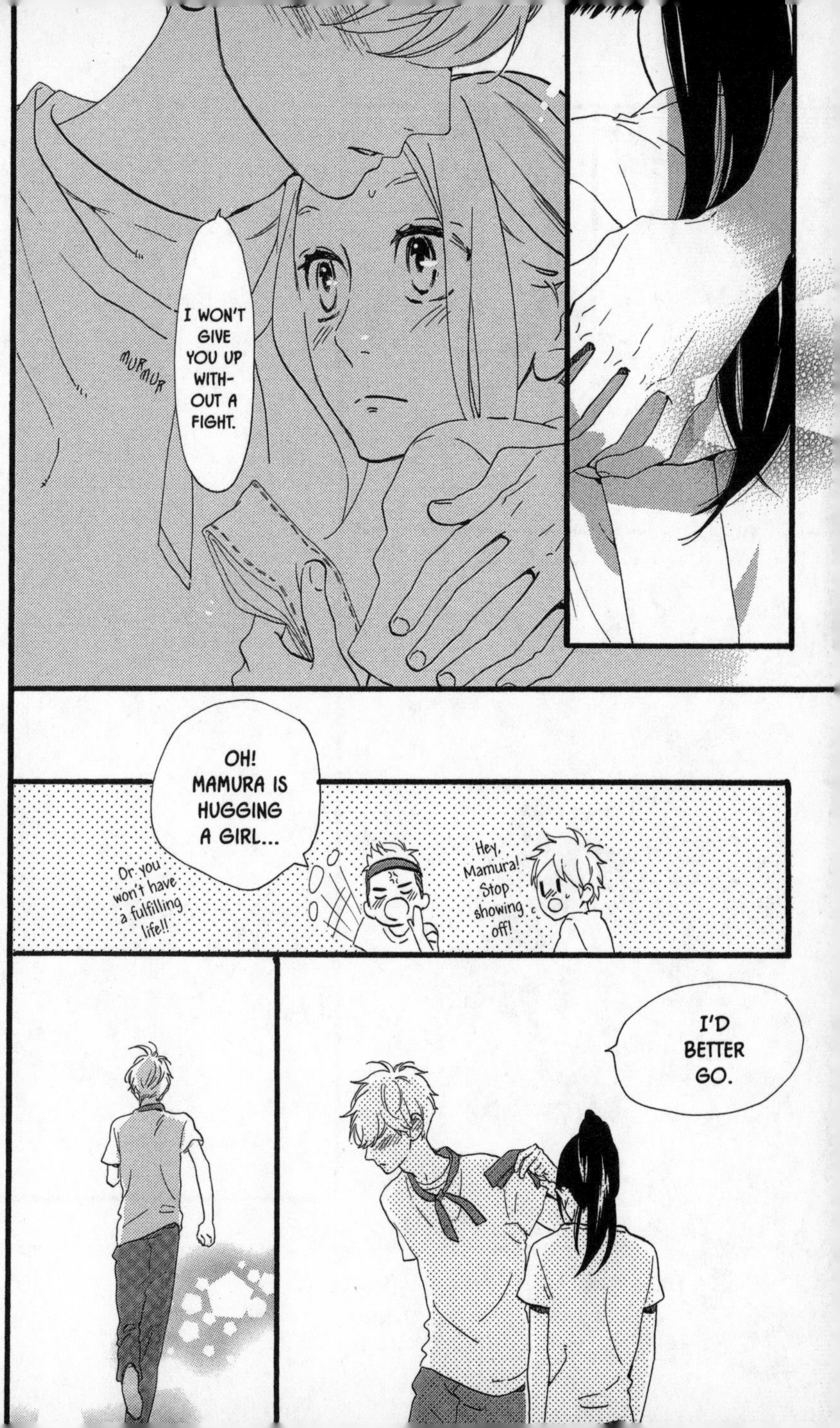
I WON'T GIVE YOU UP WITHOUT A FIGHT.
MURMUR
OH! MAMURA IS HUGGING A GIRL...
Hey, Mamura! Stop showing off!
Or you won't have a fulfilling life!!
I'D BETTER GO.

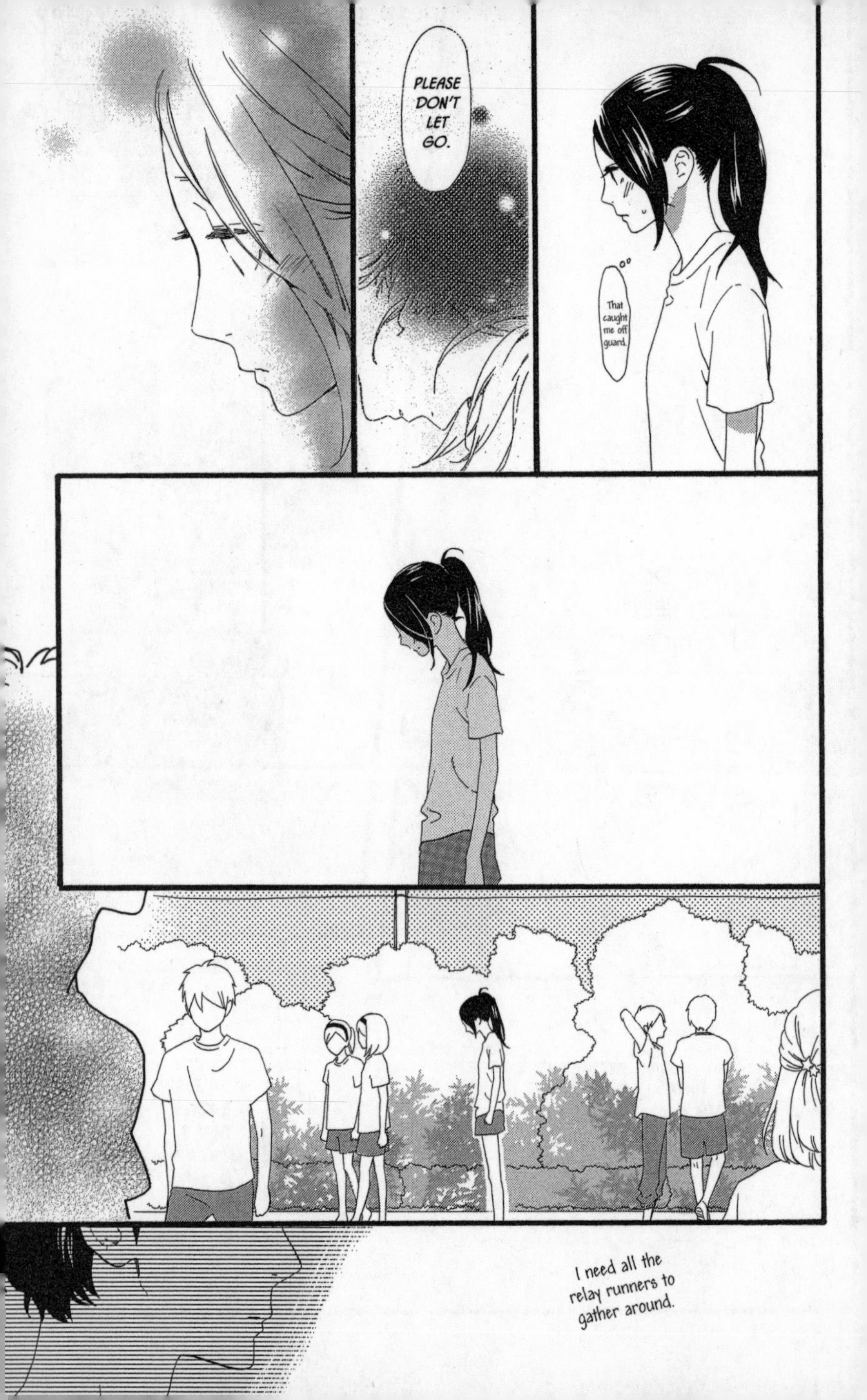
That caught me off guard.
PLEASE DON'T LET GO.
I need all the relay runners to gather around.

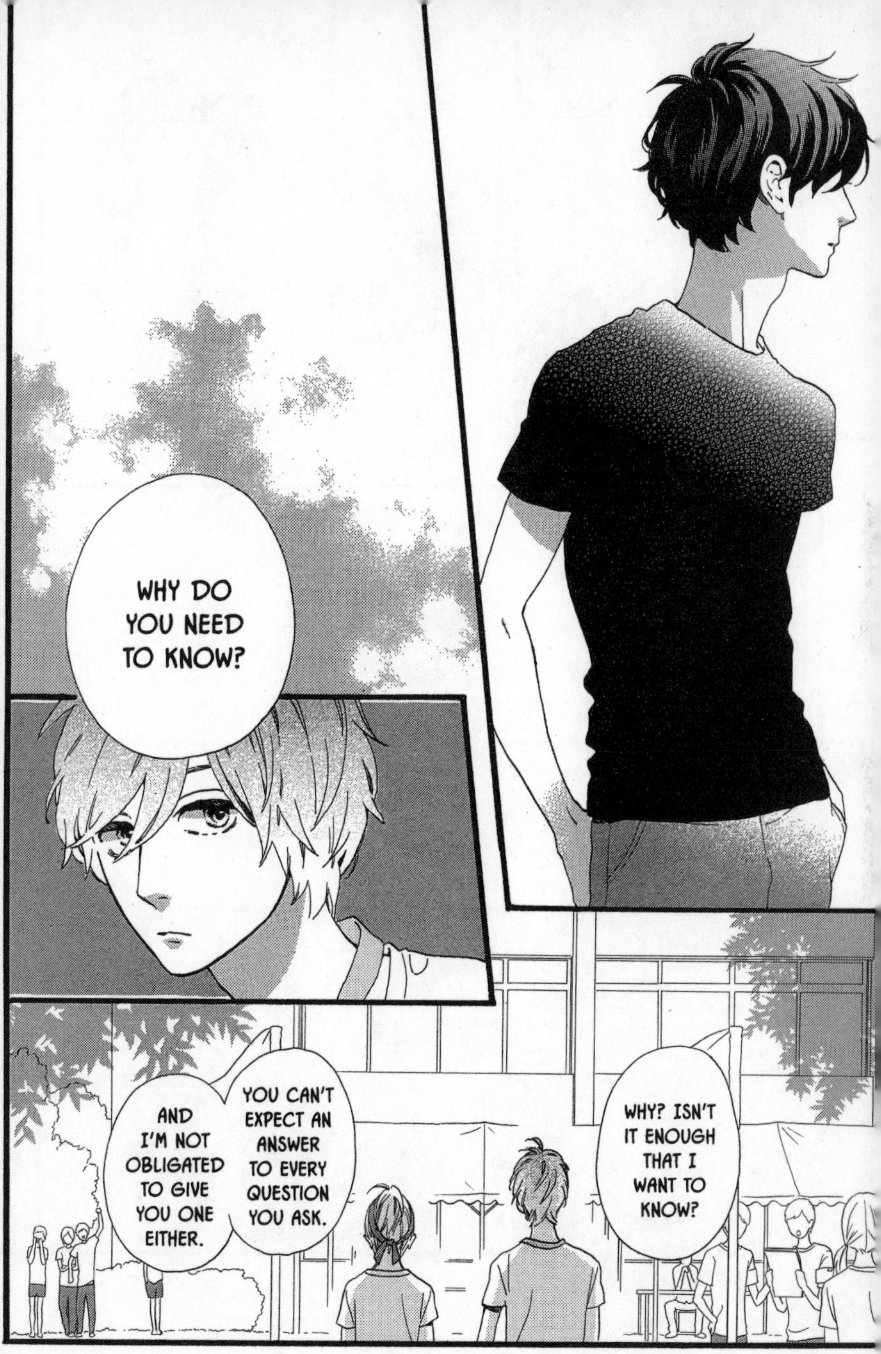
WHY DO YOU NEED TO KNOW?
WHY? ISN'T IT ENOUGH THAT I WANT TO KNOW?
YOU CAN'T EXPECT AN ANSWER TO EVERY QUESTION YOU ASK.
AND I'M NOT OBLIGATED TO GIVE YOU ONE EITHER.

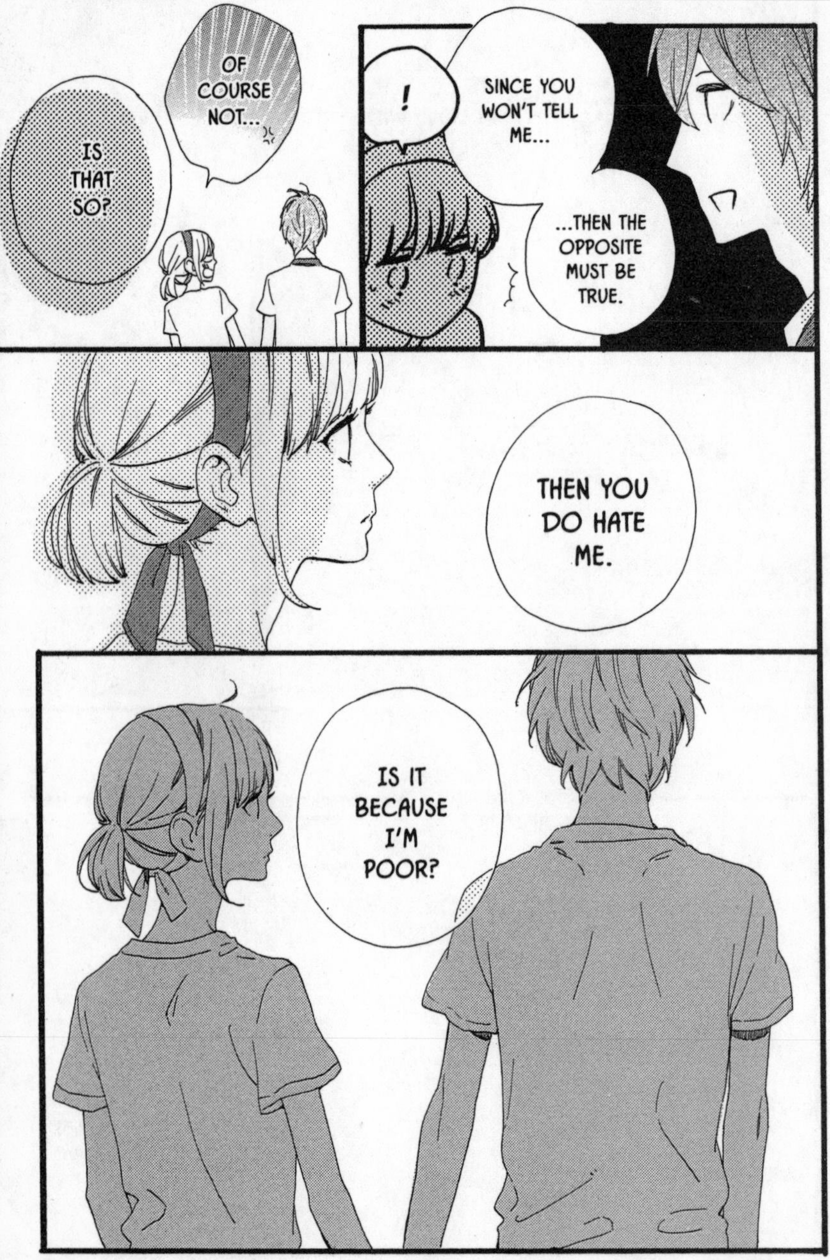
SINCE YOU WON'T TELL ME...
!
...THEN THE OPPOSITE MUST BE TRUE.
OF COURSE NOT...
IS THAT SO?
THEN YOU DO HATE ME.
IS IT BECAUSE I'M POOR?

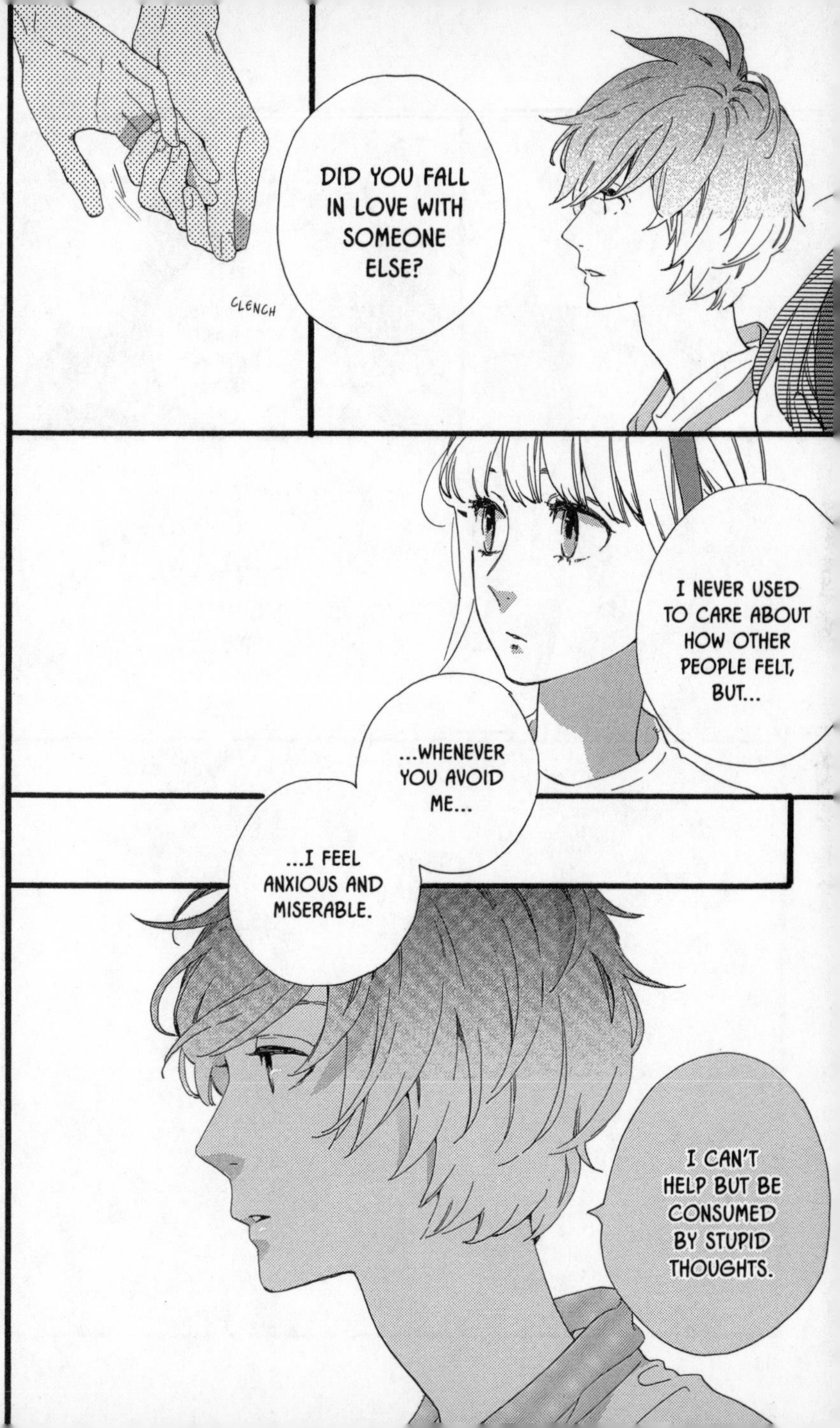
DID YOU FALL IN LOVE WITH SOMEONE ELSE?
CLENCH
I NEVER USED TO CARE ABOUT HOW OTHER PEOPLE FELT, BUT...
...WHENEVER YOU AVOID ME...
...I FEEL ANXIOUS AND MISERABLE.
I CAN'T HELP BUT BE CONSUMED BY STUPID THOUGHTS.

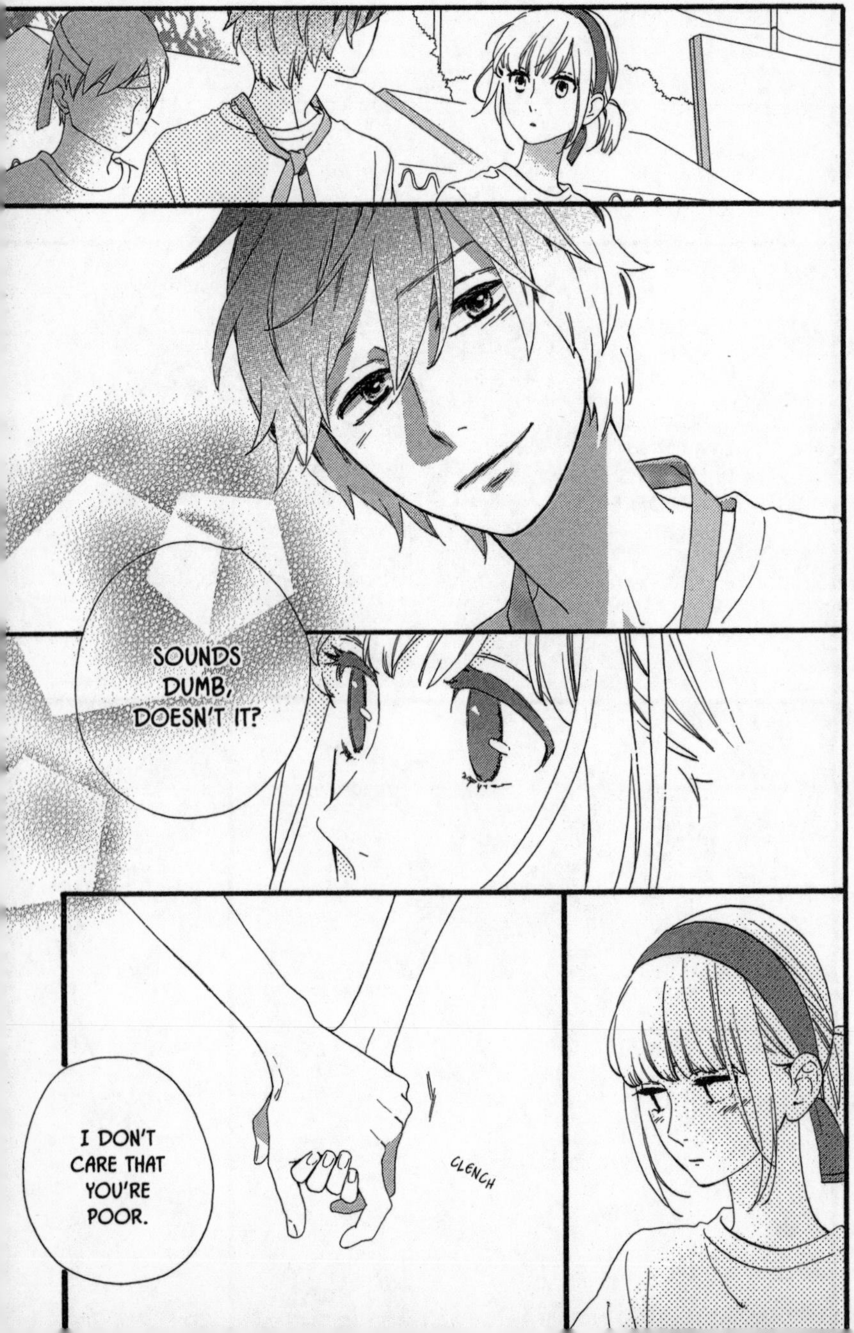
SOUNDS DUMB, DOESN'T IT?
CLENCH
I DON'T CARE THAT YOU'RE POOR.

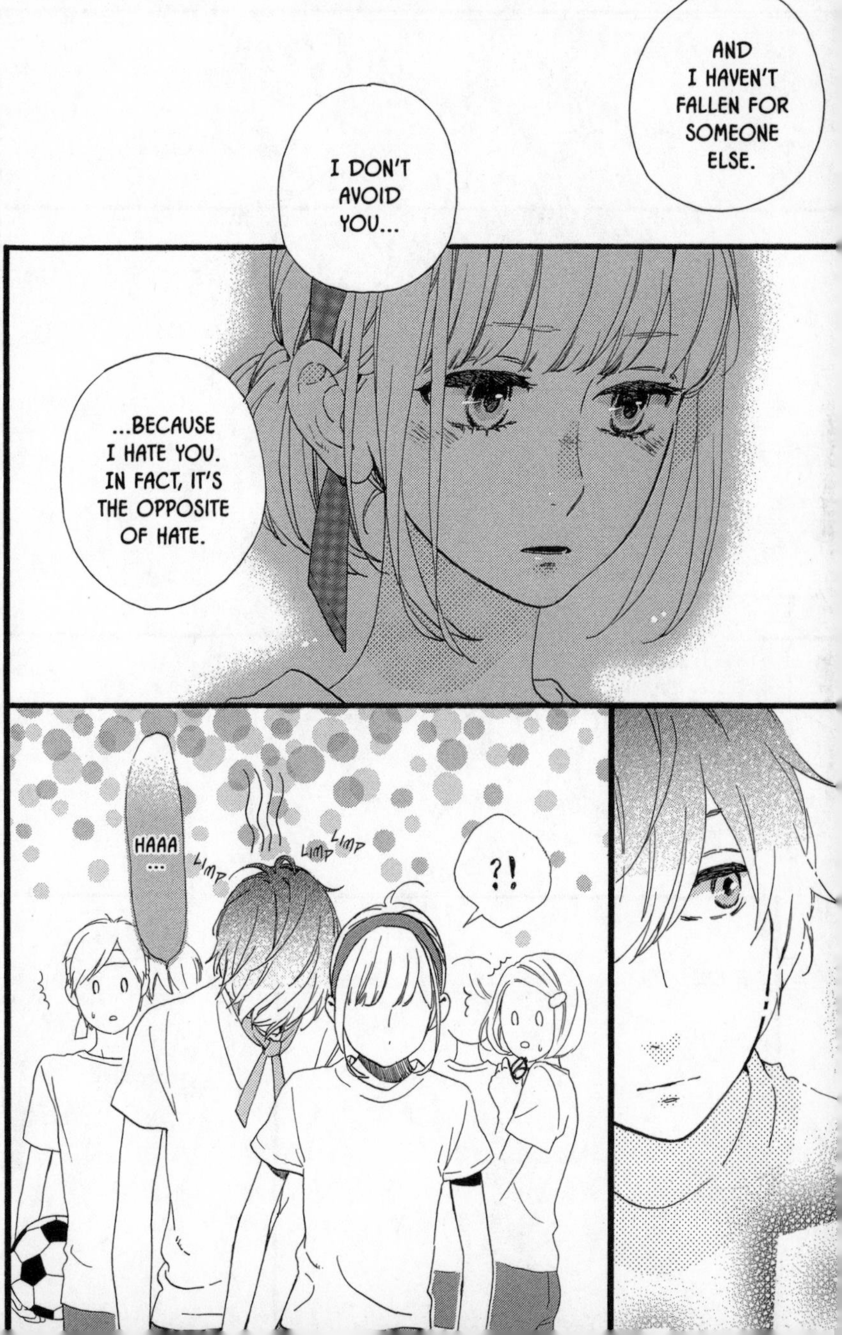
AND I HAVEN'T FALLEN FOR SOMEONE ELSE.
I DON'T AVOID YOU...
...BECAUSE I HATE YOU. IN FACT, IT'S THE OPPOSITE OF HATE.
?!
LIMP LIMP
LIMP
HAAA...

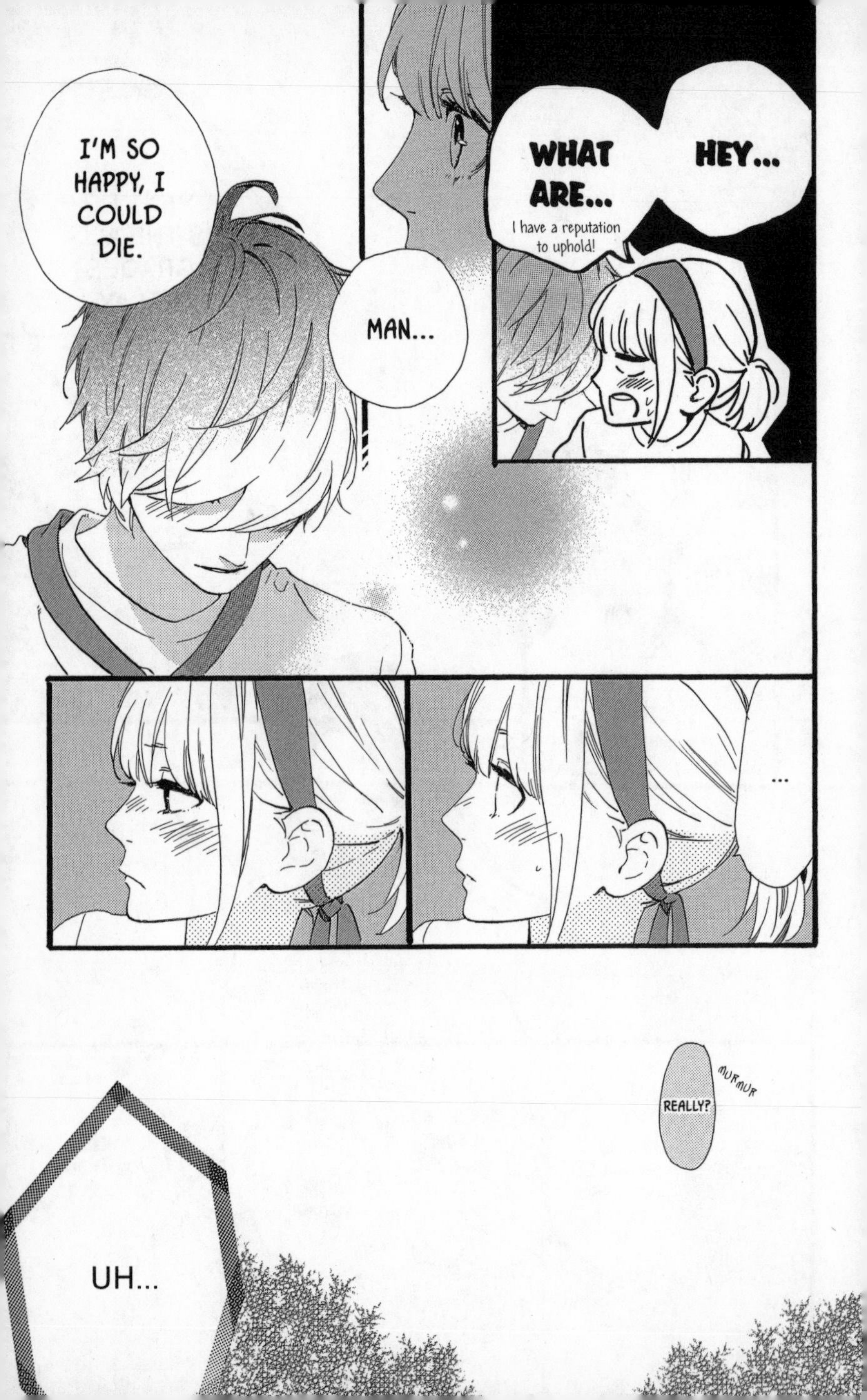
HEY...
WHAT ARE...
I have a reputation to uphold!
MAN...
I'M SO HAPPY, I COULD DIE.
...
MURMUR
REALLY?
UH...

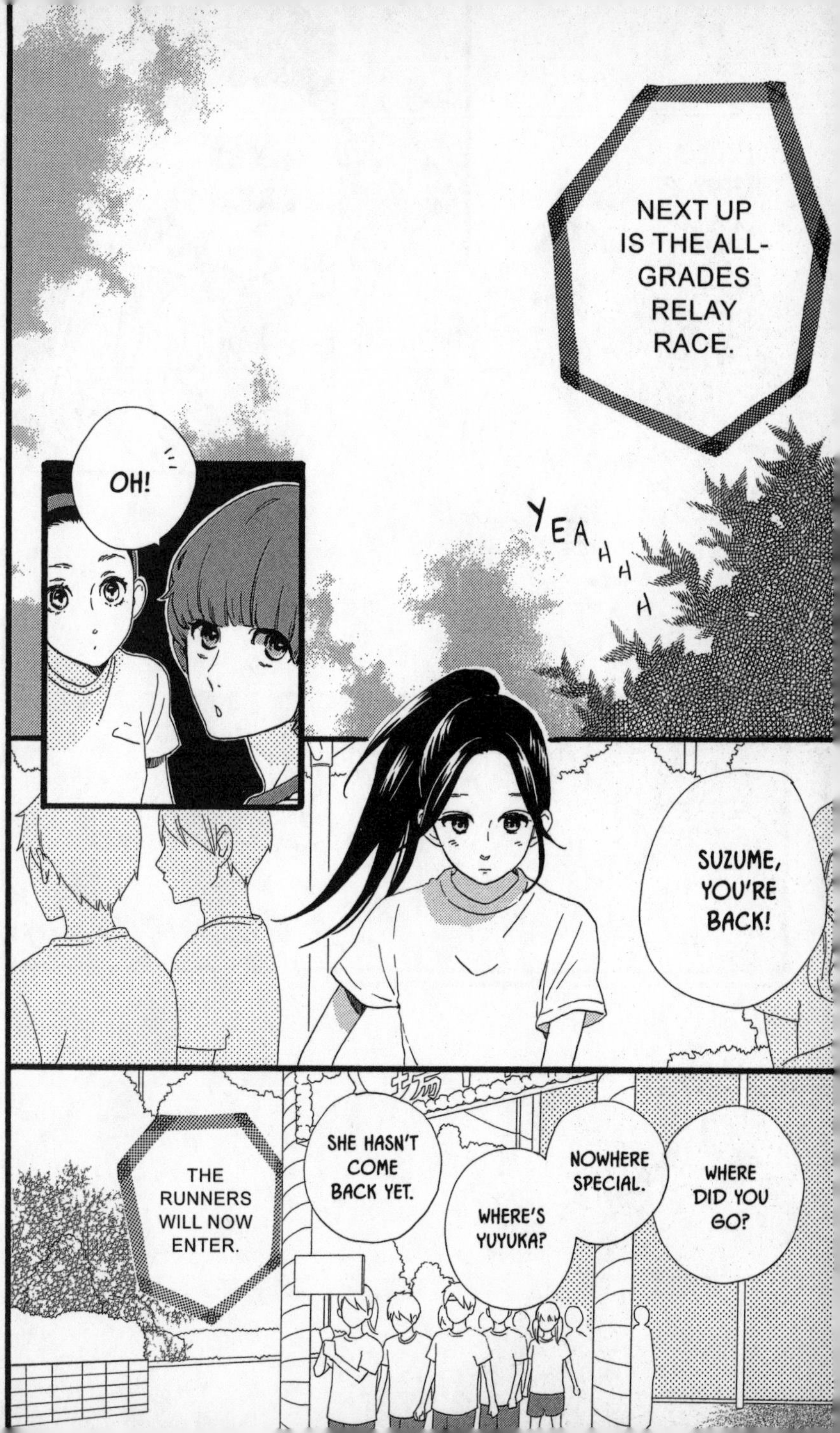
NEXT UP IS THE ALL-GRADES RELAY RACE.
YEAHHH
OH!
SUZUME, YOU'RE BACK!
WHERE DID YOU GO?
NOWHERE SPECIAL.
WHERE'S YUYUKA?
SHE HASN'T COME BACK YET.
THE RUNNERS WILL NOW ENTER.

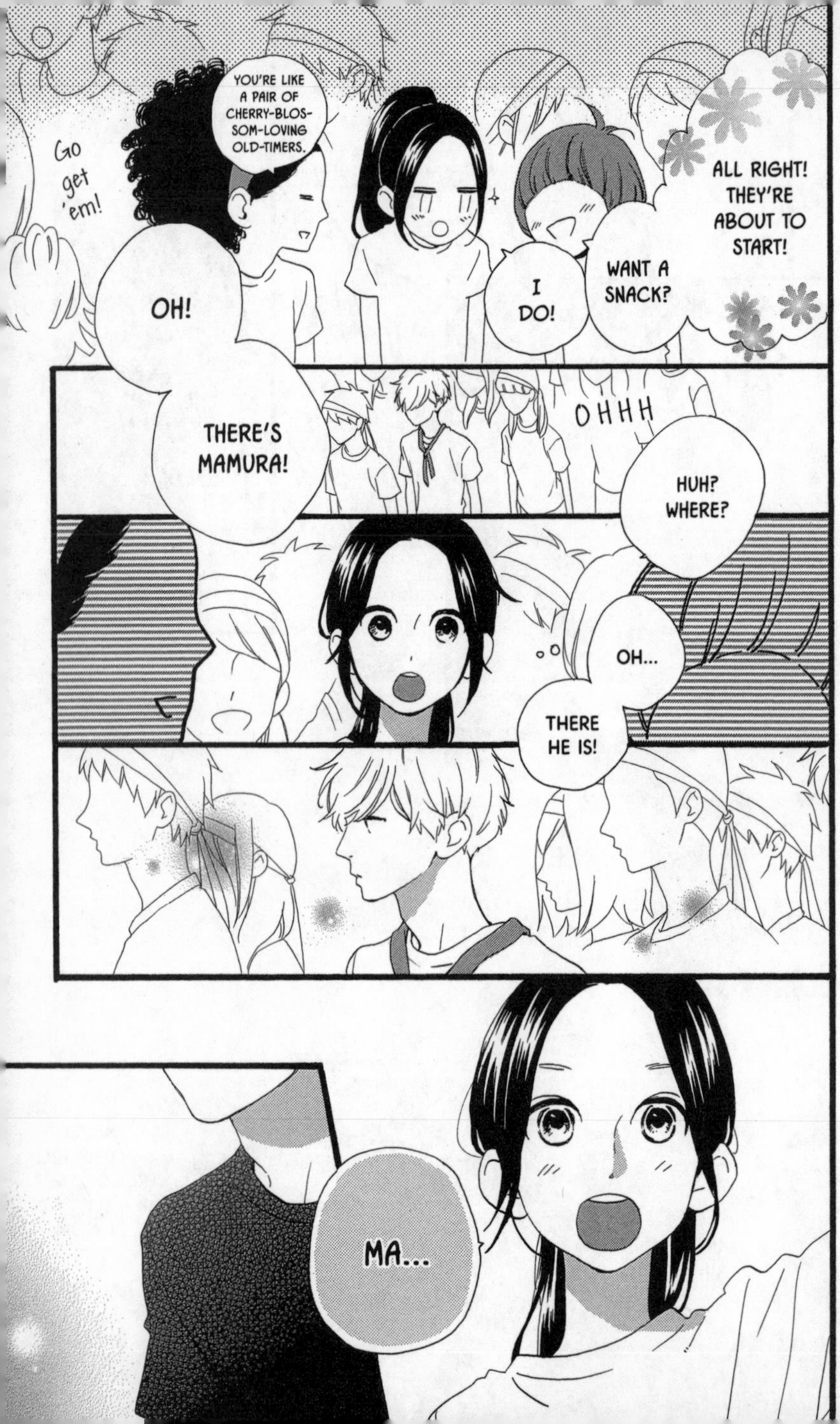
ALL RIGHT! THEY'RE ABOUT TO START!
WANT A SNACK?
I DO!
YOU'RE LIKE A PAIR OF CHERRY-BLOSSOM-LOVING OLD-TIMERS.
Go get 'em!
OH!
THERE'S MAMURA!
OHHH
HUH? WHERE?
OH...
THERE HE IS!
MA...

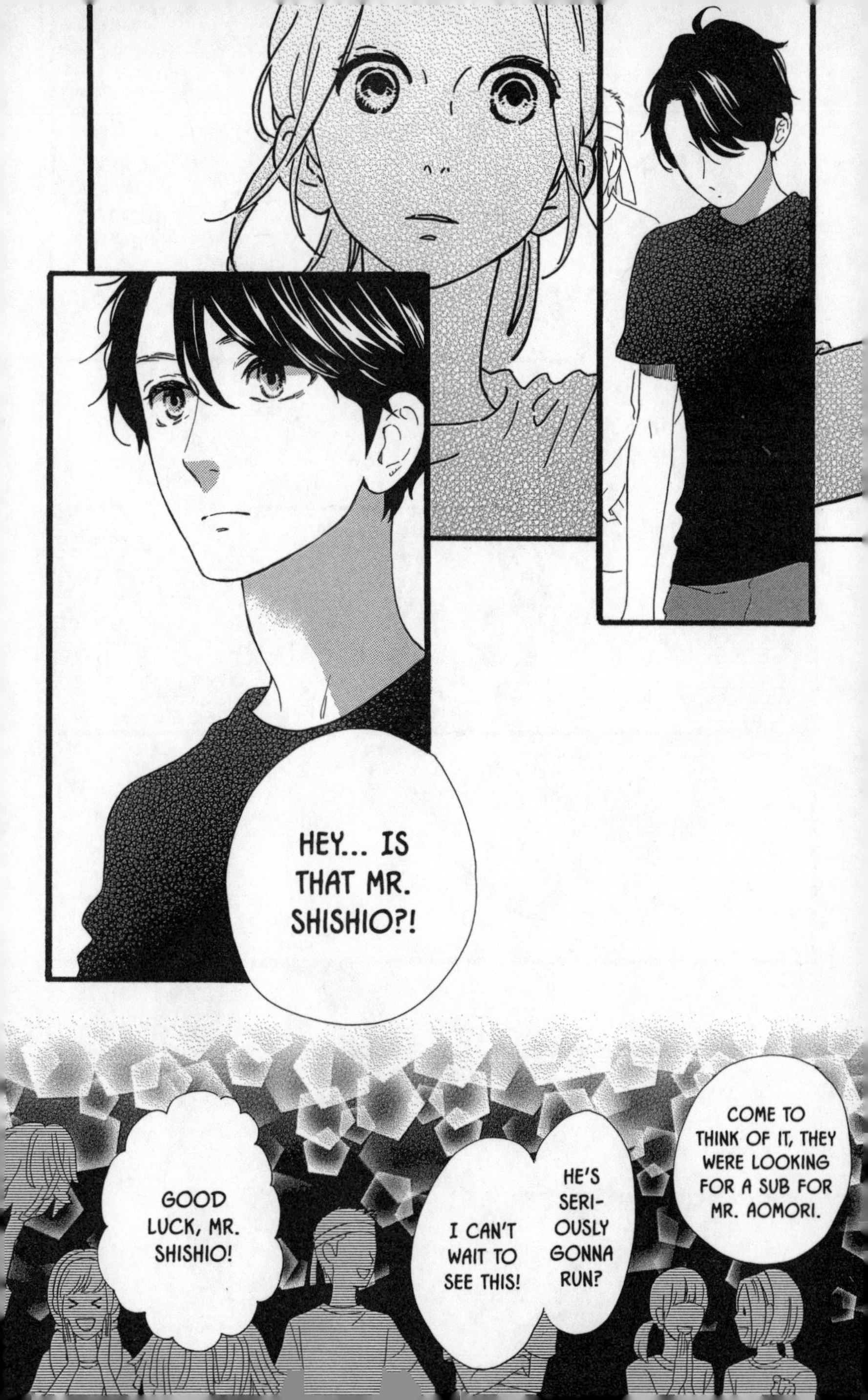
HEY... IS THAT MR. SHISHIO?!
COME TO THINK OF IT, THEY WERE LOOKING FOR A SUB FOR MR. AOMORI.
HE'S SERI-OUSLY GONNA RUN?
I CAN'T WAIT TO SEE THIS!
GOOD LUCK, MR. SHISHIO!

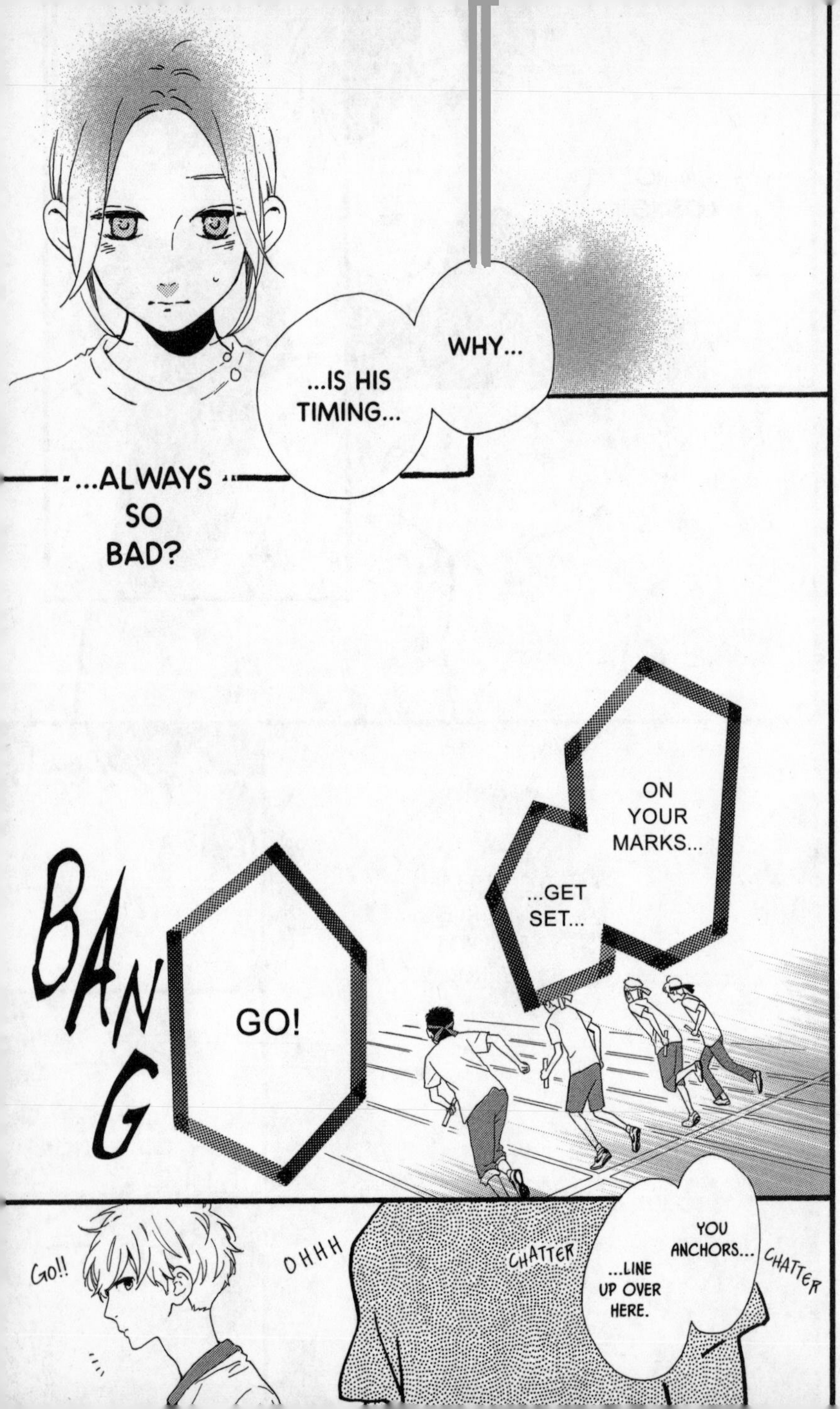
WHY...
...IS HIS TIMING...
...ALWAYS SO BAD?
ON YOUR MARKS...
...GET SET...
GO!
BANG
CHATTER
YOU ANCHORS...
...LINE UP OVER HERE.
CHATTER
OHHH
Go!!

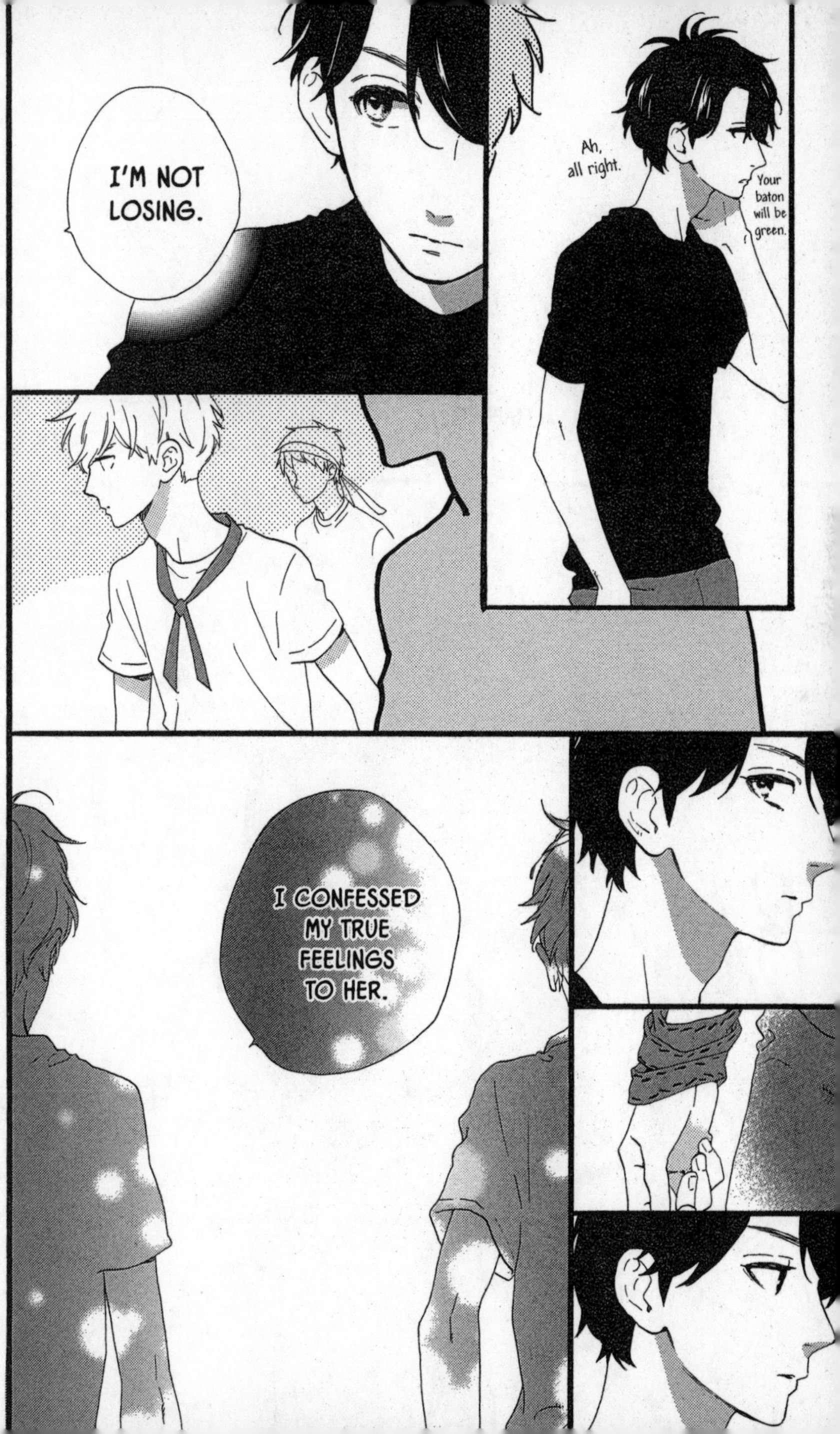
Your baton will be green.
Ah, all right.
I'M NOT LOSING.
I CONFESSED MY TRUE FEELINGS TO HER.

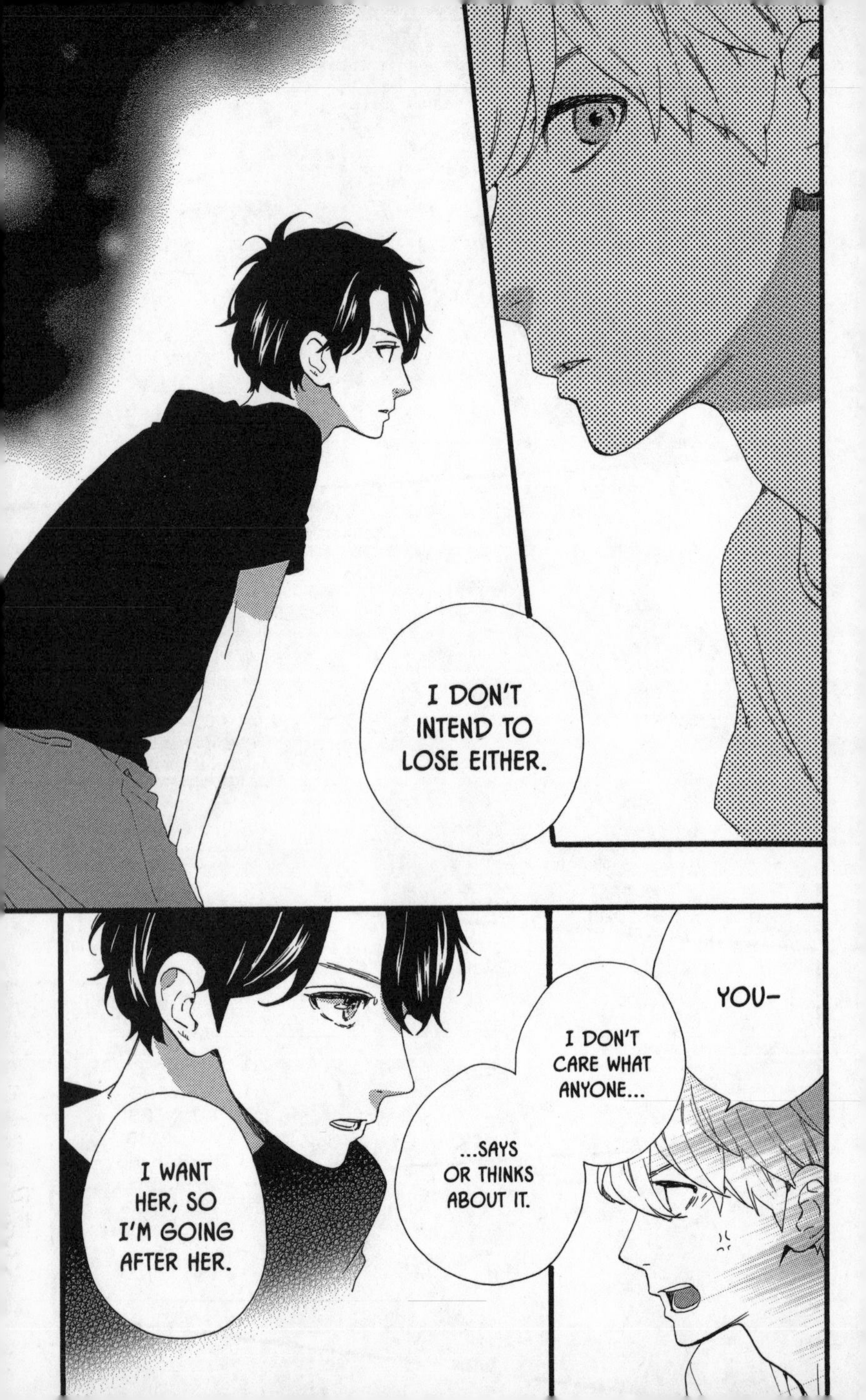
I DON'T INTEND TO LOSE EITHER.
YOU–
I DON'T CARE WHAT ANYONE...
...SAYS OR THINKS ABOUT IT.
I WANT HER, SO I'M GOING AFTER HER.

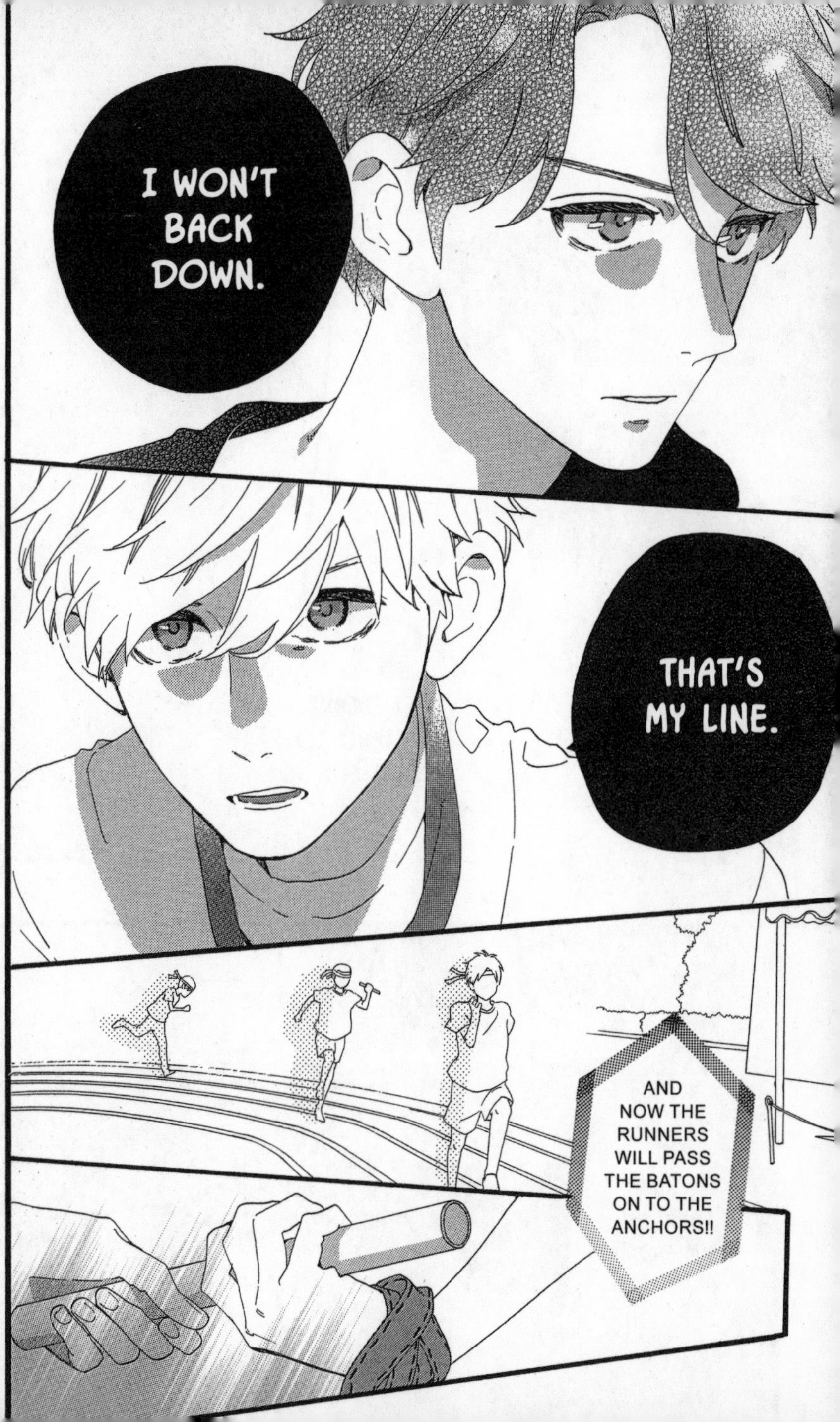
I WON'T BACK DOWN.
THAT'S MY LINE.
AND NOW THE RUNNERS WILL PASS THE BATONS ON TO THE ANCHORS!!

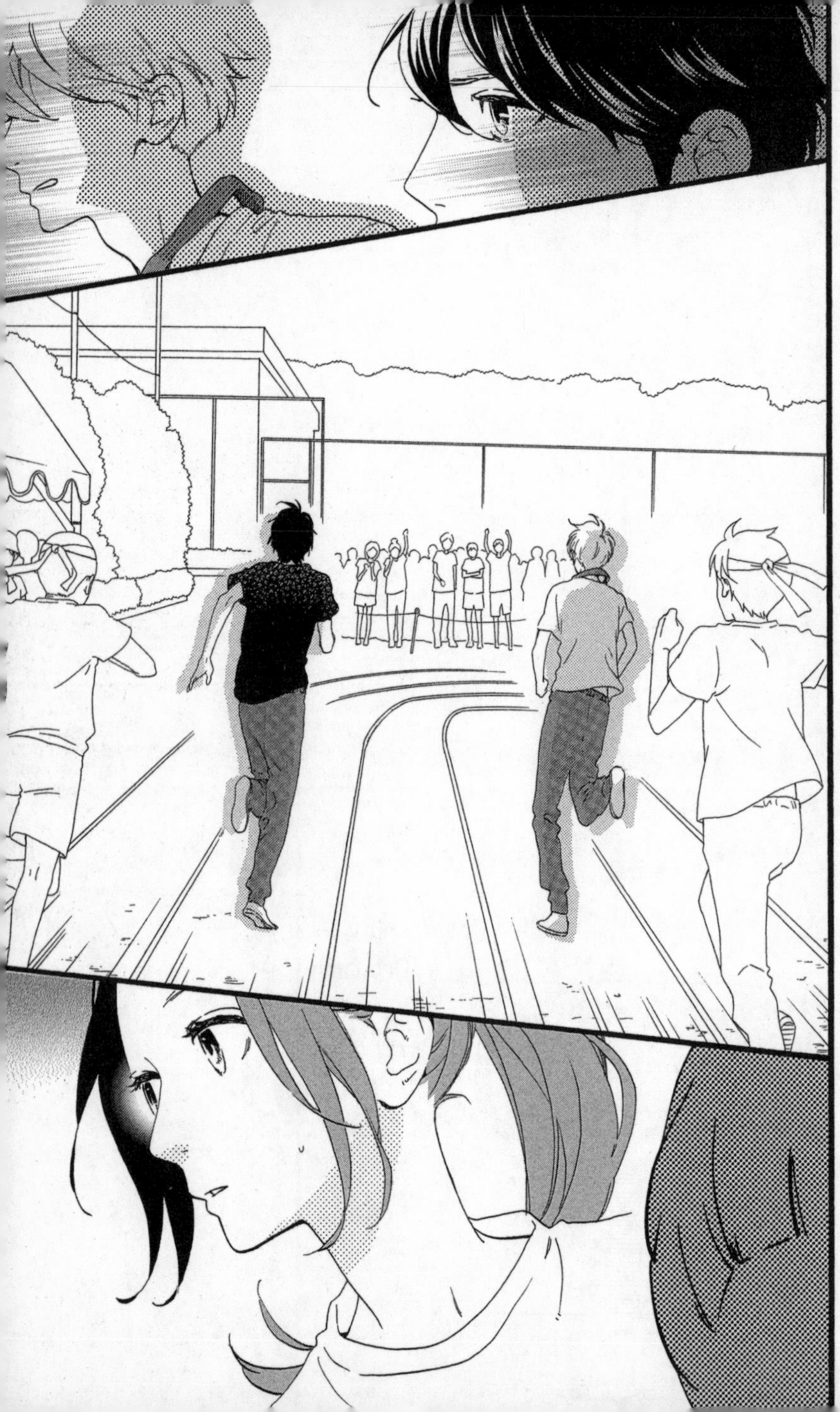

Full of vim and vigor?!
Oronamin C!!

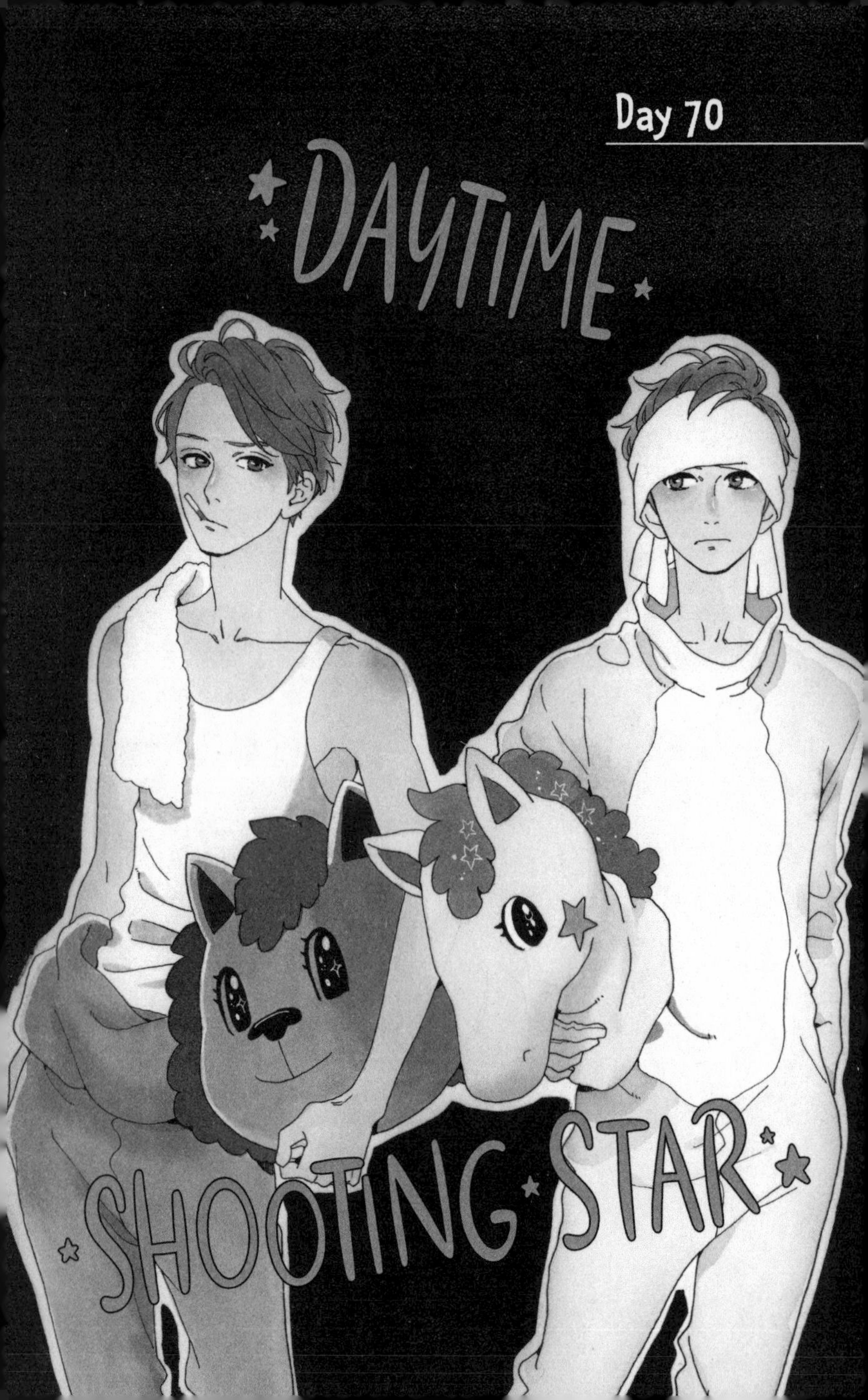
Day 70
DAYTIME
SHOOTING STAR

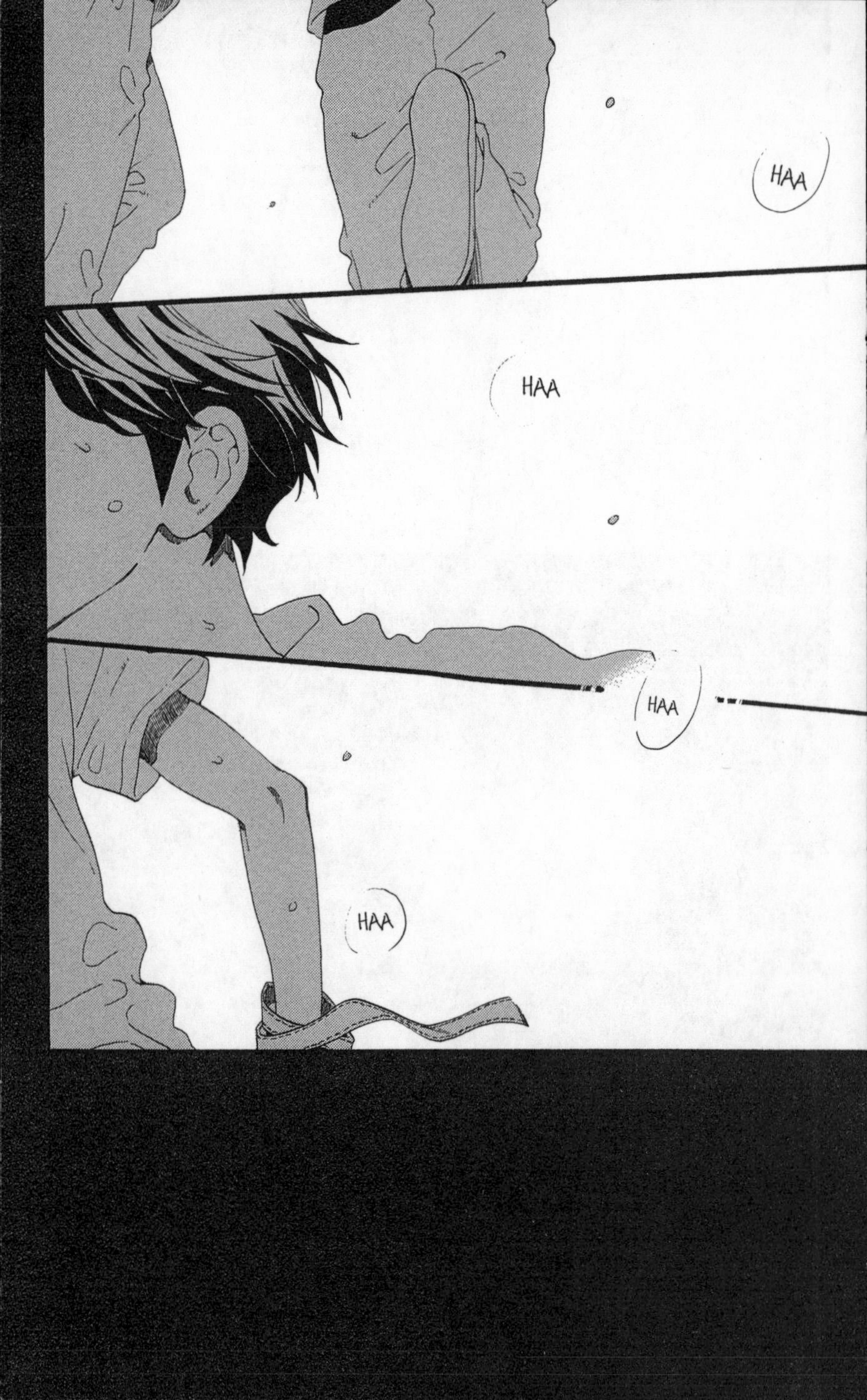
HAA
HAA
HAA
HAA

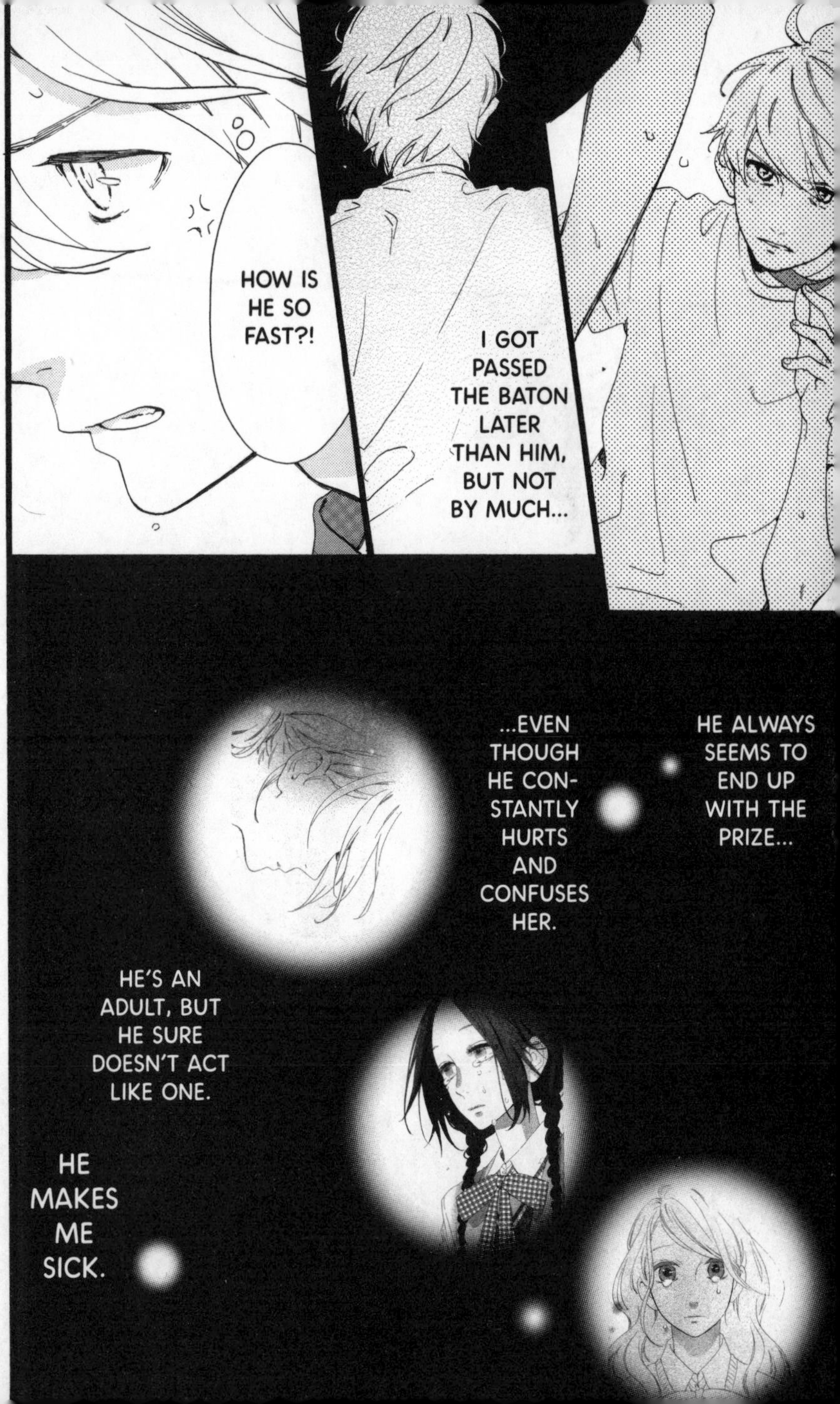
I GOT PASSED THE BATON LATER THAN HIM, BUT NOT BY MUCH...
HOW IS HE SO FAST?!
HE ALWAYS SEEMS TO END UP WITH THE PRIZE...
...EVEN THOUGH HE CON-STANTLY HURTS AND CONFUSES HER.
HE'S AN ADULT, BUT HE SURE DOESN'T ACT LIKE ONE.
HE MAKES ME SICK.

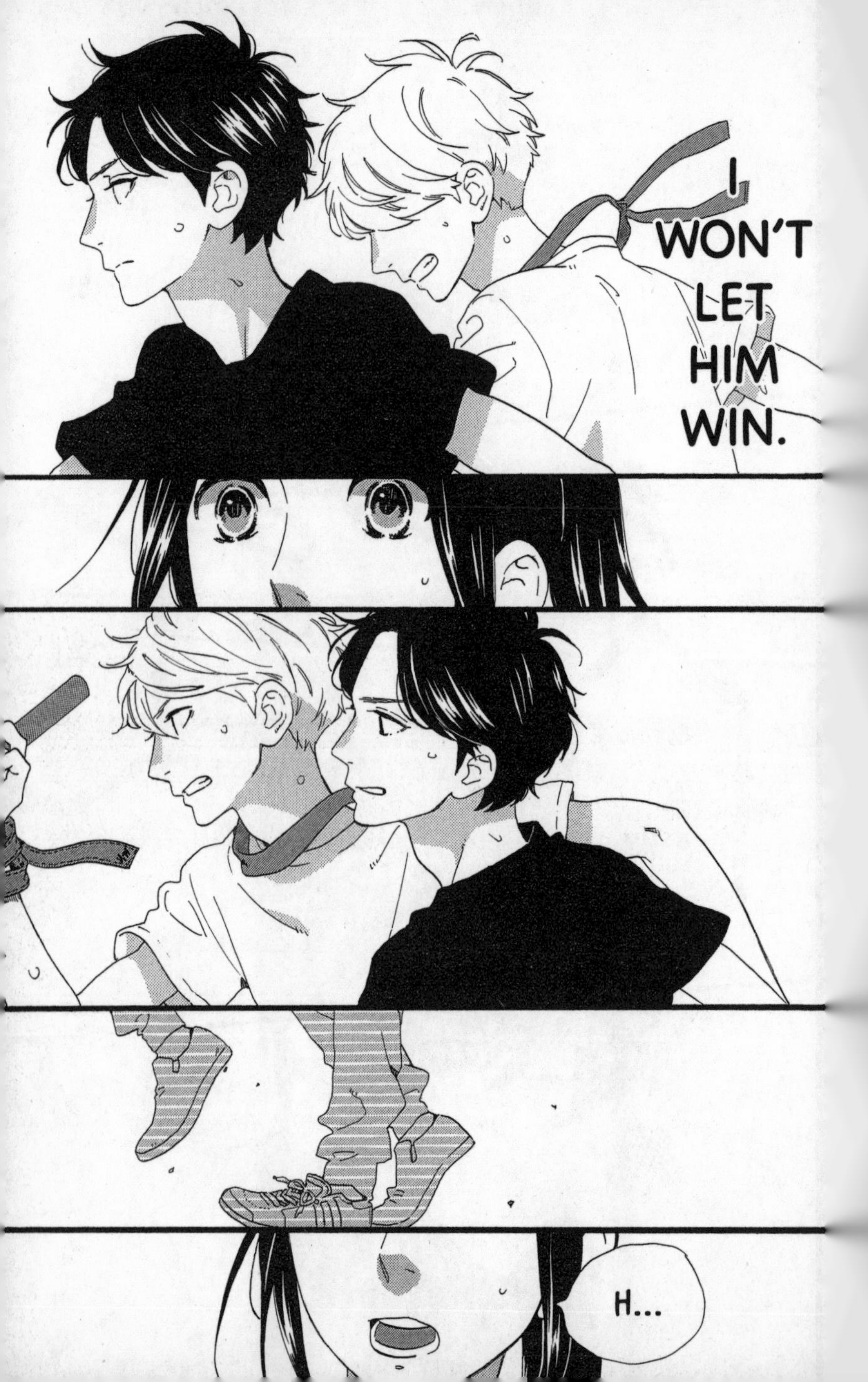
I WON'T LET HIM WIN.
H...

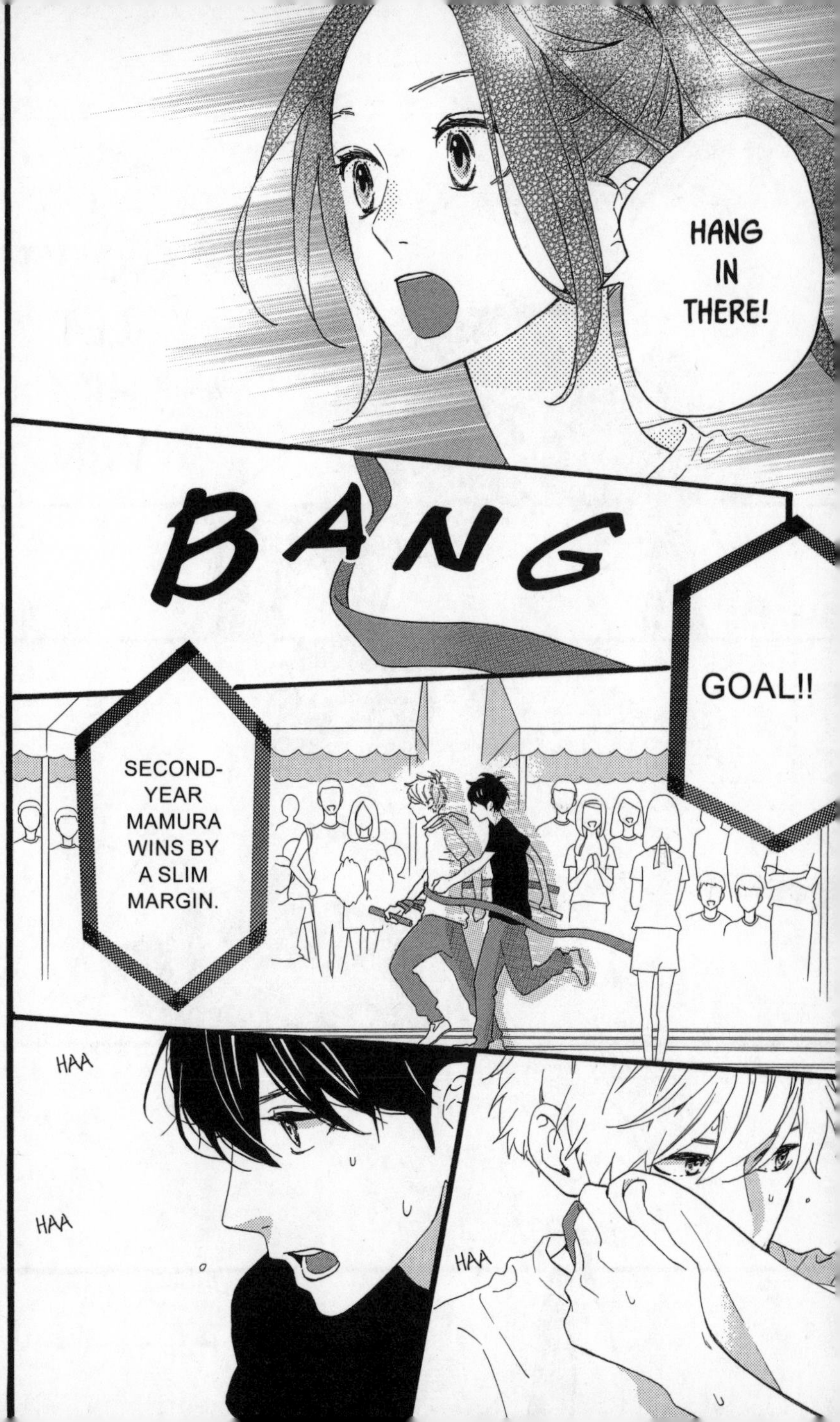
HANG IN THERE!
BANG
GOAL!!
SECOND-YEAR MAMURA WINS BY A SLIM MARGIN.
HAA
HAA
HAA

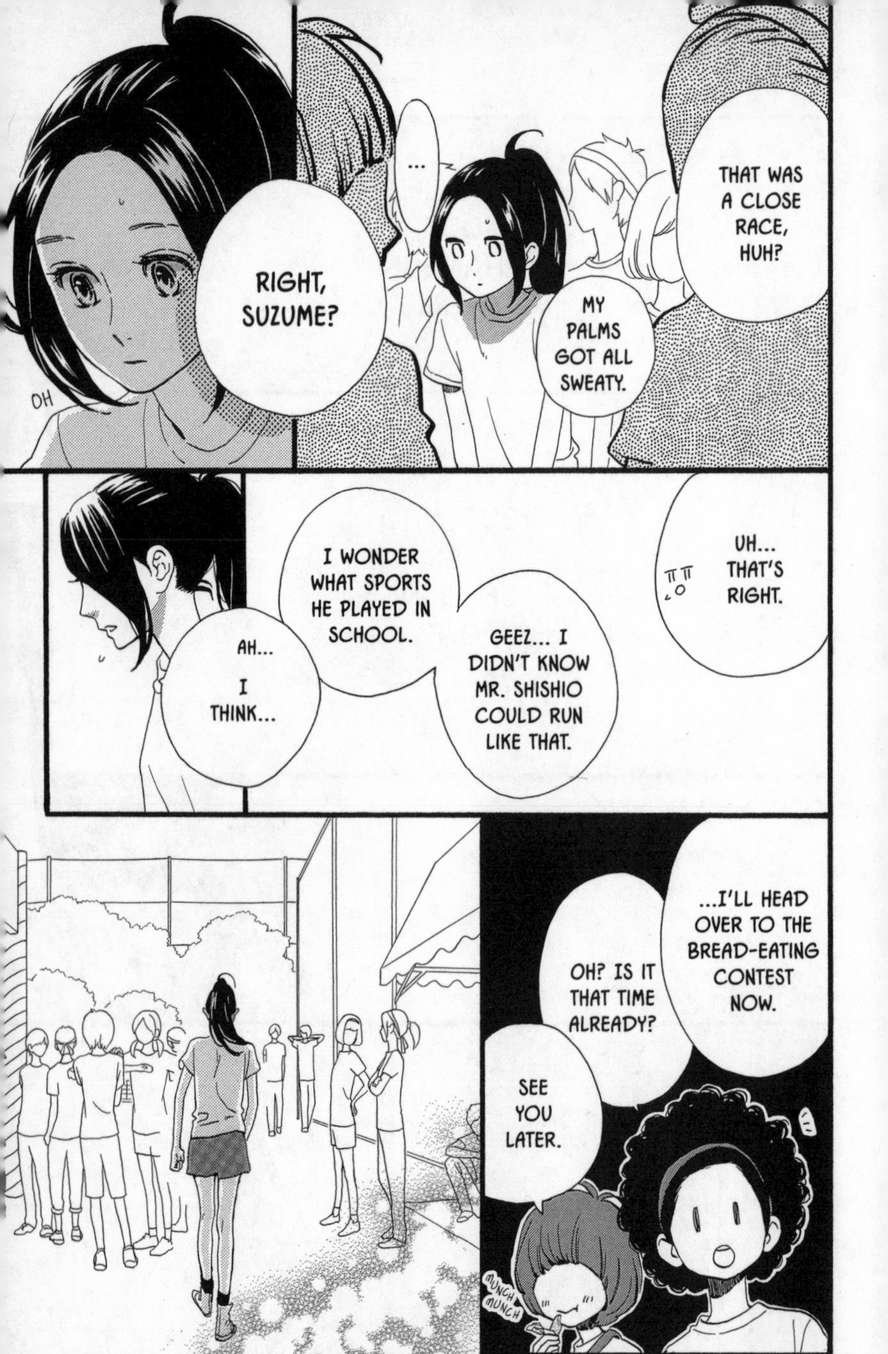
THAT WAS A CLOSE RACE, HUH?
MY PALMS GOT ALL SWEATY.
...
RIGHT, SUZUME?
OH
UH... THAT'S RIGHT.
GEEZ... I DIDN'T KNOW MR. SHISHIO COULD RUN LIKE THAT.
I WONDER WHAT SPORTS HE PLAYED IN SCHOOL.
AH... I THINK...
...I'LL HEAD OVER TO THE BREAD-EATING CONTEST NOW.
OH? IS IT THAT TIME ALREADY?
SEE YOU LATER.
MUNCH MUNCH

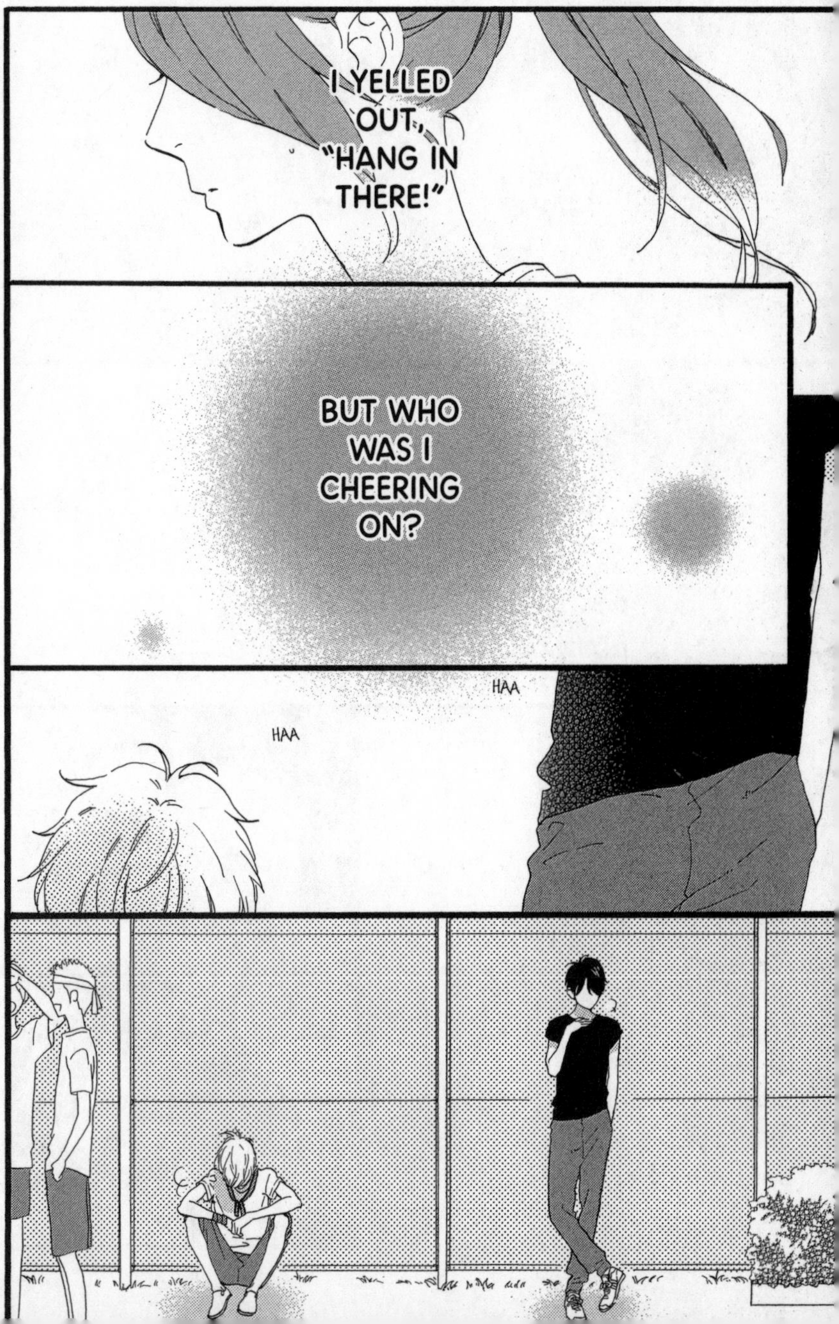
I YELLED OUT, "HANG IN THERE!"
BUT WHO WAS I CHEERING ON?
HAA
HAA

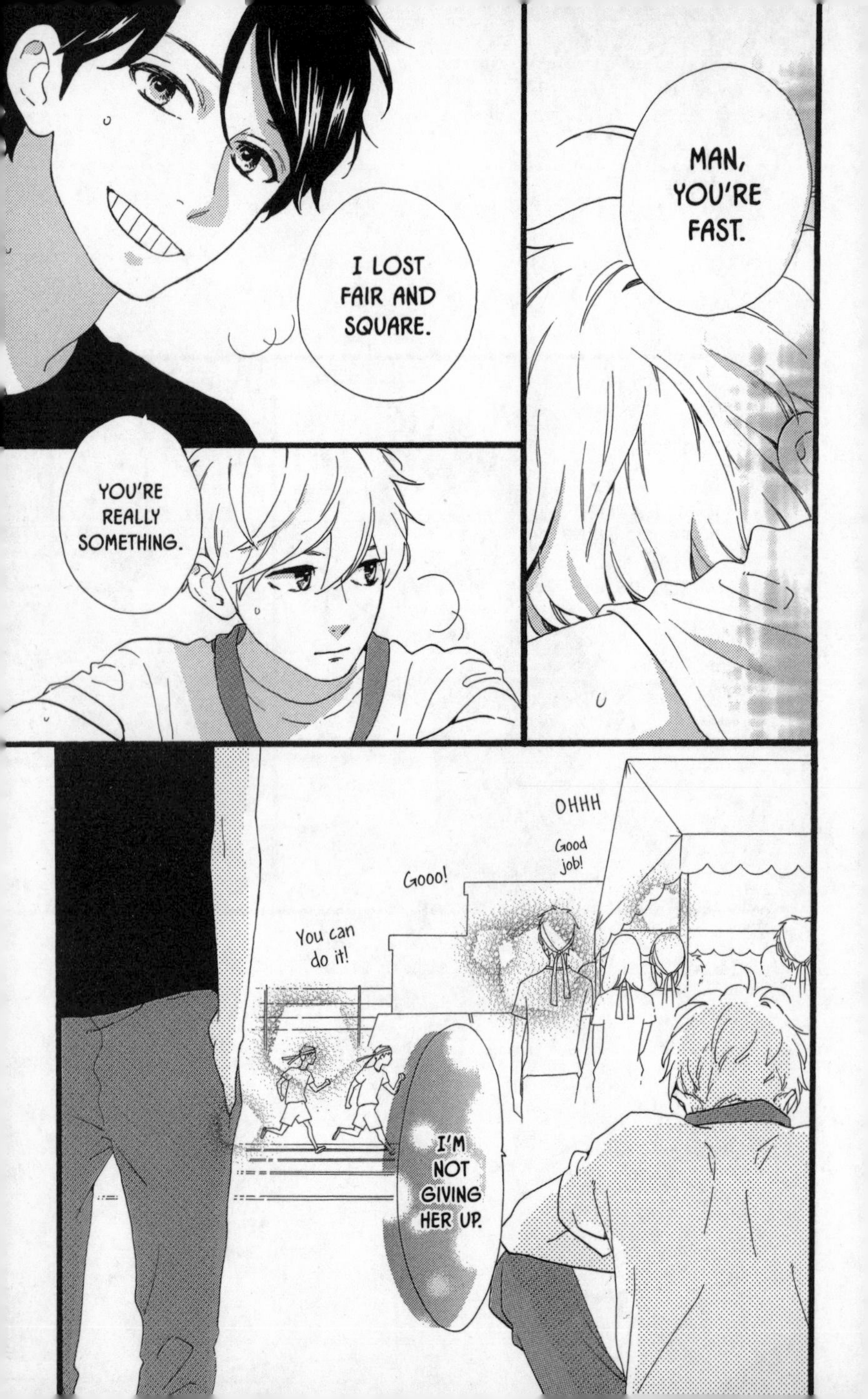
MAN, YOU'RE FAST.
I LOST FAIR AND SQUARE.
YOU'RE REALLY SOMETHING.
OHHH
Good job!
Gooo!
You can do it!
I'M NOT GIVING HER UP.

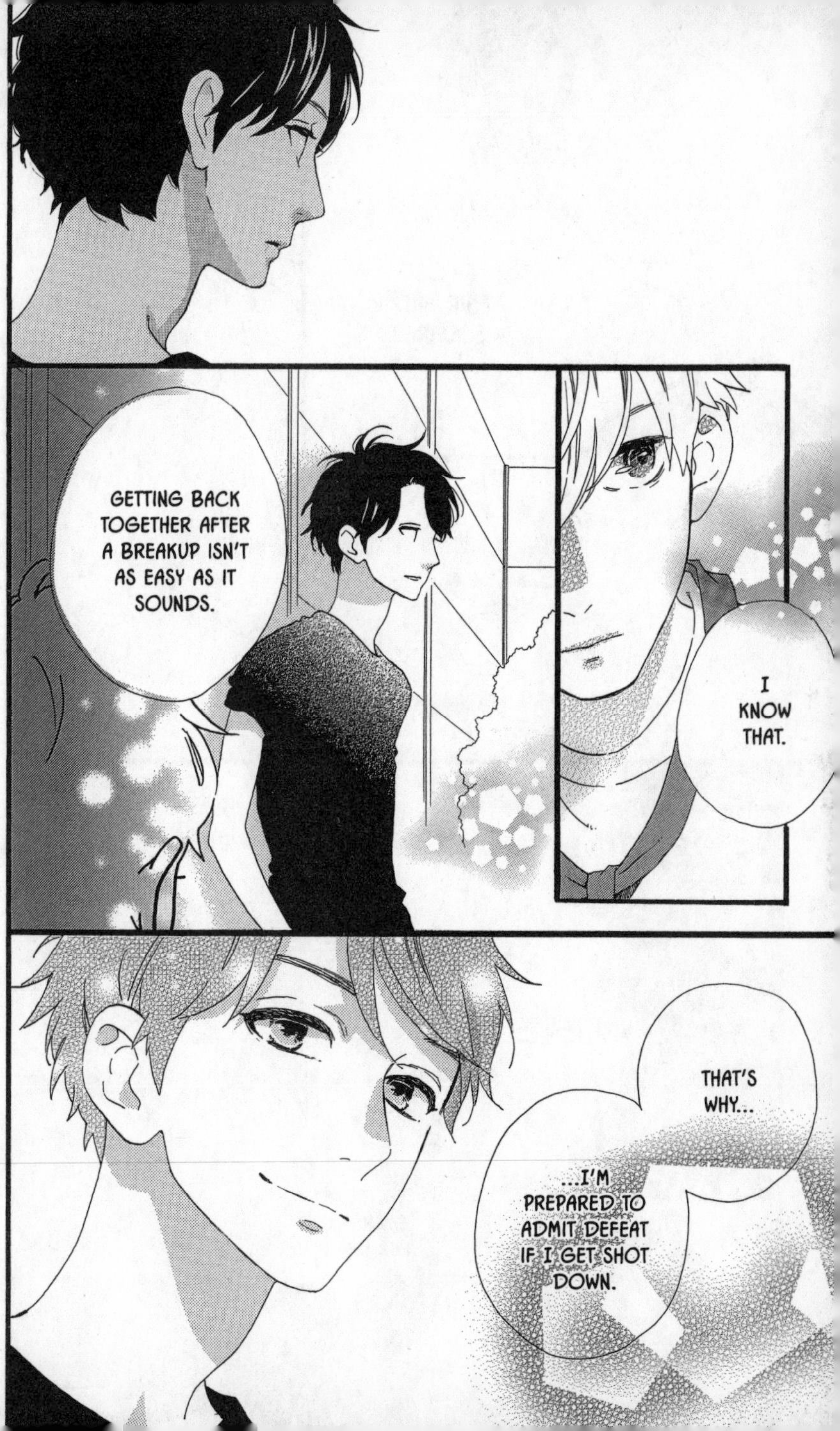
I KNOW THAT.
GETTING BACK TOGETHER AFTER A BREAKUP ISN'T AS EASY AS IT SOUNDS.
THAT'S WHY...
...I'M PREPARED TO ADMIT DEFEAT IF I GET SHOT DOWN.

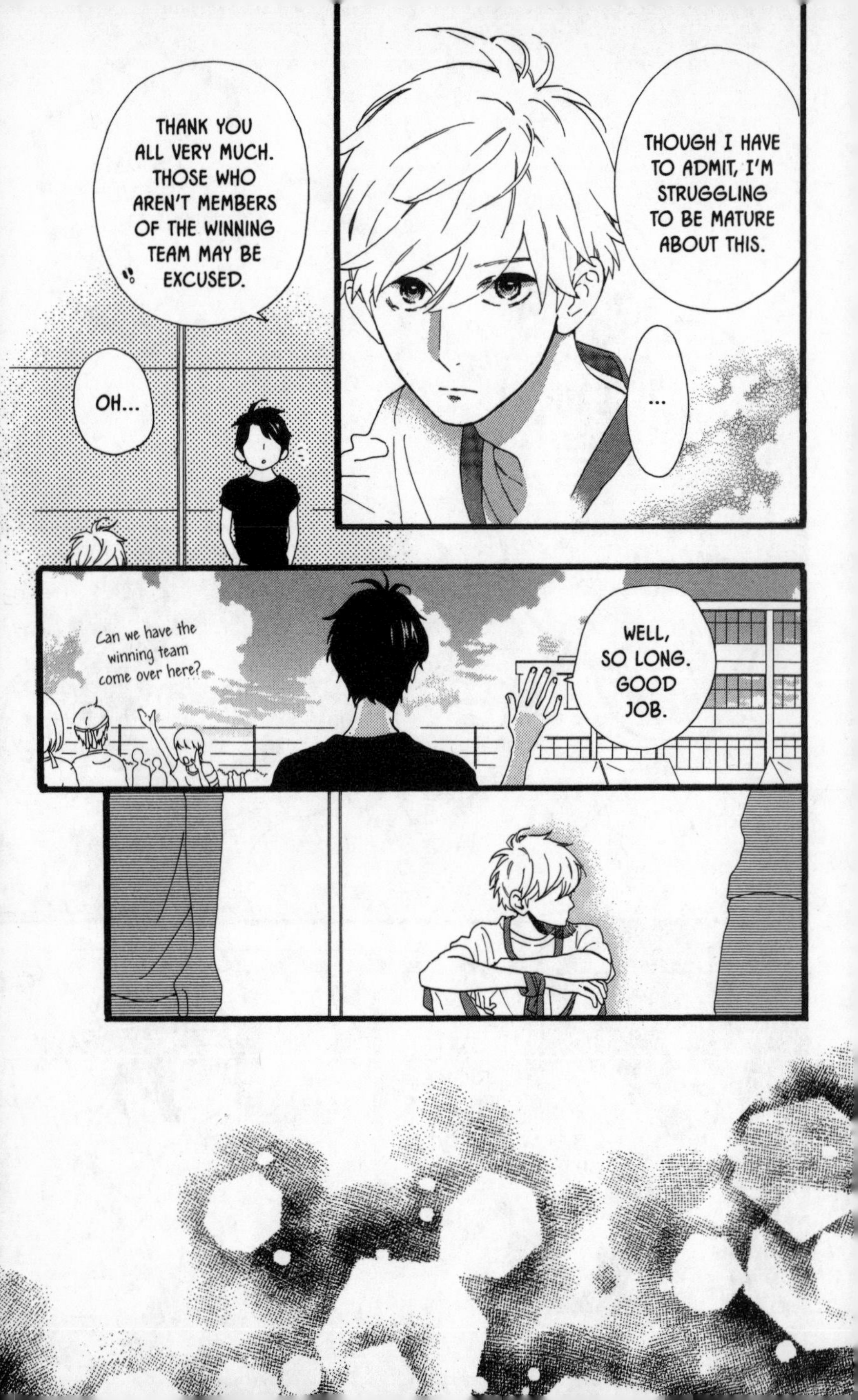
THOUGH I HAVE TO ADMIT, I'M STRUGGLING TO BE MATURE ABOUT THIS.
...
THANK YOU ALL VERY MUCH. THOSE WHO AREN'T MEMBERS OF THE WINNING TEAM MAY BE EXCUSED.
OH...
WELL, SO LONG. GOOD JOB.
Can we have the winning team come over here?

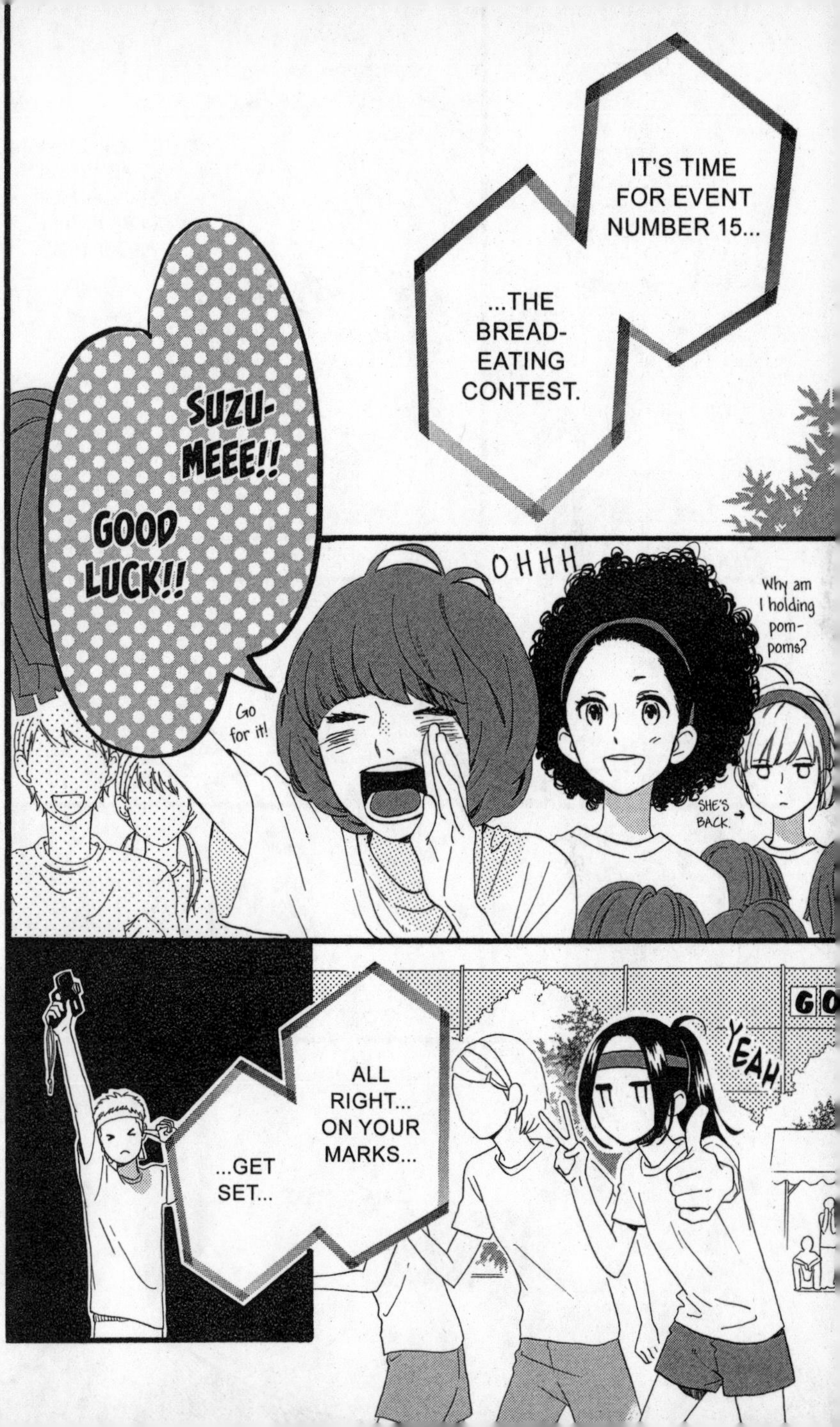
IT'S TIME FOR EVENT NUMBER 15...
...THE BREAD-EATING CONTEST.
Why am I holding pom-poms?
SHE'S BACK.
OHHH
SUZU-MEEE!! GOOD LUCK!!
Go for it!
YEAH
ALL RIGHT... ON YOUR MARKS...
...GET SET...

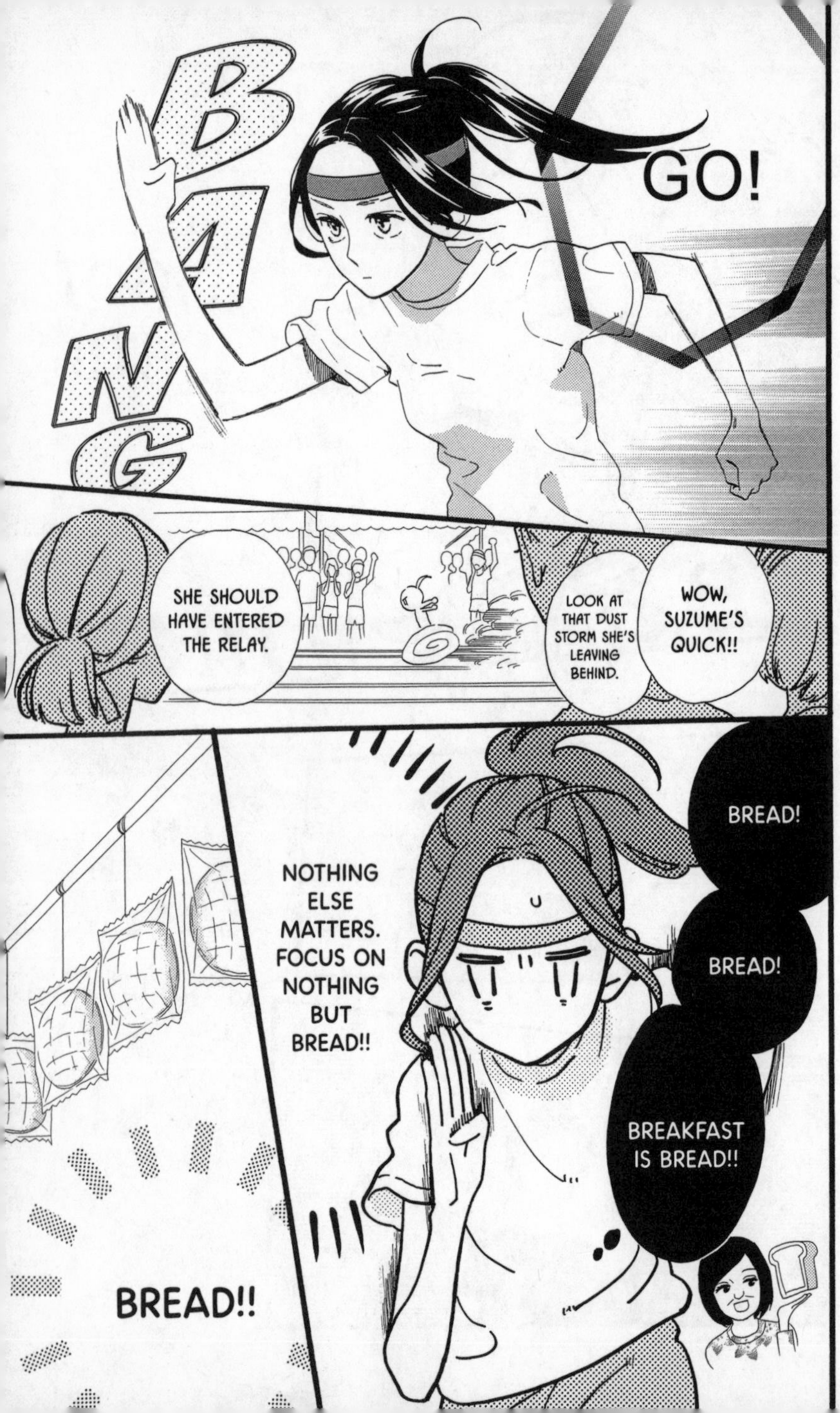
GO!
BANG
WOW, SUZUME'S QUICK!!
LOOK AT THAT DUST STORM SHE'S LEAVING BEHIND.
SHE SHOULD HAVE ENTERED THE RELAY.
BREAD!
BREAD!
BREAKFAST IS BREAD!!
NOTHING ELSE MATTERS. FOCUS ON NOTHING BUT BREAD!!
BREAD!!

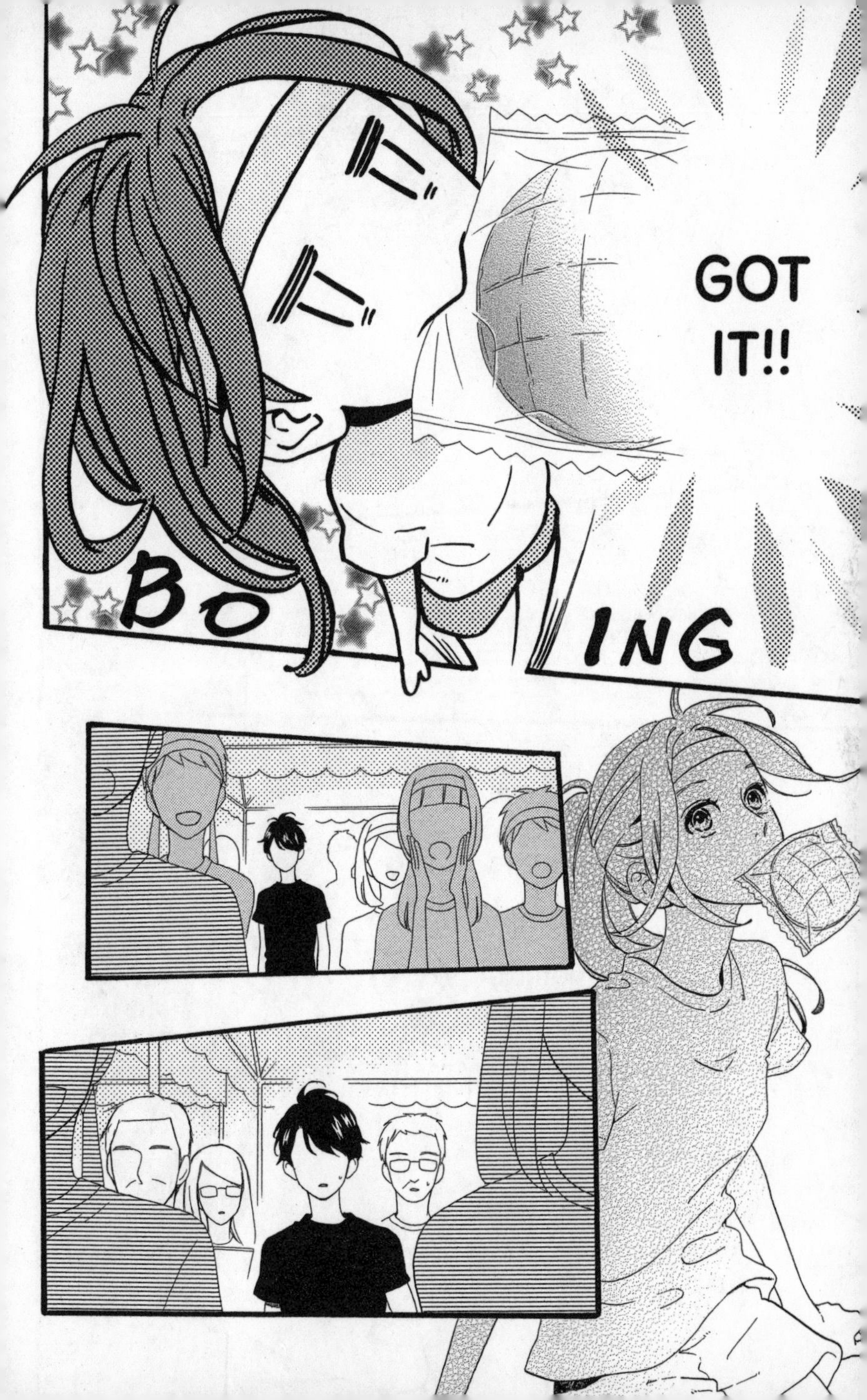
GOT IT!!
BOING

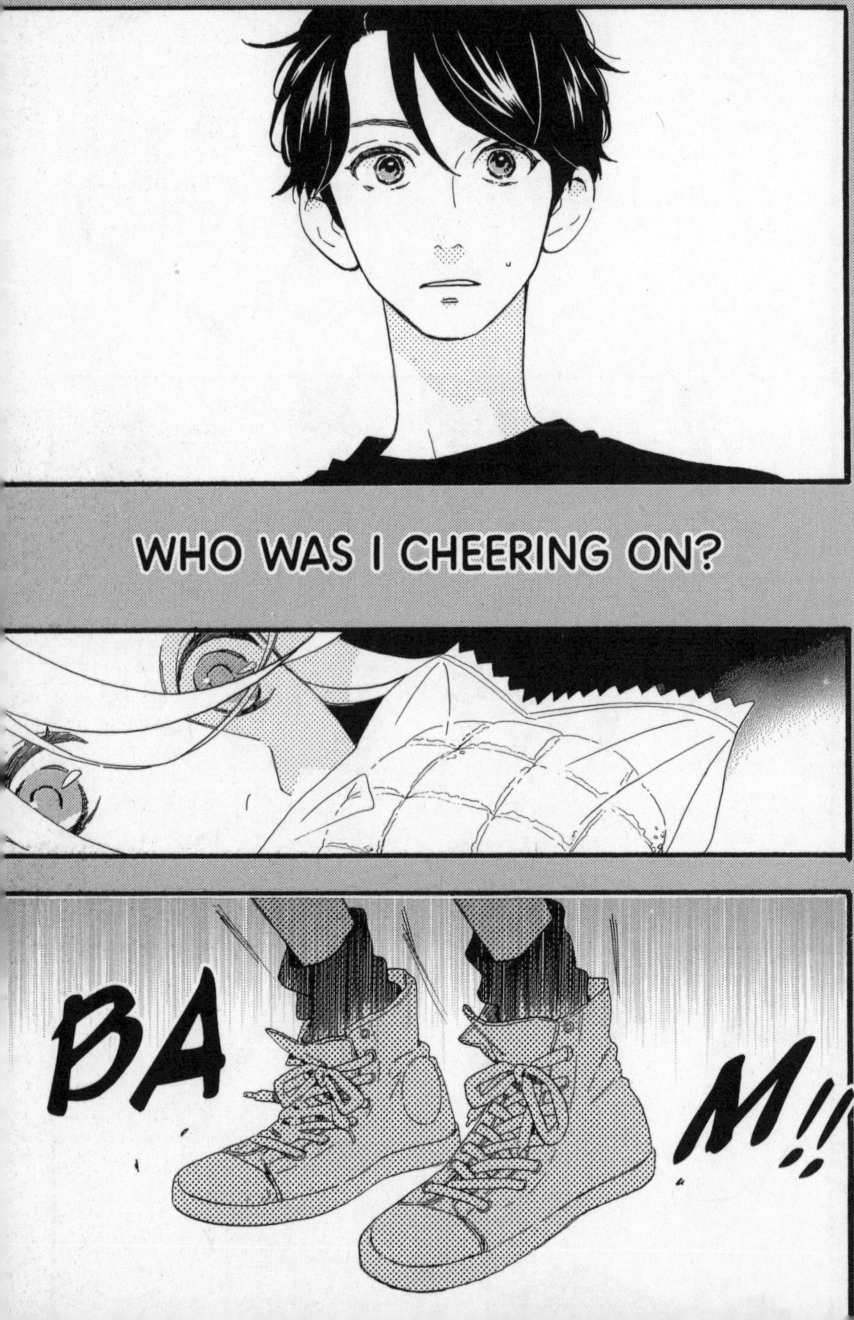
WHO WAS I CHEERING ON?
BAM!!

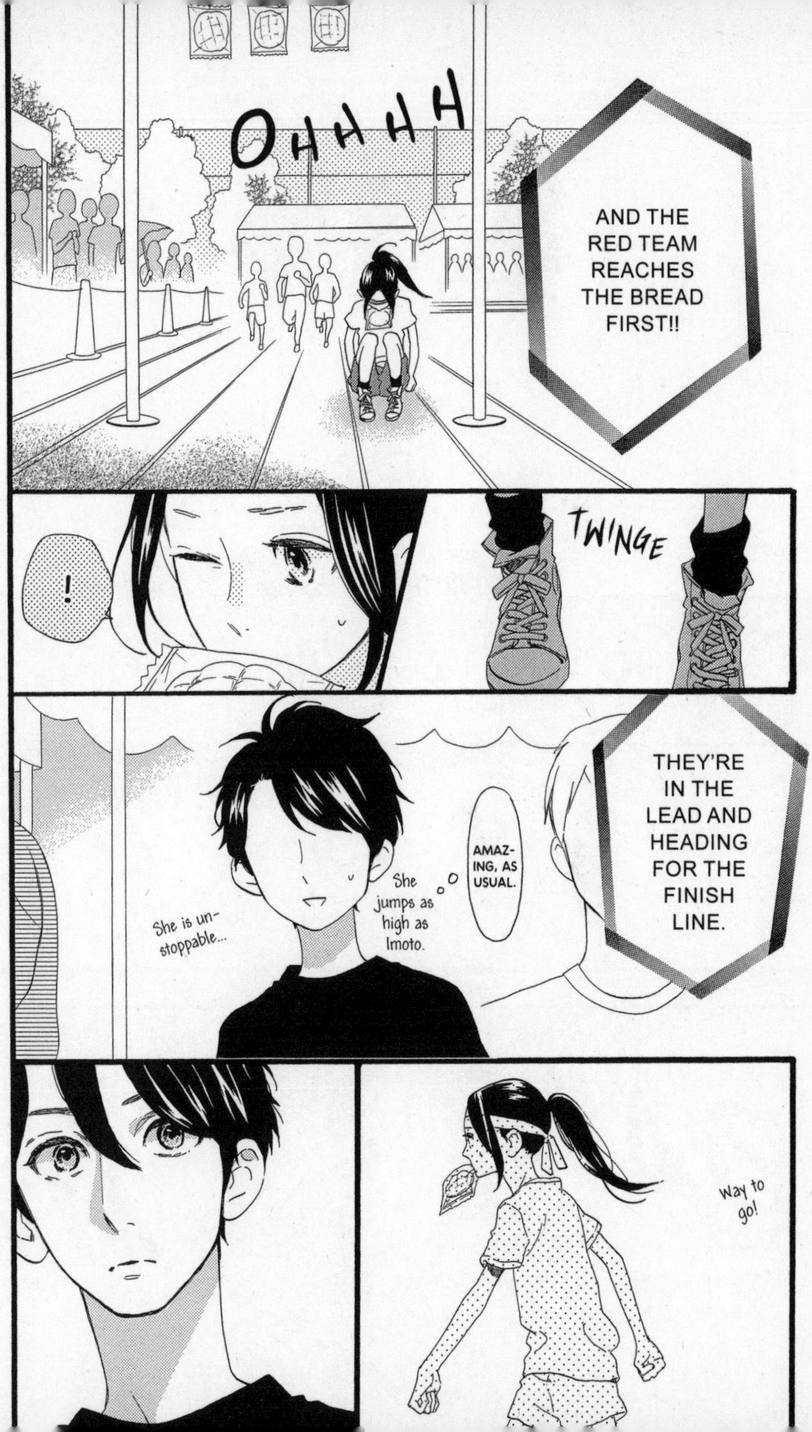
AND THE RED TEAM REACHES THE BREAD FIRST!!
OHHHH
TWINGE
!
THEY'RE IN THE LEAD AND HEADING FOR THE FINISH LINE.
AMAZ-ING, AS USUAL.
She jumps as high as Imoto.
She is un-stoppable...
Way to go!

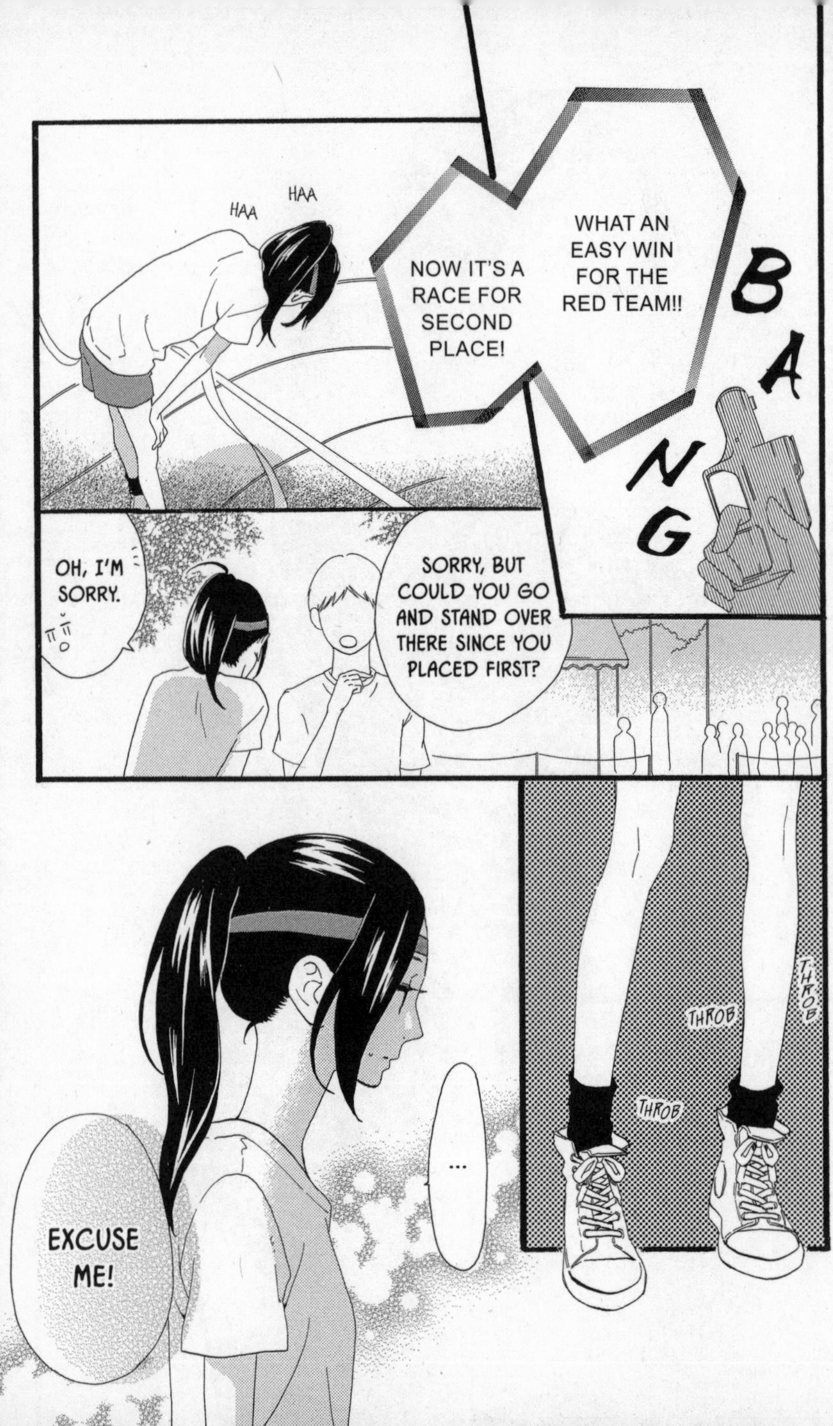
BANG
WHAT AN EASY WIN FOR THE RED TEAM!!
NOW IT'S A RACE FOR SECOND PLACE!
HAA
HAA
SORRY, BUT COULD YOU GO AND STAND OVER THERE SINCE YOU PLACED FIRST?
OH, I'M SORRY.
THROB
THROB
THROB
...
EXCUSE ME!

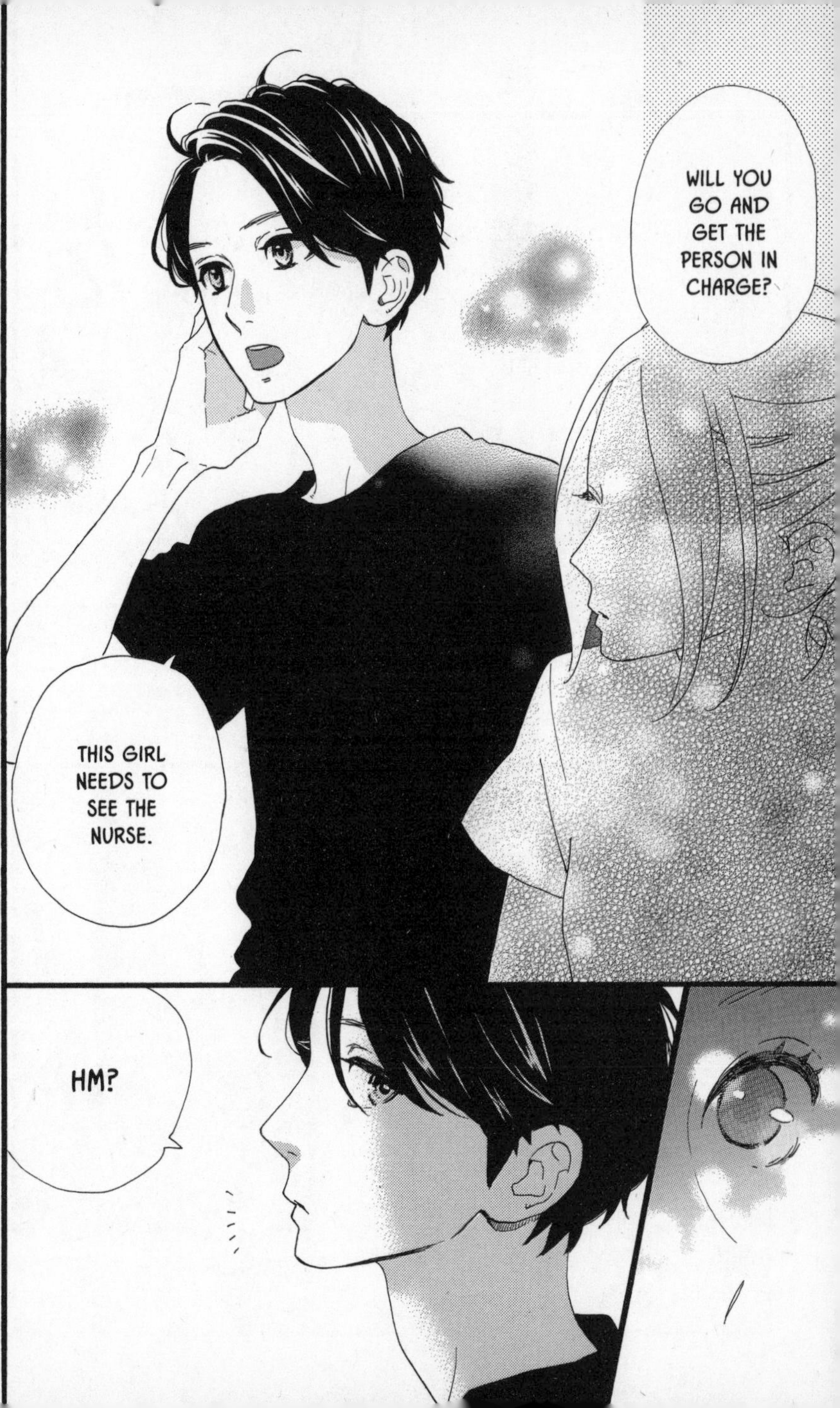
WILL YOU GO AND GET THE PERSON IN CHARGE?
THIS GIRL NEEDS TO SEE THE NURSE.
HM?

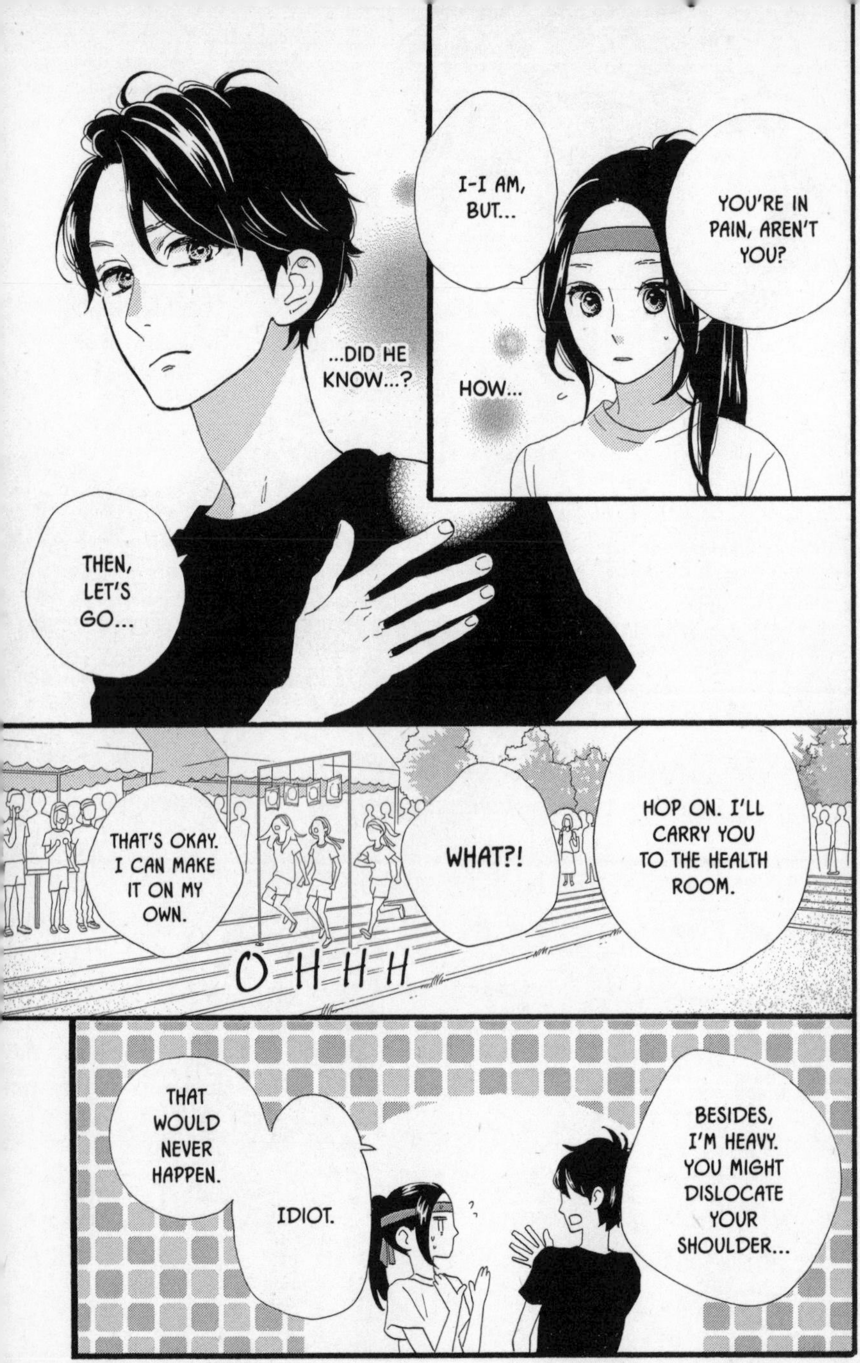
YOU'RE IN PAIN, AREN'T YOU?
I-I AM, BUT...
HOW...
...DID HE KNOW...?
THEN, LET'S GO...
HOP ON. I'LL CARRY YOU TO THE HEALTH ROOM.
WHAT?!
THAT'S OKAY. I CAN MAKE IT ON MY OWN.
OHHH
BESIDES, I'M HEAVY. YOU MIGHT DISLOCATE YOUR SHOULDER...
THAT WOULD NEVER HAPPEN.
IDIOT.

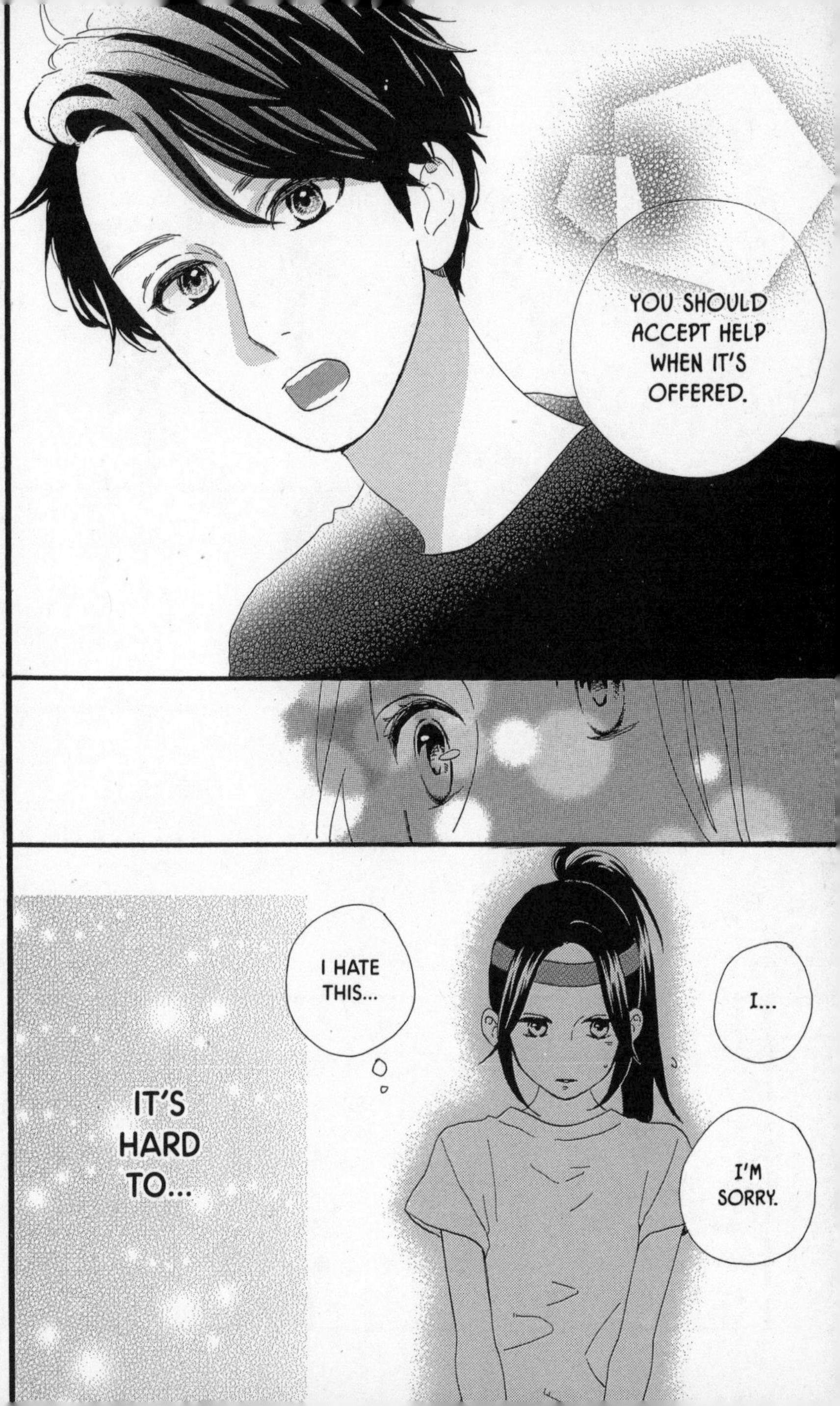
YOU SHOULD ACCEPT HELP WHEN IT'S OFFERED.
I...
I'M SORRY.
I HATE THIS...
IT'S HARD TO...

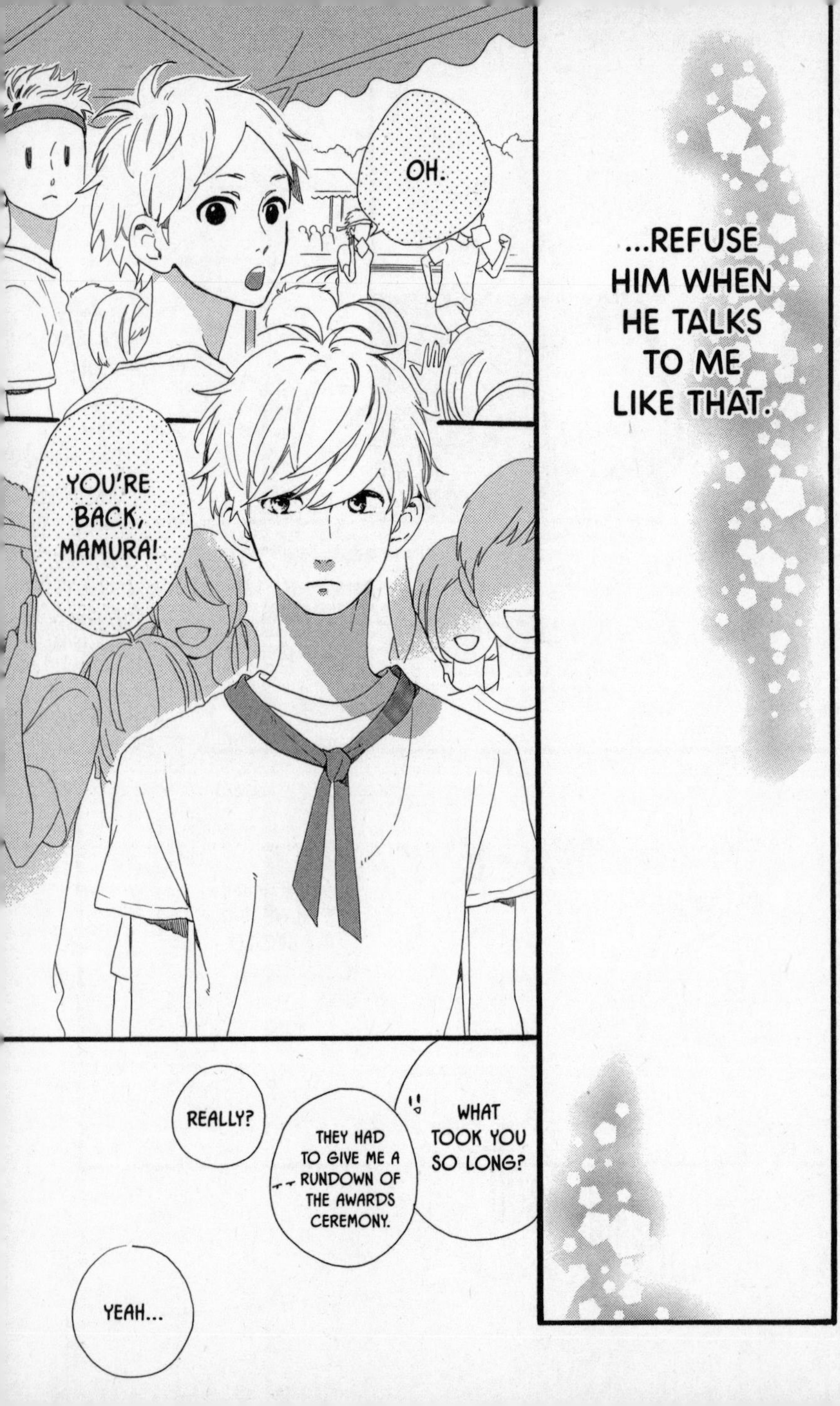
...REFUSE HIM WHEN HE TALKS TO ME LIKE THAT.
OH.
YOU'RE BACK, MAMURA!
WHAT TOOK YOU SO LONG?
THEY HAD TO GIVE ME A RUNDOWN OF THE AWARDS CEREMONY.
REALLY?
YEAH...

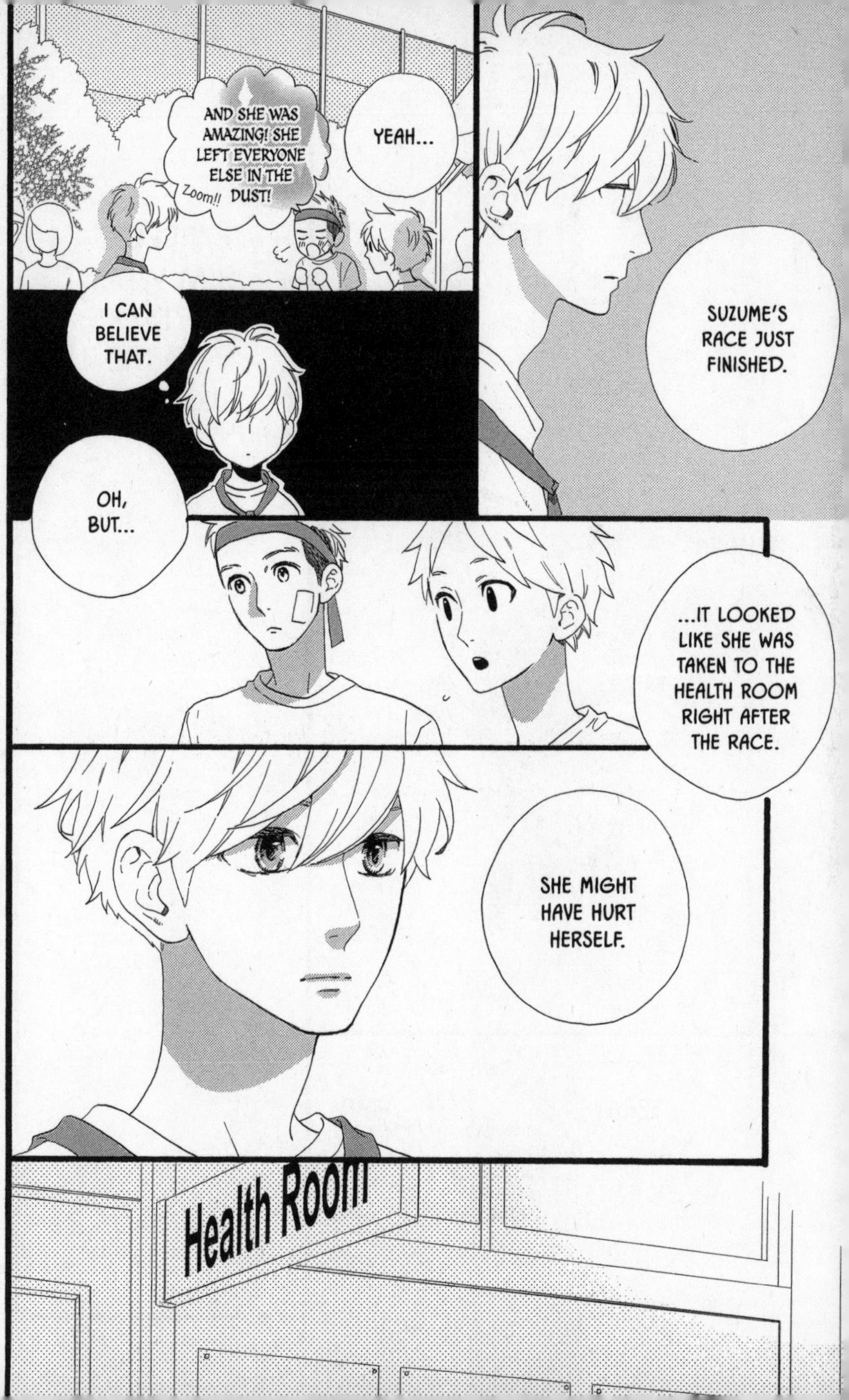

SUZUME'S RACE JUST FINISHED.
YEAH...
AND SHE WAS AMAZING! SHE LEFT EVERYONE ELSE IN THE DUST!
Zoom!!
I CAN BELIEVE THAT.
OH, BUT...
...IT LOOKED LIKE SHE WAS TAKEN TO THE HEALTH ROOM RIGHT AFTER THE RACE.
SHE MIGHT HAVE HURT HERSELF.
Health Room

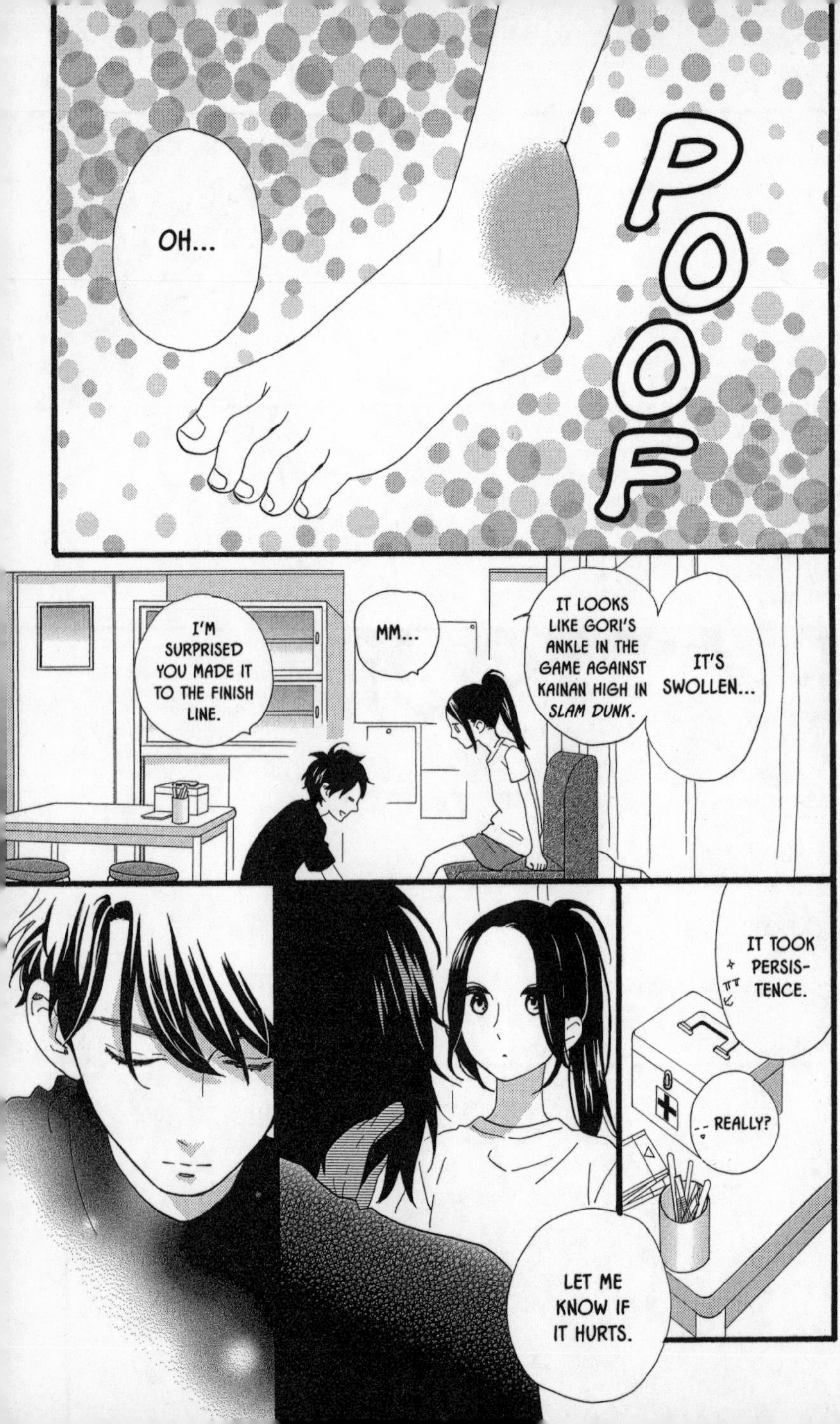
POOF
OH...
IT'S SWOLLEN...
IT LOOKS LIKE GORI'S ANKLE IN THE GAME AGAINST KAINAN HIGH IN *SLAM DUNK*.
MM...
I'M SURPRISED YOU MADE IT TO THE FINISH LINE.
IT TOOK PERSIS-TENCE.
REALLY?
LET ME KNOW IF IT HURTS.

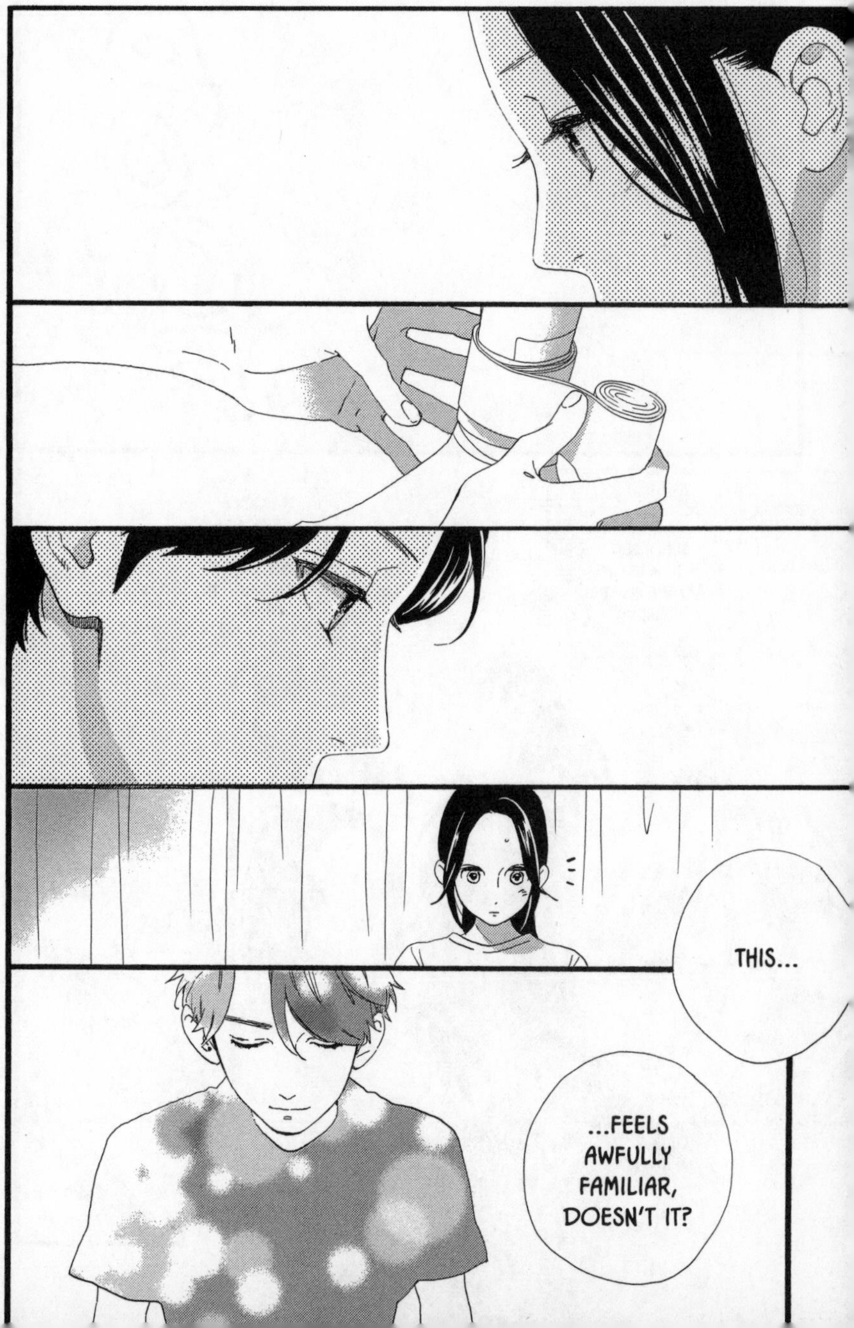
THIS...
...FEELS AWFULLY FAMILIAR, DOESN'T IT?

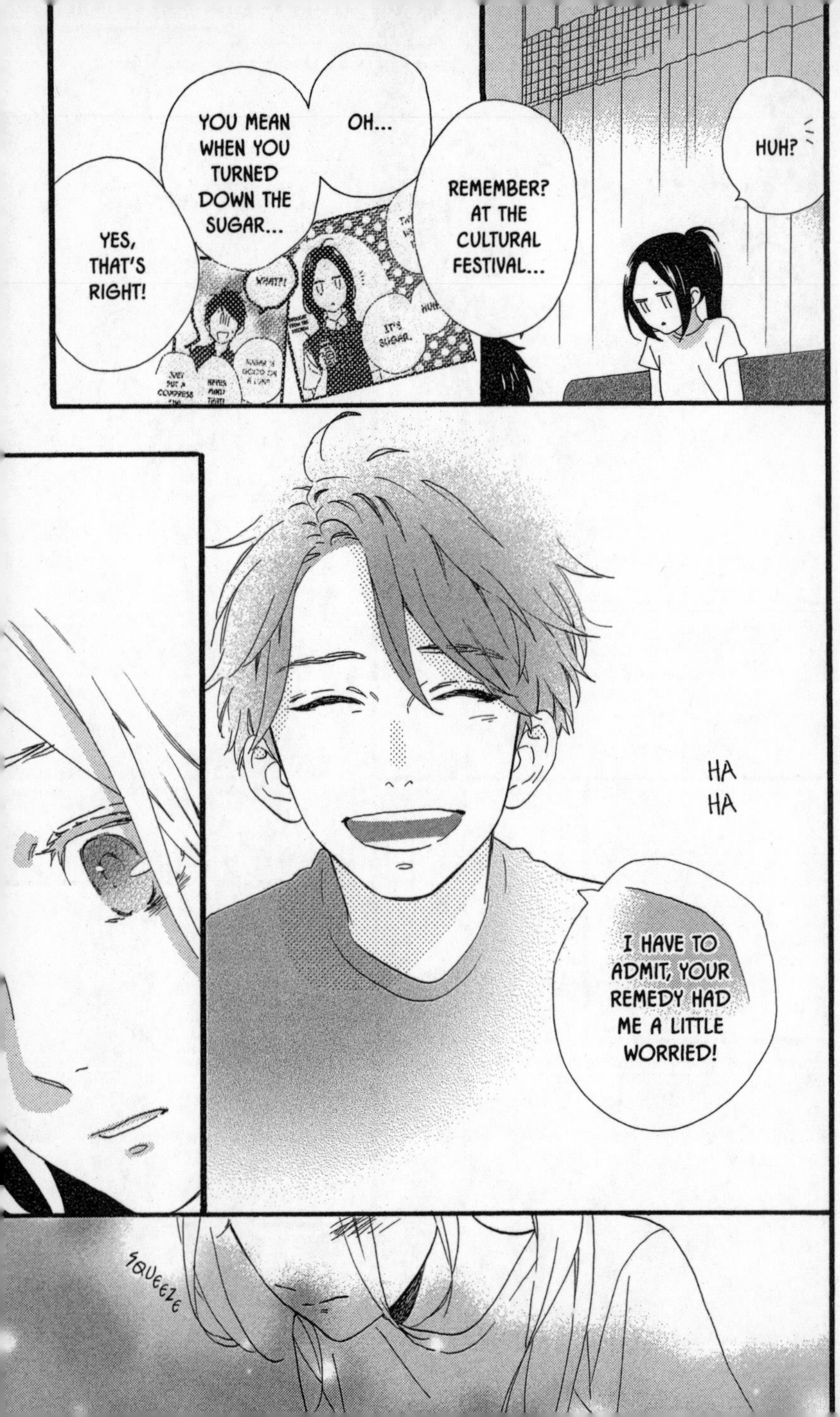
HUH?
REMEMBER? AT THE CULTURAL FESTIVAL...
OH...
YOU MEAN WHEN YOU TURNED DOWN THE SUGAR...
YES, THAT'S RIGHT!
HA HA
I HAVE TO ADMIT, YOUR REMEDY HAD ME A LITTLE WORRIED!
SQUEEZE

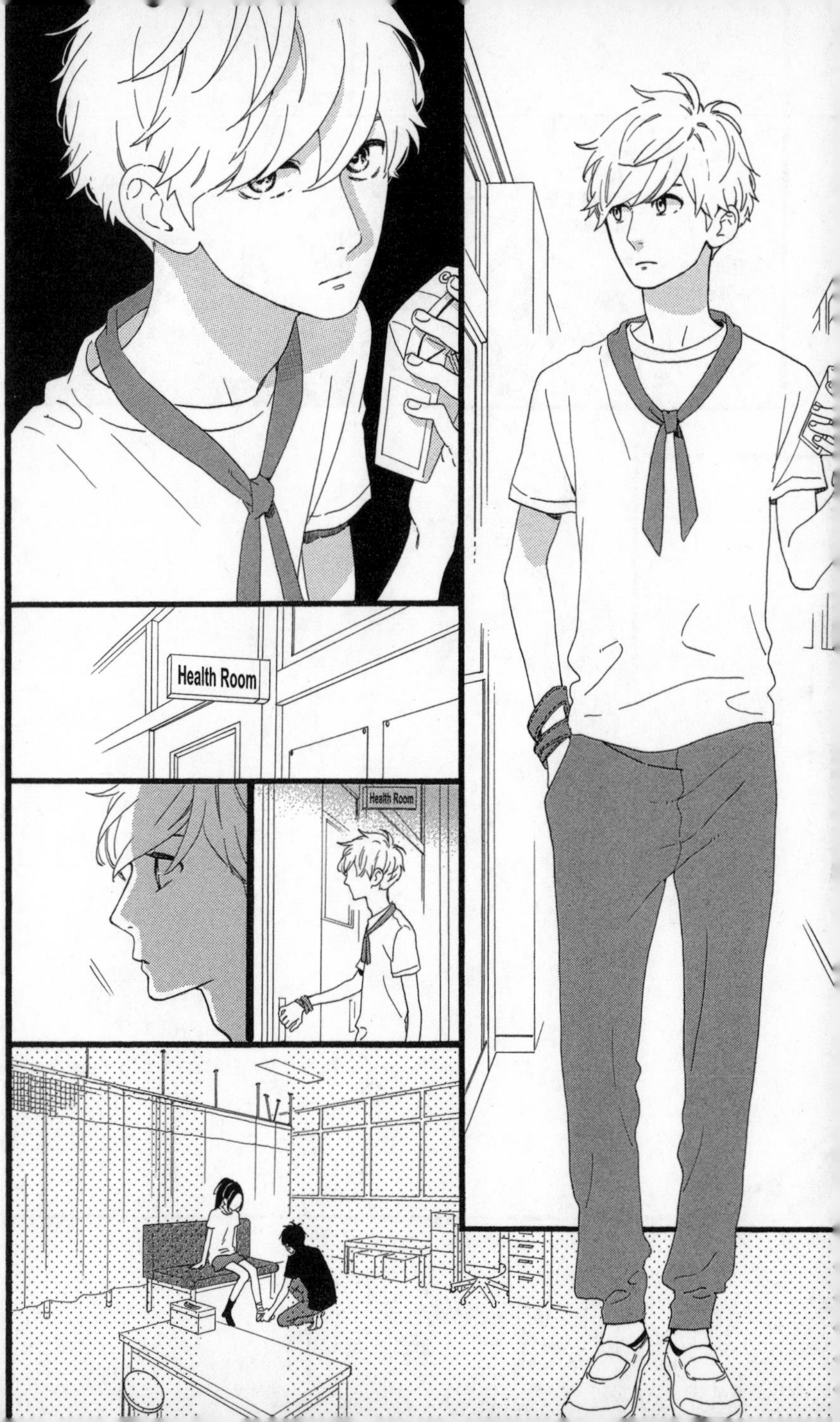
Health Room
Health Room

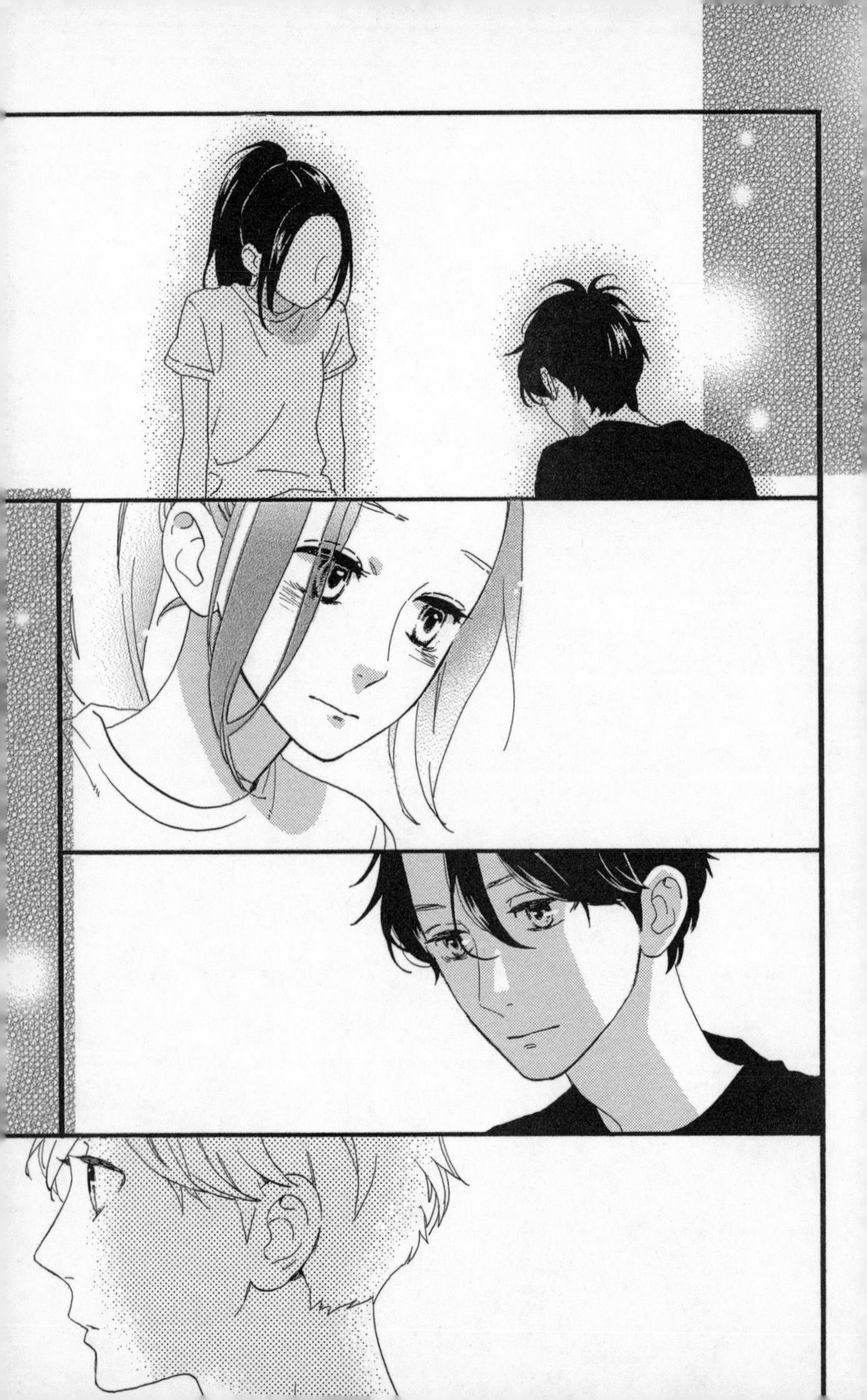

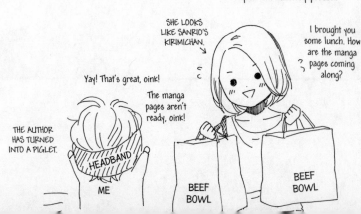

My new editor has turned into quite the delivery person.

I brought you some lunch. How are the manga pages coming along?
SHE LOOKS LIKE SANRIO'S KIRIMICHAN.
Yay! That's great, oink!
The manga pages aren't ready, oink!
THE AUTHOR HAS TURNED INTO A PIGLET.
HEADBAND
ME
BEEF BOWL
BEEF BOWL

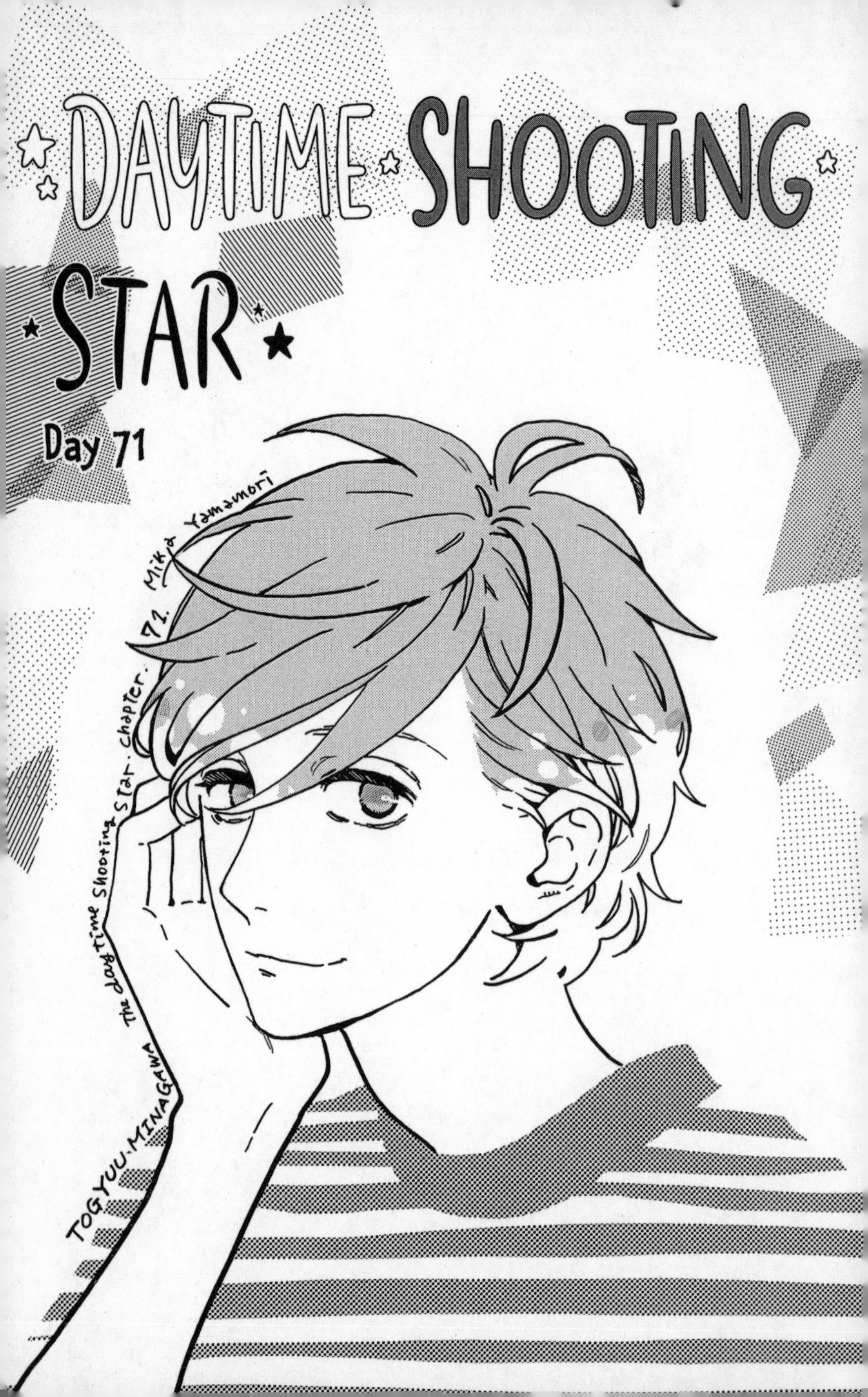
DAYTIME SHOOTING STAR
Day 71
TOGYUU-MINAGAWA The daytime shooting star chapter. 71. Mika Yamamori

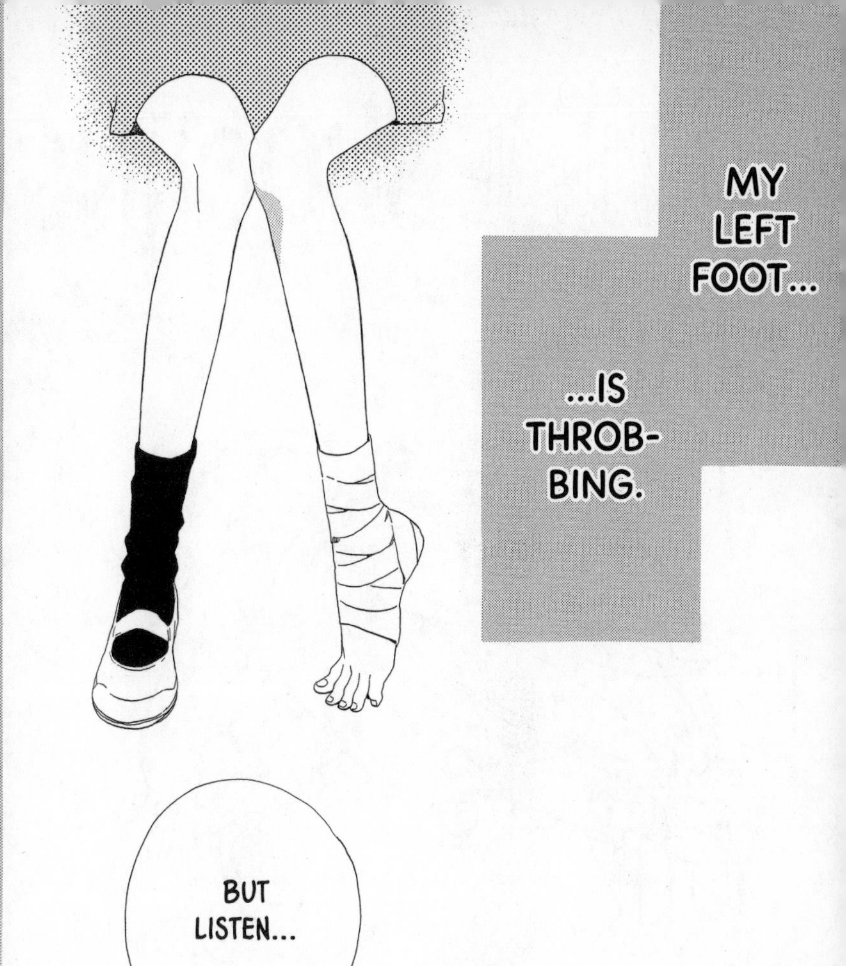
MY LEFT FOOT...
...IS THROB-BING.
BUT LISTEN...

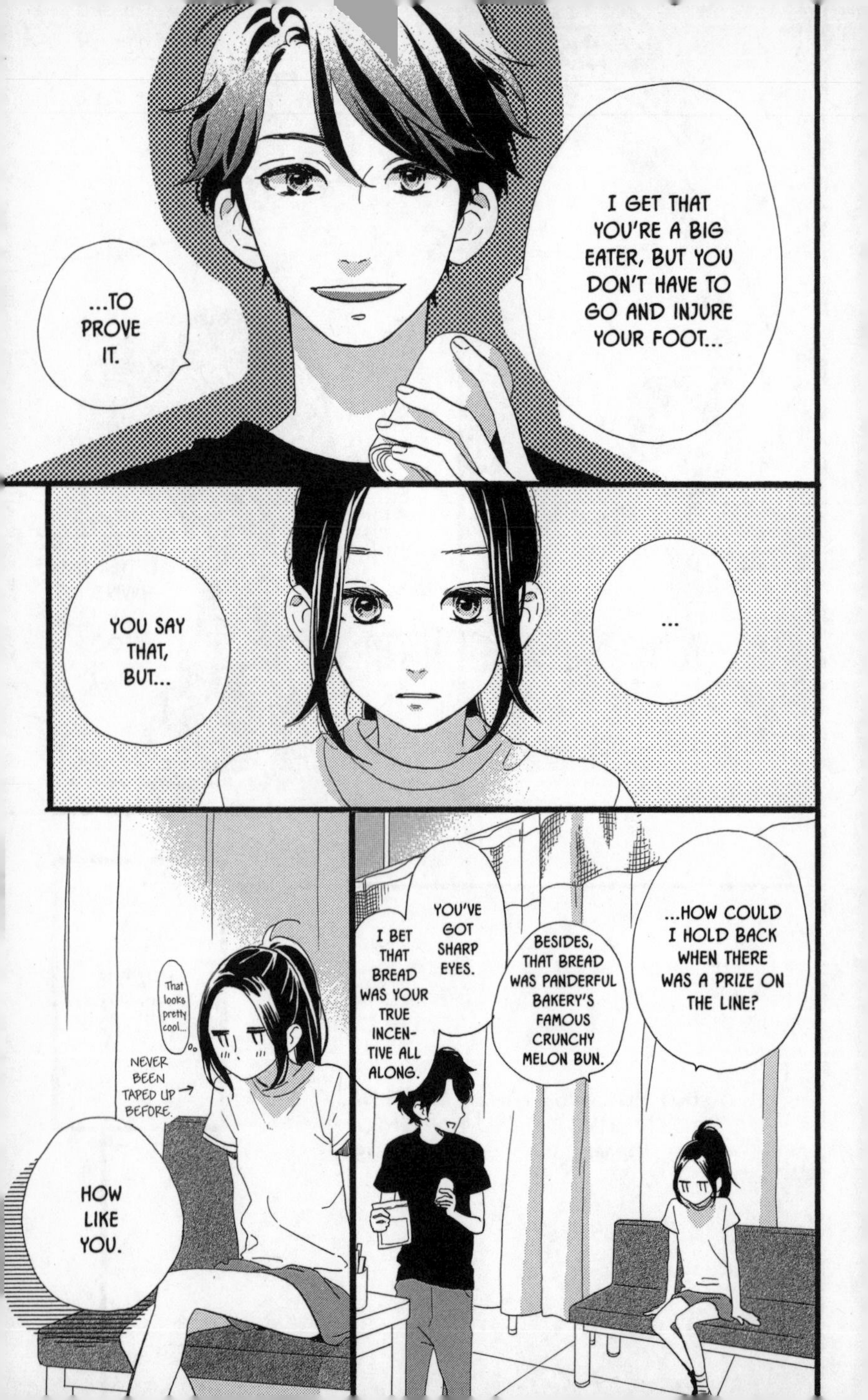
I GET THAT YOU'RE A BIG EATER, BUT YOU DON'T HAVE TO GO AND INJURE YOUR FOOT...
...TO PROVE IT.
...
YOU SAY THAT, BUT...
...HOW COULD I HOLD BACK WHEN THERE WAS A PRIZE ON THE LINE?
BESIDES, THAT BREAD WAS PANDERFUL BAKERY'S FAMOUS CRUNCHY MELON BUN.
YOU'VE GOT SHARP EYES.
I BET THAT BREAD WAS YOUR TRUE INCEN-TIVE ALL ALONG.
That looks pretty cool...
NEVER BEEN TAPED UP BEFORE.
HOW LIKE YOU.

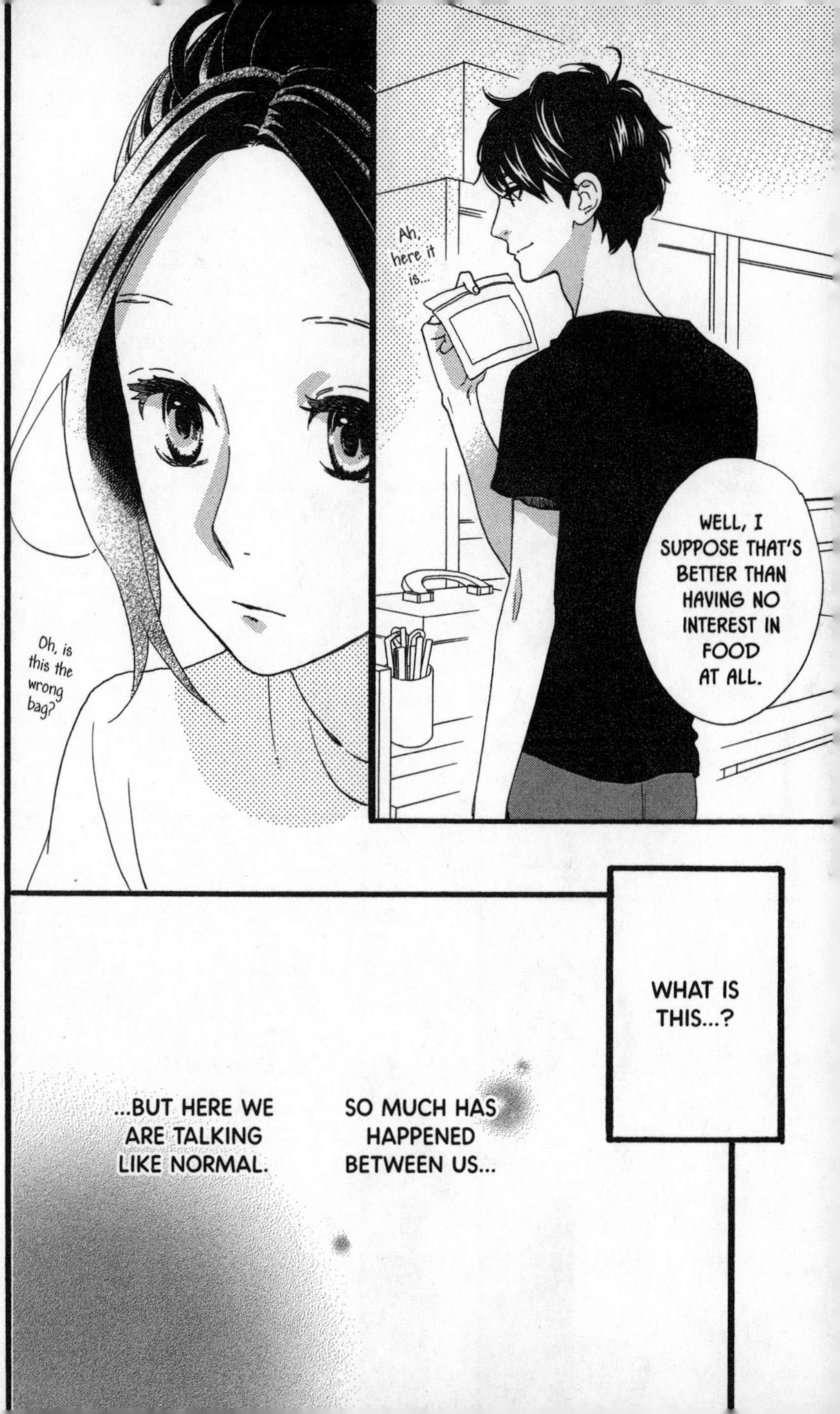
Ah, here it is...
WELL, I SUPPOSE THAT'S BETTER THAN HAVING NO INTEREST IN FOOD AT ALL.
Oh, is this the wrong bag?
WHAT IS THIS...?
SO MUCH HAS HAPPENED BETWEEN US...
...BUT HERE WE ARE TALKING LIKE NORMAL.

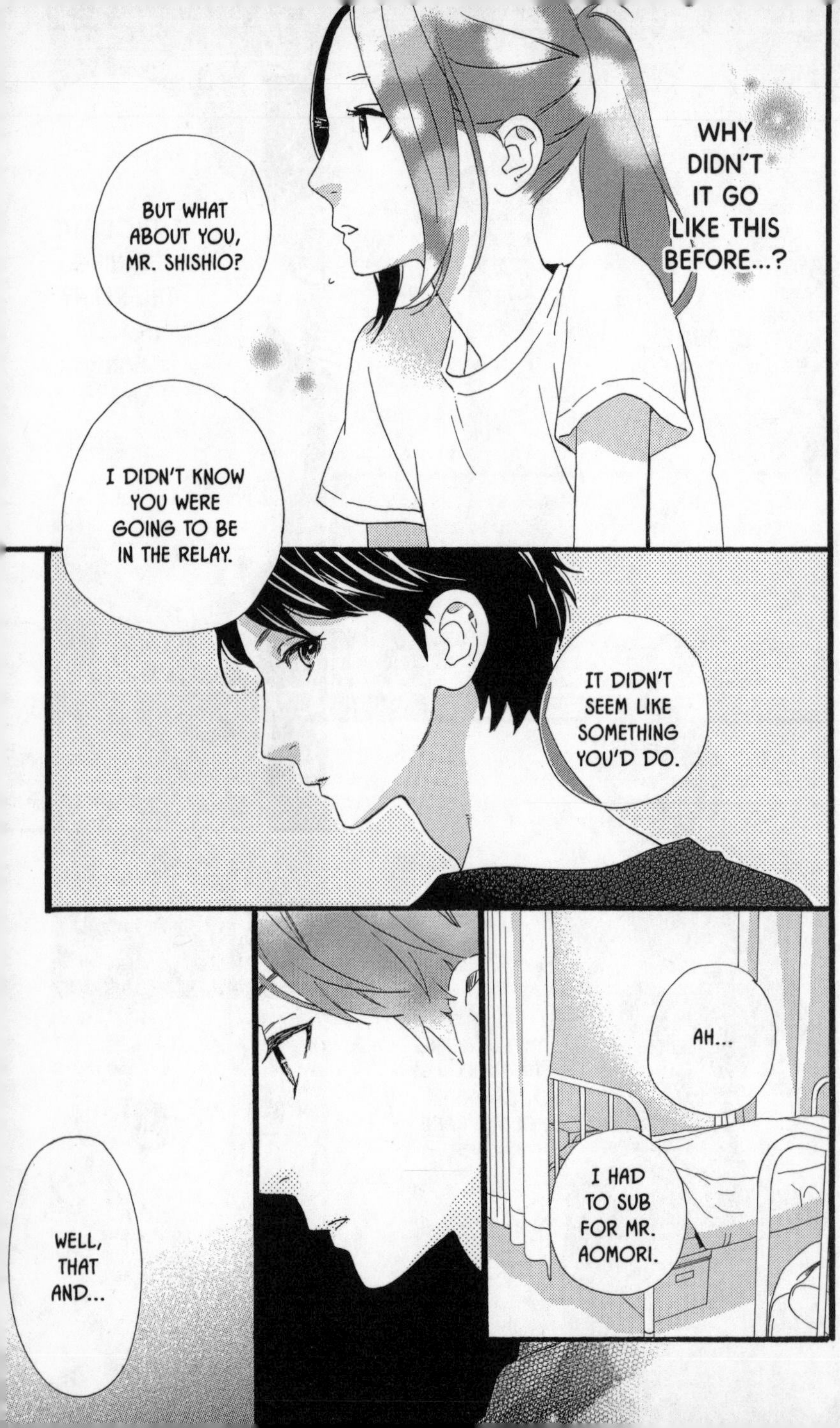
WHY DIDN'T IT GO LIKE THIS BEFORE...?
BUT WHAT ABOUT YOU, MR. SHISHIO?
I DIDN'T KNOW YOU WERE GOING TO BE IN THE RELAY.
IT DIDN'T SEEM LIKE SOMETHING YOU'D DO.
AH...
I HAD TO SUB FOR MR. AOMORI.
WELL, THAT AND...

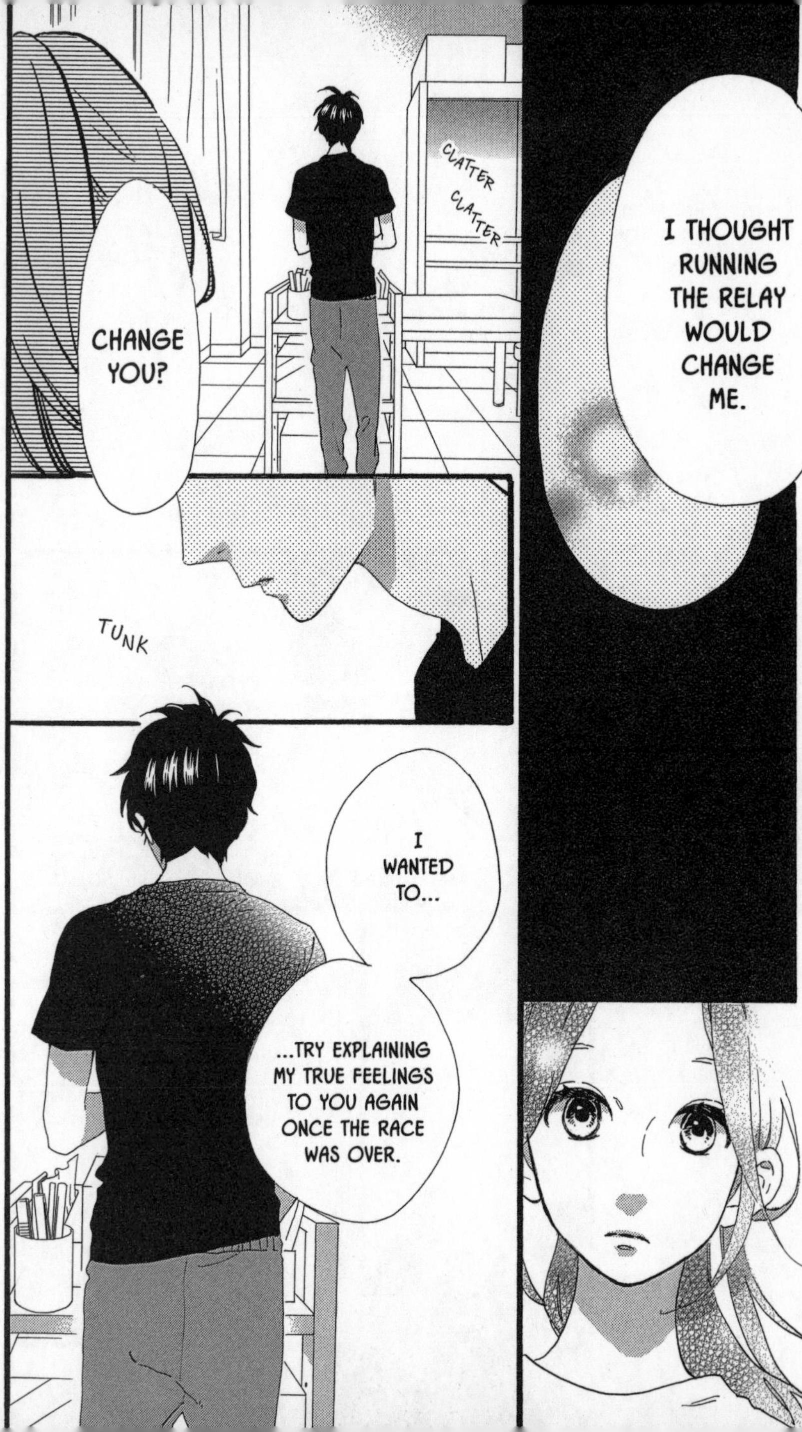
I THOUGHT RUNNING THE RELAY WOULD CHANGE ME.
CLATTER
CLATTER
CHANGE YOU?
TUNK
I WANTED TO...
...TRY EXPLAINING MY TRUE FEELINGS TO YOU AGAIN ONCE THE RACE WAS OVER.

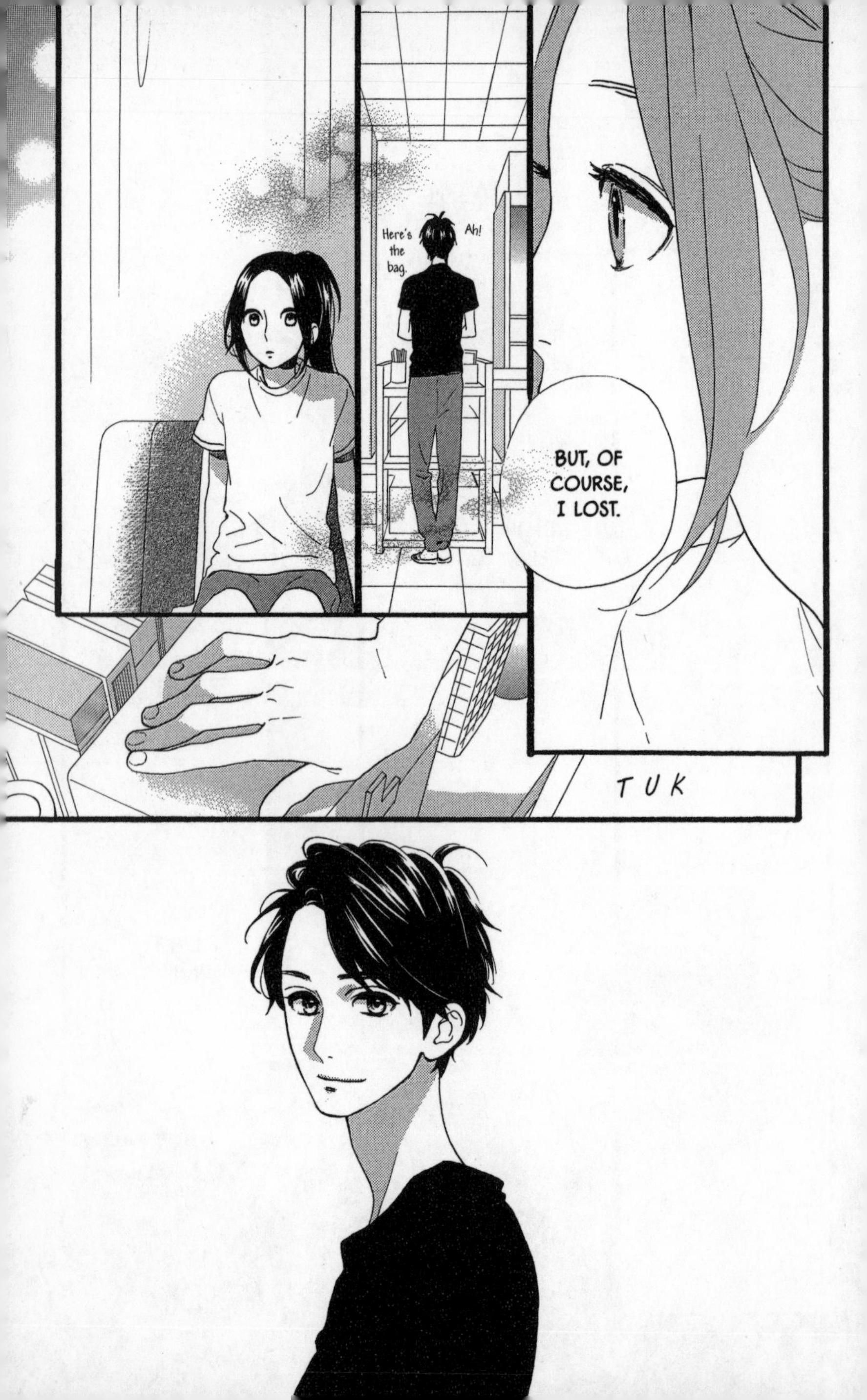
BUT, OF COURSE, I LOST.
Ah!
Here's the bag.
TUK

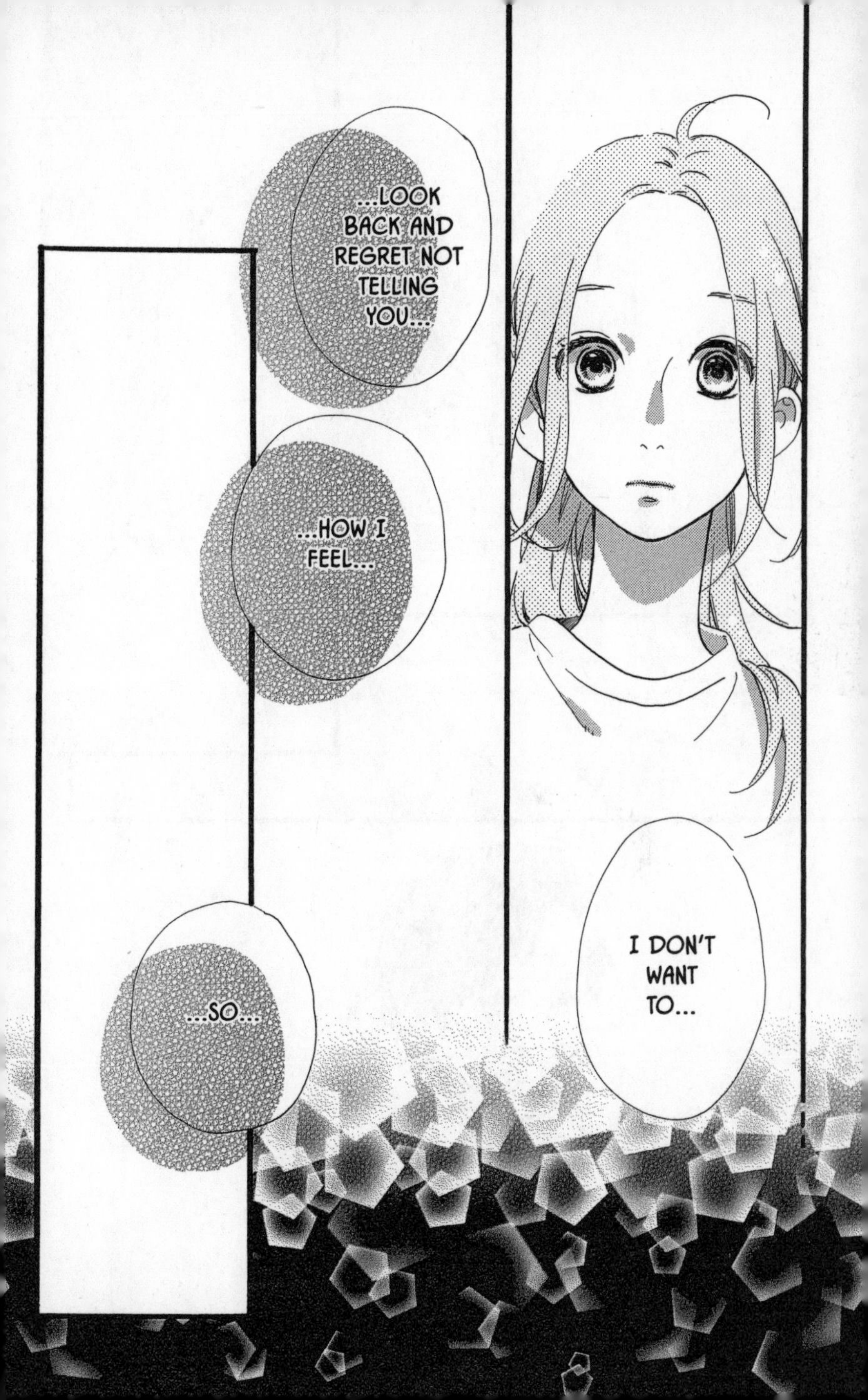
I DON'T WANT TO...
...LOOK BACK AND REGRET NOT TELLING YOU...
...HOW I FEEL...
...SO...

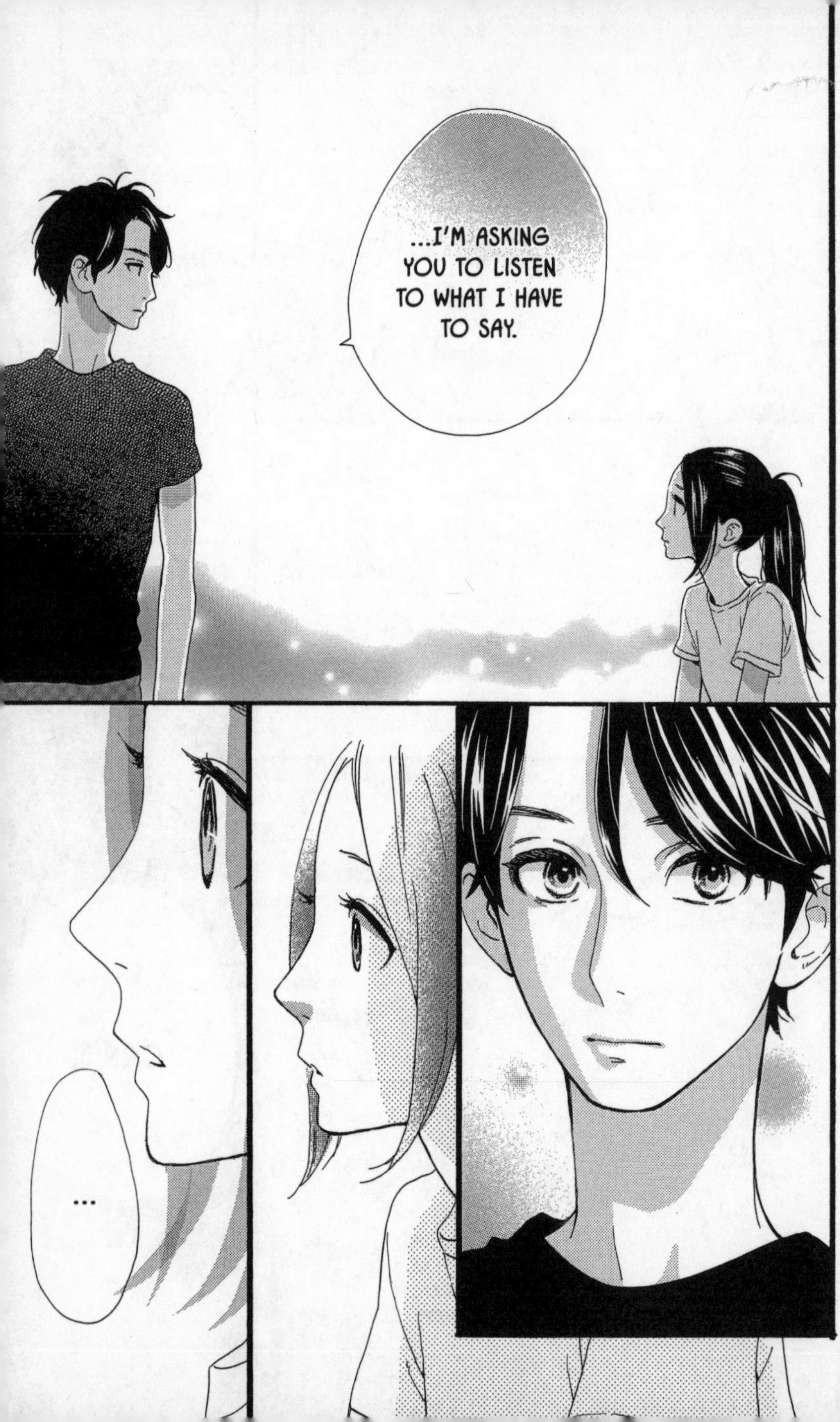
...I'M ASKING YOU TO LISTEN TO WHAT I HAVE TO SAY.
...

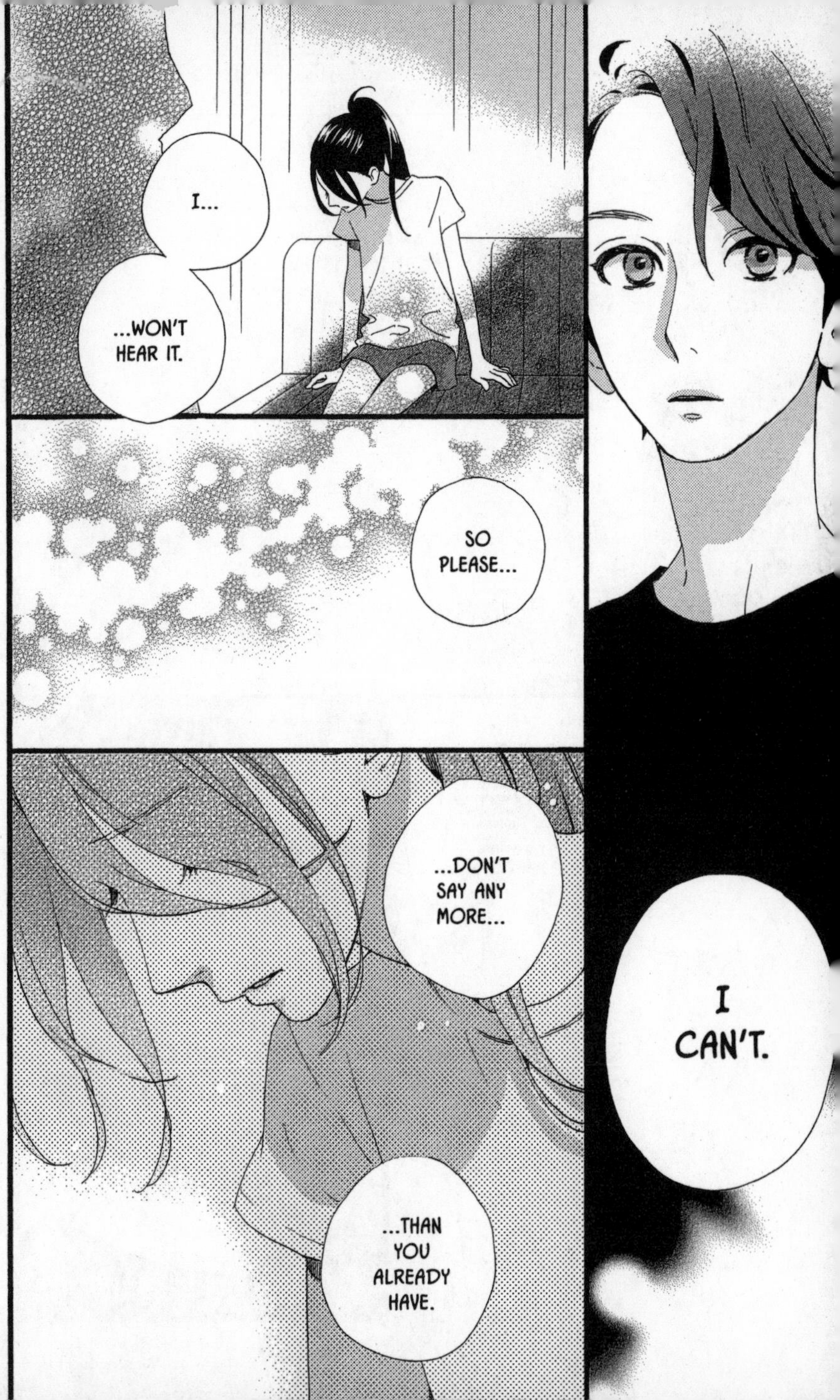
I...
...WON'T HEAR IT.
SO PLEASE...
...DON'T SAY ANY MORE...
...THAN YOU ALREADY HAVE.
I CAN'T.

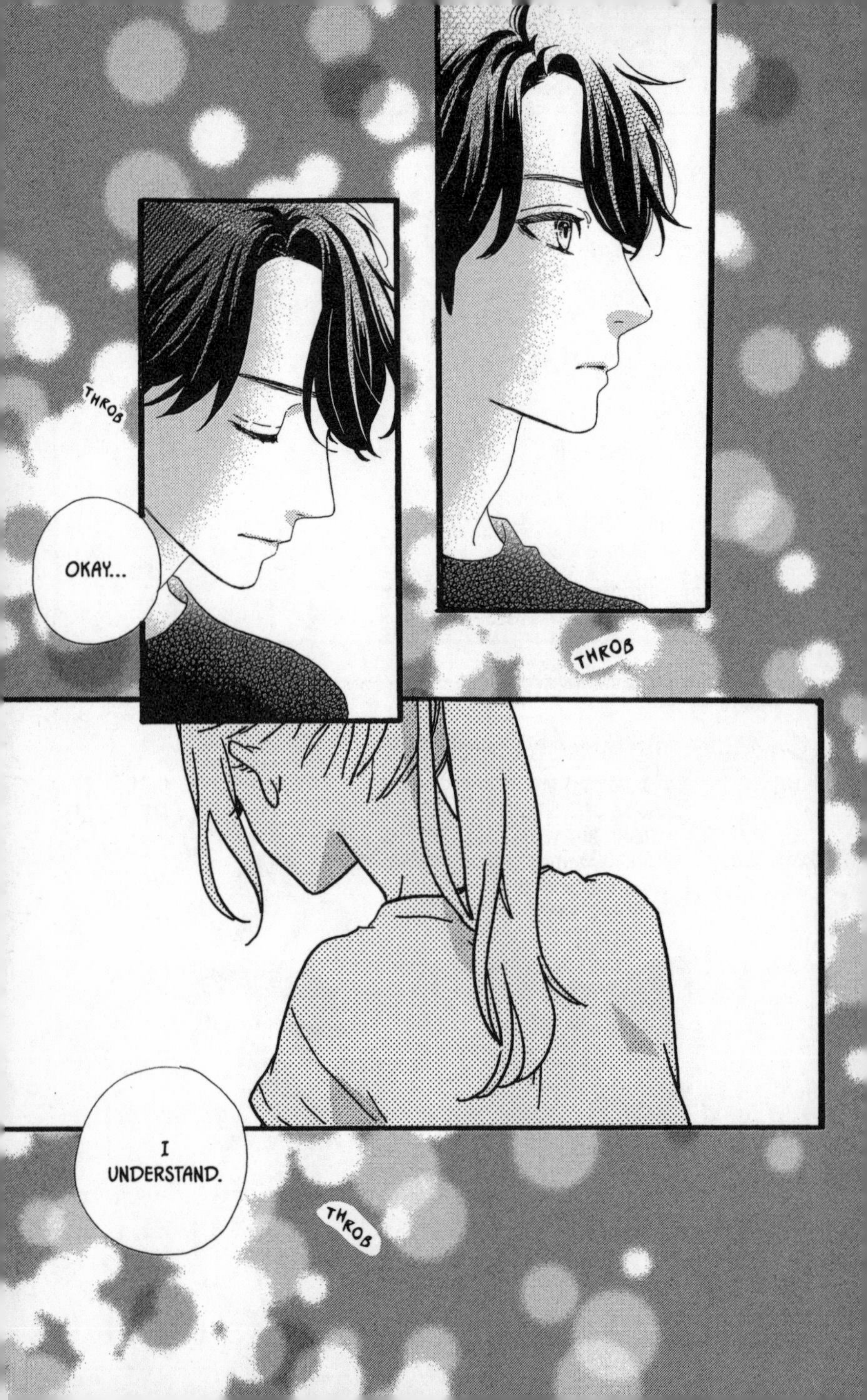
THROB
OKAY...
THROB
I UNDERSTAND.
THROB

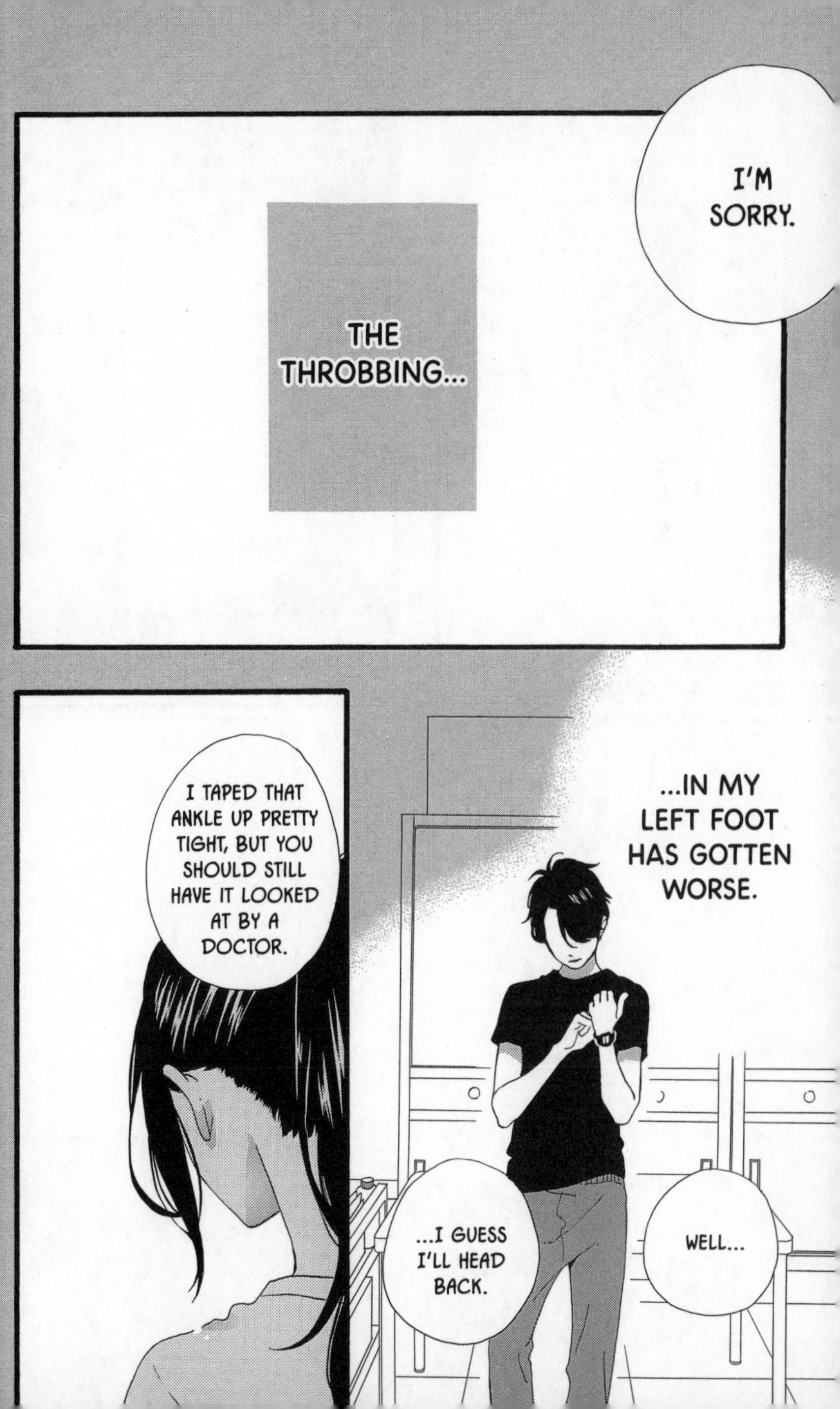
I'M SORRY.
THE THROBBING...
...IN MY LEFT FOOT HAS GOTTEN WORSE.
WELL...
...I GUESS I'LL HEAD BACK.
I TAPED THAT ANKLE UP PRETTY TIGHT, BUT YOU SHOULD STILL HAVE IT LOOKED AT BY A DOCTOR.

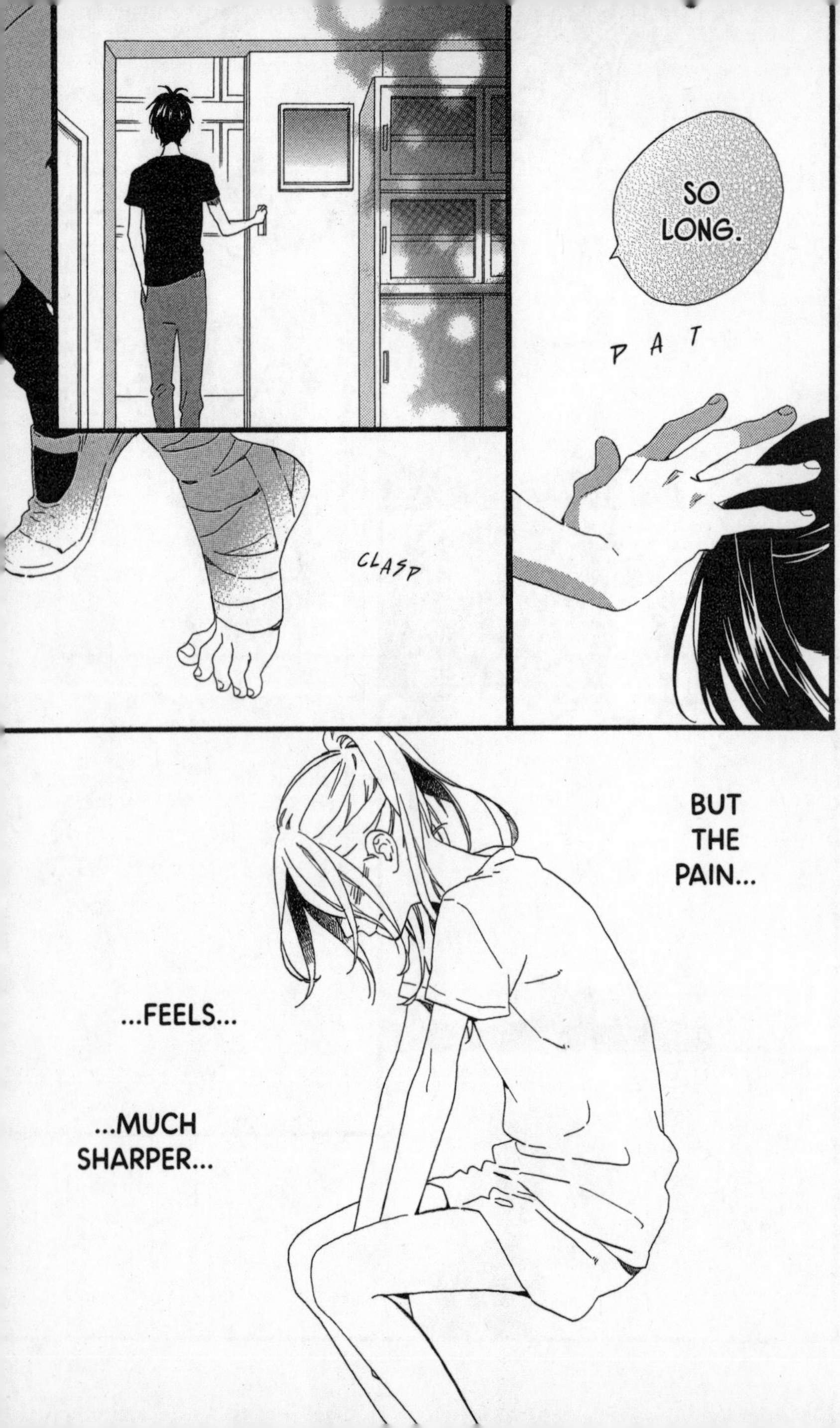
SO LONG.
PAT
CLASP
BUT THE PAIN...
...FEELS...
...MUCH SHARPER...

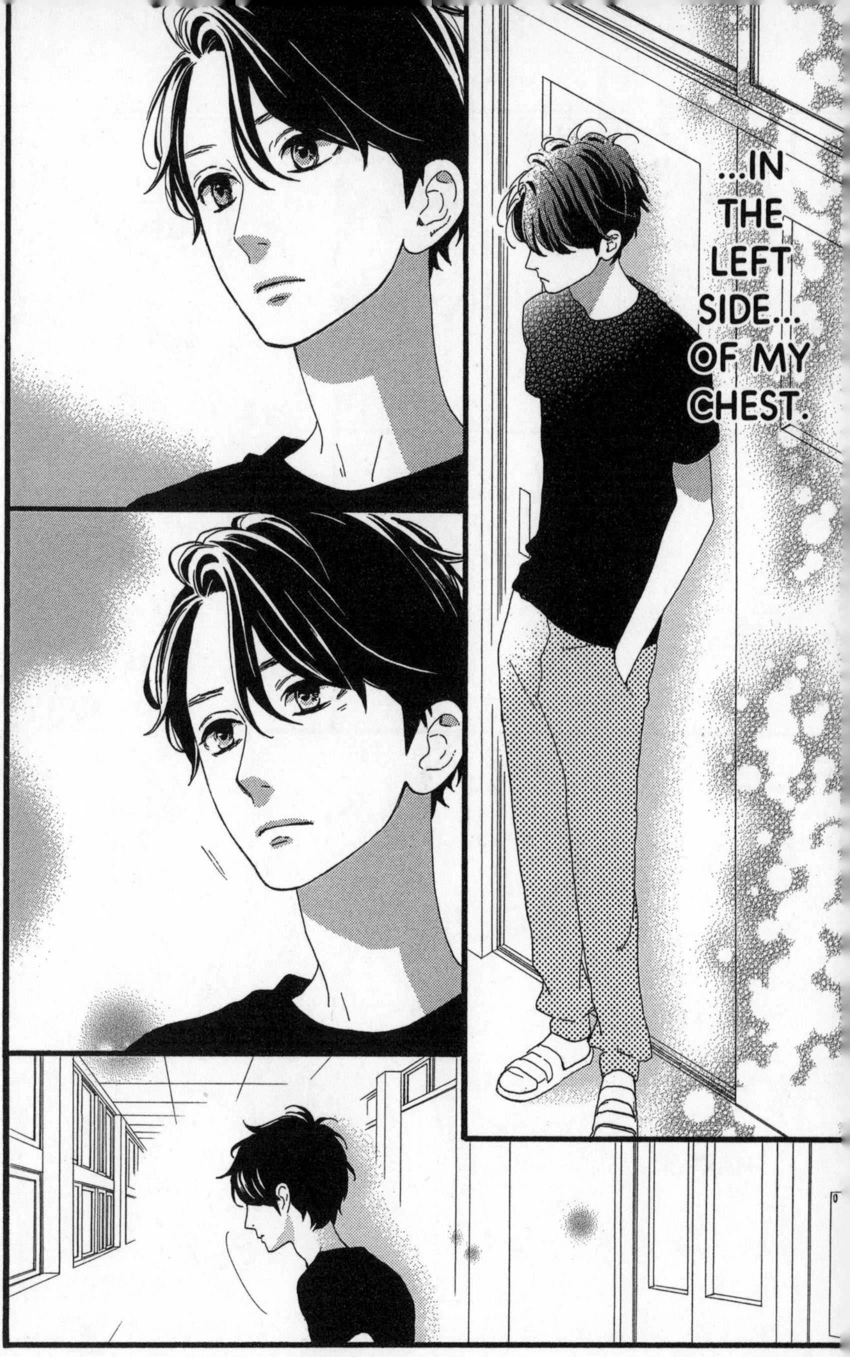
...IN THE LEFT SIDE... OF MY CHEST.

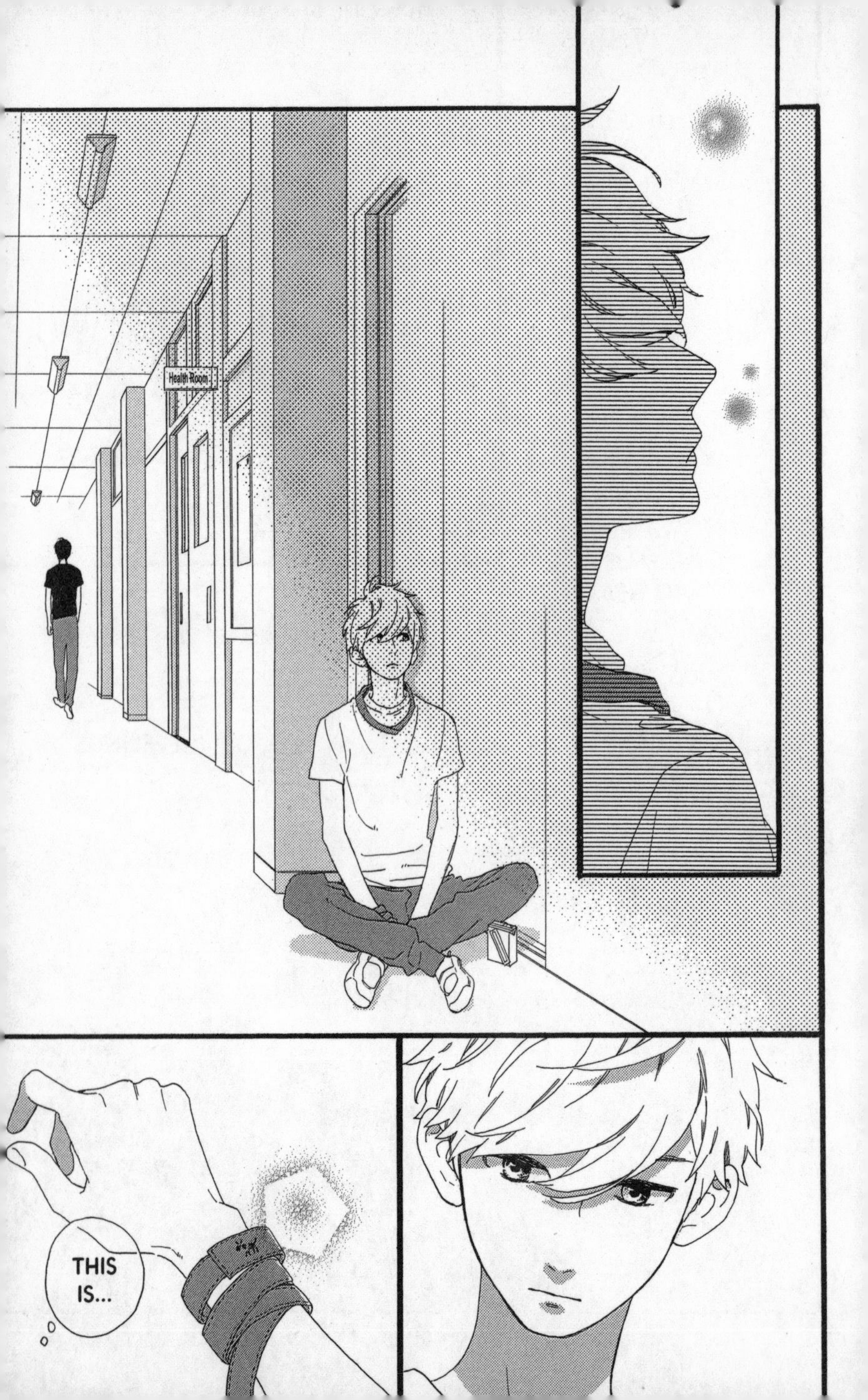
Health Room
THIS IS...

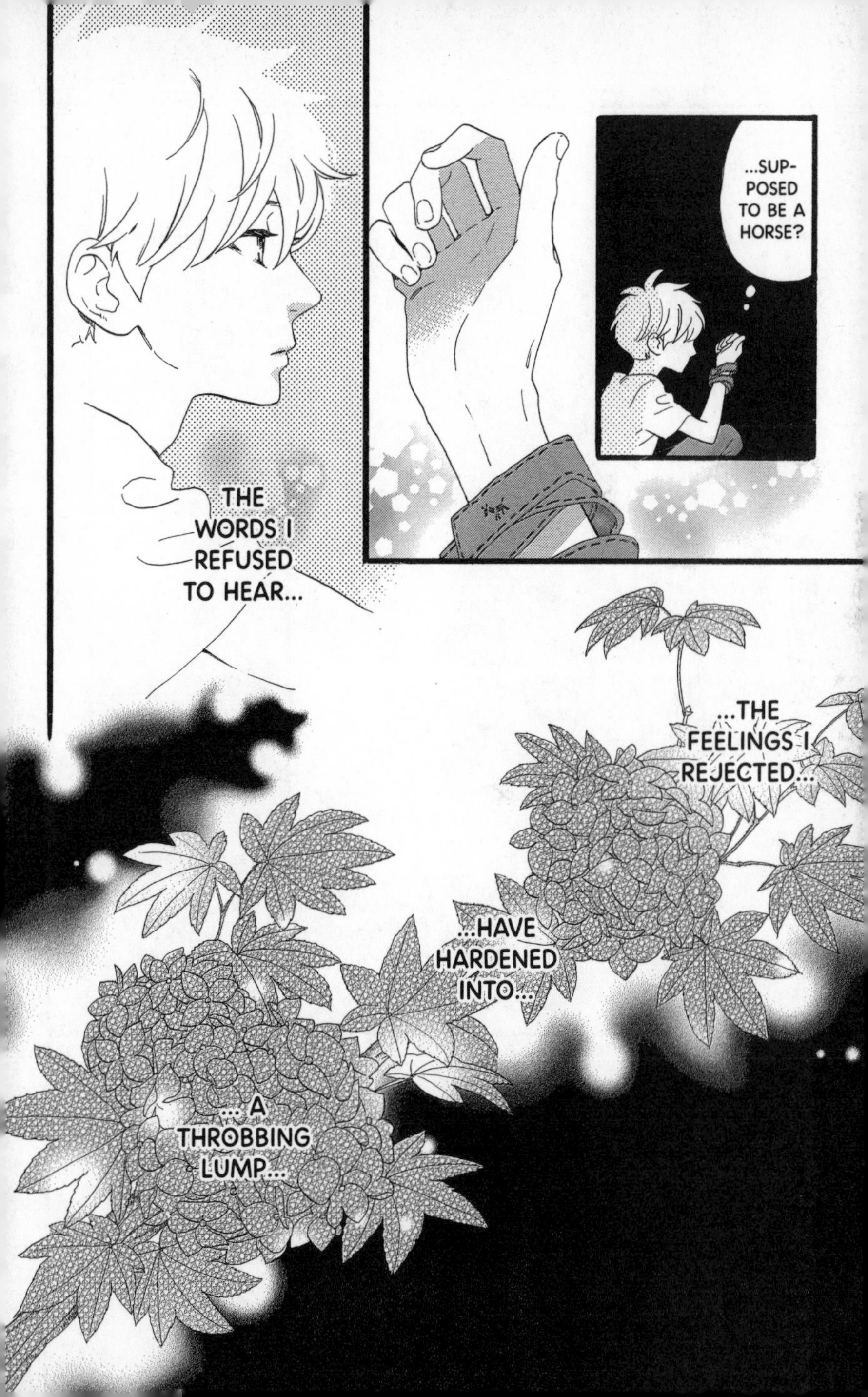
...SUP-
POSED
TO BE A
HORSE?
THE WORDS I REFUSED TO HEAR...
...THE FEELINGS I REJECTED...
...HAVE HARDENED INTO...
... A THROBBING LUMP...

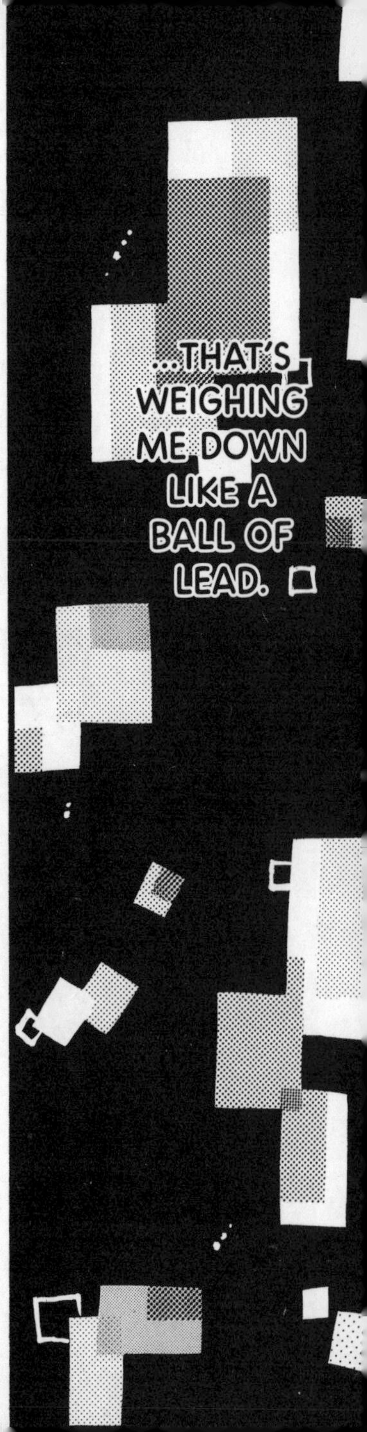
...THAT'S WEIGHING ME DOWN LIKE A BALL OF LEAD.

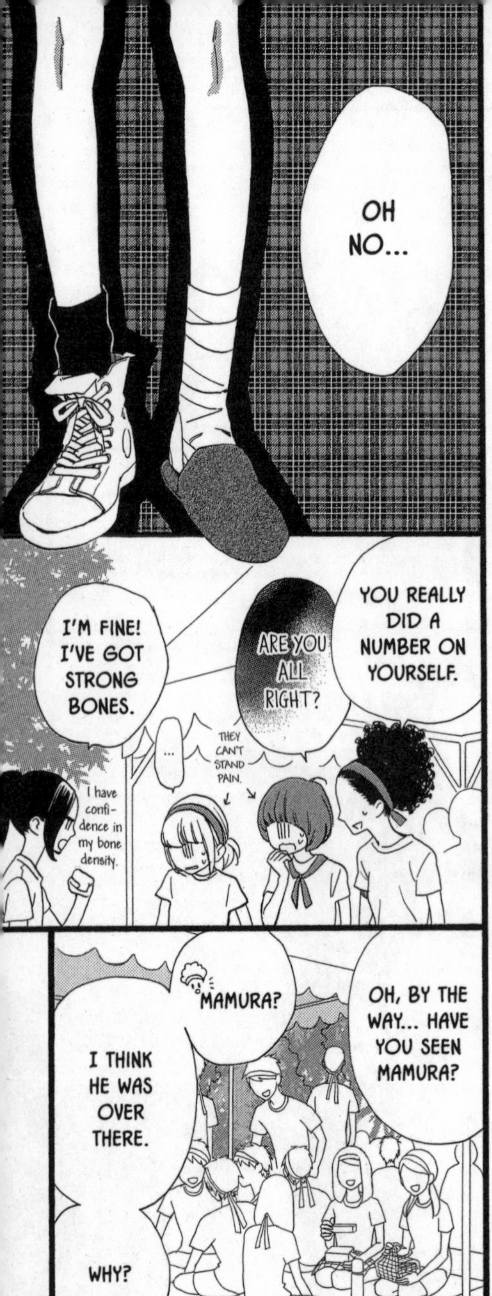
OH NO...
YOU REALLY DID A NUMBER ON YOURSELF.
ARE YOU ALL RIGHT?
THEY CAN'T STAND PAIN.
...
I'M FINE! I'VE GOT STRONG BONES.
I have confidence in my bone density.
OH, BY THE WAY... HAVE YOU SEEN MAMURA?
MAMURA?
I THINK HE WAS OVER THERE.
WHY?

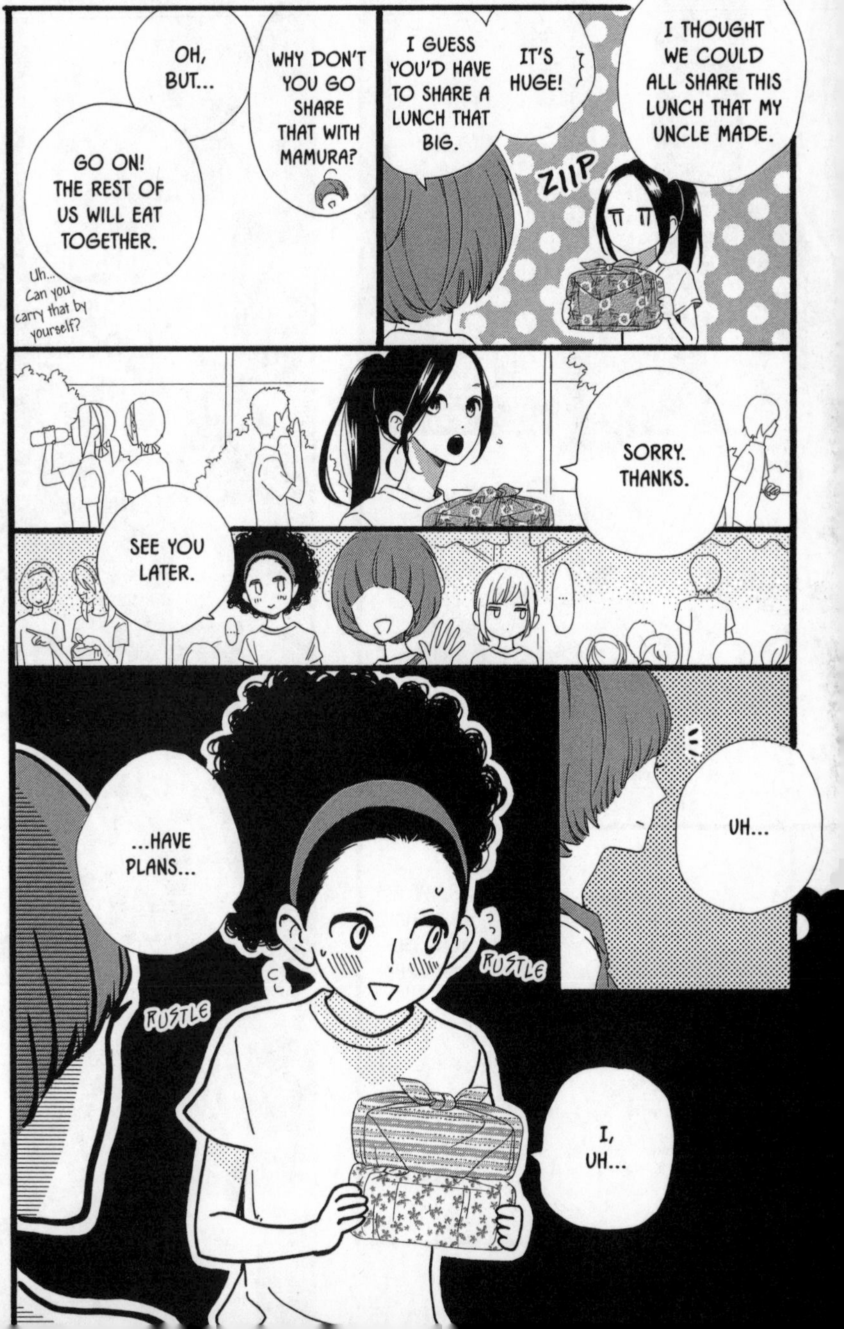
I THOUGHT WE COULD ALL SHARE THIS LUNCH THAT MY UNCLE MADE.
ZIIP
IT'S HUGE!
I GUESS YOU'D HAVE TO SHARE A LUNCH THAT BIG.
WHY DON'T YOU GO SHARE THAT WITH MAMURA?
OH, BUT...
GO ON! THE REST OF US WILL EAT TOGETHER.
Uh... Can you carry that by yourself?
SORRY. THANKS.
...
SEE YOU LATER.
...
UH...
I, UH...
...HAVE PLANS...
RUSTLE
RUSTLE

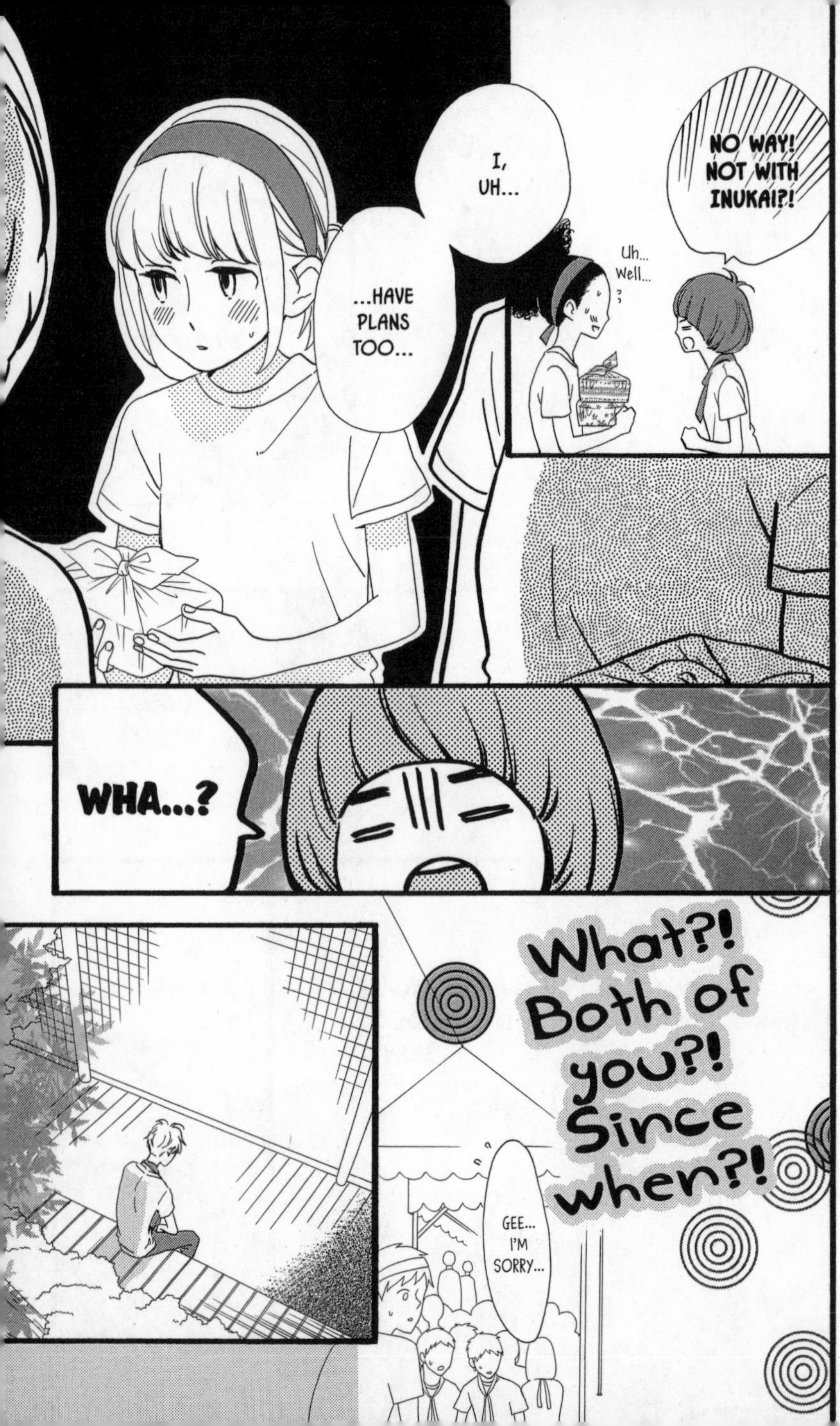
NO WAY! NOT WITH INUKAI?!
Uh... Well...
I, UH...
...HAVE PLANS TOO...
WHA...?
What?! Both of you?! Since when?!
GEE... I'M SORRY...

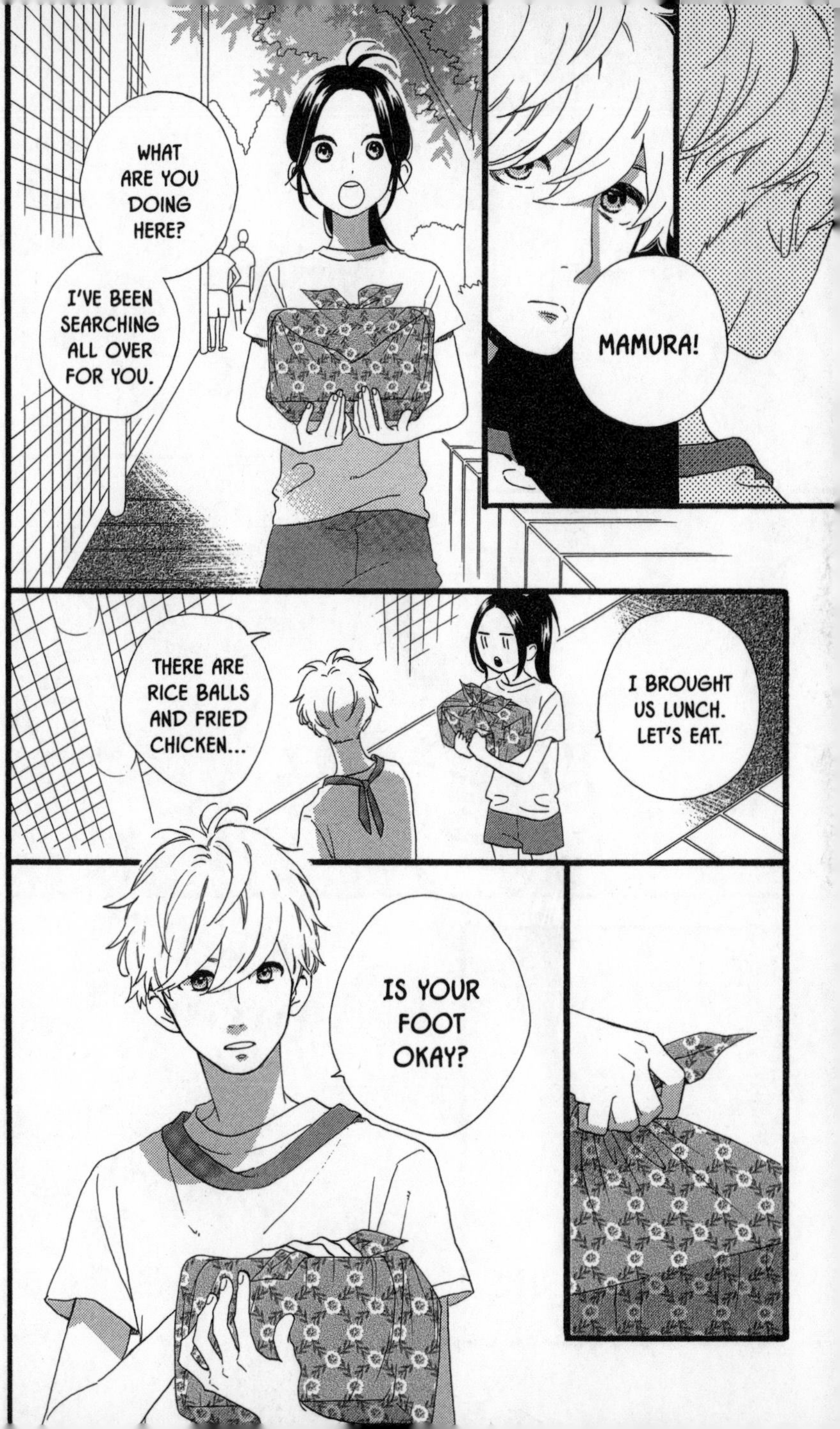
MAMURA!
WHAT ARE YOU DOING HERE?
I'VE BEEN SEARCHING ALL OVER FOR YOU.
I BROUGHT US LUNCH. LET'S EAT.
THERE ARE RICE BALLS AND FRIED CHICKEN...
IS YOUR FOOT OKAY?

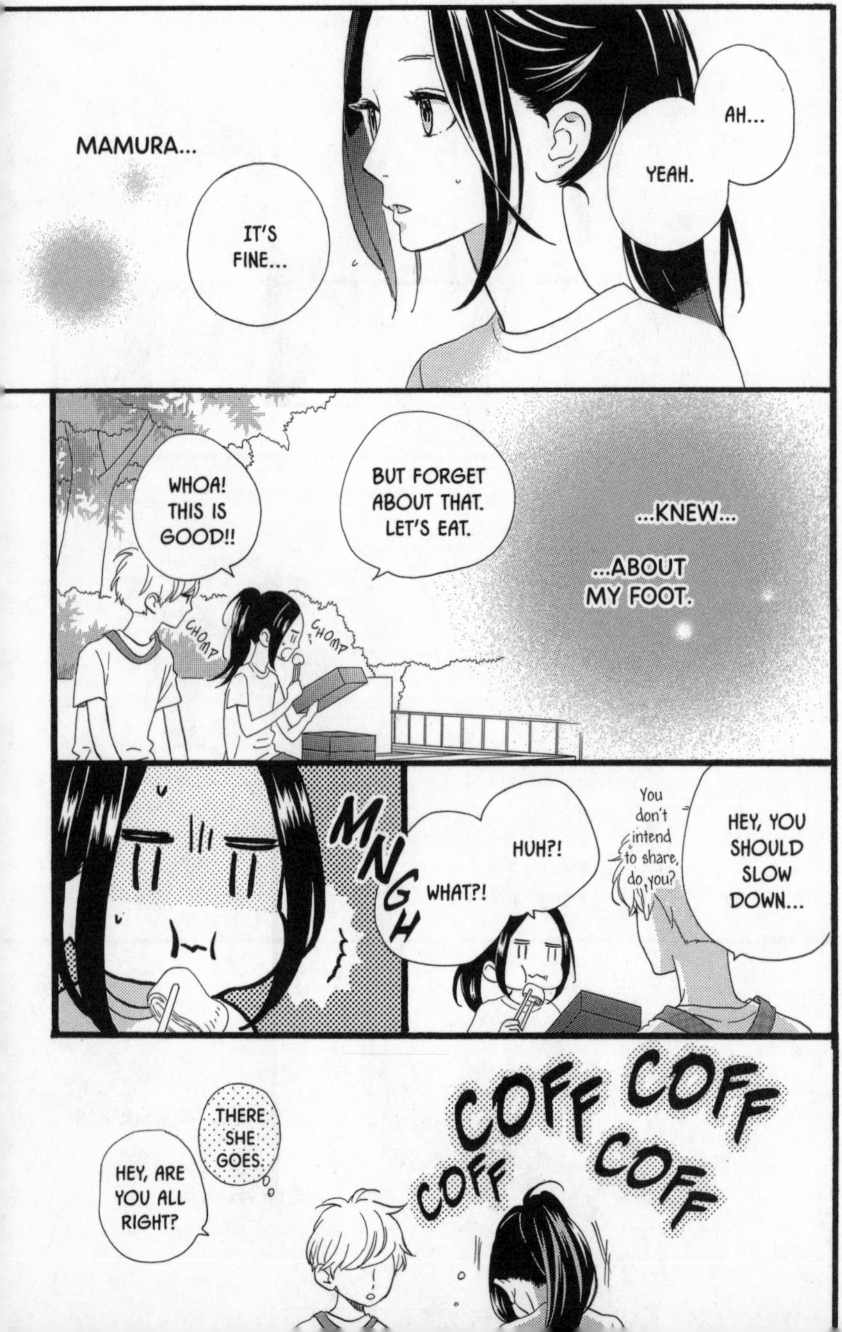
AH... YEAH.
IT'S FINE...
MAMURA...
...KNEW...
...ABOUT MY FOOT.
BUT FORGET ABOUT THAT. LET'S EAT.
CHOMP
CHOMP
WHOA! THIS IS GOOD!!
HEY, YOU SHOULD SLOW DOWN...
You don't intend to share, do you?
HUH?! WHAT?!
MNGH
COFF COFF COFF COFF
THERE SHE GOES.
HEY, ARE YOU ALL RIGHT?

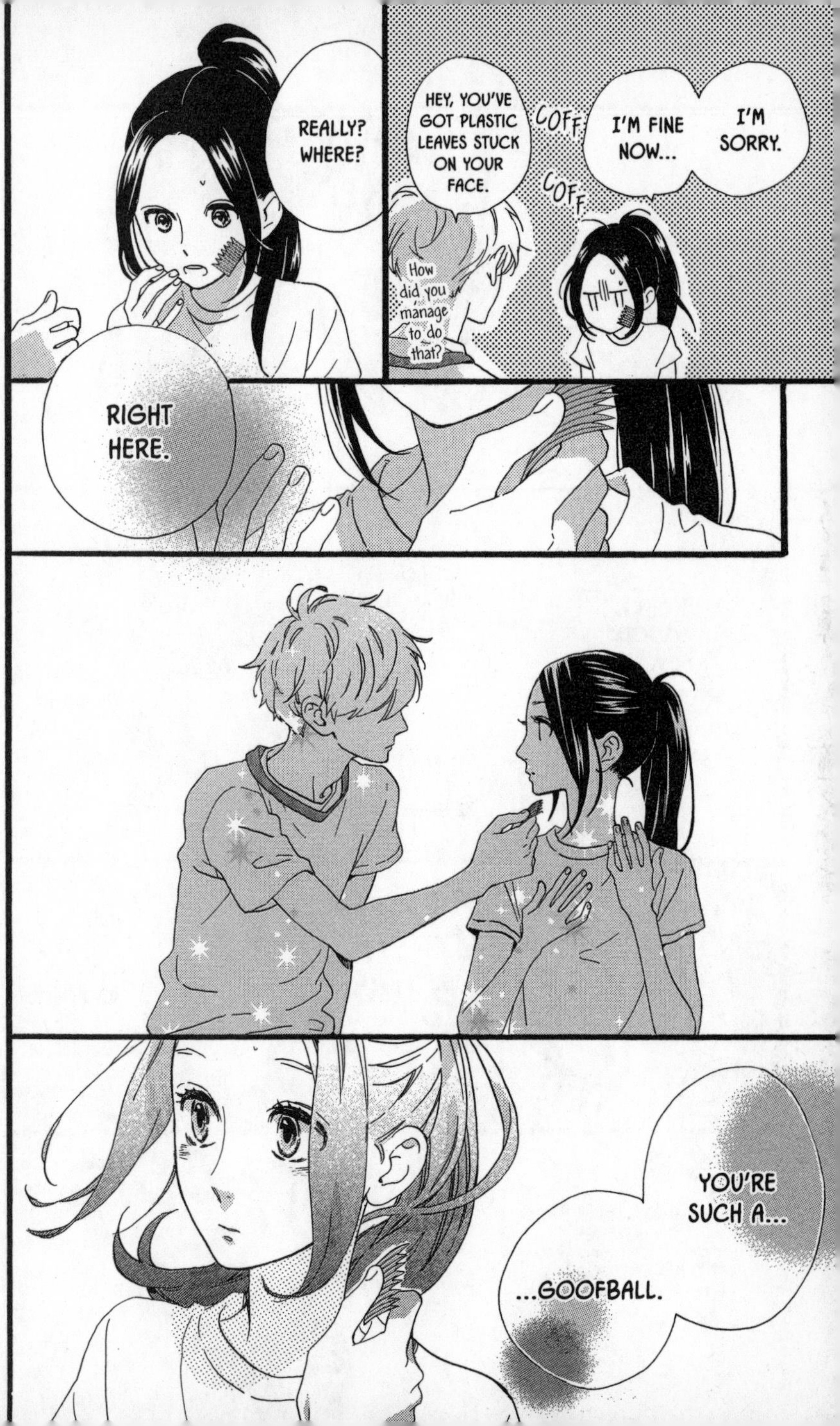
I'M SORRY.
I'M FINE NOW...
COFF
HEY, YOU'VE GOT PLASTIC LEAVES STUCK ON YOUR FACE.
COFF
How did you manage to do that?
REALLY? WHERE?
RIGHT HERE.
YOU'RE SUCH A...
...GOOFBALL.

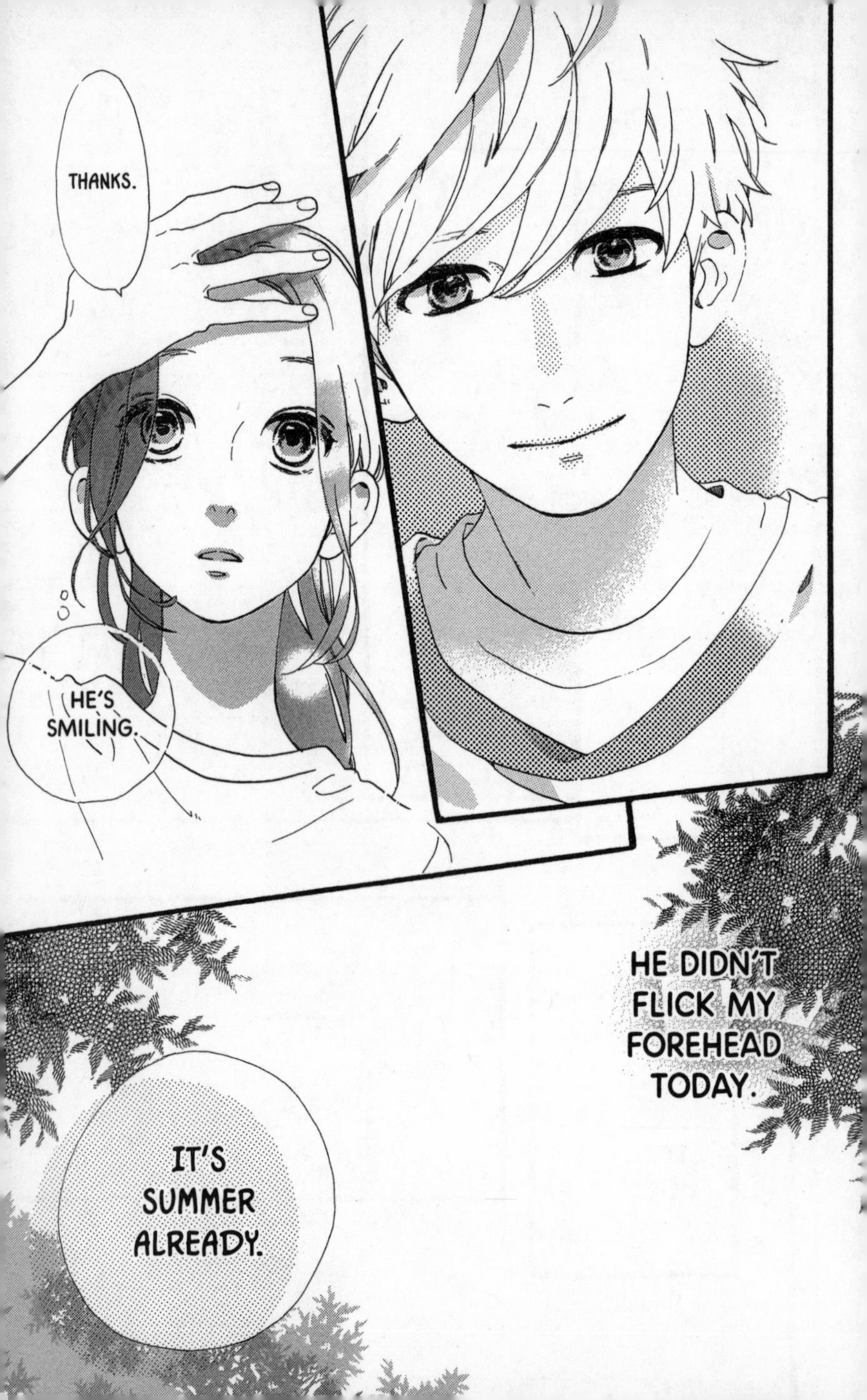
THANKS.
HE'S SMILING.
HE DIDN'T FLICK MY FOREHEAD TODAY.
IT'S SUMMER ALREADY.

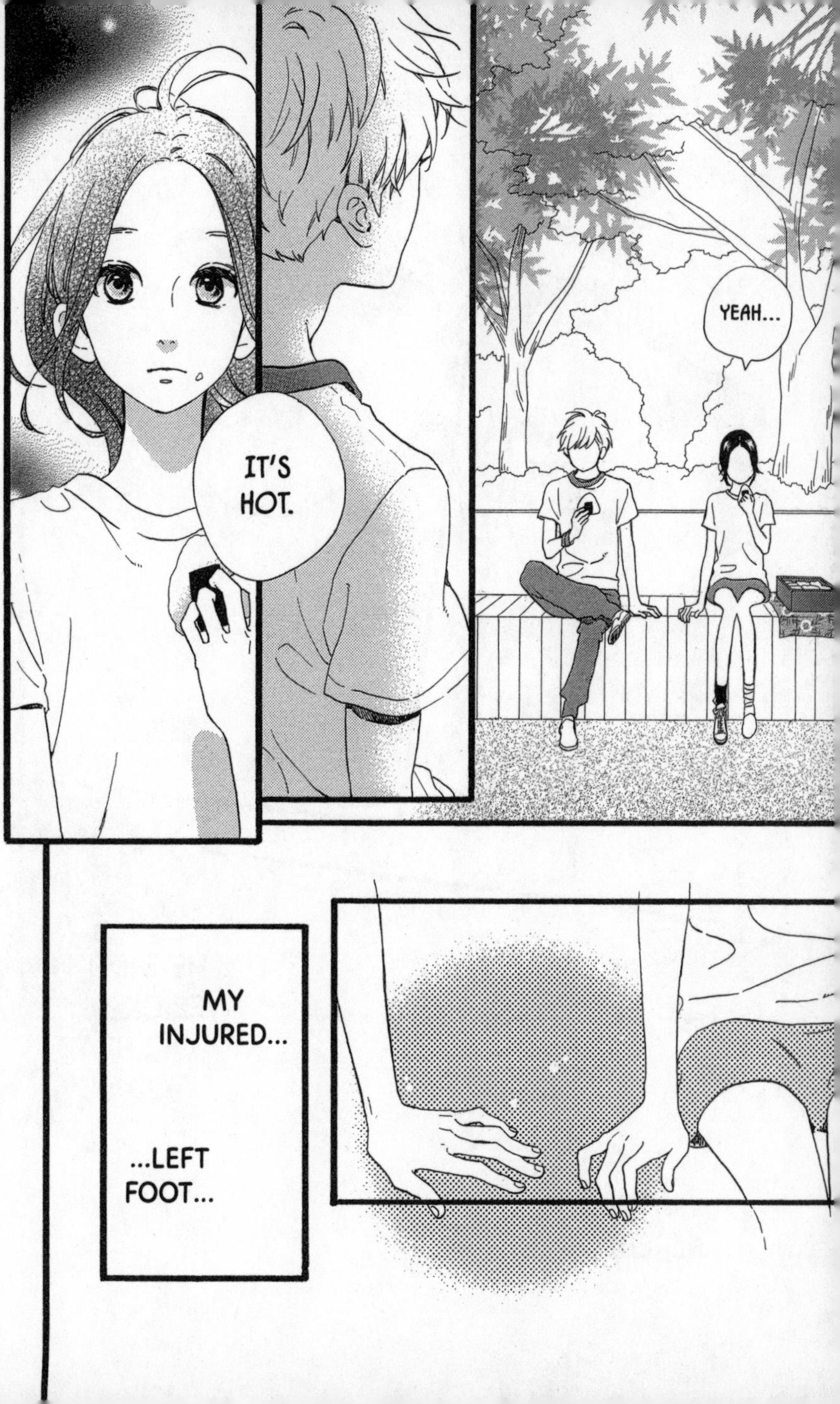
YEAH...
IT'S HOT.
MY INJURED...
...LEFT FOOT...

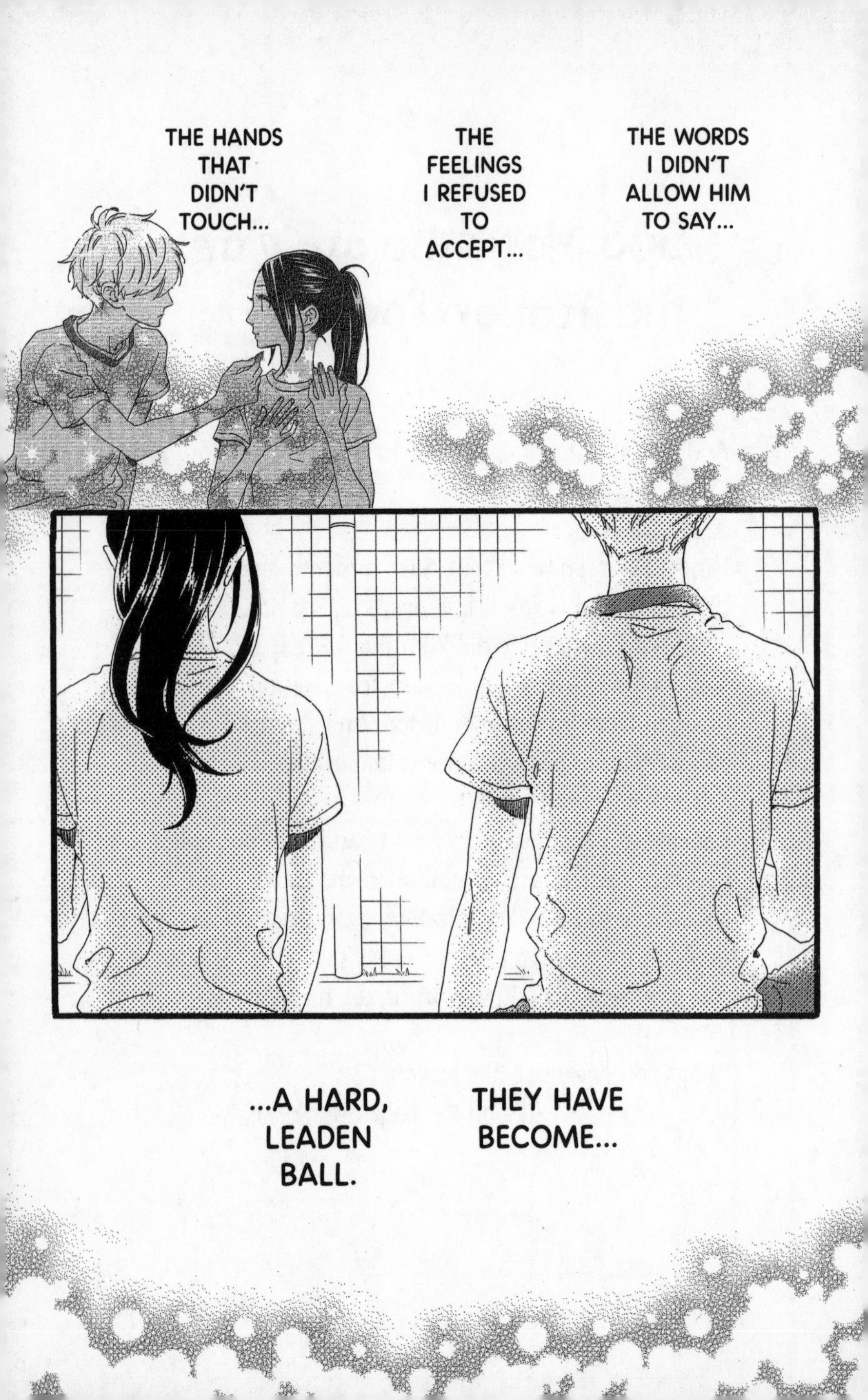
THE WORDS I DIDN'T ALLOW HIM TO SAY...
THE FEELINGS I REFUSED TO ACCEPT...
THE HANDS THAT DIDN'T TOUCH...
THEY HAVE BECOME...
...A HARD, LEADEN BALL.

# Suu Morishita drew an illustration for me.

And so, Suu Morishita agreed to do an illustration. ♫
Thank you so much! ♫

I think I've seen her about twice a month since the
beginning of this year!! She drops by my house more
often than my friends do! With the way she moves about,
you wouldn't believe she lives in the country!! We have
plans to meet up this month too. And the next! It's almost
like we're in a long-distance relationship!

Looking at her illustration now, I can't help but notice
how cute my characters look when she draws them. If
she had drawn *Daytime Shooting Star*, the story probably
wouldn't have become so sorid. My favorite character in
*Hibi Chocho* is Ichi. Please let us see more of him.

I hope you enjoy her illustration. ♫

(It's on the page after next.)

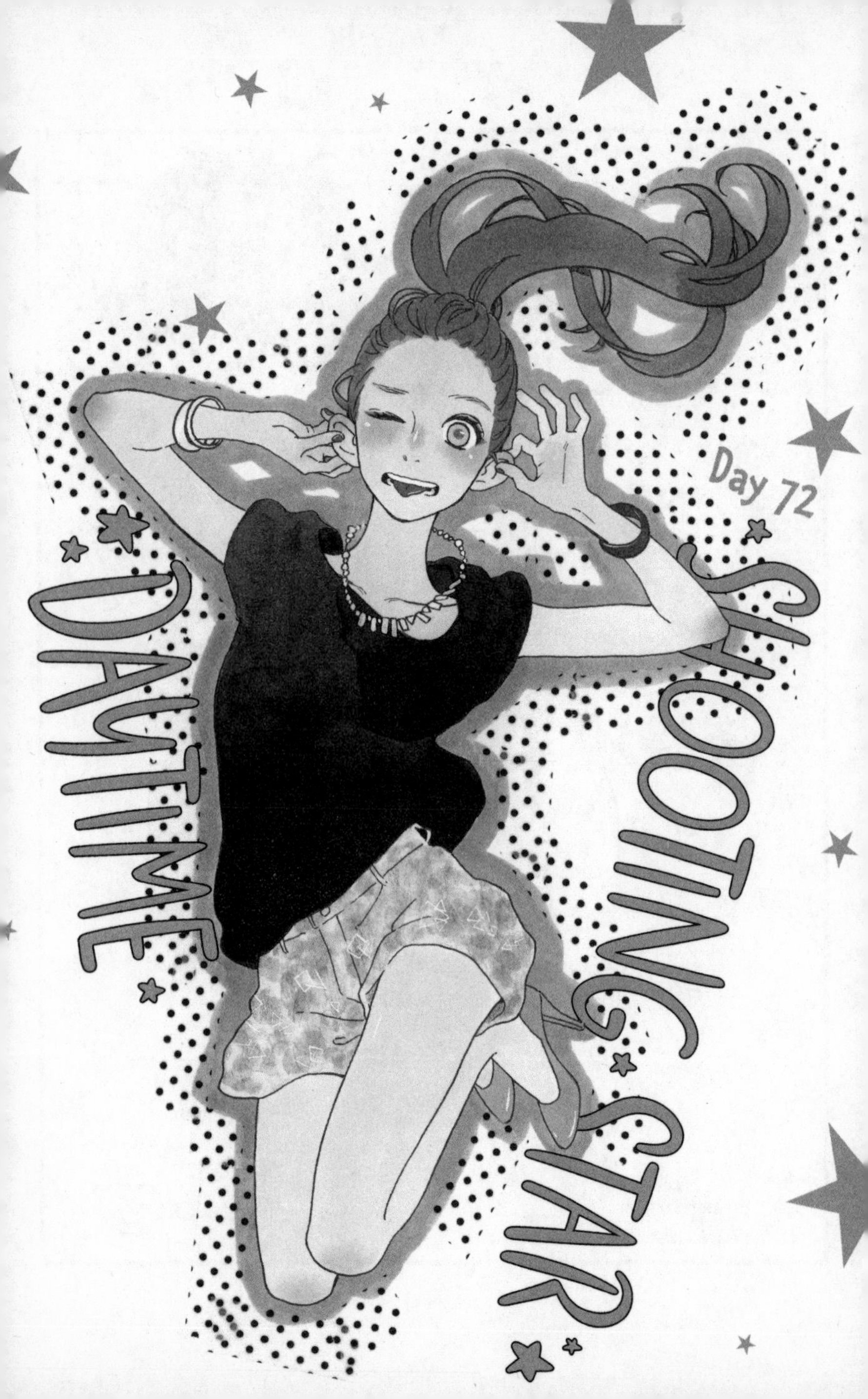
Day 72
SHOOTING STAR
DAYTIME

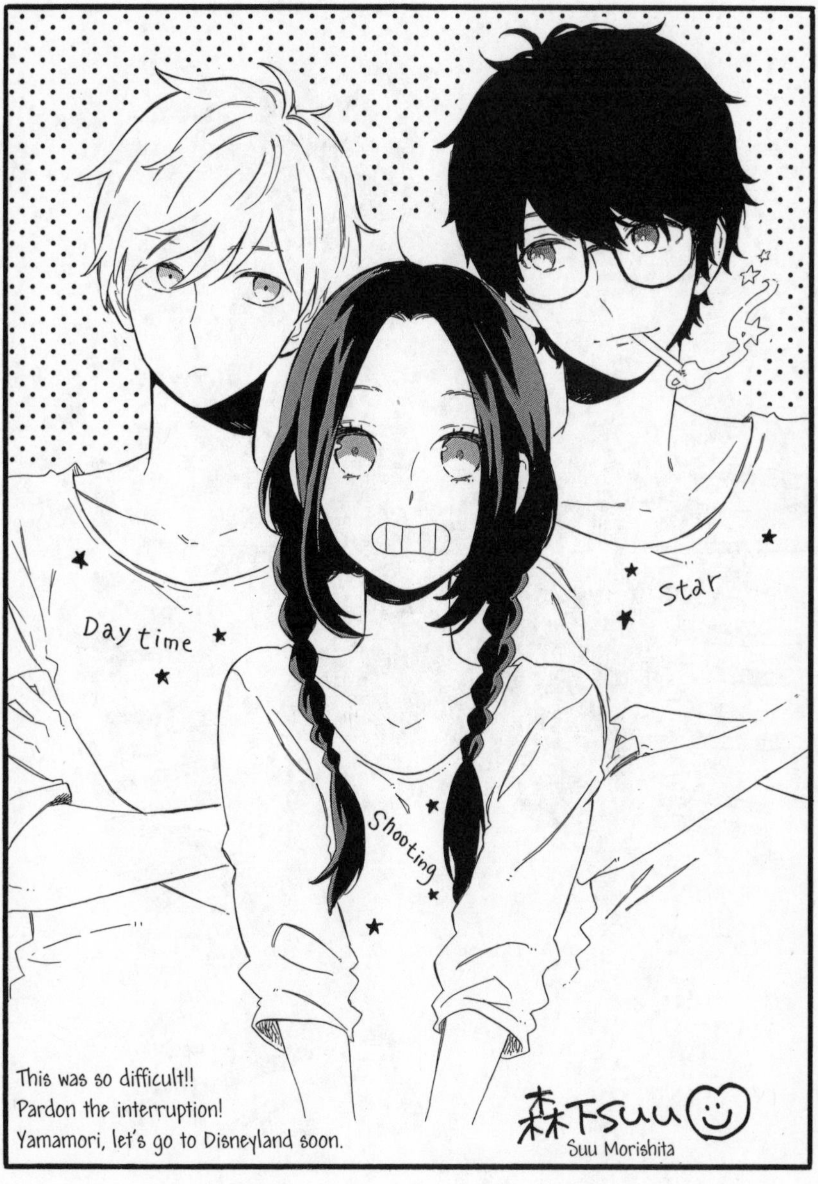
Daytime
Shooting
Star
This was so difficult!!
Pardon the interruption!
Yamamori, let's go to Disneyland soon.
森下suu
Suu Morishita

SPORTS DAY CAME AND WENT AND SO DID OUR TESTS.

I WAS SO BUSY TRYING TO SORT OUT MY FEELINGS...

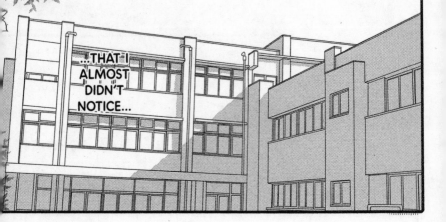

...THAT I ALMOST DIDN'T NOTICE...

DAYTIME SHOOTING STAR

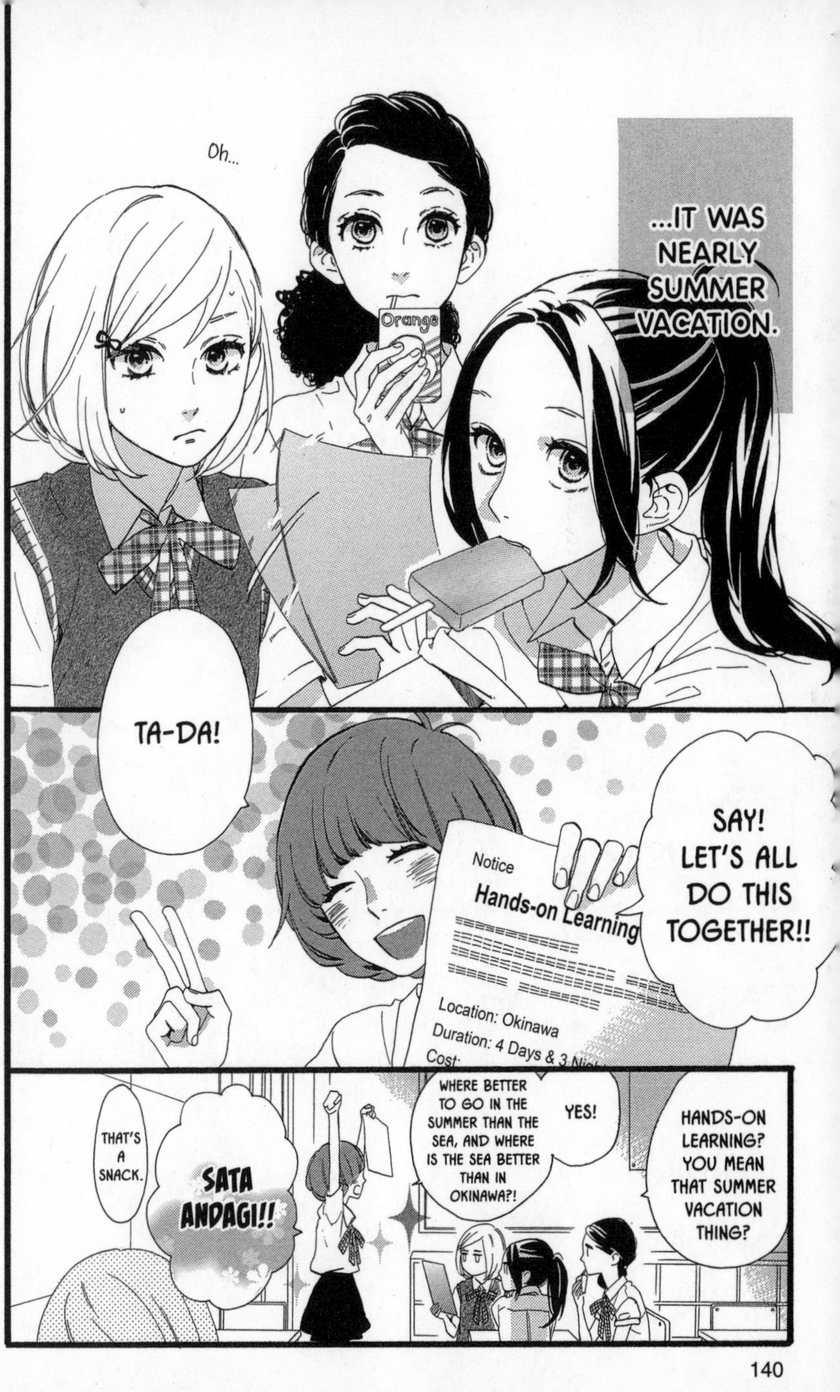
...IT WAS NEARLY SUMMER VACATION.
Oh...
SAY! LET'S ALL DO THIS TOGETHER!!
Notice
Hands-on Learning
Location: Okinawa
TA-DA!
HANDS-ON LEARNING? YOU MEAN THAT SUMMER VACATION THING?
YES!
WHERE BETTER TO GO IN THE SUMMER THAN THE SEA, AND WHERE IS THE SEA BETTER THAN IN OKINAWA?!
SATA ANDAGI!!
THAT'S A SNACK.

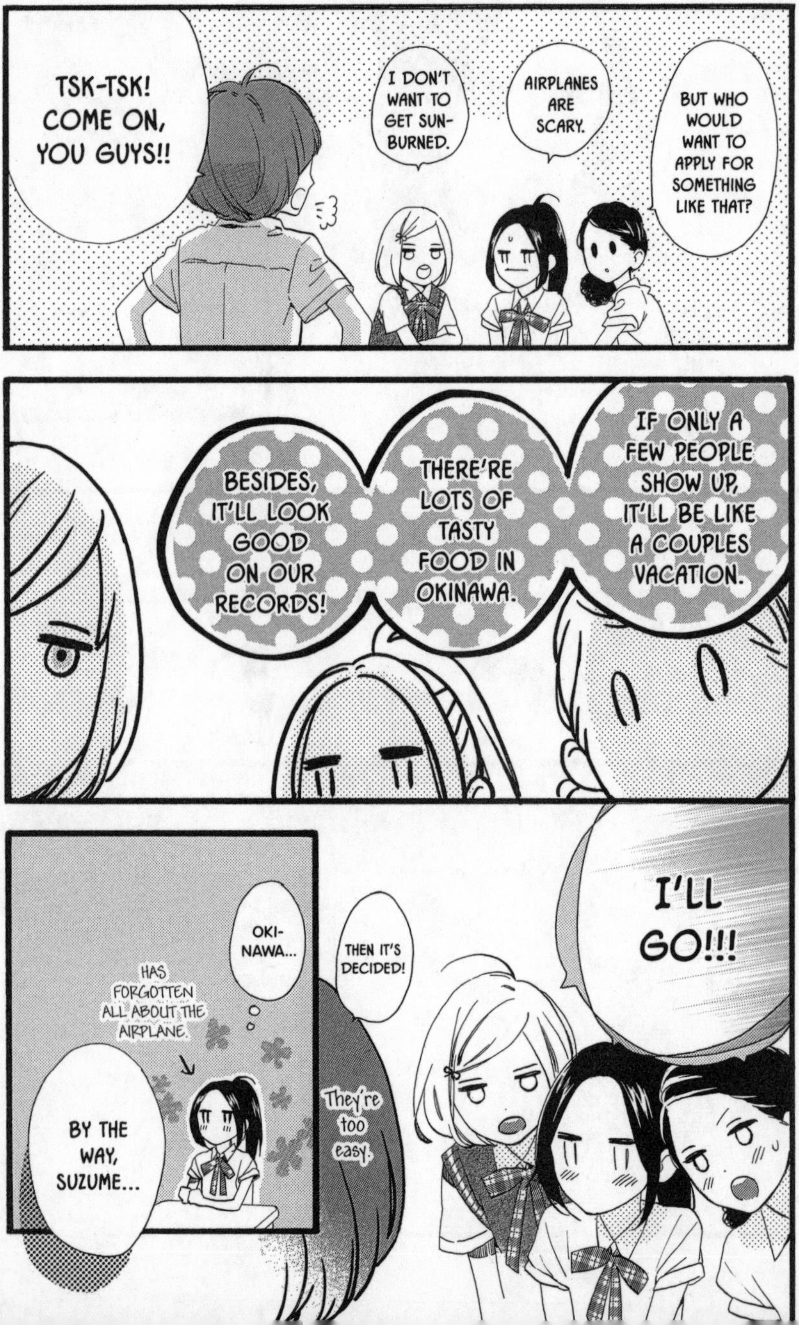
BUT WHO WOULD WANT TO APPLY FOR SOMETHING LIKE THAT?
AIRPLANES ARE SCARY.
I DON'T WANT TO GET SUN-BURNED.
TSK-TSK! COME ON, YOU GUYS!!
IF ONLY A FEW PEOPLE SHOW UP, IT'LL BE LIKE A COUPLES VACATION.
THERE'RE LOTS OF TASTY FOOD IN OKINAWA.
BESIDES, IT'LL LOOK GOOD ON OUR RECORDS!
I'LL GO!!!
THEN IT'S DECIDED!
They're too easy.
OKI-NAWA...
HAS FORGOTTEN ALL ABOUT THE AIRPLANE.
BY THE WAY, SUZUME...

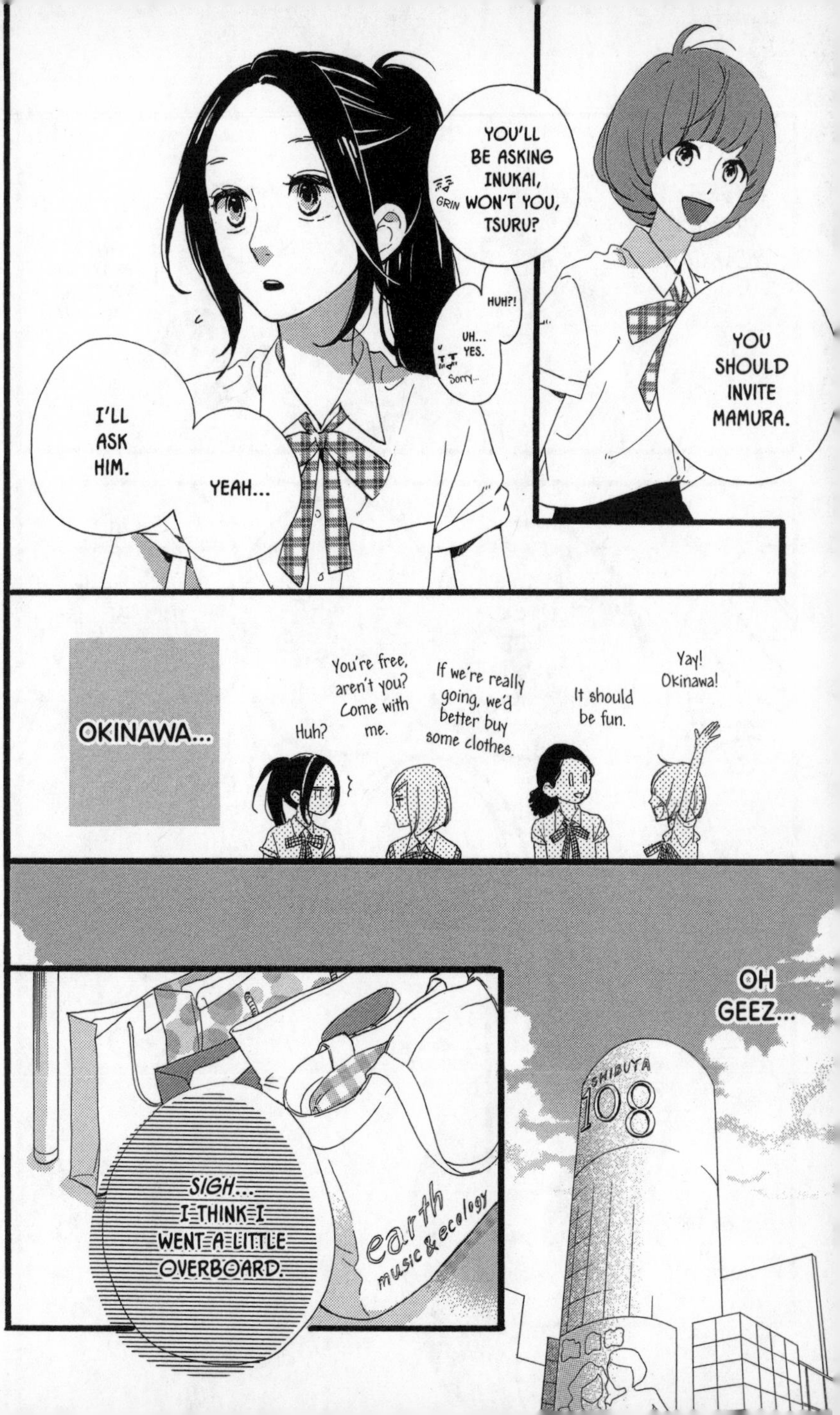
YOU'LL BE ASKING INUKAI, WON'T YOU, TSURU?
GRIN
HUH?!
UH... YES.
Sorry...
YOU SHOULD INVITE MAMURA.
I'LL ASK HIM.
YEAH...
Yay! Okinawa!
It should be fun.
If we're really going, we'd better buy some clothes.
You're free, aren't you? Come with me.
Huh?
OKINAWA...
OH GEEZ...
SHIBUYA
108
SIGH... I THINK I WENT A LITTLE OVERBOARD.
earth music & ecology

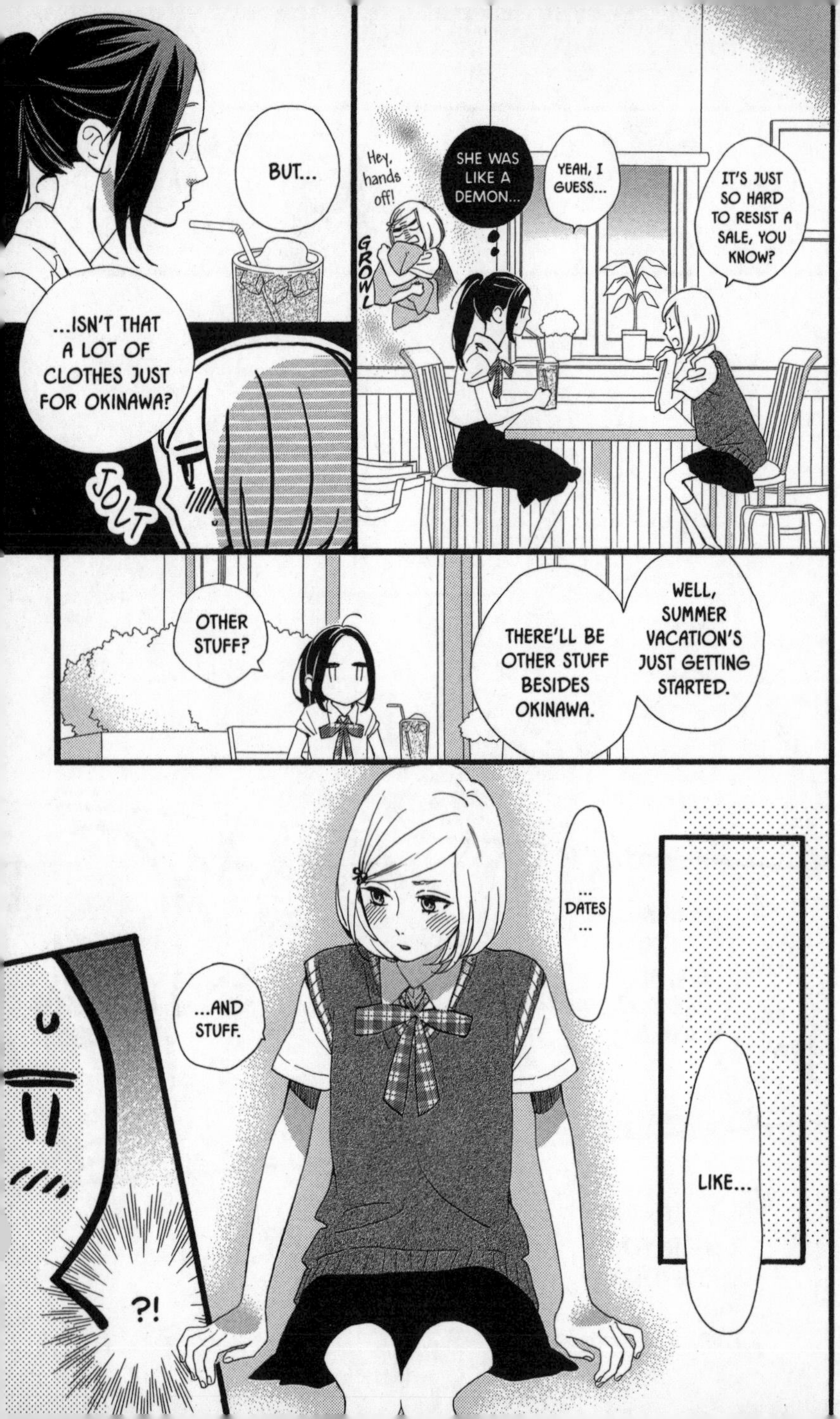
IT'S JUST SO HARD TO RESIST A SALE, YOU KNOW?
YEAH, I GUESS...
SHE WAS LIKE A DEMON...
Hey, hands off!
GROWL
BUT...
...ISN'T THAT A LOT OF CLOTHES JUST FOR OKINAWA?
JOLT
WELL, SUMMER VACATION'S JUST GETTING STARTED.
THERE'LL BE OTHER STUFF BESIDES OKINAWA.
OTHER STUFF?
LIKE...
...DATES...
...AND STUFF.
?!

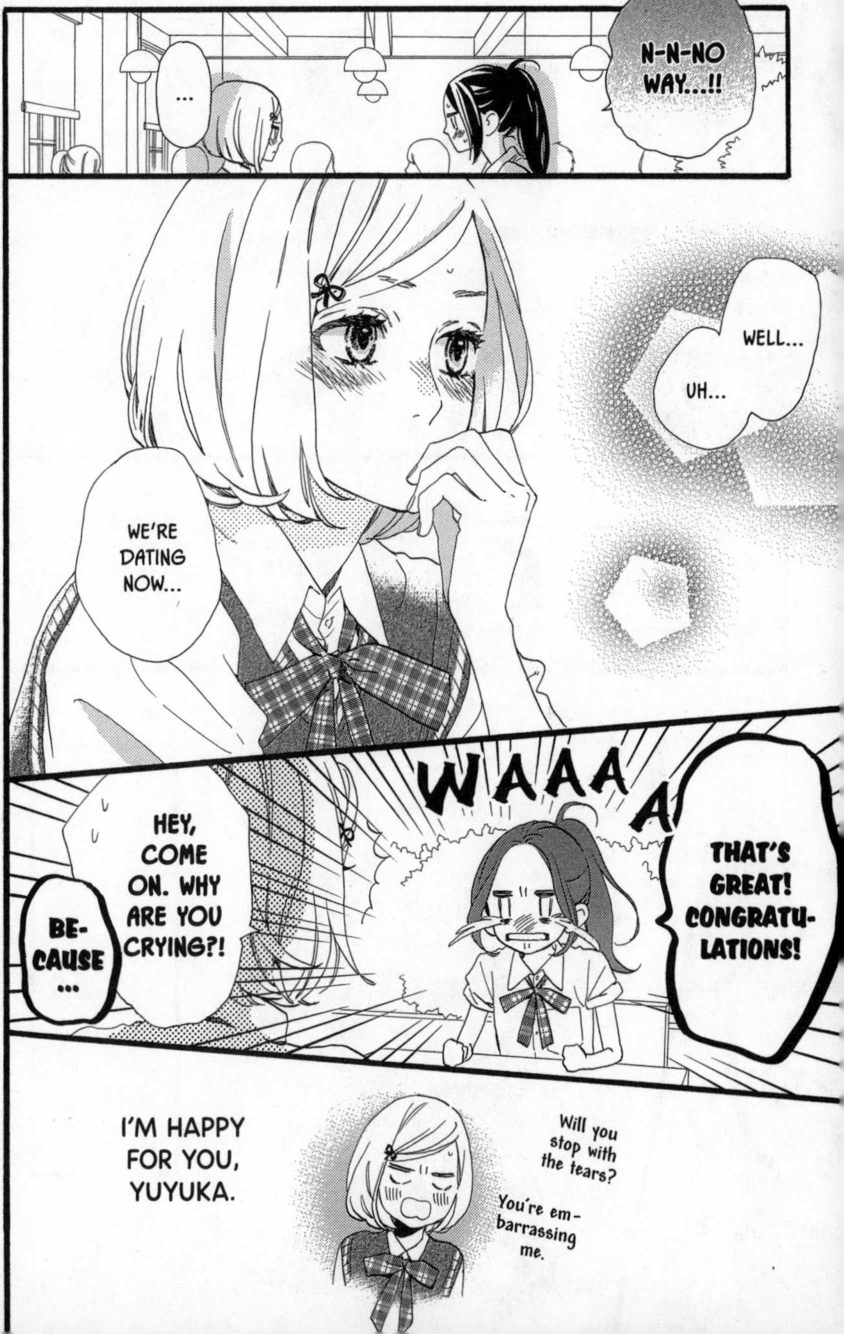
N-N-NO WAY...!!
...
WELL... UH...
WE'RE DATING NOW...
WAAAA
THAT'S GREAT! CONGRATU-LATIONS!
HEY, COME ON. WHY ARE YOU CRYING?!
BE-CAUSE ...
Will you stop with the tears?
You're em-barrassing me.
I'M HAPPY FOR YOU, YUYUKA.

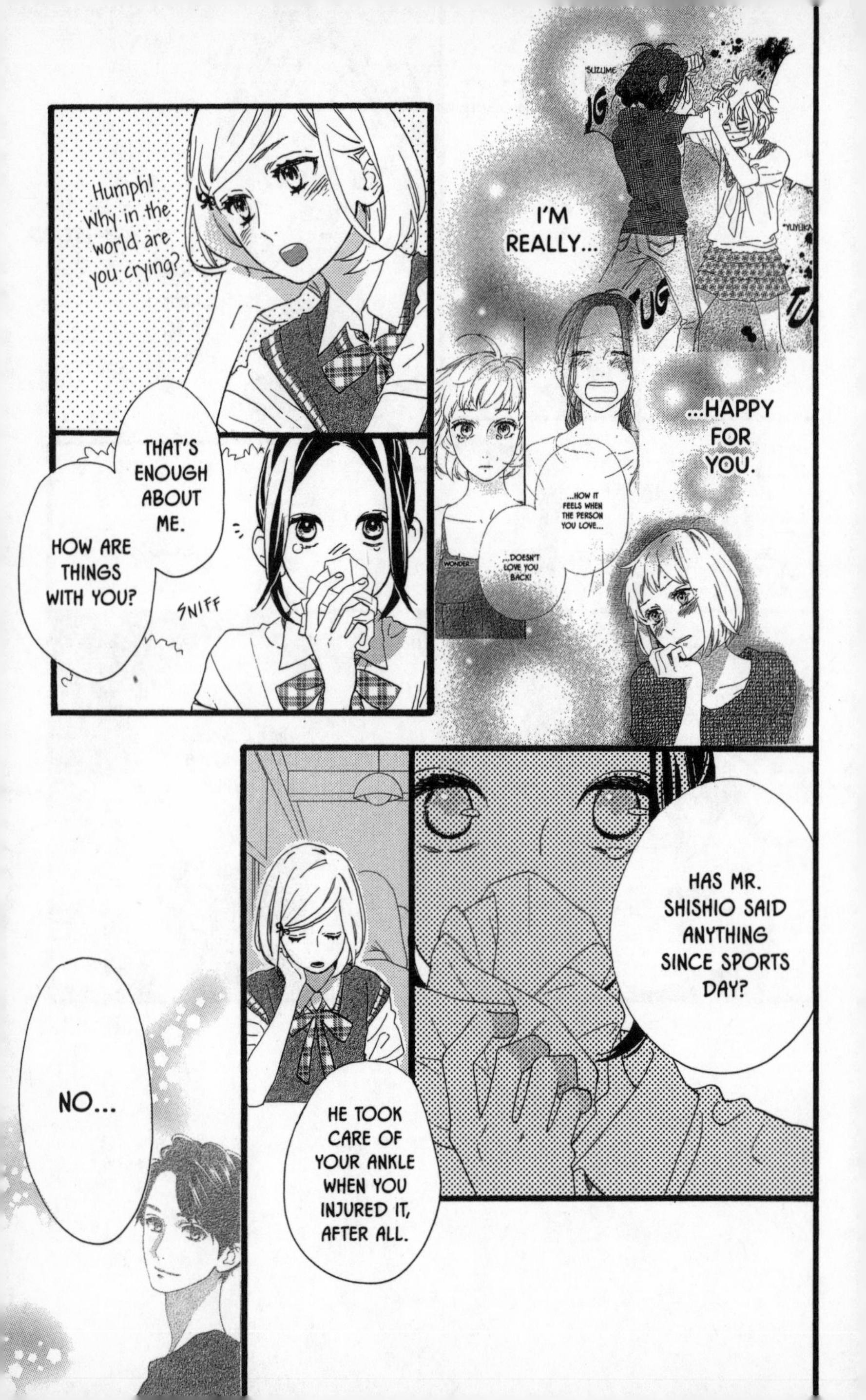
*YUYUKA
*SUZUME
TUG
I'M REALLY...
...HAPPY FOR YOU.
I WONDER...
...HOW IT FEELS WHEN THE PERSON YOU LOVE...
...DOESN'T LOVE YOU BACK!
Humph! Why in the world are you crying?
THAT'S ENOUGH ABOUT ME.
HOW ARE THINGS WITH YOU?
SNIFF
HAS MR. SHISHIO SAID ANYTHING SINCE SPORTS DAY?
HE TOOK CARE OF YOUR ANKLE WHEN YOU INJURED IT, AFTER ALL.
NO...

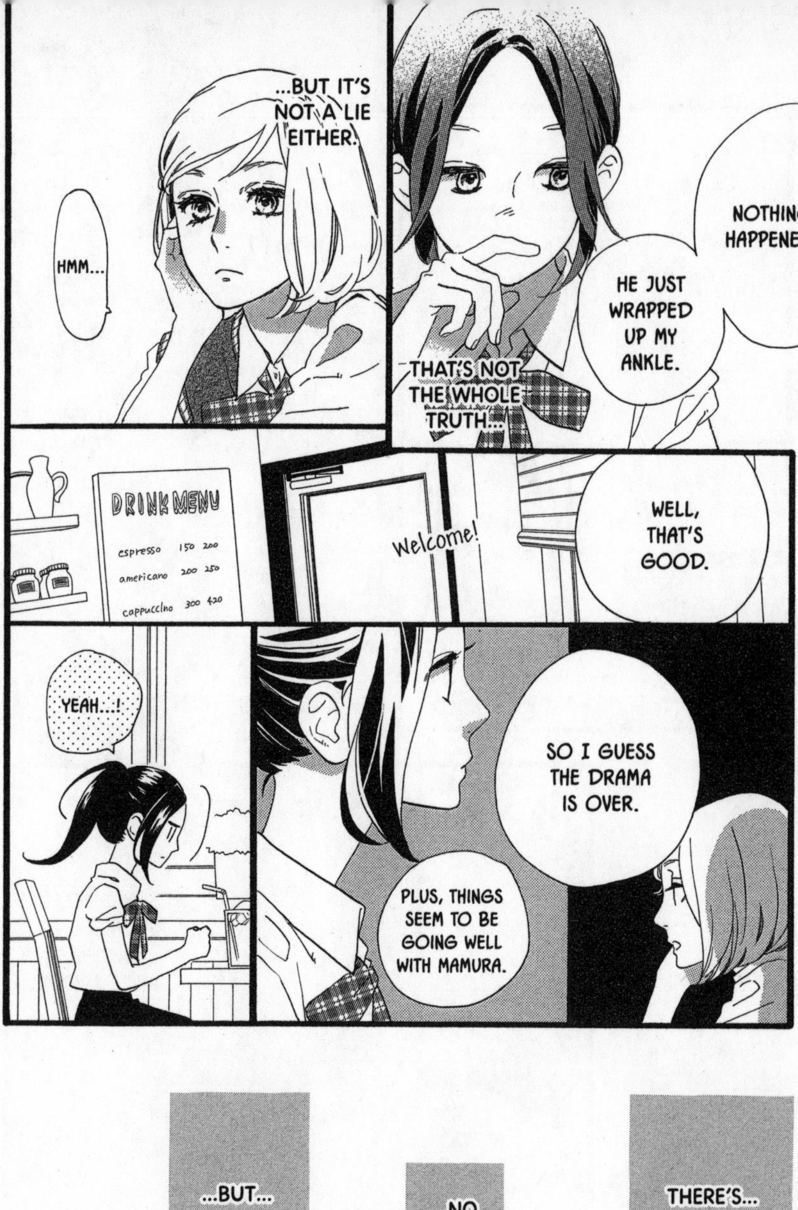
NOTHING HAPPENED.
HE JUST WRAPPED UP MY ANKLE.
THAT'S NOT THE WHOLE TRUTH...
...BUT IT'S NOT A LIE EITHER.
HMM...
WELL, THAT'S GOOD.
Welcome!
DRINK MENU
espresso 150 200
americano 200 250
cappuccino 300 420
SO I GUESS THE DRAMA IS OVER.
PLUS, THINGS SEEM TO BE GOING WELL WITH MAMURA.
YEAH...!
THERE'S...
...NO DRAMA...
...BUT...

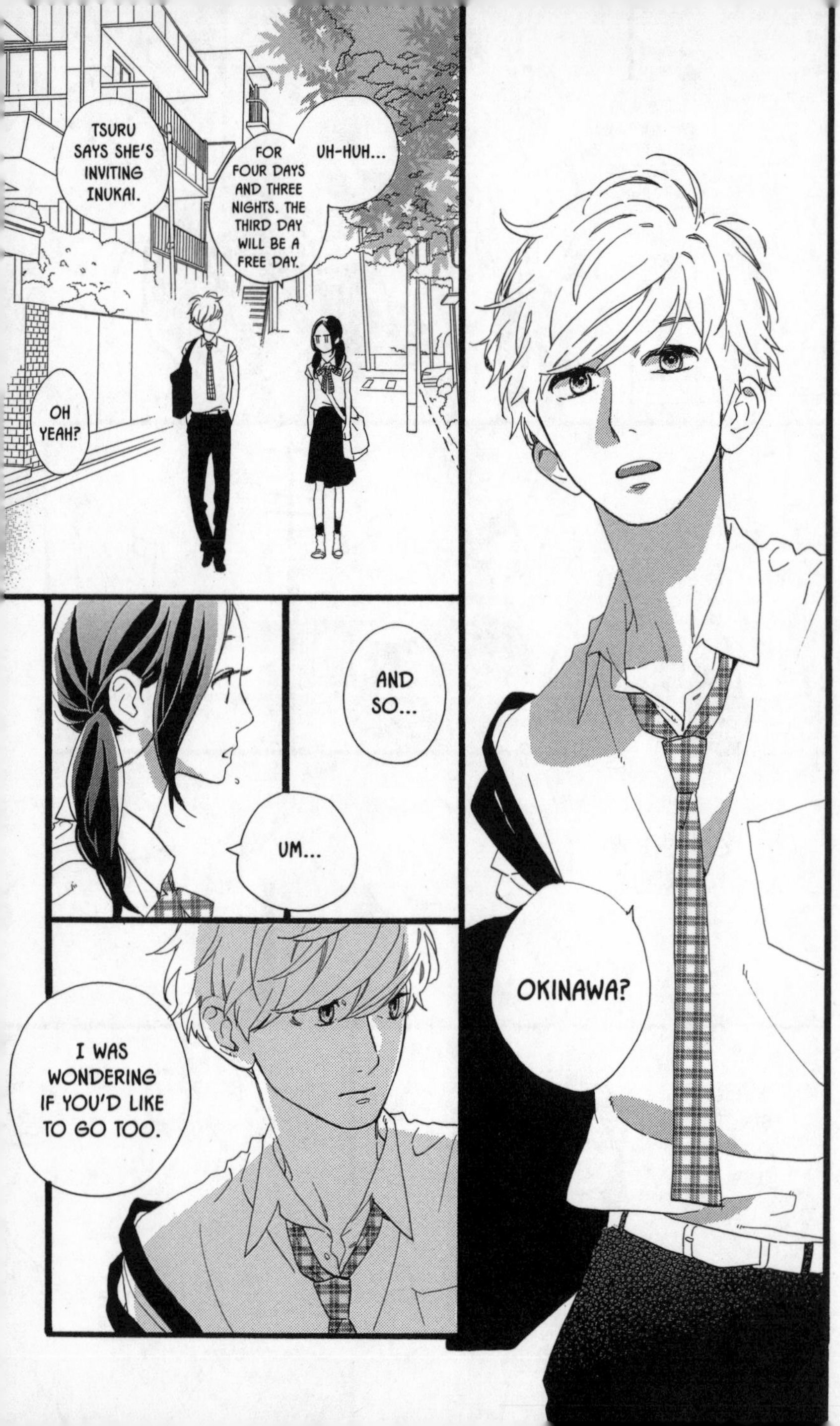
OKINAWA?
UH-HUH...
FOR FOUR DAYS AND THREE NIGHTS. THE THIRD DAY WILL BE A FREE DAY.
TSURU SAYS SHE'S INVITING INUKAI.
OH YEAH?
AND SO...
UM...
I WAS WONDERING IF YOU'D LIKE TO GO TOO.

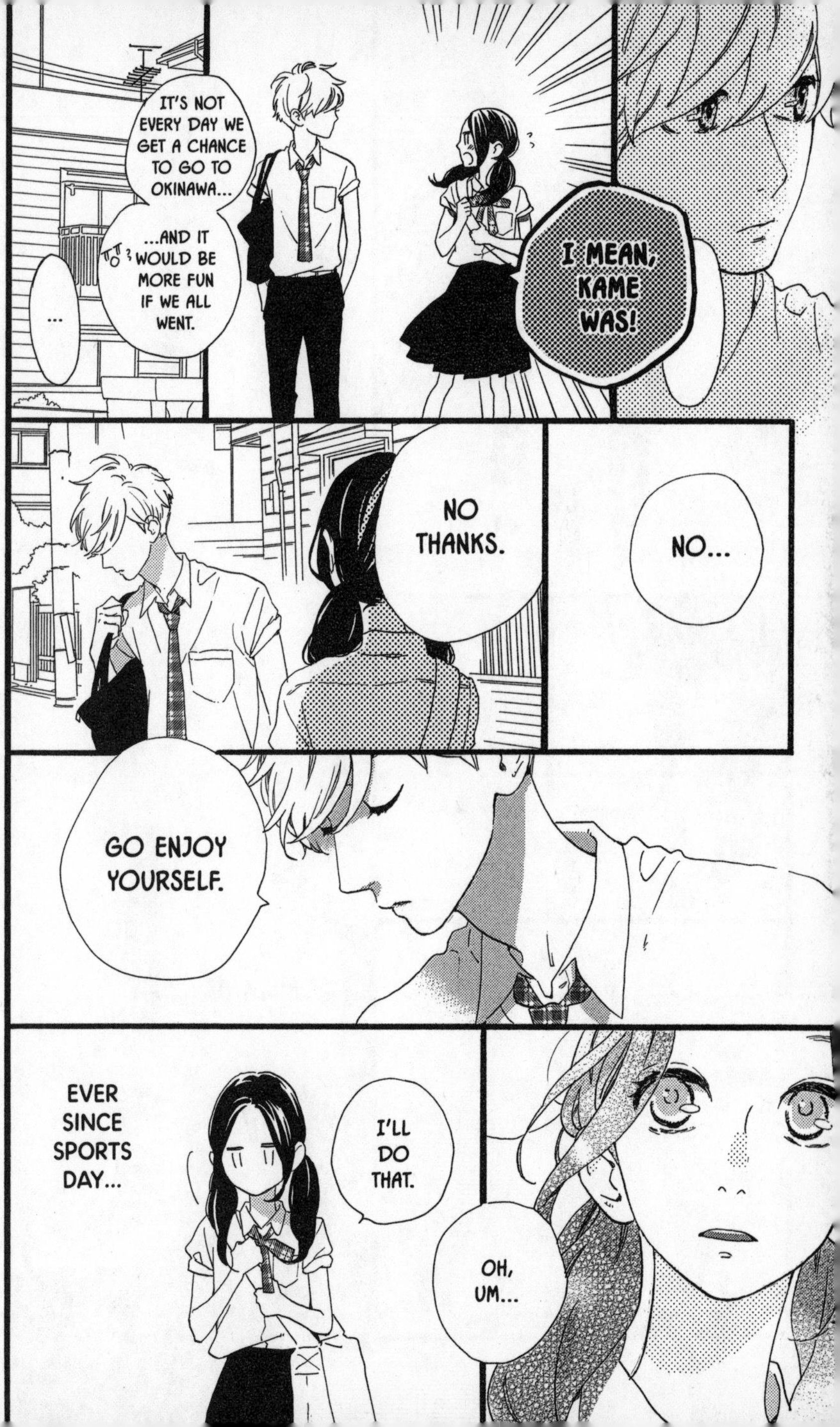
I MEAN, KAME WAS!
IT'S NOT EVERY DAY WE GET A CHANCE TO GO TO OKINAWA...
...AND IT WOULD BE MORE FUN IF WE ALL WENT.
...
NO...
NO THANKS.
GO ENJOY YOURSELF.
OH, UM...
I'LL DO THAT.
EVER SINCE SPORTS DAY...

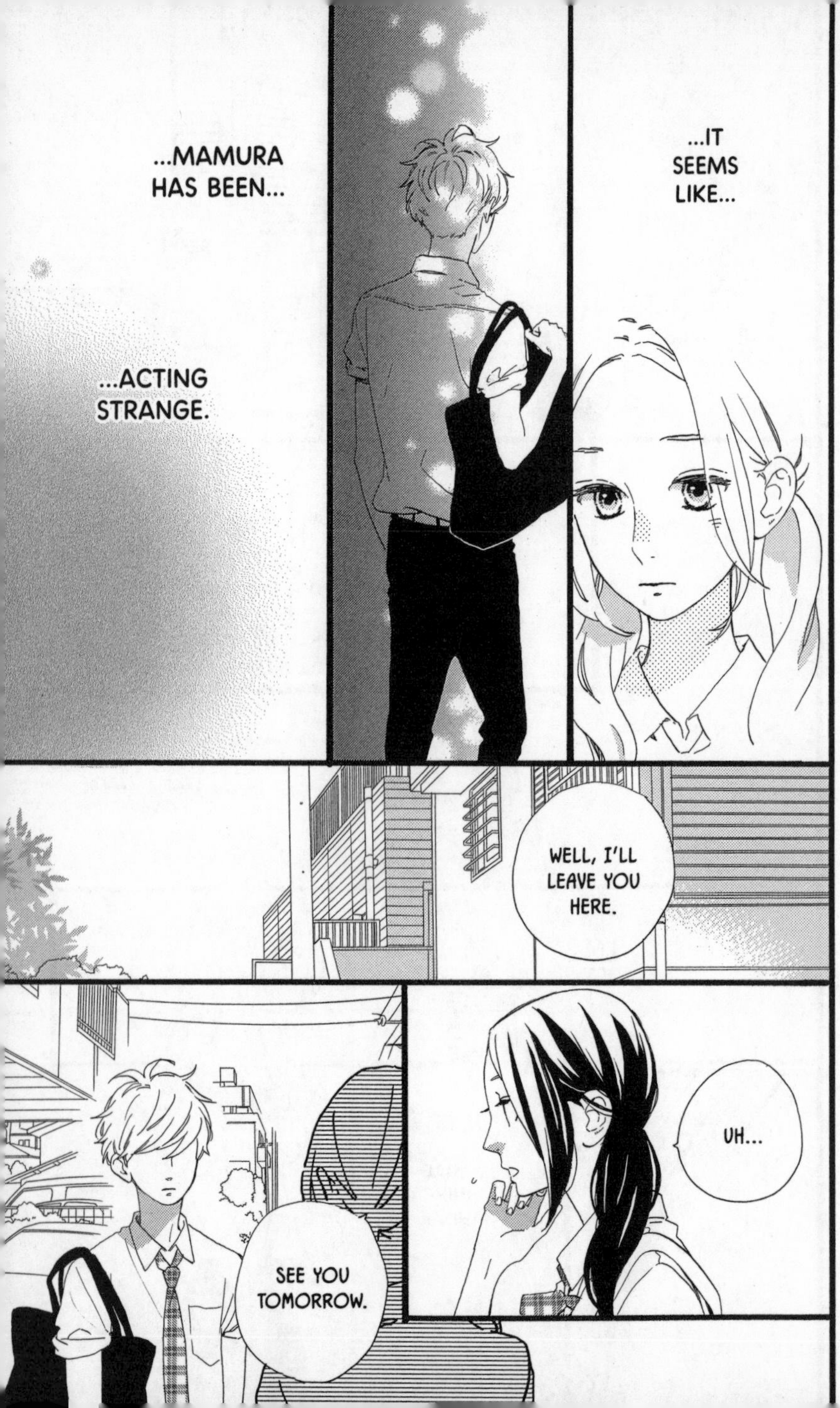
...IT SEEMS LIKE...
...MAMURA HAS BEEN...
...ACTING STRANGE.
WELL, I'LL LEAVE YOU HERE.
UH...
SEE YOU TOMORROW.

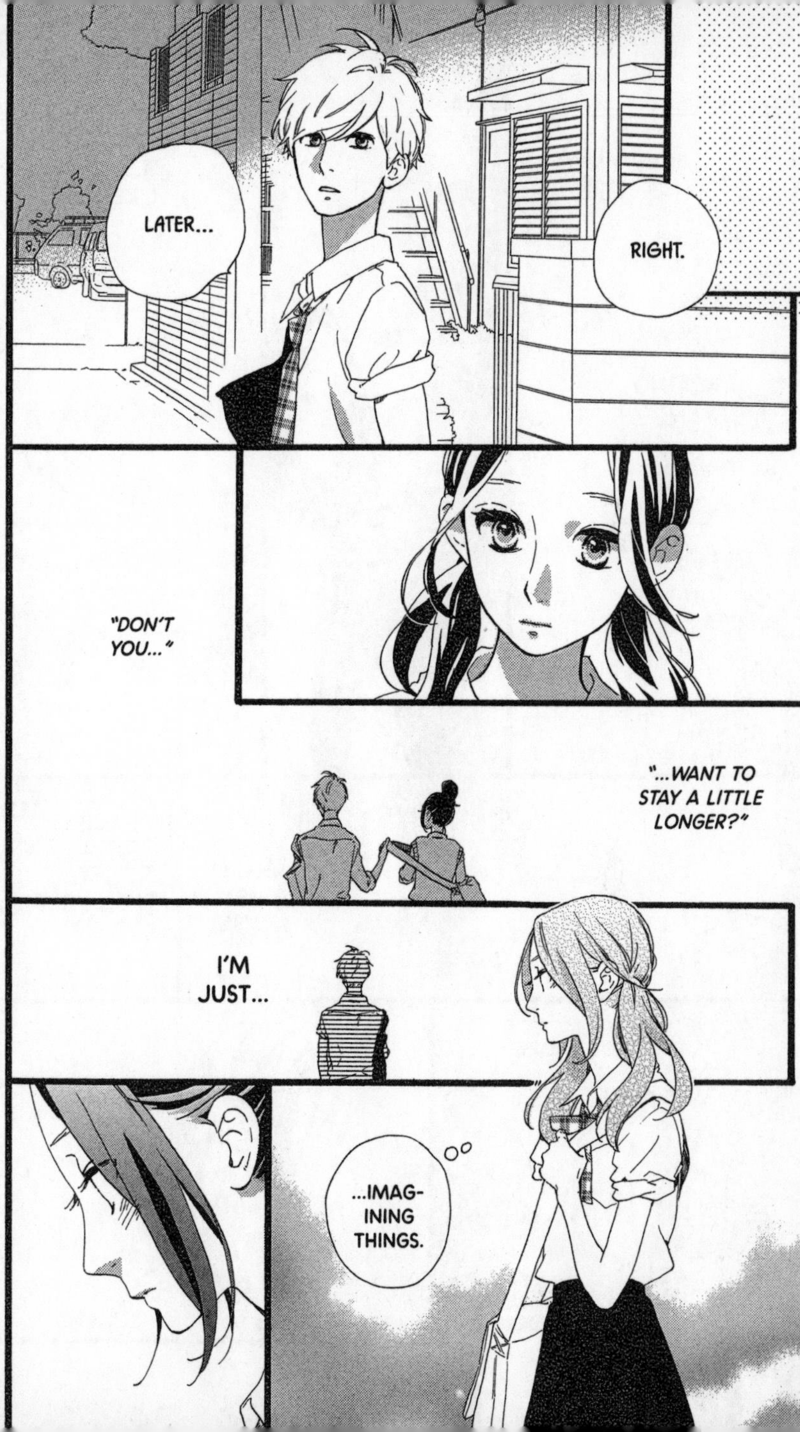
RIGHT.
LATER...
"DON'T YOU..."
"...WANT TO STAY A LITTLE LONGER?"
I'M JUST...
...IMAG-ING THINGS.

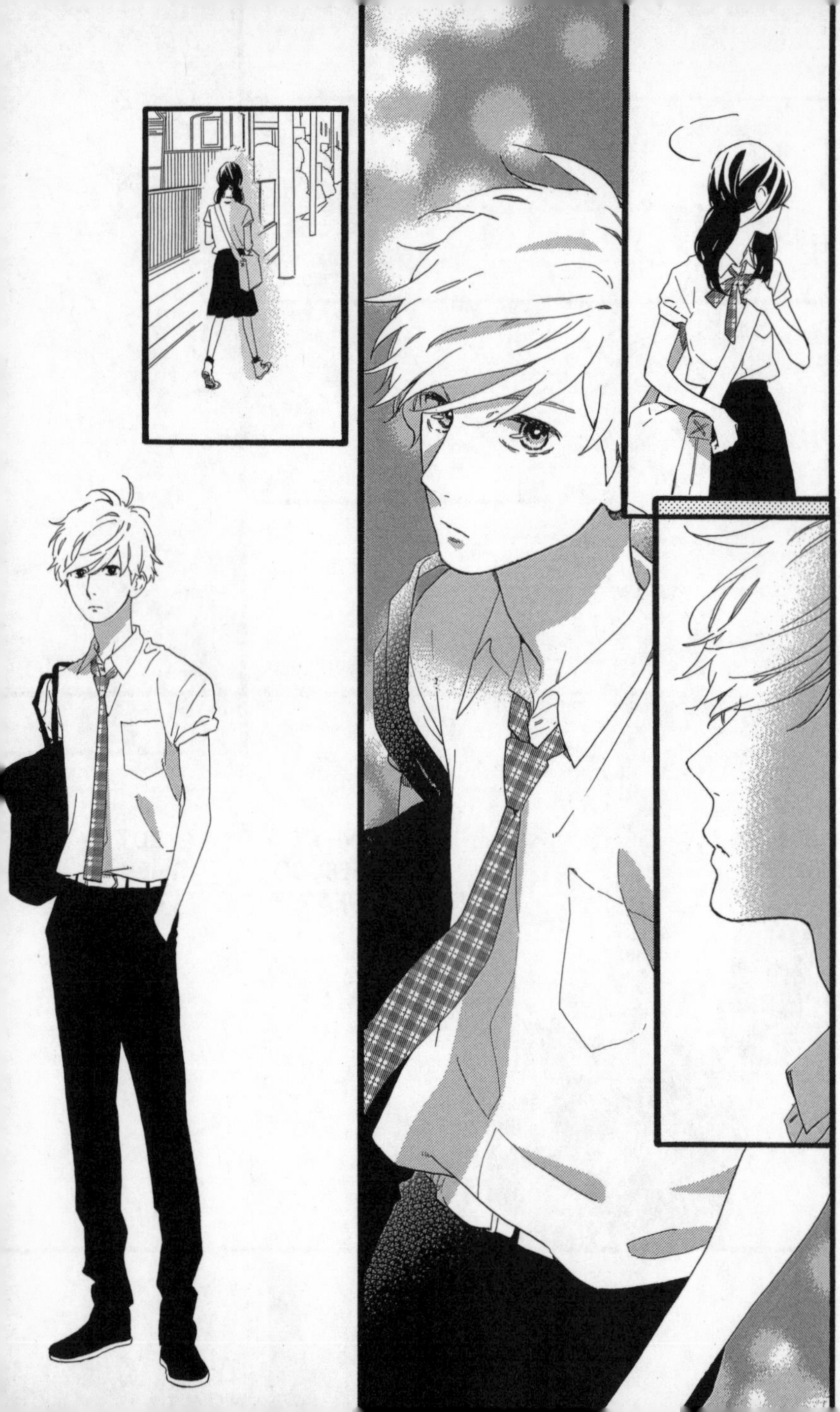

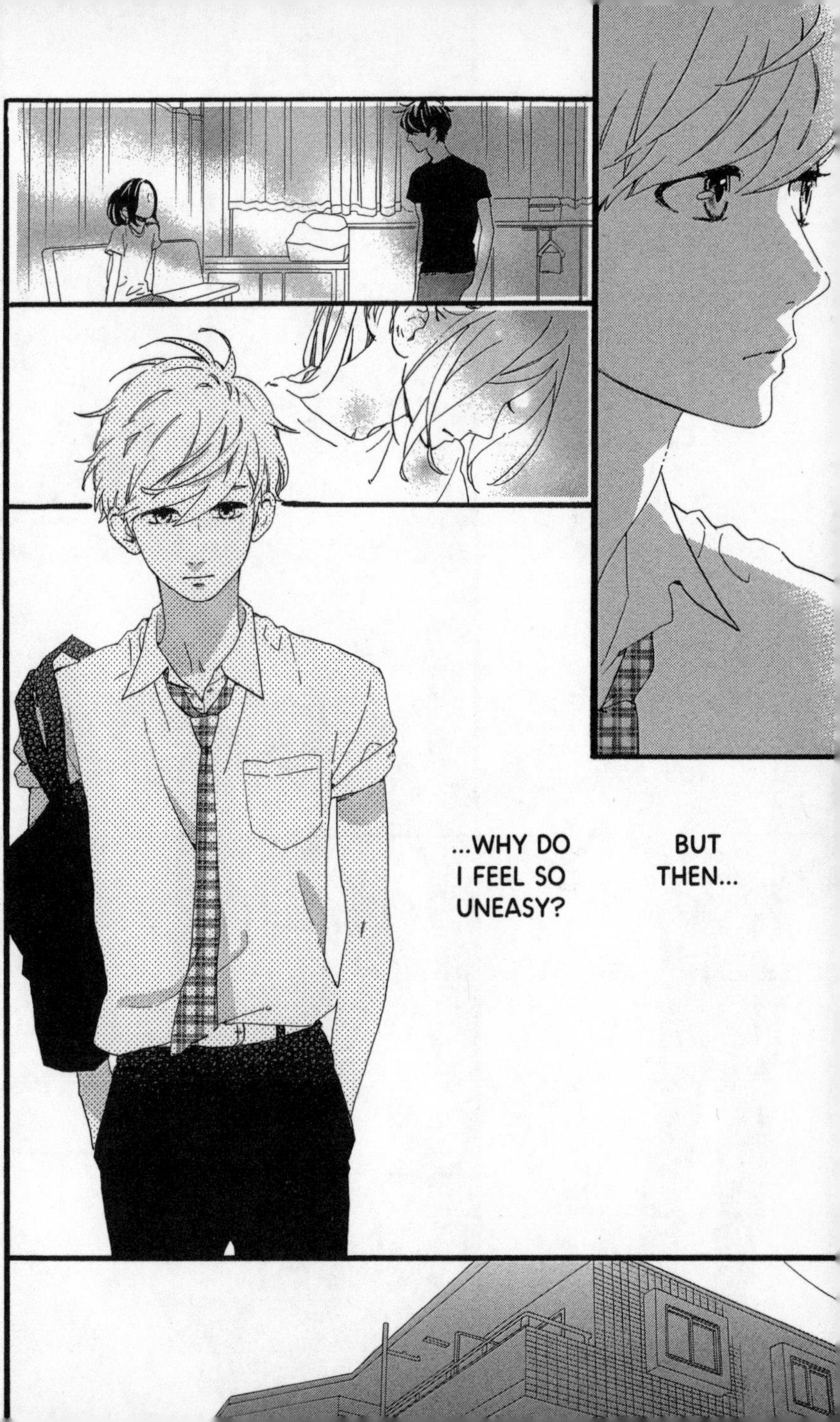
BUT THEN...
...WHY DO I FEEL SO UNEASY?

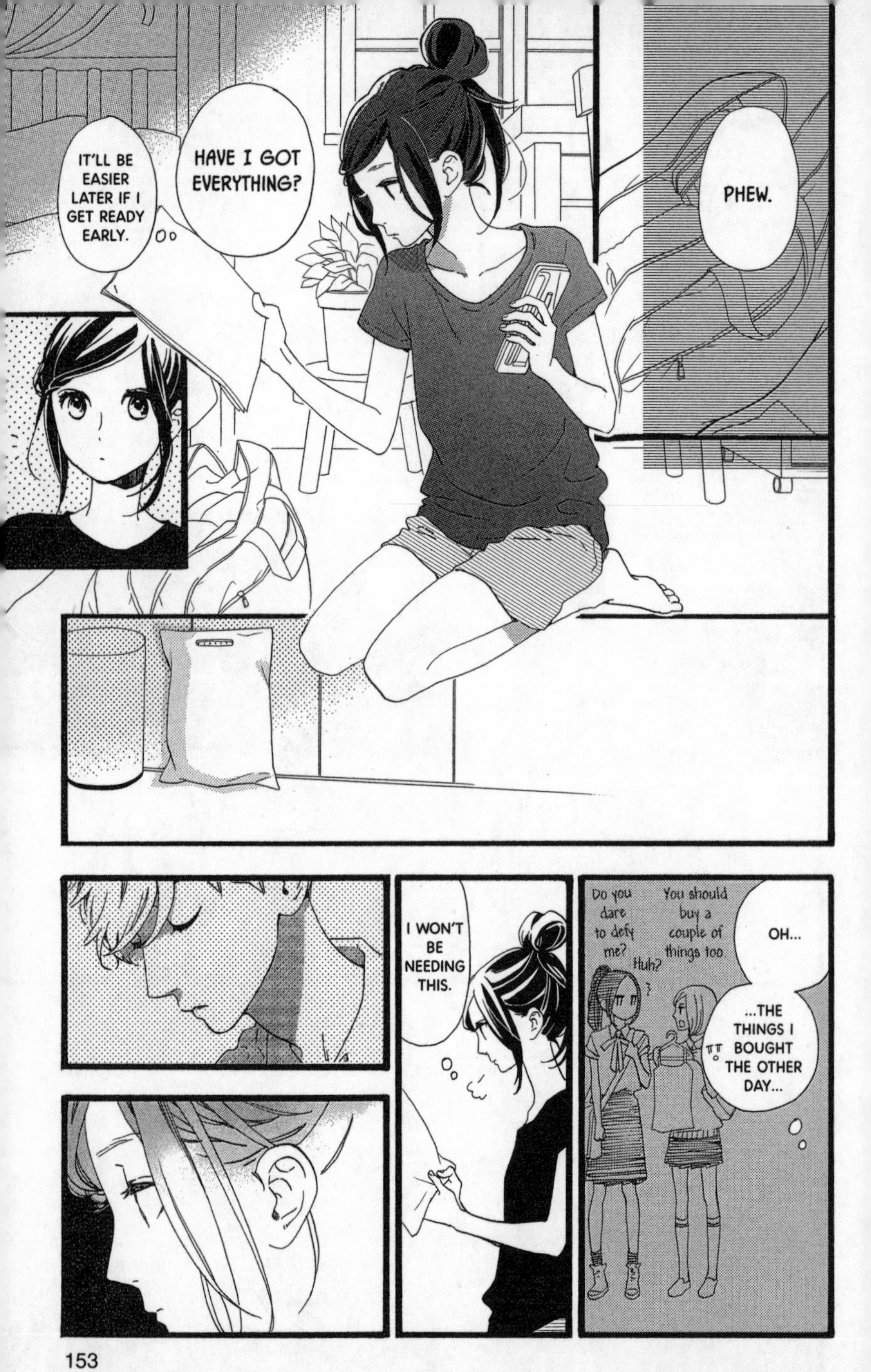
PHEW.
HAVE I GOT EVERYTHING?
IT'LL BE EASIER LATER IF I GET READY EARLY.
OH...
...THE THINGS I BOUGHT THE OTHER DAY...
You should buy a couple of things too
Huh?
Do you dare to defy me?
I WON'T BE NEEDING THIS.

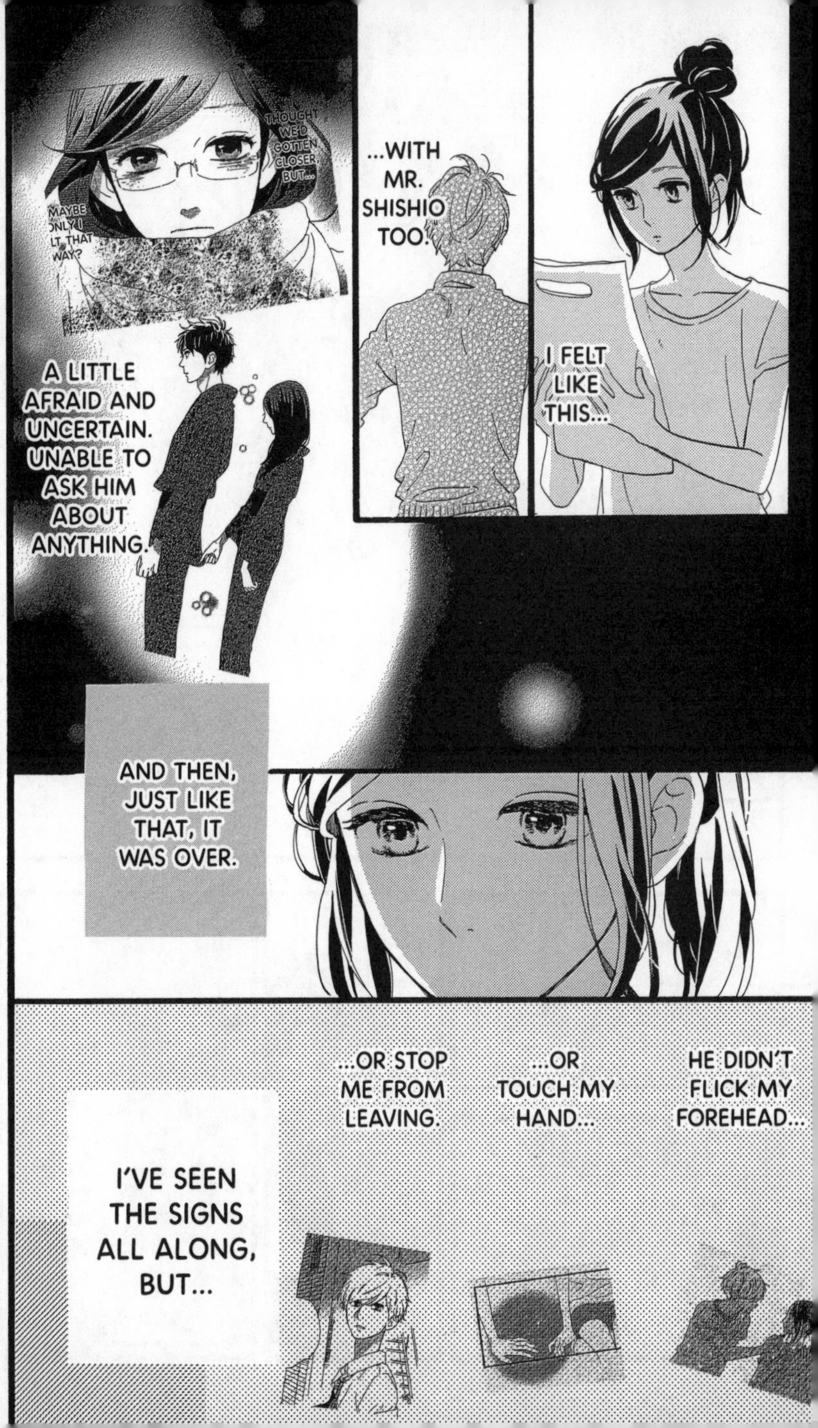
I FELT LIKE THIS...
...WITH MR. SHISHIO TOO.
THOUGHT WE'D GOTTEN CLOSER, BUT...
MAYBE ONLY I LT THAT WAY?
A LITTLE AFRAID AND UNCERTAIN. UNABLE TO ASK HIM ABOUT ANYTHING.
AND THEN, JUST LIKE THAT, IT WAS OVER.
HE DIDN'T FLICK MY FOREHEAD...
...OR TOUCH MY HAND...
...OR STOP ME FROM LEAVING.
I'VE SEEN THE SIGNS ALL ALONG, BUT...

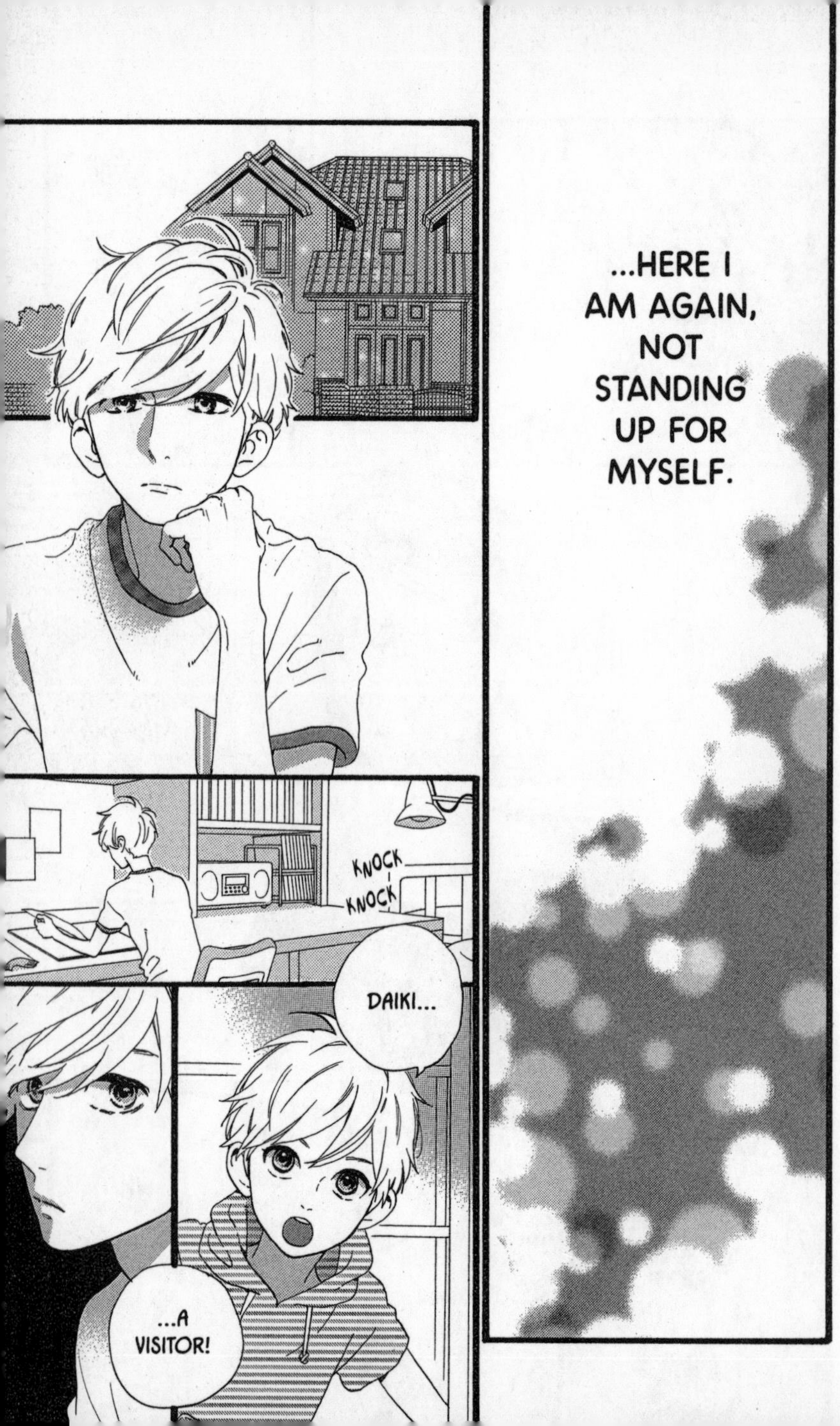
...HERE I AM AGAIN, NOT STANDING UP FOR MYSELF.
KNOCK KNOCK
DAIKI...
...A VISITOR!

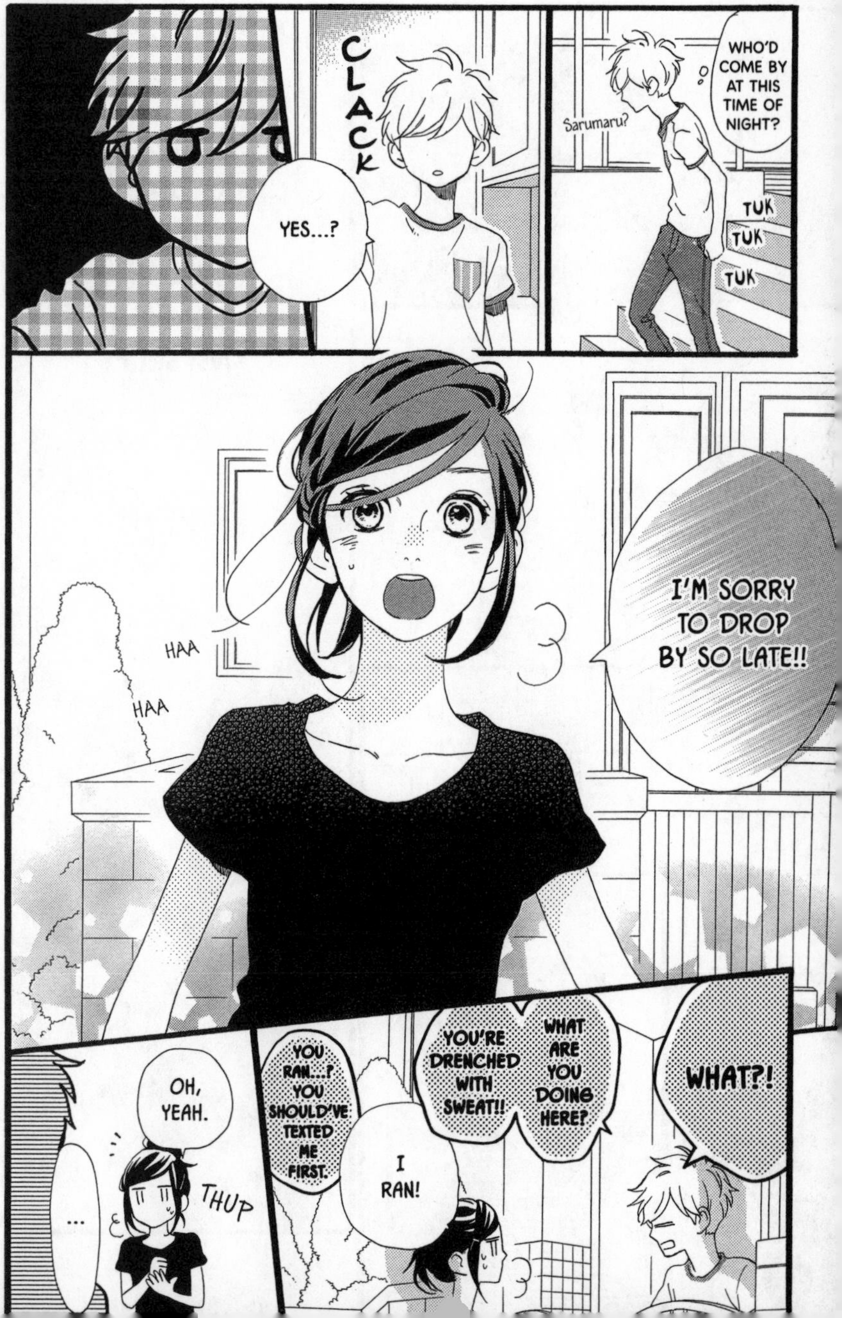
WHO'D COME BY AT THIS TIME OF NIGHT?
Sarumaru?
TUK
TUK
TUK
CLACK
YES...?
I'M SORRY TO DROP BY SO LATE!!
HAA
HAA
WHAT?!
WHAT ARE YOU DOING HERE?
YOU'RE DRENCHED WITH SWEAT!!
I RAN!
YOU RAN...? YOU SHOULD'VE TEXTED ME FIRST.
OH, YEAH.
THUP
...

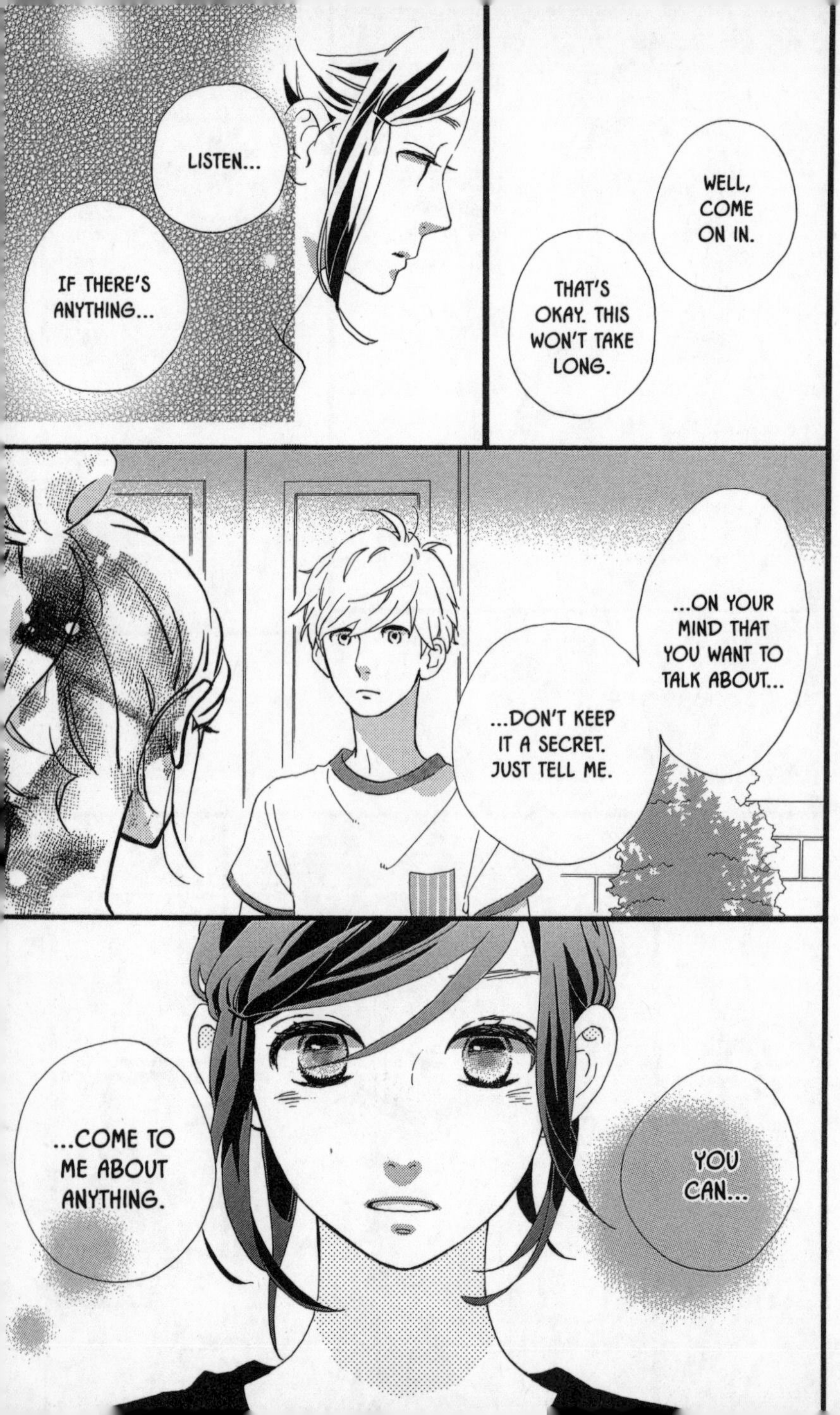
WELL, COME ON IN.
THAT'S OKAY. THIS WON'T TAKE LONG.
LISTEN...
IF THERE'S ANYTHING...
...ON YOUR MIND THAT YOU WANT TO TALK ABOUT...
...DON'T KEEP IT A SECRET. JUST TELL ME.
YOU CAN...
...COME TO ME ABOUT ANYTHING.

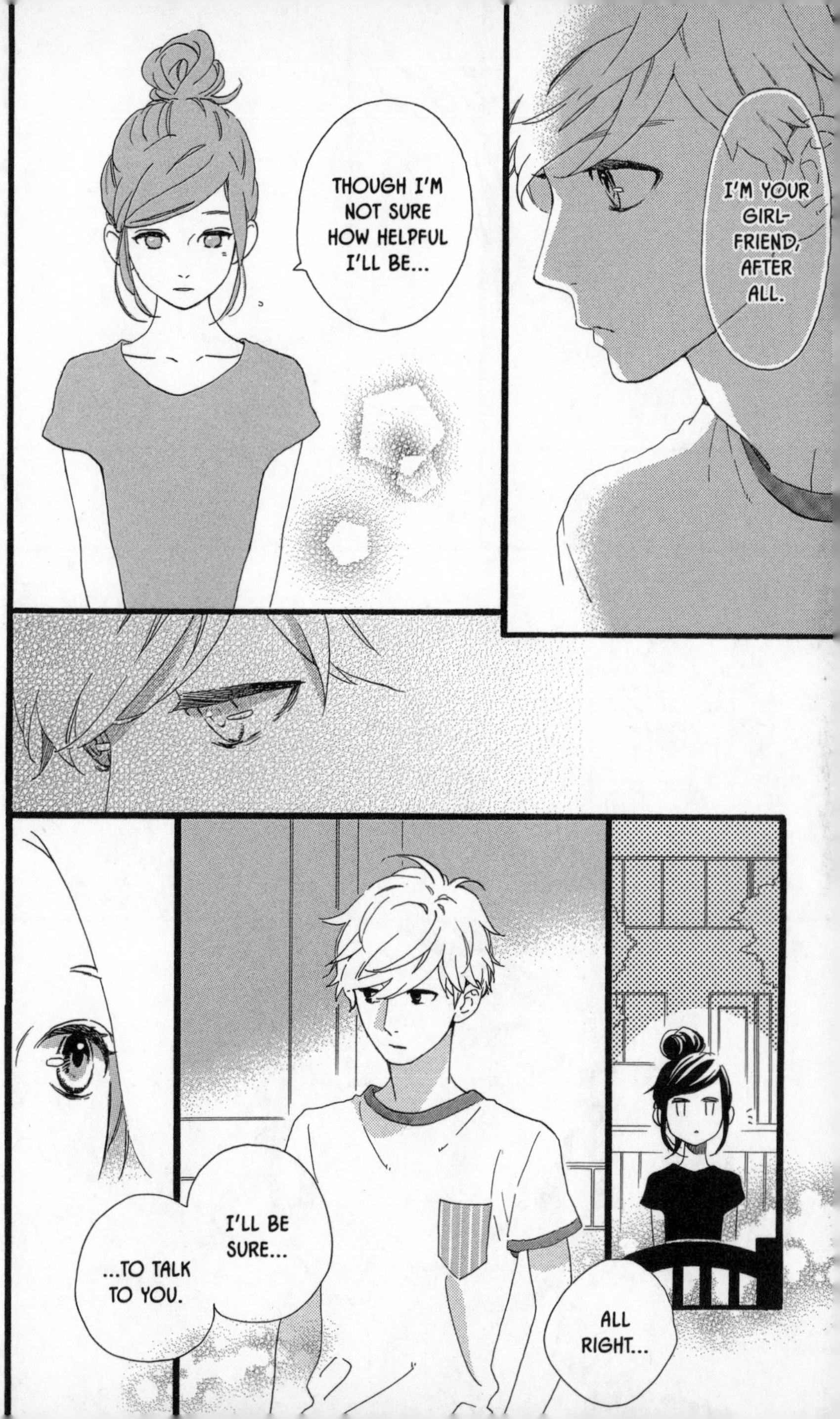
I'M YOUR GIRLFRIEND, AFTER ALL.
THOUGH I'M NOT SURE HOW HELPFUL I'LL BE...
ALL RIGHT...
I'LL BE SURE...
...TO TALK TO YOU.

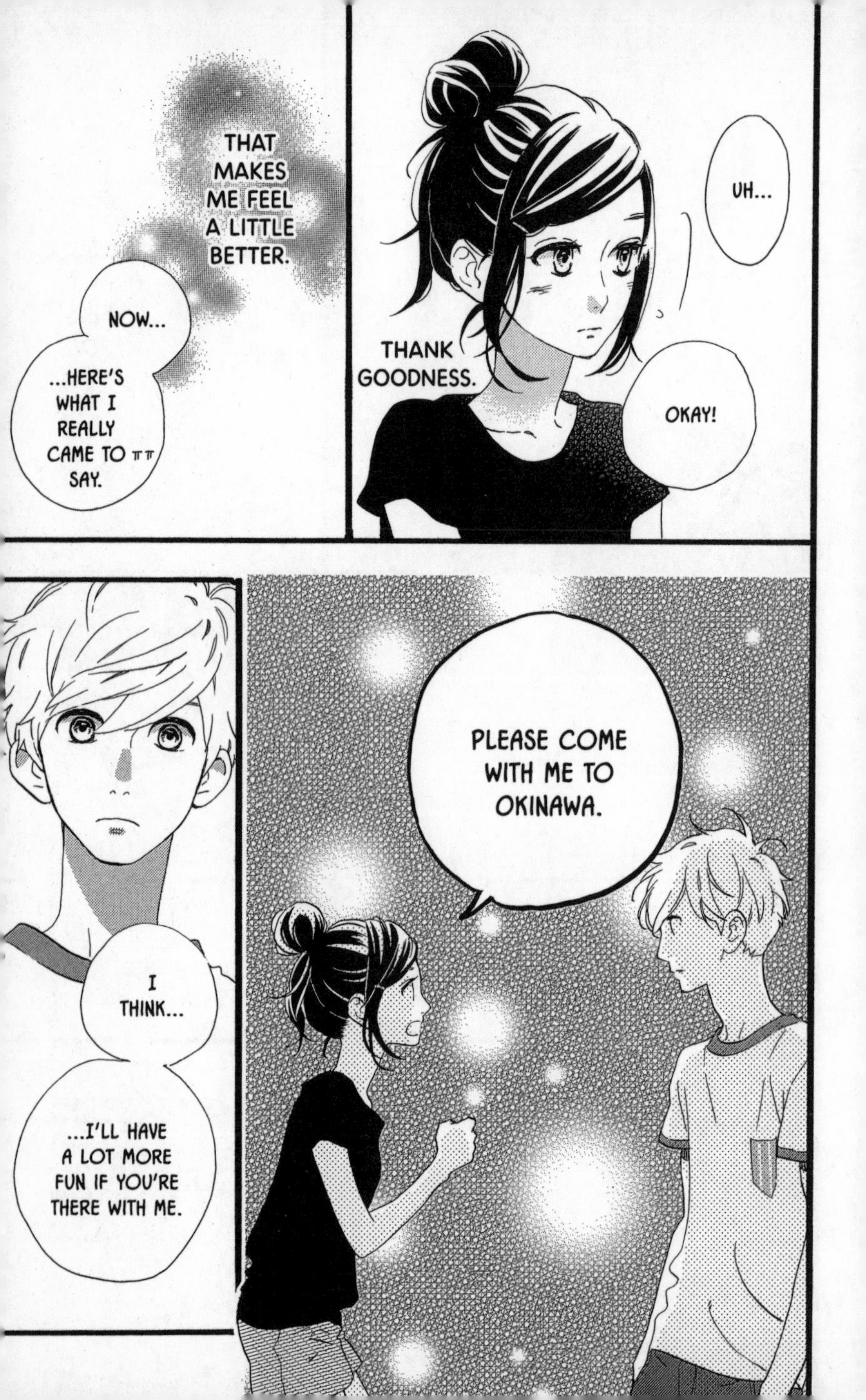
UH...
OKAY!
THANK GOODNESS.
THAT MAKES ME FEEL A LITTLE BETTER.
NOW...
...HERE'S WHAT I REALLY CAME TO SAY.
PLEASE COME WITH ME TO OKINAWA.
I THINK...
...I'LL HAVE A LOT MORE FUN IF YOU'RE THERE WITH ME.

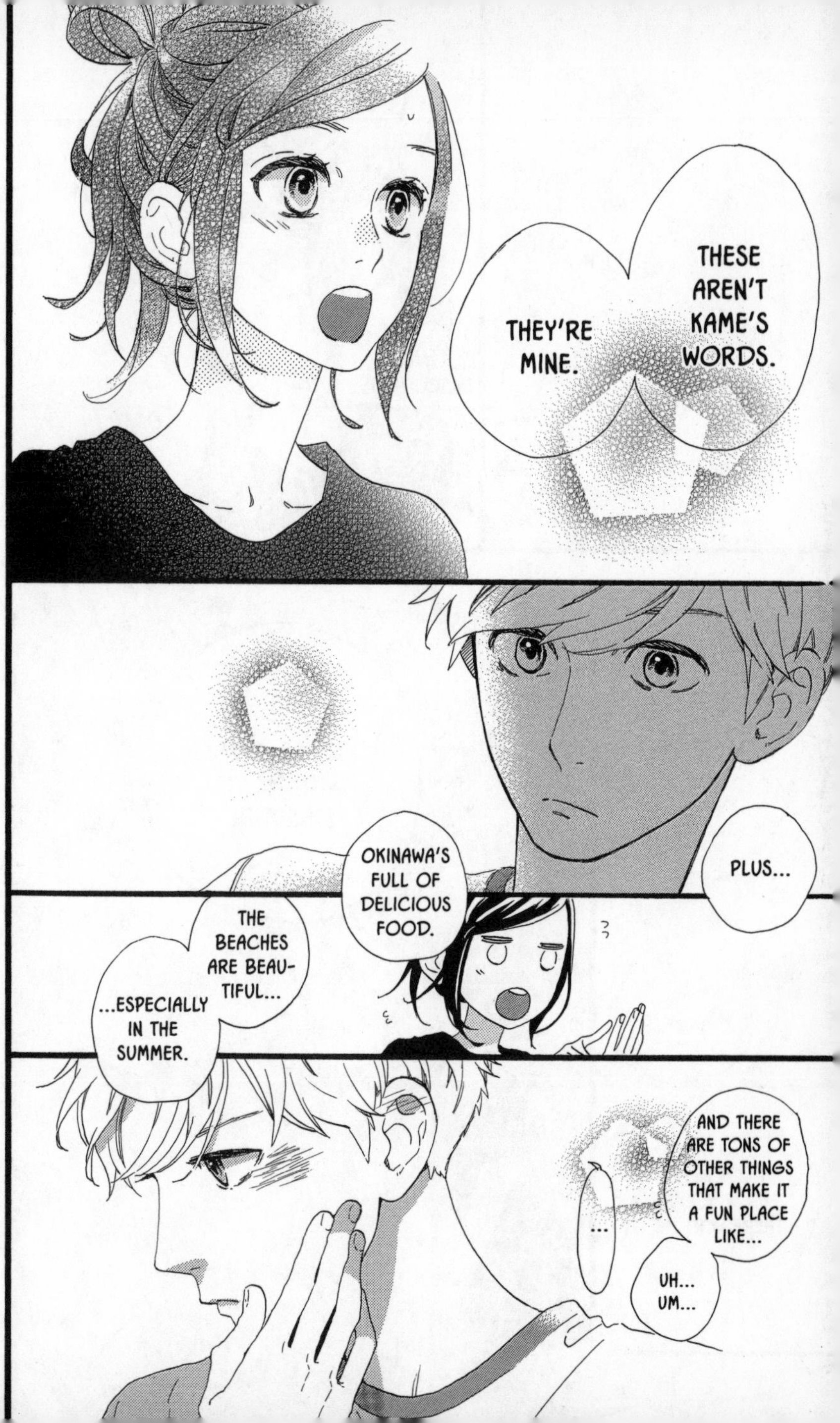
THESE AREN'T KAME'S WORDS.
THEY'RE MINE.
PLUS...
OKINAWA'S FULL OF DELICIOUS FOOD.
THE BEACHES ARE BEAU-TIFUL...
...ESPECIALLY IN THE SUMMER.
AND THERE ARE TONS OF OTHER THINGS THAT MAKE IT A FUN PLACE LIKE...
...
UH... UM...

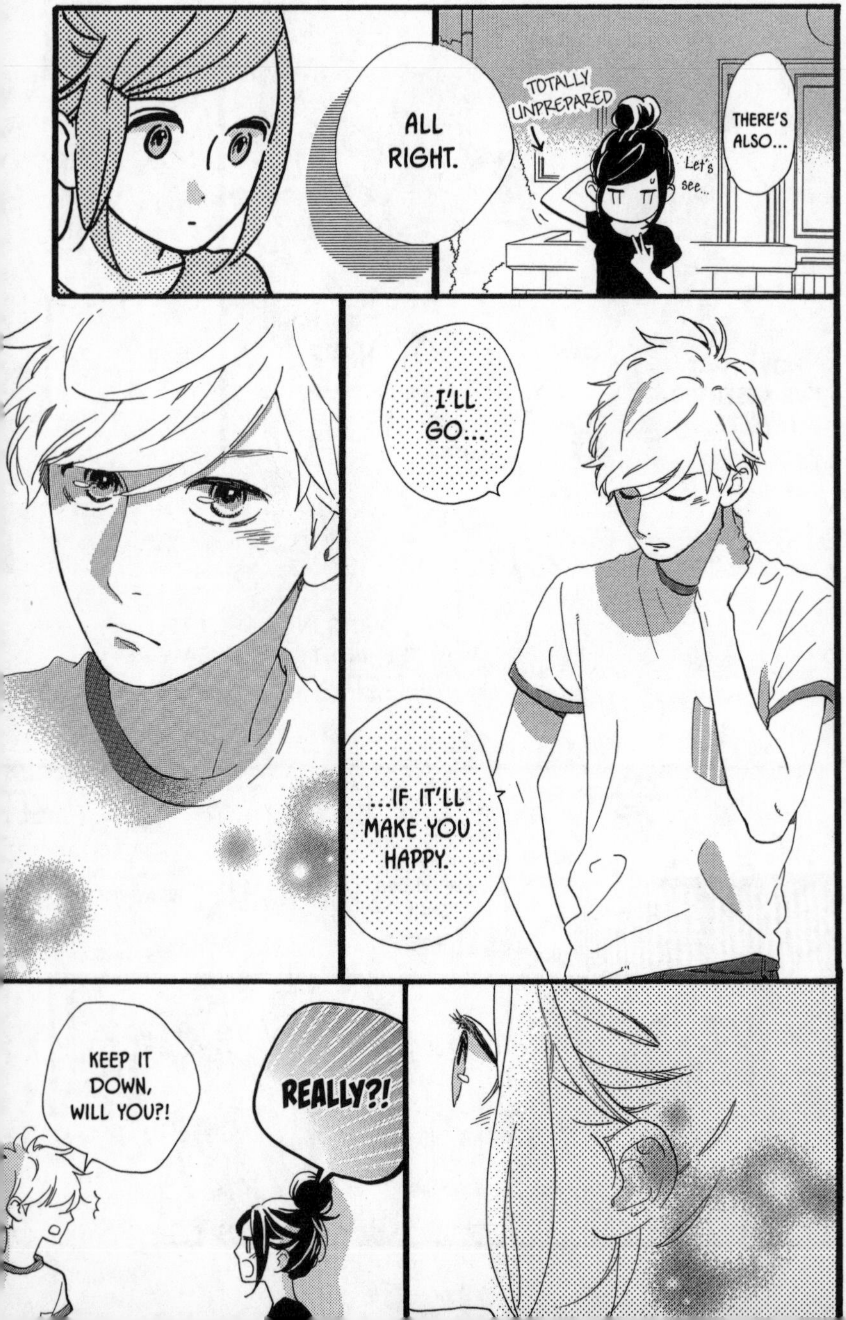
THERE'S ALSO...
Let's see...
TOTALLY UNPREPARED
ALL RIGHT.
I'LL GO...
...IF IT'LL MAKE YOU HAPPY.
REALLY?!
KEEP IT DOWN, WILL YOU?!

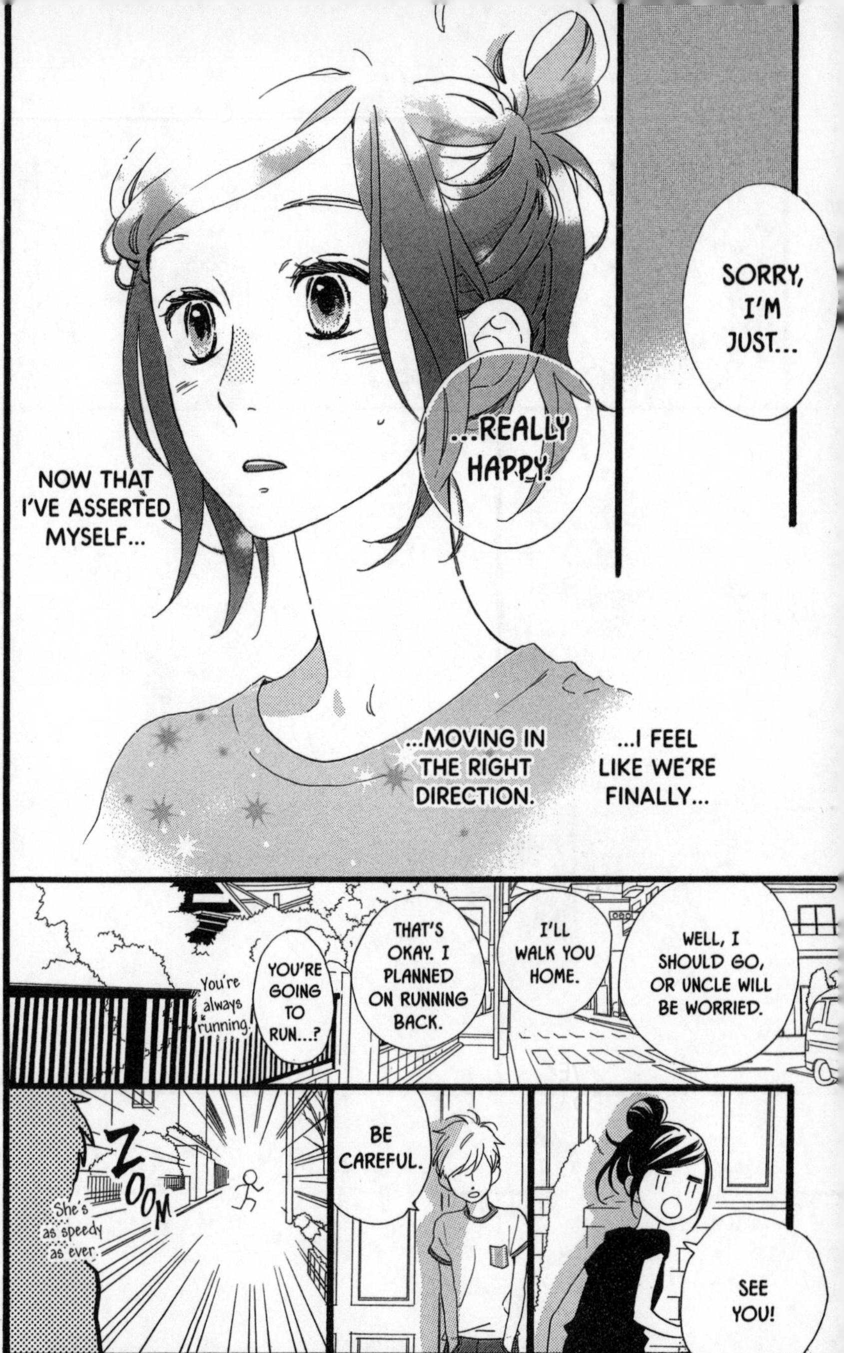
SORRY, I'M JUST...
...REALLY HAPPY.
NOW THAT I'VE ASSERTED MYSELF...
...I FEEL LIKE WE'RE FINALLY...
...MOVING IN THE RIGHT DIRECTION.
WELL, I SHOULD GO, OR UNCLE WILL BE WORRIED.
I'LL WALK YOU HOME.
THAT'S OKAY. I PLANNED ON RUNNING BACK.
YOU'RE GOING TO RUN...?
You're always running.
SEE YOU!
BE CAREFUL.
ZOOM
She's as speedy as ever.

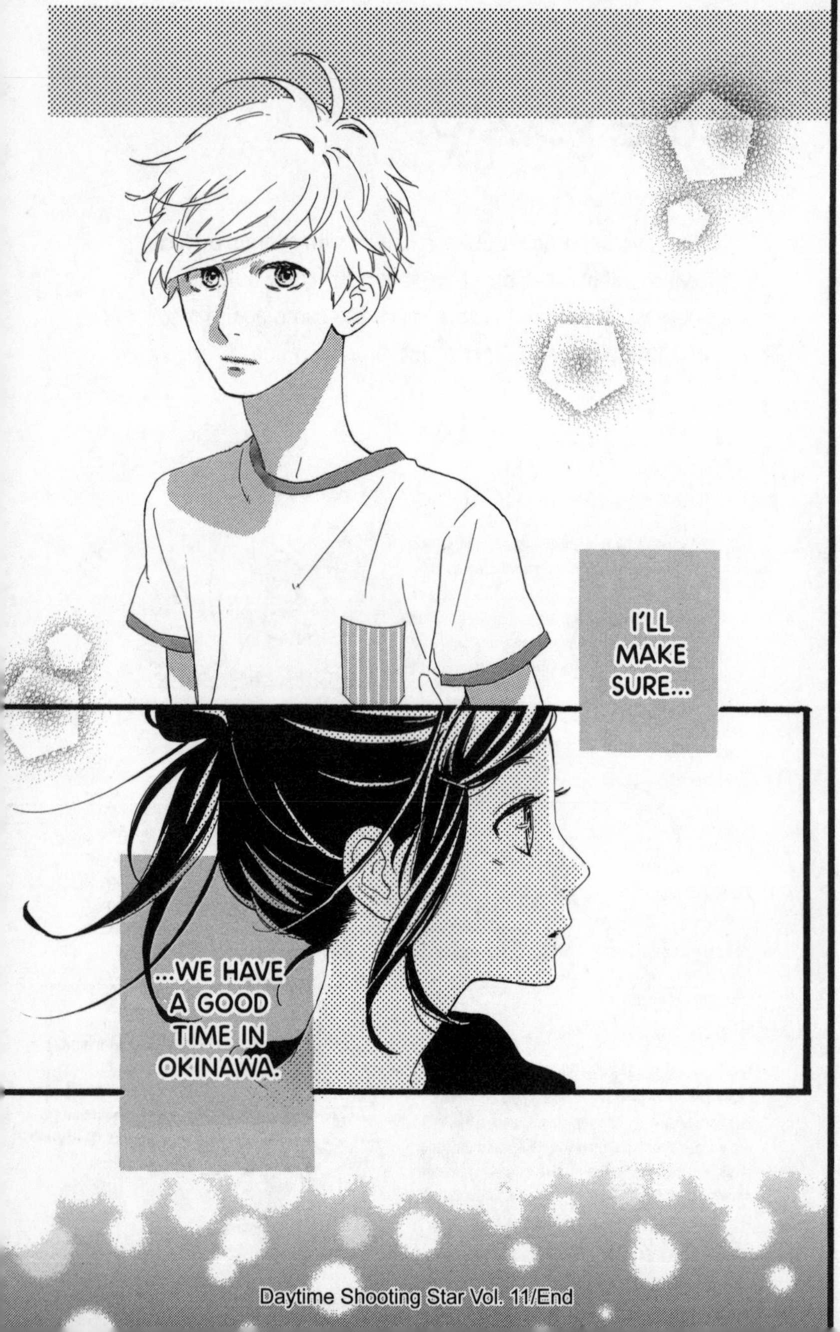
I'LL MAKE SURE...
...WE HAVE A GOOD TIME IN OKINAWA.

Daytime Shooting Star Vol. 11/End

# Idle gossip.

Lately, I've been going out for drinks with Momoko Koda, Masako Shitara and Suu Morishita (all fellow authors). I guess we get along because we're the same age. It's so much fun. We spend most of the time laughing.

• Momoko Koda •

Machida's high-energy queen, Koda, joined a gym to lose weight and ended up quitting after one day. Full of passion, she once got into a fervent debate about the Torumekian army in *Nausicaä* at a wrap party and was scolded by her editor about it. She's such a carefree, fun person.

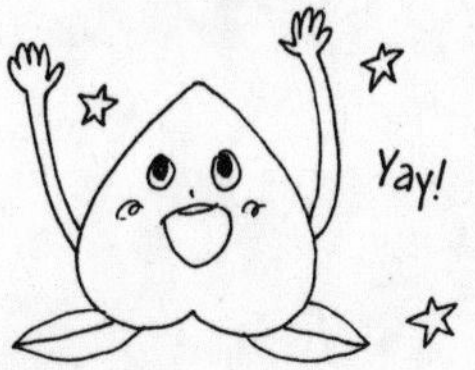
Yay!

Her series *Sensei Kunshu* is currently running in *Bessatsu Margaret.*

• Masako Shitara •

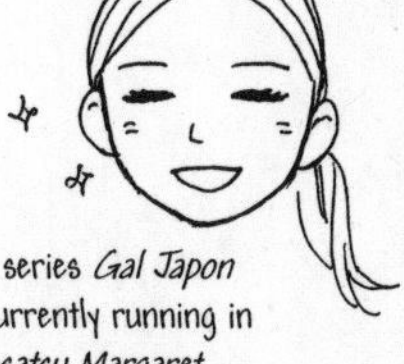

Her series *Gal Japon* is currently running in *Bessatsu Margaret.*

Those who meet her for the first time almost always exclaim, "You mean, she's the one who writes *Gal Japon*?" That goes to show you how different she is from her work. On the surface, she looks like a pretty office worker, but in reality, she is an obsessive gamer. She is always ranked at the top in my *LINE: Tsum Tsum* game. It's also a little-known fact that she's a voracious eater and smells like peaches.

• Nachiyan (Suu Morishita) •

She's around 30, but the gingham dresses she wears are so stylish. She's always two or three chapters ahead on her projects. I have a theory that she's from another dimension. Her communication skills are top-notch. No matter how early or late I email her, she replies right away. I don't know when she finds time to sleep. Sometimes I think there might actually be two of her.

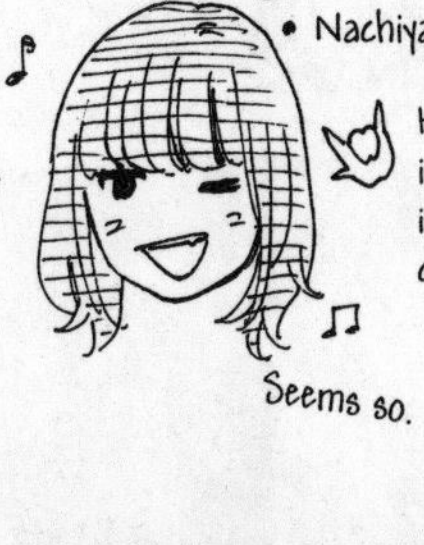
Seems so.

Her series *Hibi Chocho* is currently running in *Margaret.* (She's in charge of the art)

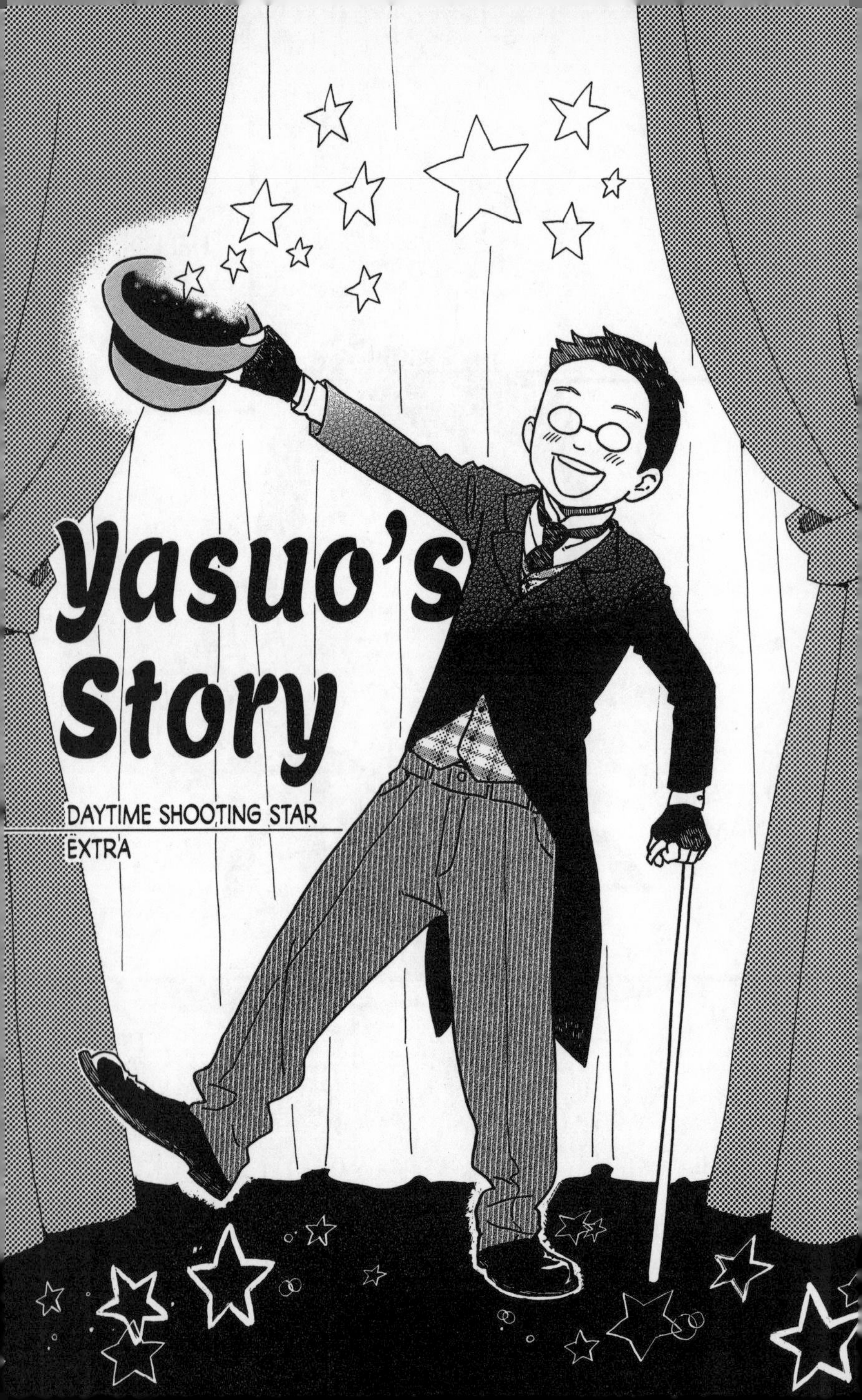
Yasuo's Story
DAYTIME SHOOTING STAR
EXTRA

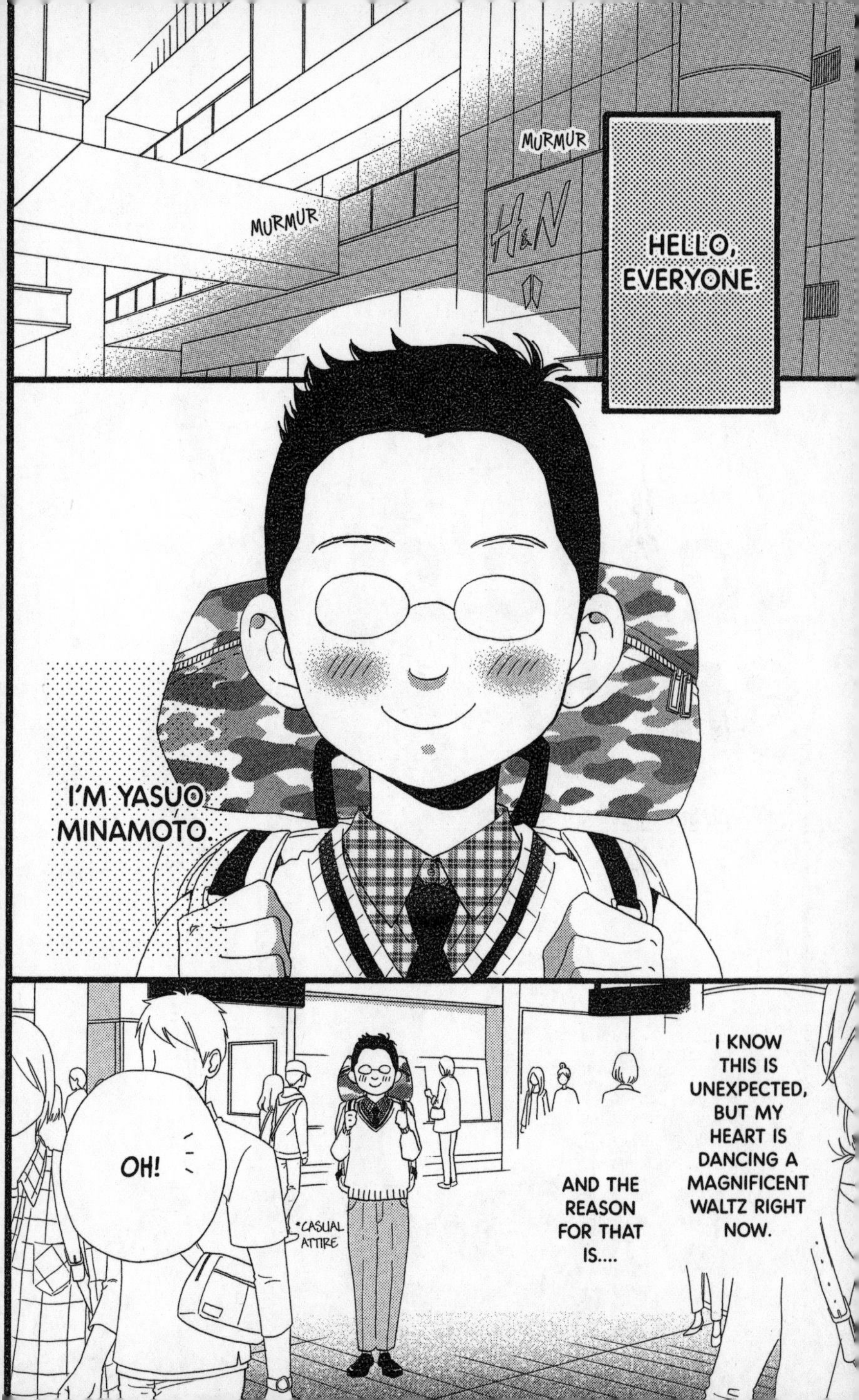
HELLO, EVERYONE.
MURMUR
MURMUR
I'M YASUO MINAMOTO.
I KNOW THIS IS UNEXPECTED, BUT MY HEART IS DANCING A MAGNIFICENT WALTZ RIGHT NOW.
AND THE REASON FOR THAT IS....
*CASUAL ATTIRE
OH!

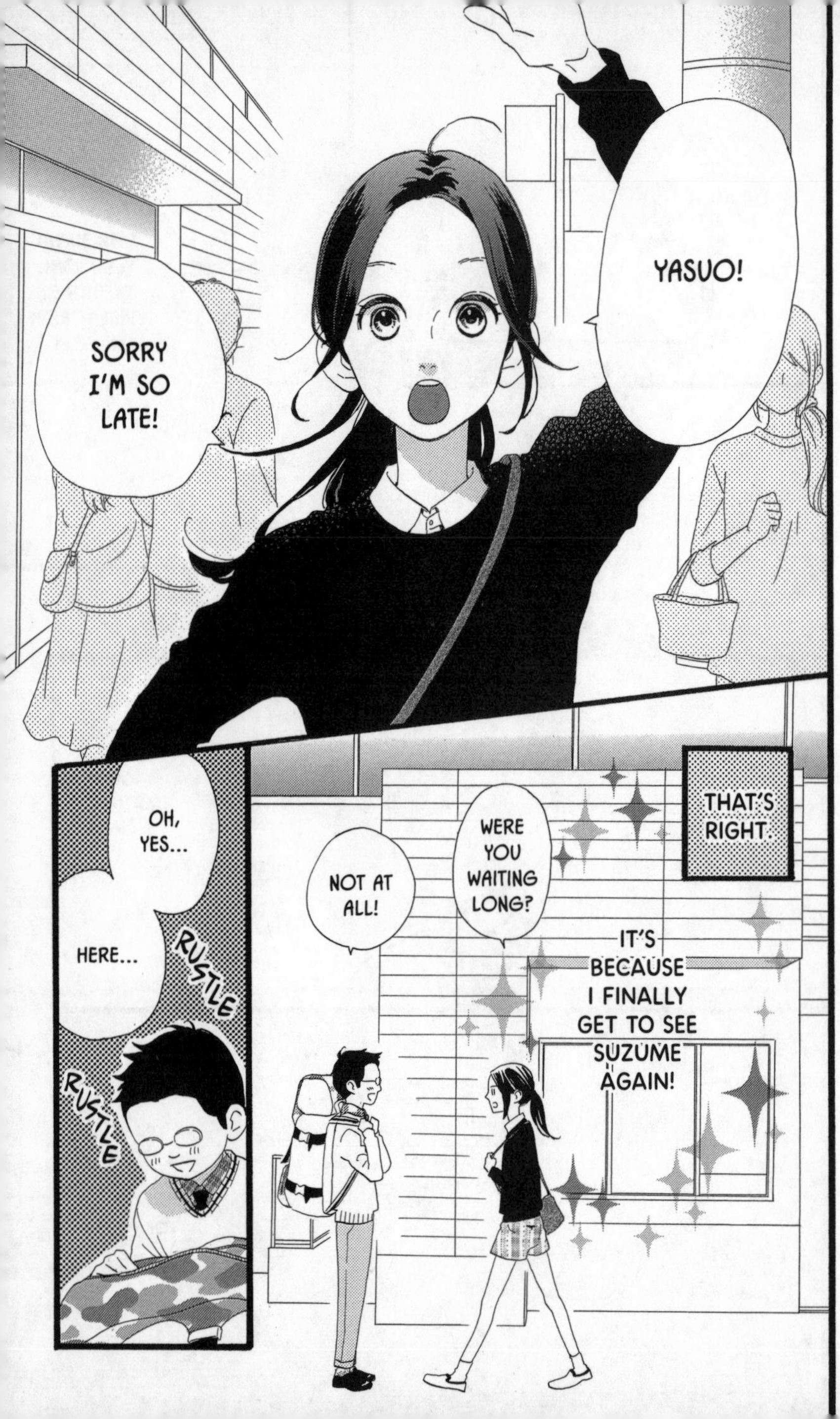
YASUO!
SORRY I'M SO LATE!
THAT'S RIGHT.
WERE YOU WAITING LONG?
NOT AT ALL!
IT'S BECAUSE I FINALLY GET TO SEE SUZUME AGAIN!
OH, YES...
HERE...
RUSTLE
RUSTLE

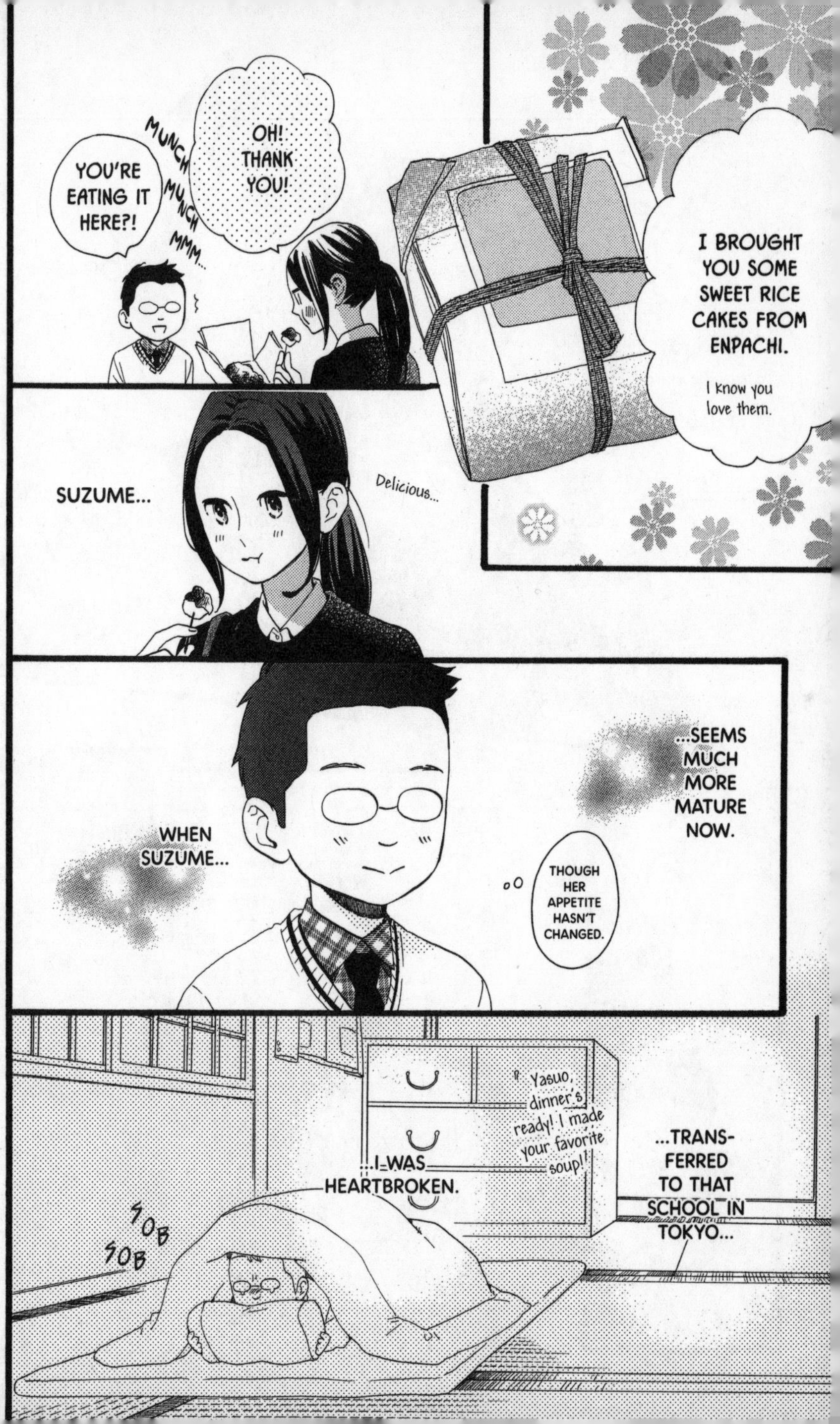
I BROUGHT YOU SOME SWEET RICE CAKES FROM ENPACHI.
I know you love them.
OH! THANK YOU!
MUNCH MUNCH MMM...
YOU'RE EATING IT HERE?!
Delicious...
SUZUME...
...SEEMS MUCH MORE MATURE NOW.
THOUGH HER APPETITE HASN'T CHANGED.
WHEN SUZUME...
...TRANS-FERRED TO THAT SCHOOL IN TOKYO...
Yasuo, dinner's ready! I made your favorite soup!
...I WAS HEARTBROKEN.
SOB SOB

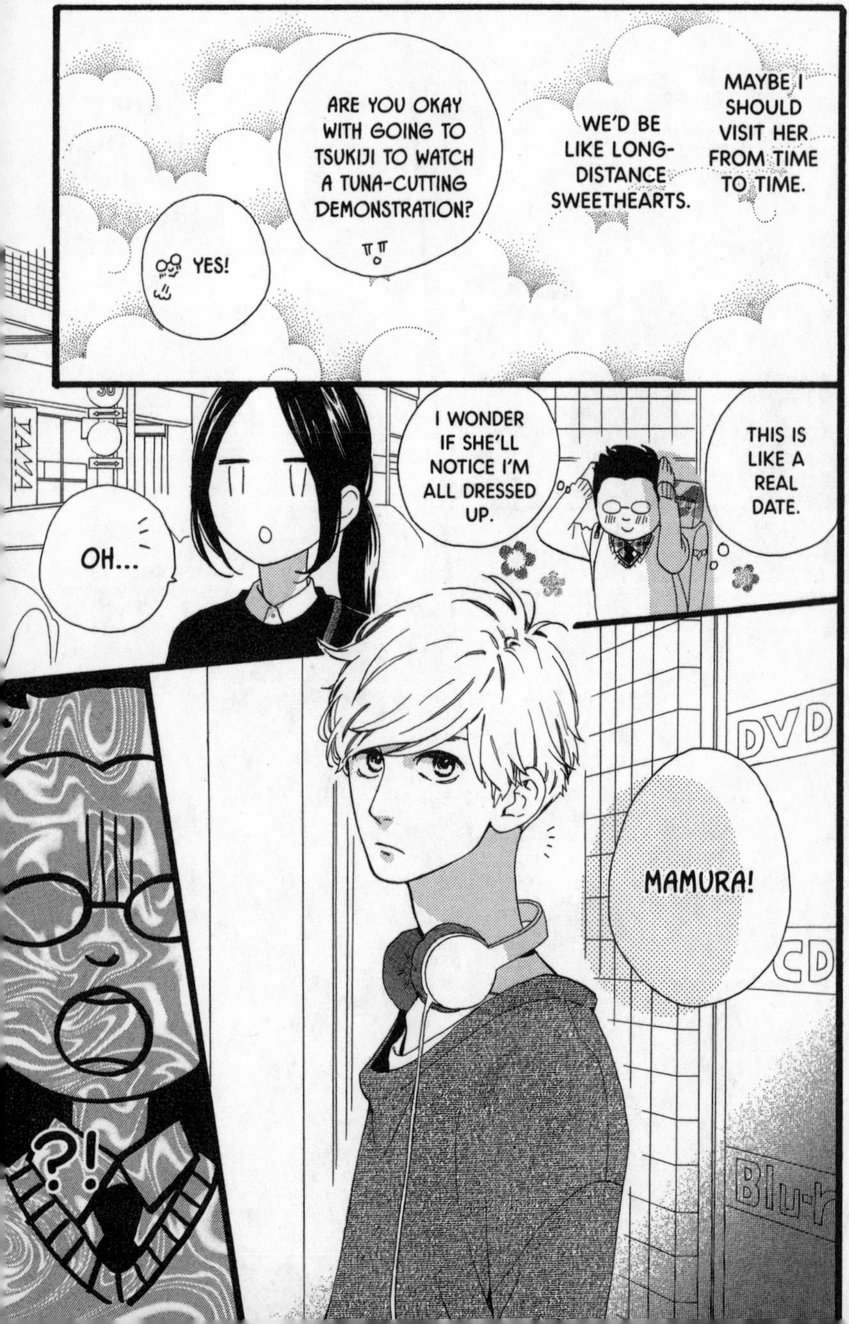

MAYBE I SHOULD VISIT HER FROM TIME TO TIME.
WE'D BE LIKE LONG-DISTANCE SWEETHEARTS.
ARE YOU OKAY WITH GOING TO TSUKIJI TO WATCH A TUNA-CUTTING DEMONSTRATION?
YES!
THIS IS LIKE A REAL DATE.
I WONDER IF SHE'LL NOTICE I'M ALL DRESSED UP.
OH...
DVD
MAMURA!
CD
?!

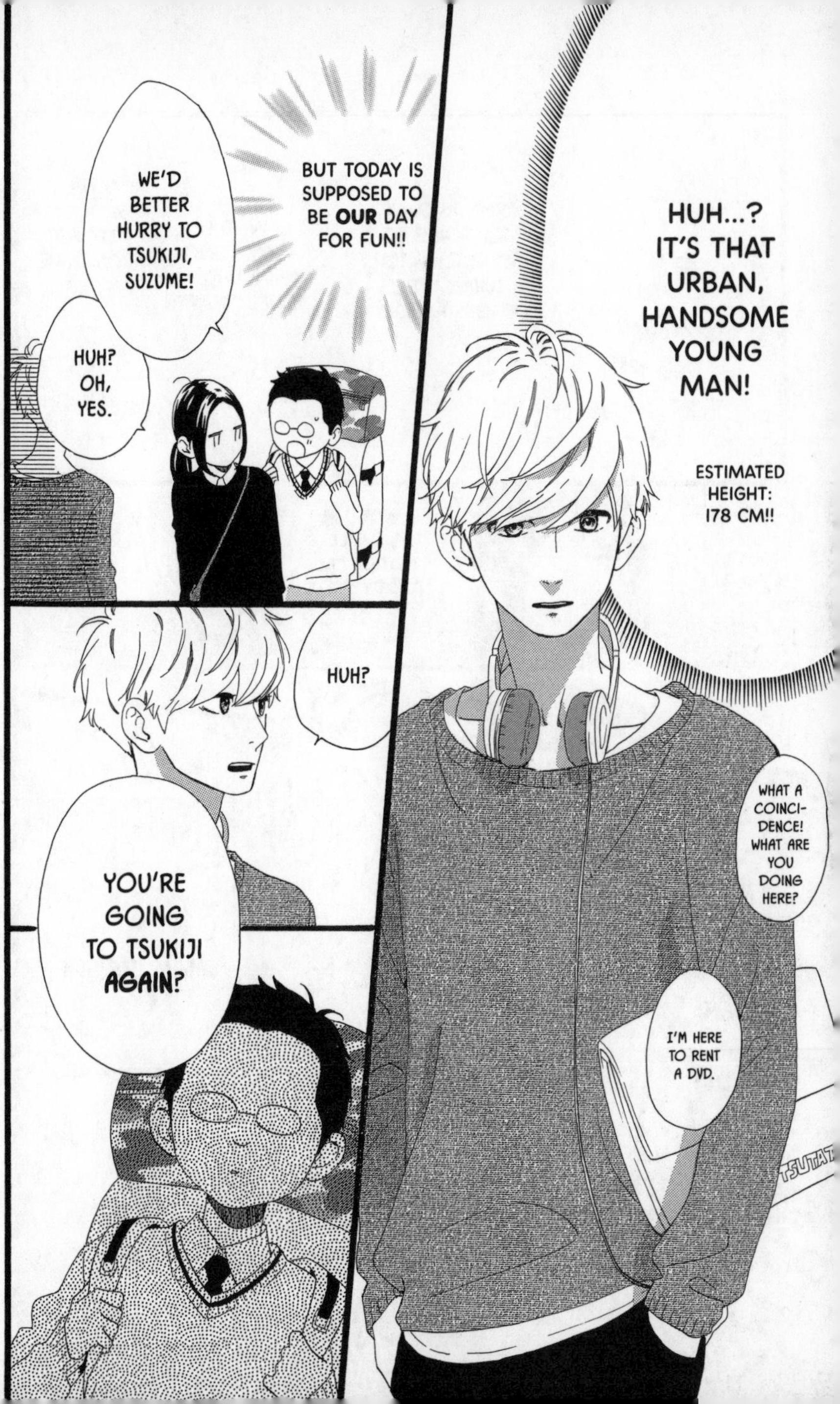
HUH...? IT'S THAT URBAN, HANDSOME YOUNG MAN!
ESTIMATED HEIGHT: 178 CM!!
WHAT A COINCI-DENCE! WHAT ARE YOU DOING HERE?
I'M HERE TO RENT A DVD.
BUT TODAY IS SUPPOSED TO BE **OUR** DAY FOR FUN!!
WE'D BETTER HURRY TO TSUKIJI, SUZUME!
HUH? OH, YES.
HUH?
YOU'RE GOING TO TSUKIJI **AGAIN**?

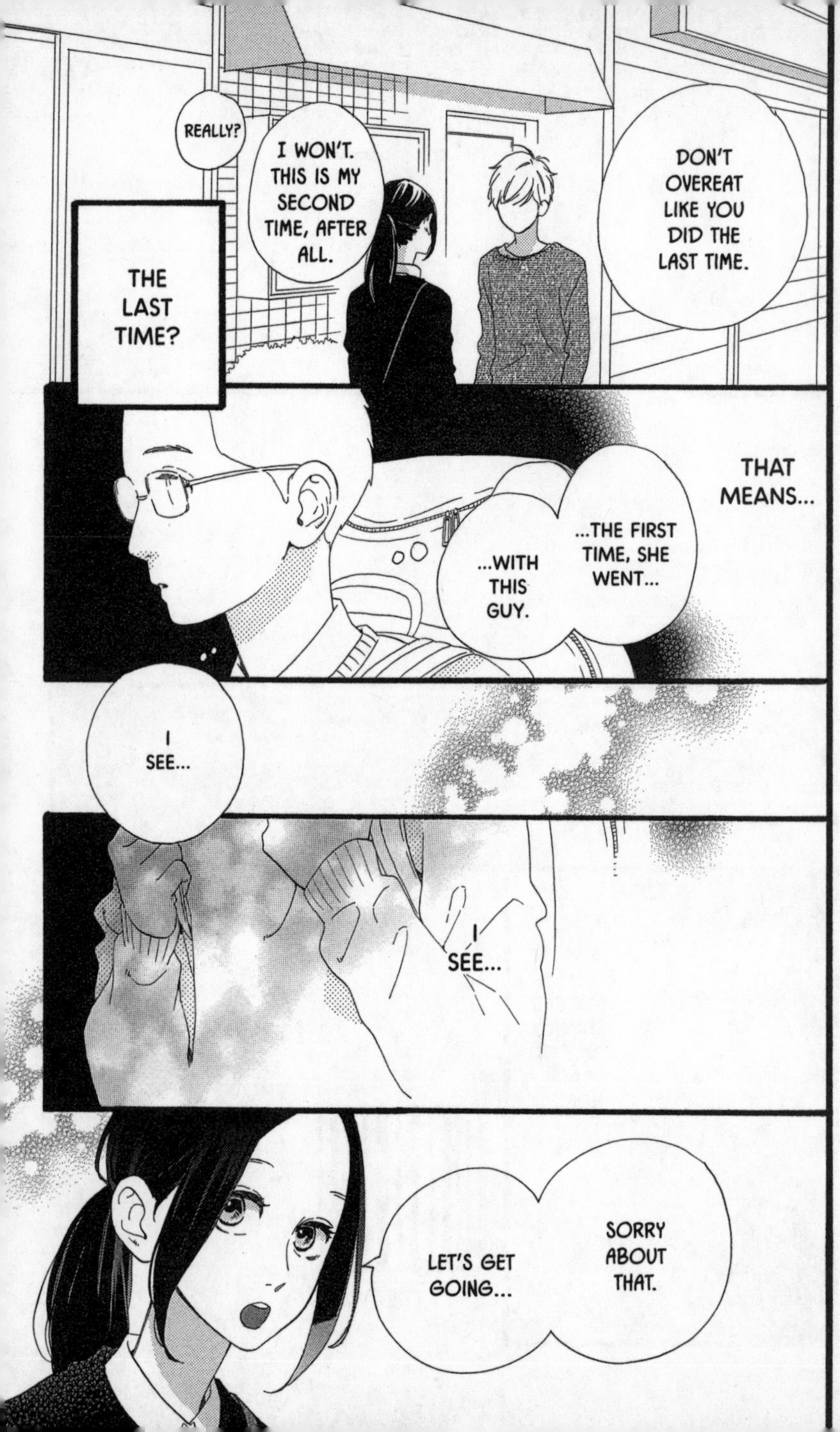
DON'T OVEREAT LIKE YOU DID THE LAST TIME.
I WON'T. THIS IS MY SECOND TIME, AFTER ALL.
REALLY?
THE LAST TIME?
THAT MEANS...
...THE FIRST TIME, SHE WENT...
...WITH THIS GUY.
I SEE...
I SEE...
SORRY ABOUT THAT.
LET'S GET GOING...

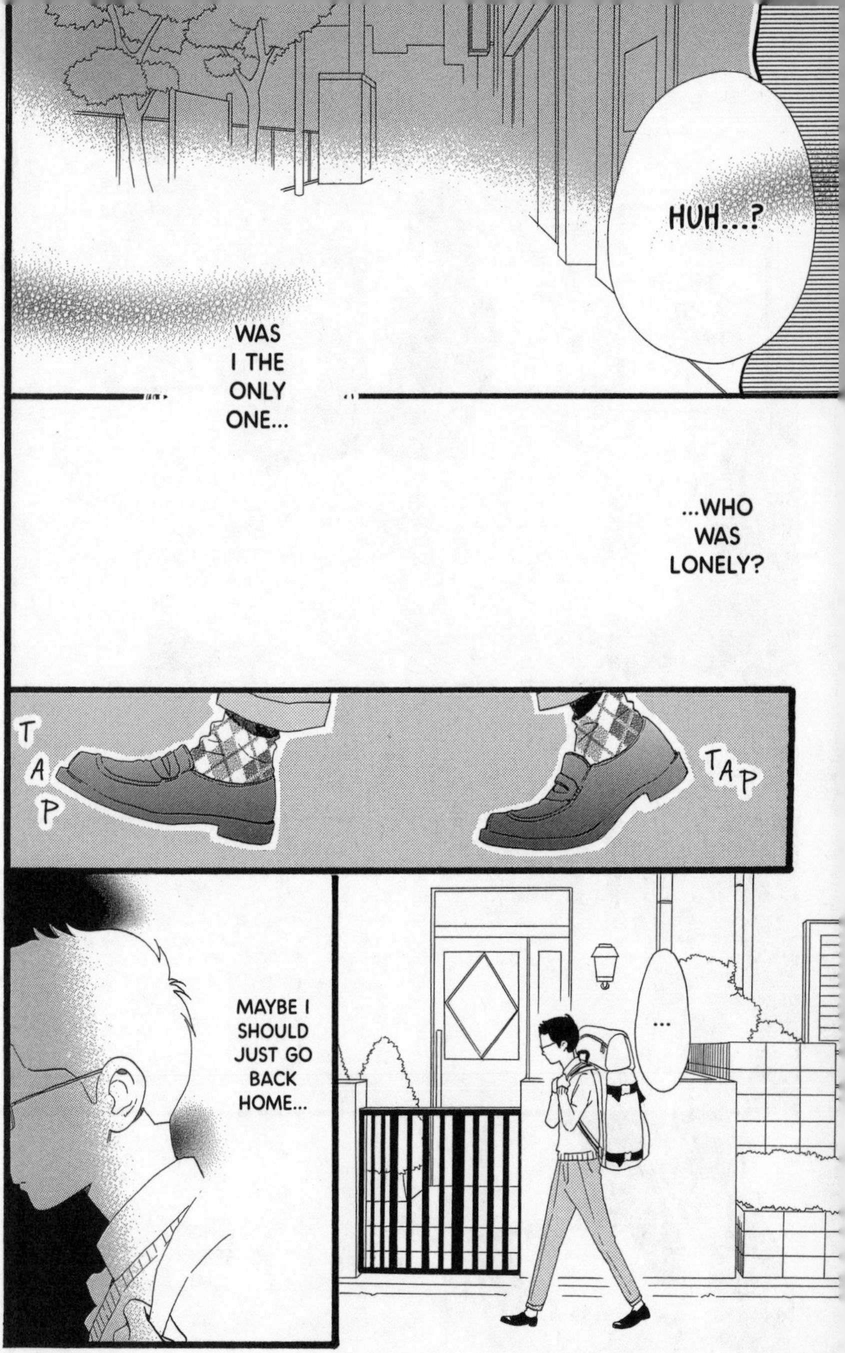

HUH...?
WAS I THE ONLY ONE...
...WHO WAS LONELY?
TAP
TAP
...
MAYBE I SHOULD JUST GO BACK HOME...

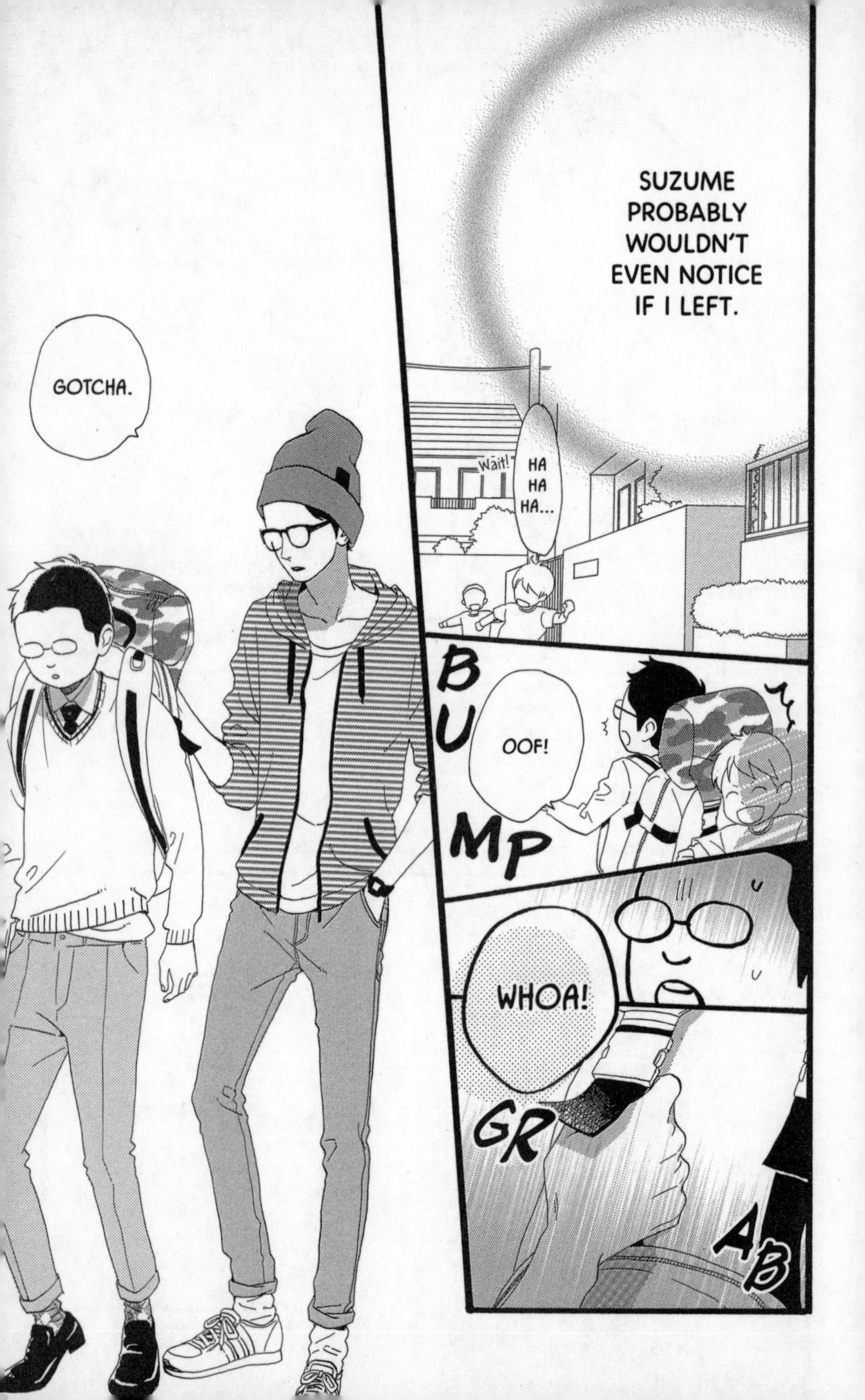
SUZUME PROBABLY WOULDN'T EVEN NOTICE IF I LEFT.
HA HA HA...
Wait!
BUMP
OOF!
WHOA!
GRAB
GOTCHA.

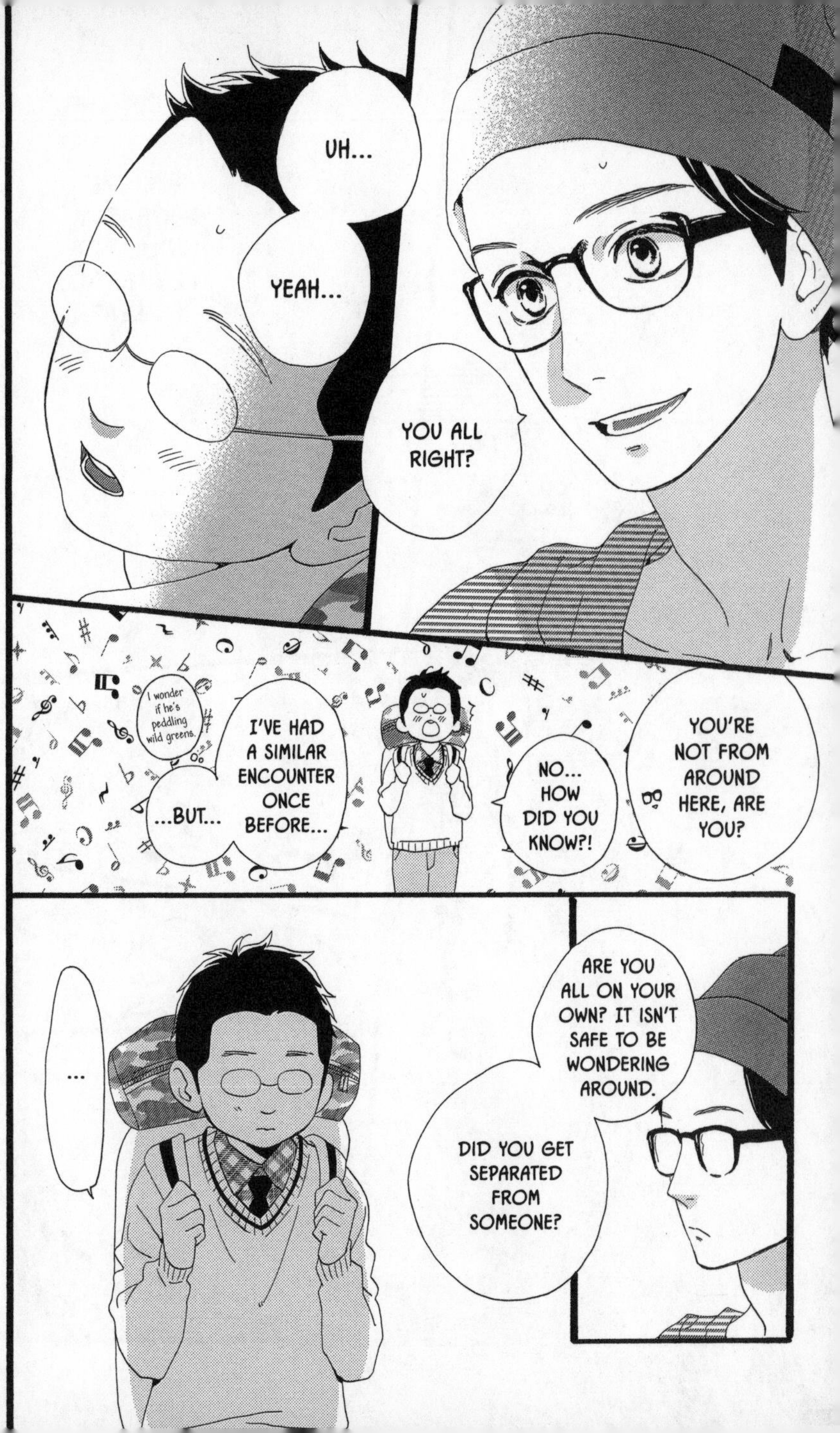
YOU ALL RIGHT?
UH...
YEAH...
YOU'RE NOT FROM AROUND HERE, ARE YOU?
NO... HOW DID YOU KNOW?!
I'VE HAD A SIMILAR ENCOUNTER ONCE BEFORE...
...BUT...
I wonder if he's peddling wild greens.
ARE YOU ALL ON YOUR OWN? IT ISN'T SAFE TO BE WONDERING AROUND.
DID YOU GET SEPARATED FROM SOMEONE?
...

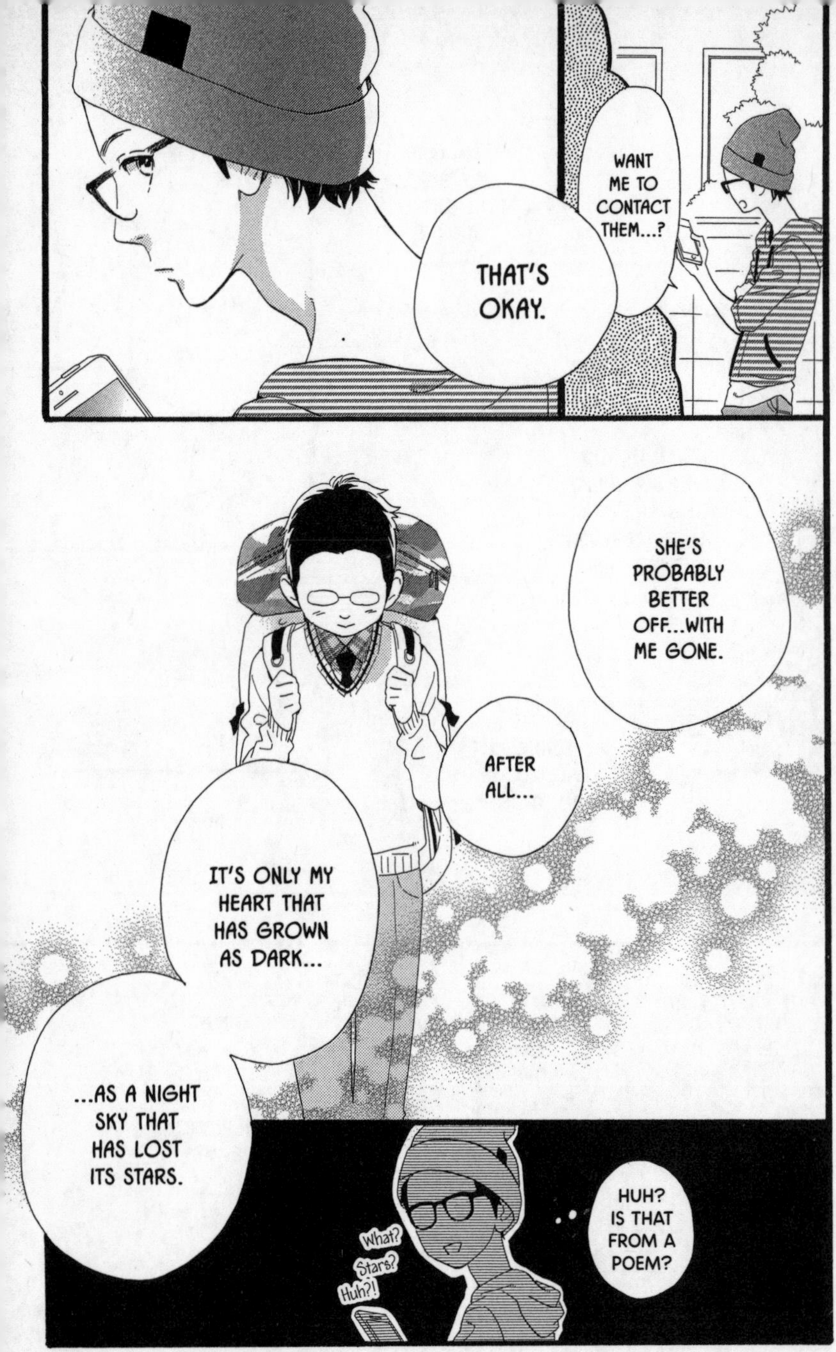
WANT ME TO CONTACT THEM...?
THAT'S OKAY.
SHE'S PROBABLY BETTER OFF...WITH ME GONE.
AFTER ALL...
IT'S ONLY MY HEART THAT HAS GROWN AS DARK...
...AS A NIGHT SKY THAT HAS LOST ITS STARS.
HUH? IS THAT FROM A POEM?
What? Stars? Huh?!

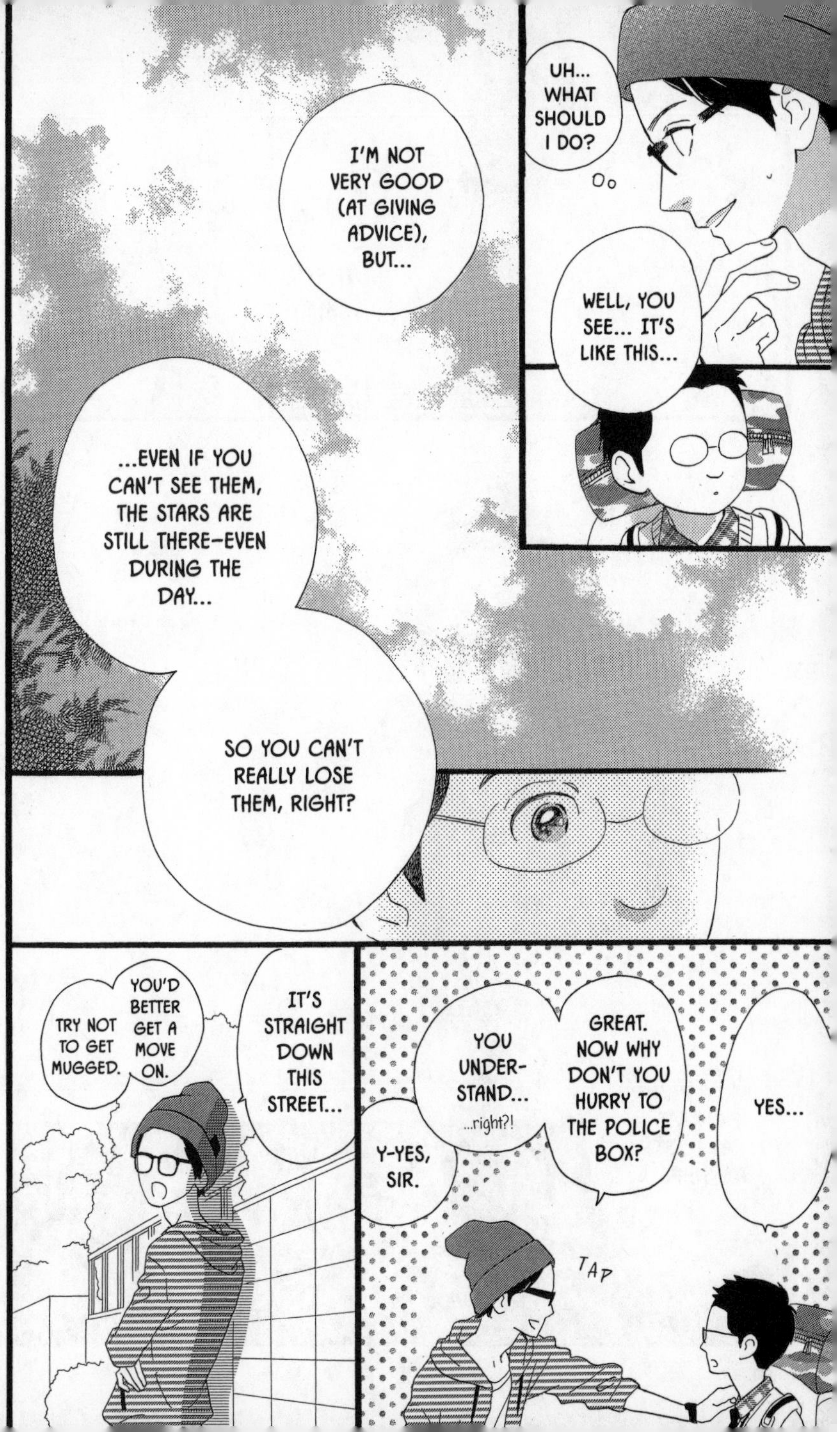
UH... WHAT SHOULD I DO?
WELL, YOU SEE... IT'S LIKE THIS...
I'M NOT VERY GOOD (AT GIVING ADVICE), BUT...
...EVEN IF YOU CAN'T SEE THEM, THE STARS ARE STILL THERE—EVEN DURING THE DAY...
SO YOU CAN'T REALLY LOSE THEM, RIGHT?
YES...
GREAT. NOW WHY DON'T YOU HURRY TO THE POLICE BOX?
YOU UNDER-STAND...
...right?!
Y-YES, SIR.
TAP
IT'S STRAIGHT DOWN THIS STREET...
YOU'D BETTER GET A MOVE ON.
TRY NOT TO GET MUGGED.

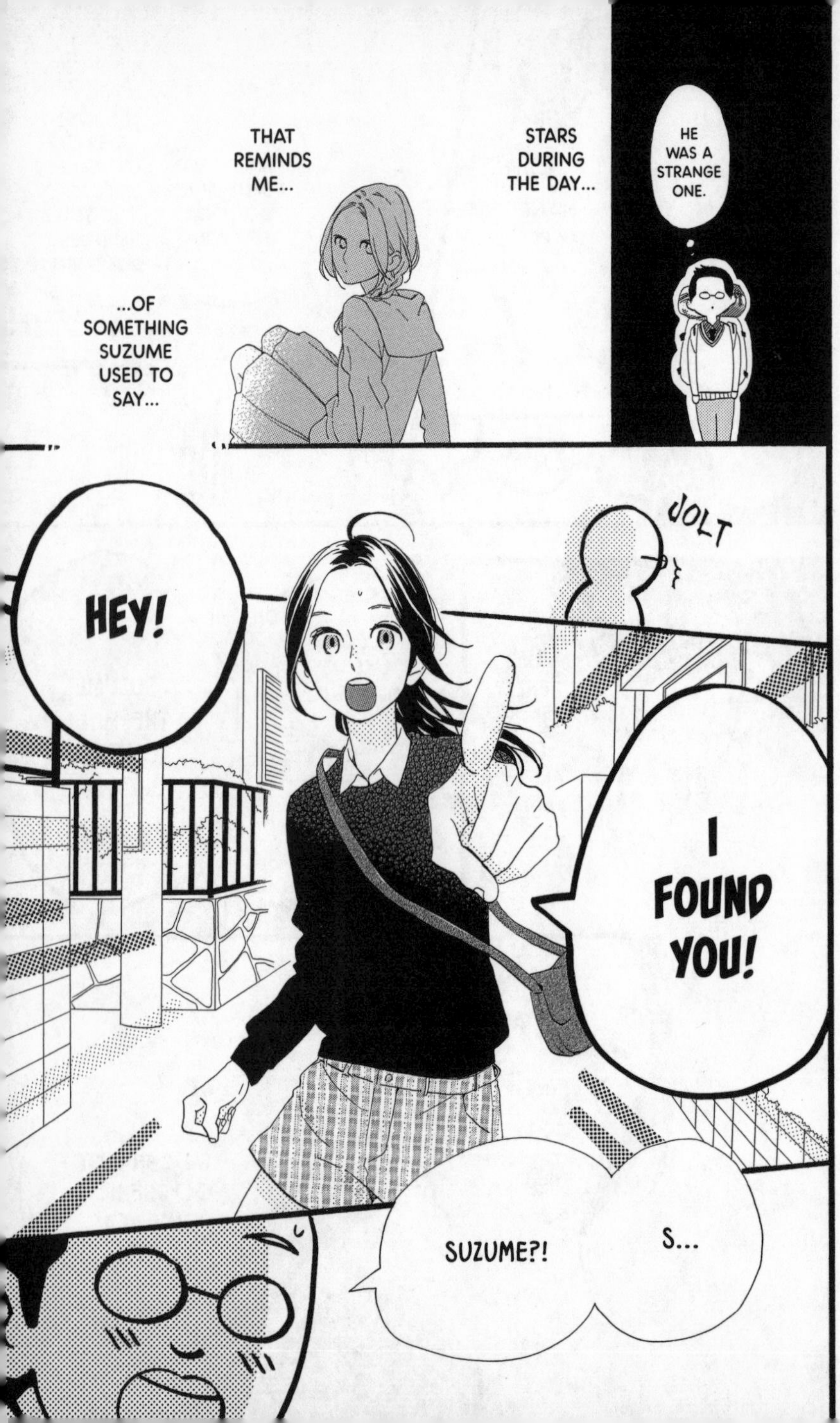

HE WAS A STRANGE ONE.
STARS DURING THE DAY...
THAT REMINDS ME...
...OF SOMETHING SUZUME USED TO SAY...
JOLT
HEY!
I FOUND YOU!
S...
SUZUME?!

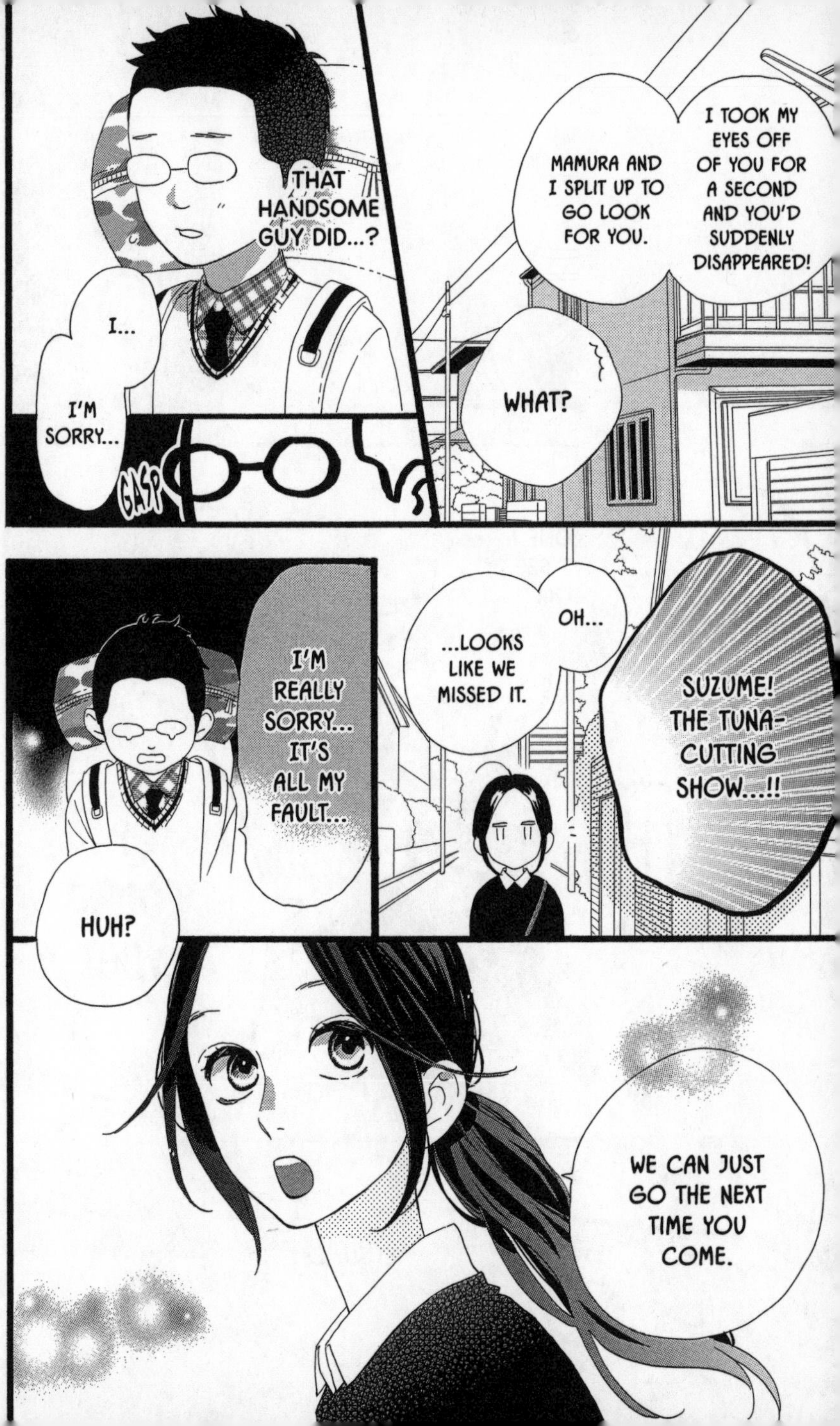
I TOOK MY EYES OFF OF YOU FOR A SECOND AND YOU'D SUDDENLY DISAPPEARED!
MAMURA AND I SPLIT UP TO GO LOOK FOR YOU.
WHAT?
THAT HANDSOME GUY DID...?
GASP
I...
I'M SORRY...
SUZUME! THE TUNA-CUTTING SHOW...!!
OH...
...LOOKS LIKE WE MISSED IT.
I'M REALLY SORRY... IT'S ALL MY FAULT...
HUH?
WE CAN JUST GO THE NEXT TIME YOU COME.

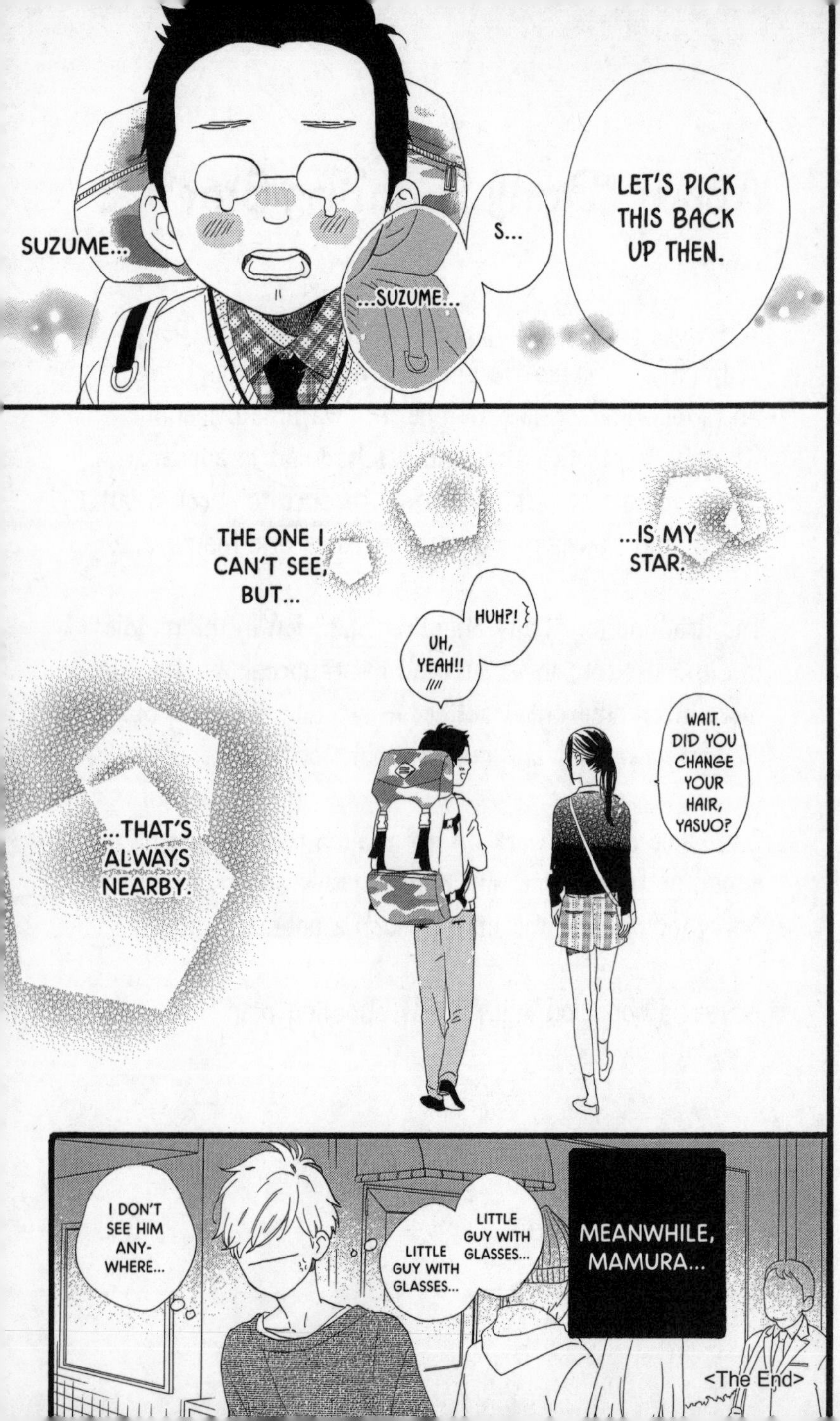
LET'S PICK THIS BACK UP THEN.
S...
...SUZUME...
SUZUME...
...IS MY STAR.
THE ONE I CAN'T SEE, BUT...
HUH?!
UH, YEAH!!
WAIT. DID YOU CHANGE YOUR HAIR, YASUO?
...THAT'S ALWAYS NEARBY.
MEANWHILE, MAMURA...
LITTLE GUY WITH GLASSES...
LITTLE GUY WITH GLASSES...
I DON'T SEE HIM ANY-WHERE...
<The End>

# About "Daily Shooting Star"

This story contains elements from *Hibi Chocho* (Daily Butterfly). I created the storyboard for this short, and Suu Morishita created the one for "Daytime Chocho" (Daytime Butterfly). That one is scheduled to appear in a future volume of *Hibi Chocho*, so be sure to check it out. ♪ Suiren and Kawasumi run into Suzume and Mamura. ♪

The deadline for "Daily Shooting Star" fell in the middle of Golden Week, so we were all in an uproar. We had to meet three different deadlines—for "Hibi Shooting Star," "Daytime Chocho" and our original stories.

Suu came over to work on her manga pages, but she ended up helping me with mine! I really appreciate it! Sorry for stealing the time of such a popular author!!

Anyway, I hope you enjoy "Daily Shooting Star"!

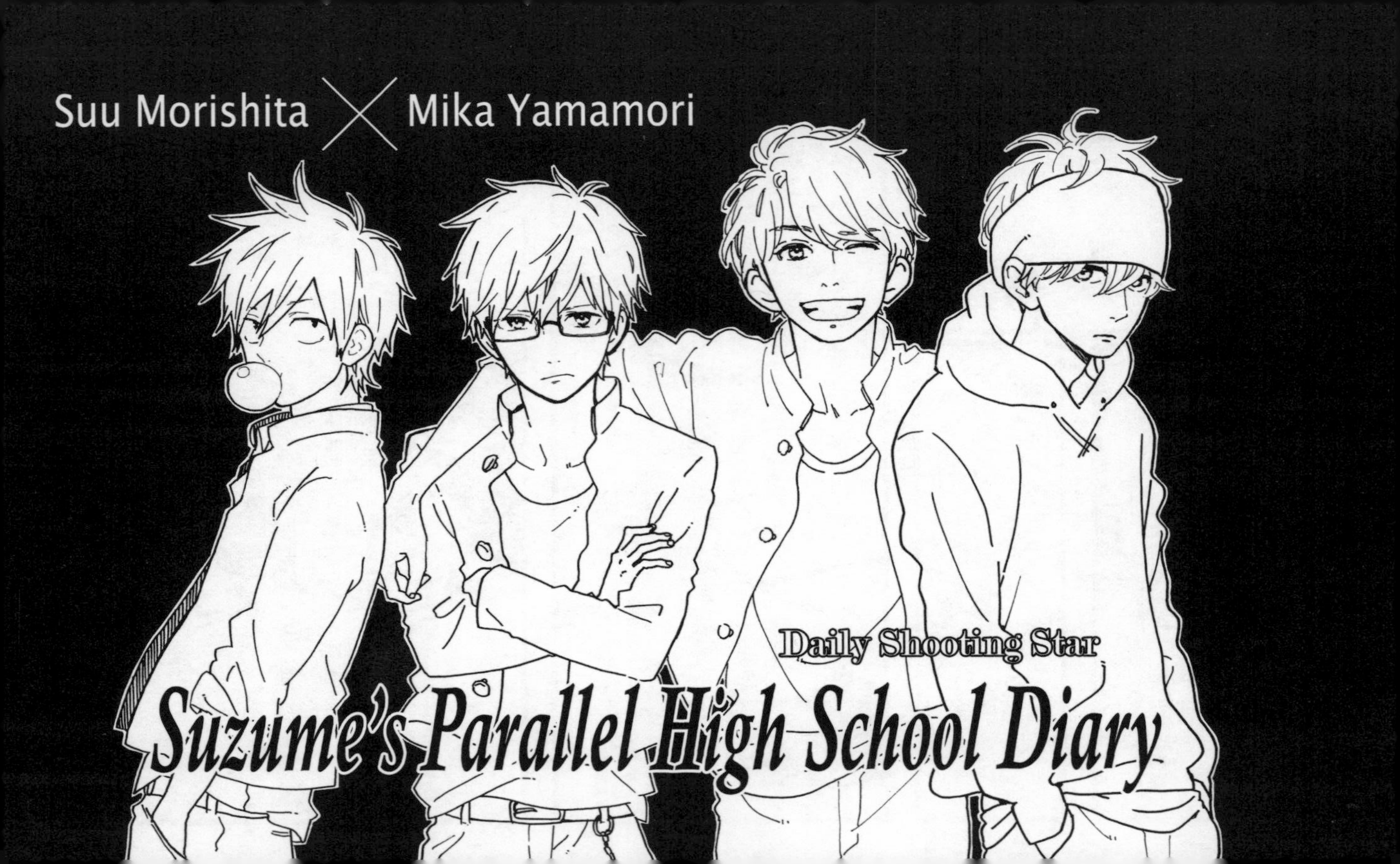
Suu Morishita × Mika Yamamori
Daily Shooting Star
Suzume's Parallel High School Diary

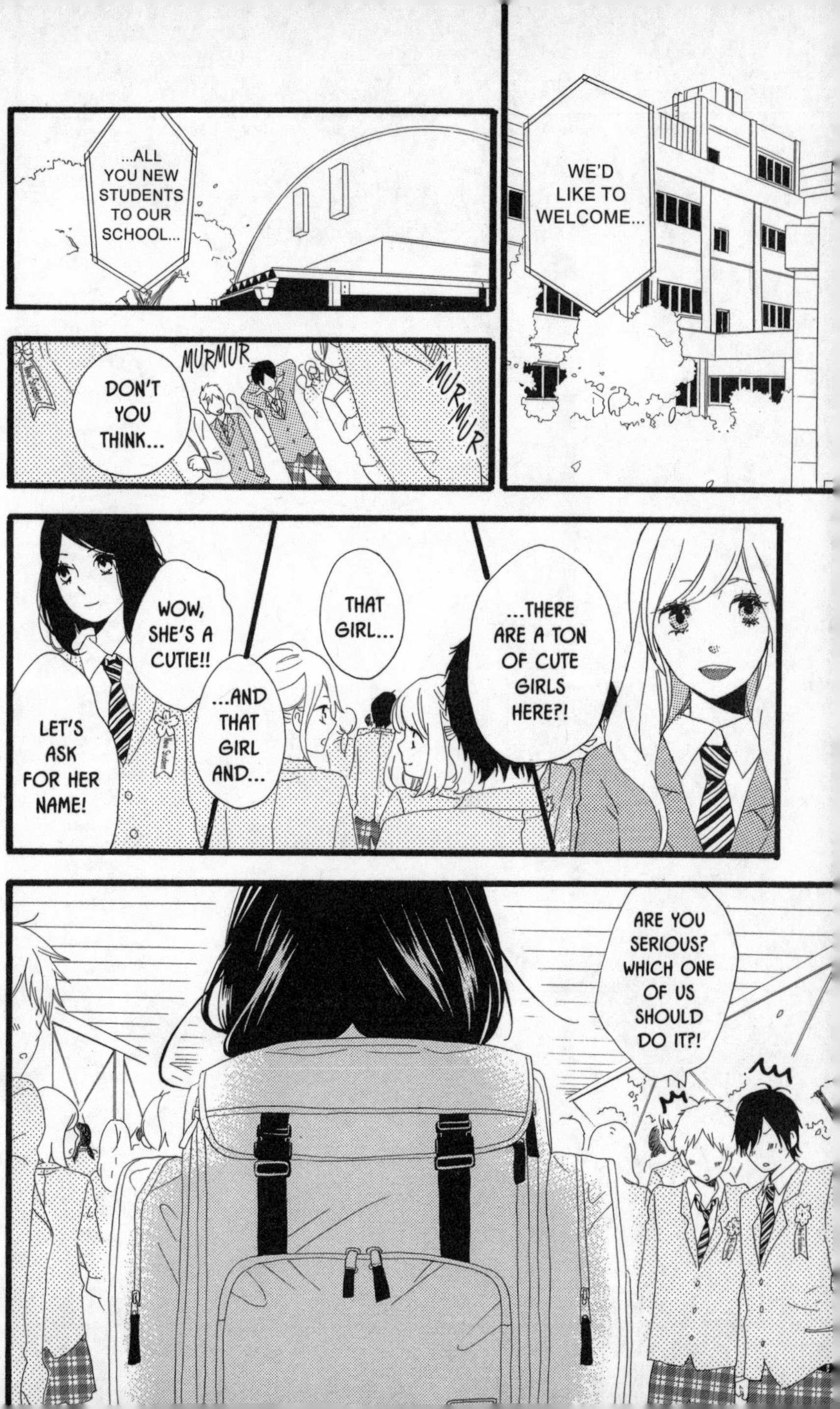
WE'D LIKE TO WELCOME...
...ALL YOU NEW STUDENTS TO OUR SCHOOL...
MURMUR
MURMUR
DON'T YOU THINK...
...THERE ARE A TON OF CUTE GIRLS HERE?!
THAT GIRL...
...AND THAT GIRL AND...
WOW, SHE'S A CUTIE!!
LET'S ASK FOR HER NAME!
ARE YOU SERIOUS? WHICH ONE OF US SHOULD DO IT?!

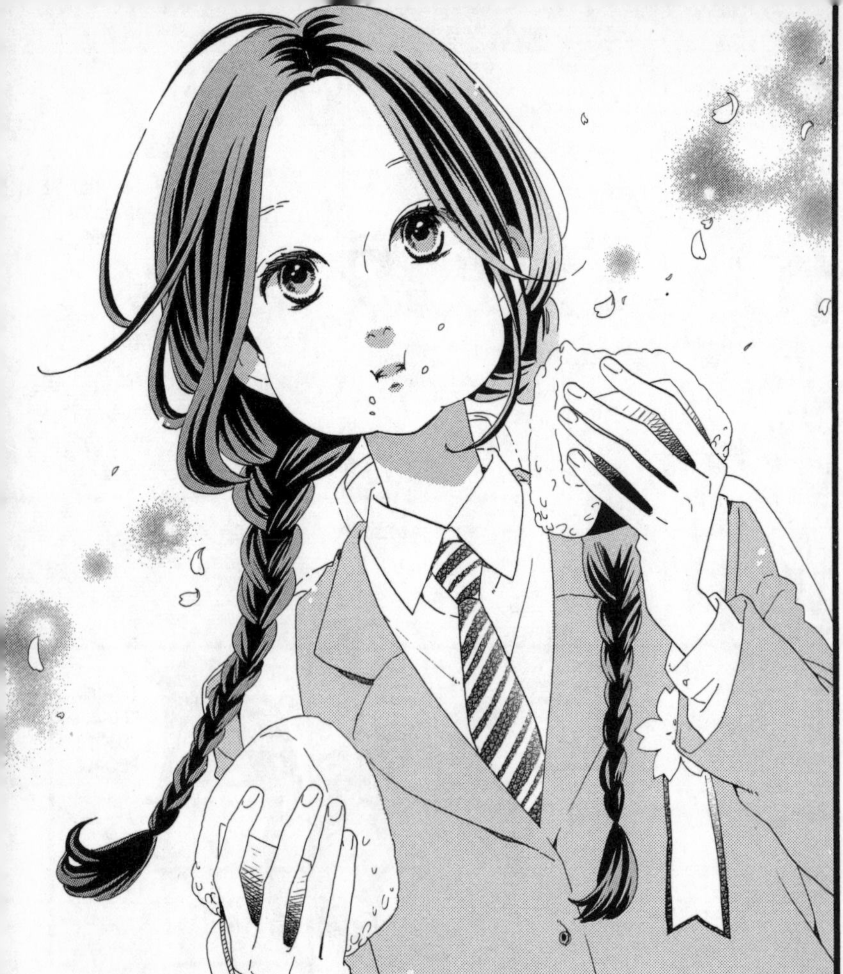

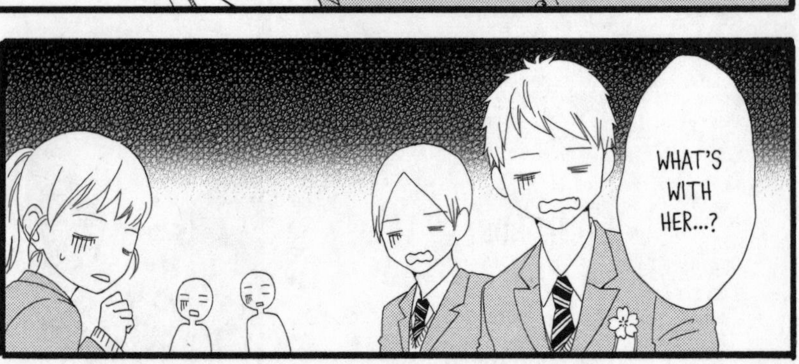
WHAT'S WITH HER...?

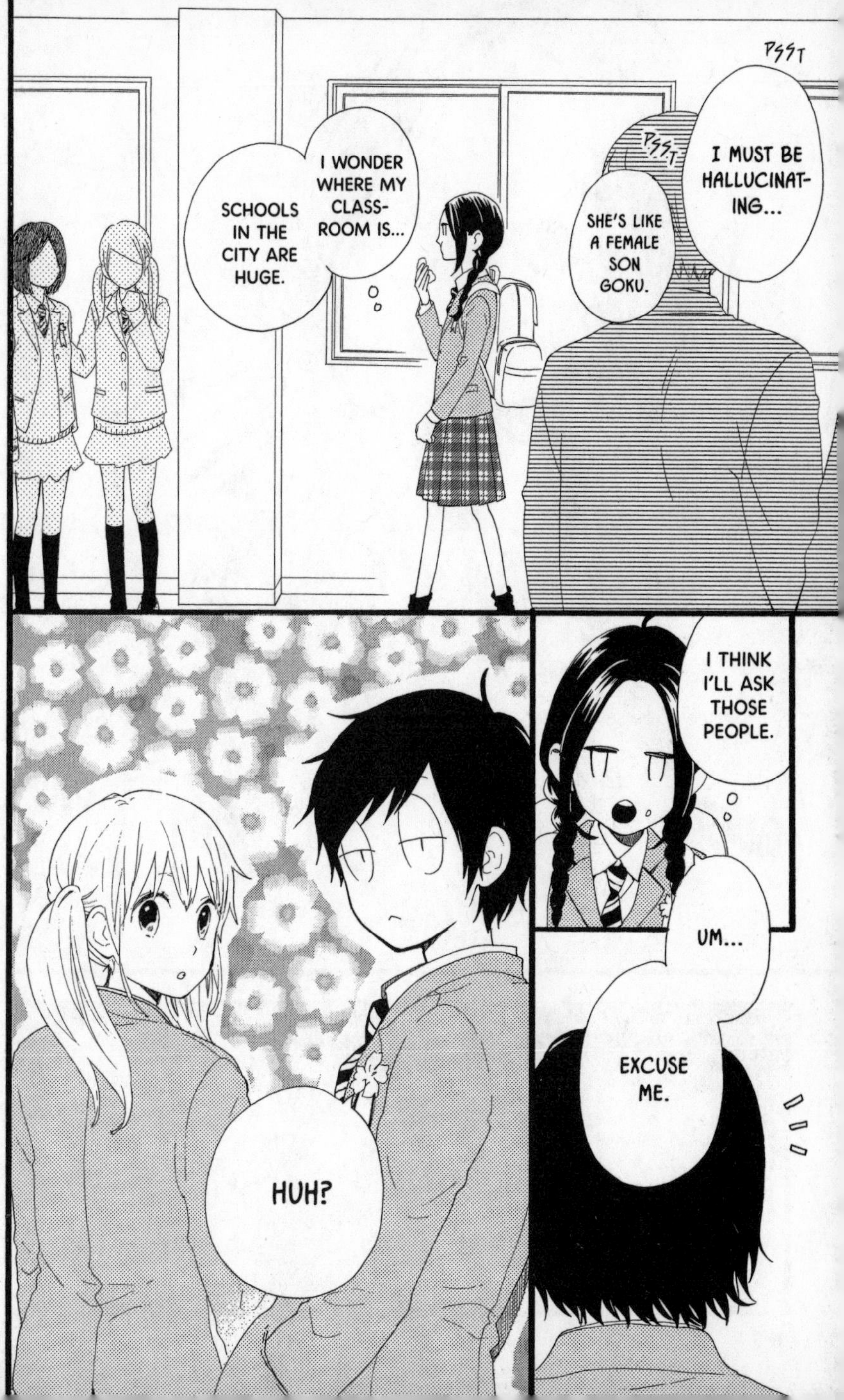
PSST
I MUST BE HALLUCINATING...
PSST
SHE'S LIKE A FEMALE SON GOKU.
I WONDER WHERE MY CLASSROOM IS...
SCHOOLS IN THE CITY ARE HUGE.
I THINK I'LL ASK THOSE PEOPLE.
UM...
EXCUSE ME.
HUH?

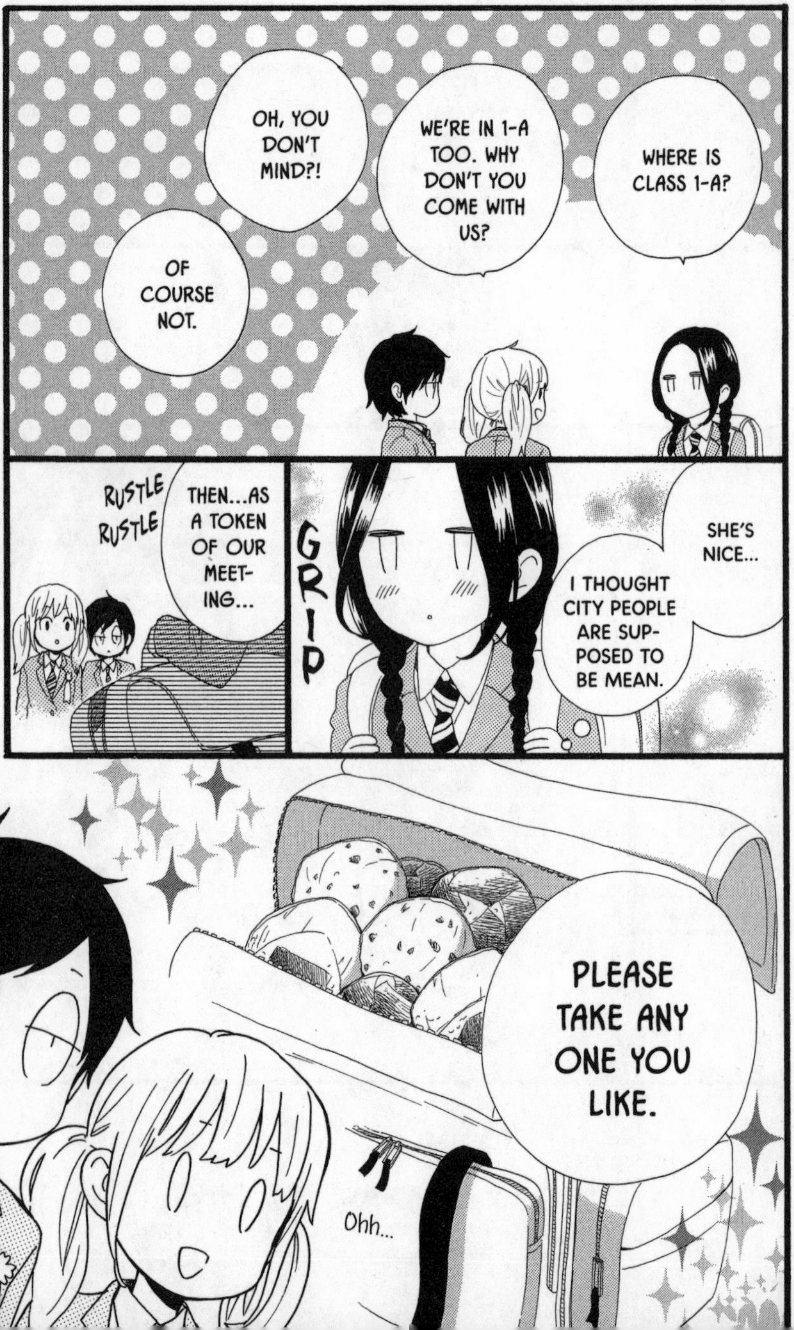
WHERE IS CLASS 1-A?
WE'RE IN 1-A TOO. WHY DON'T YOU COME WITH US?
OH, YOU DON'T MIND?!
OF COURSE NOT.
SHE'S NICE...
I THOUGHT CITY PEOPLE ARE SUPPOSED TO BE MEAN.
GRIP
THEN...AS A TOKEN OF OUR MEETING...
RUSTLE RUSTLE
PLEASE TAKE ANY ONE YOU LIKE.
Ohh...

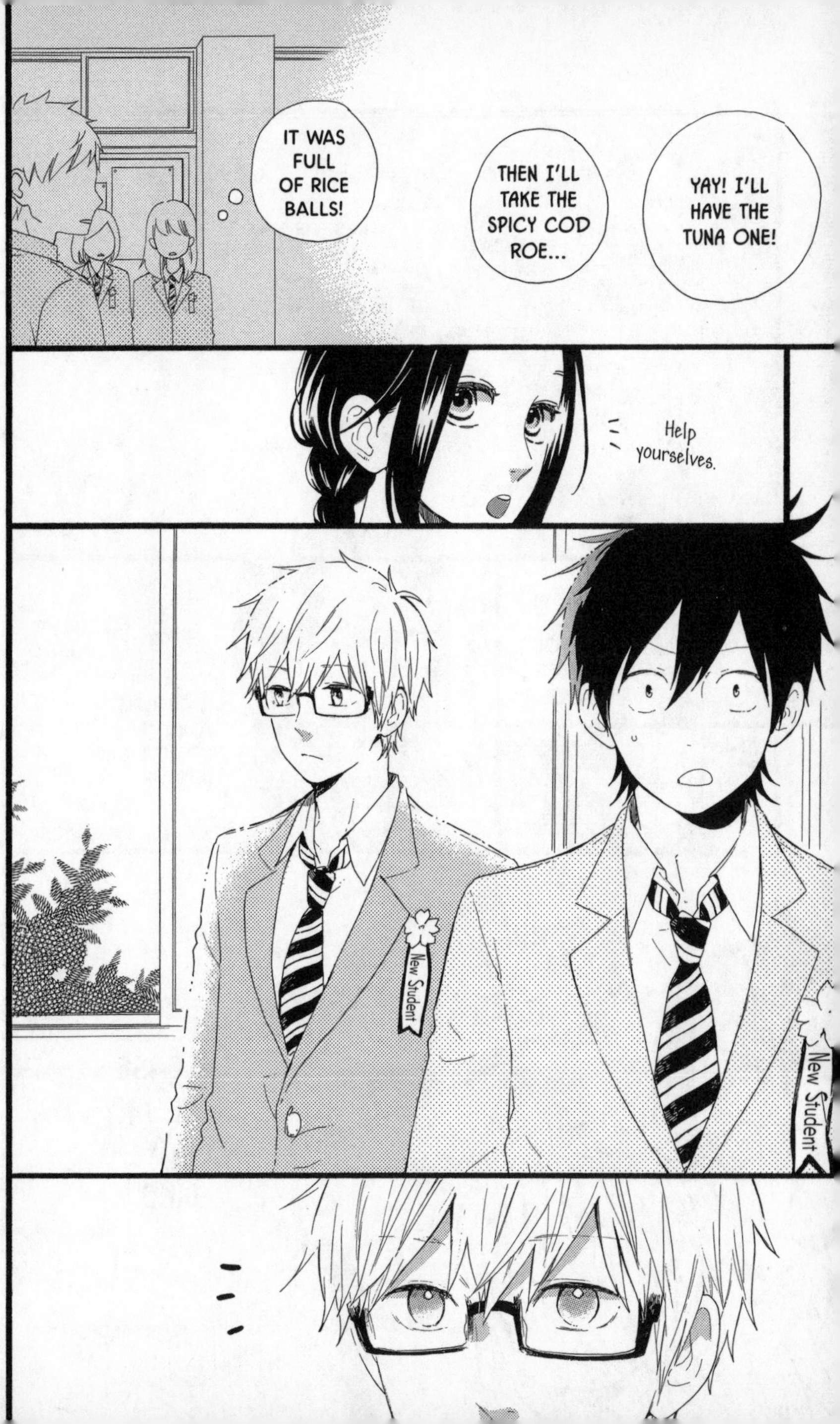
YAY! I'LL HAVE THE TUNA ONE!
THEN I'LL TAKE THE SPICY COD ROE...
IT WAS FULL OF RICE BALLS!
Help yourselves.
New Student
New Student

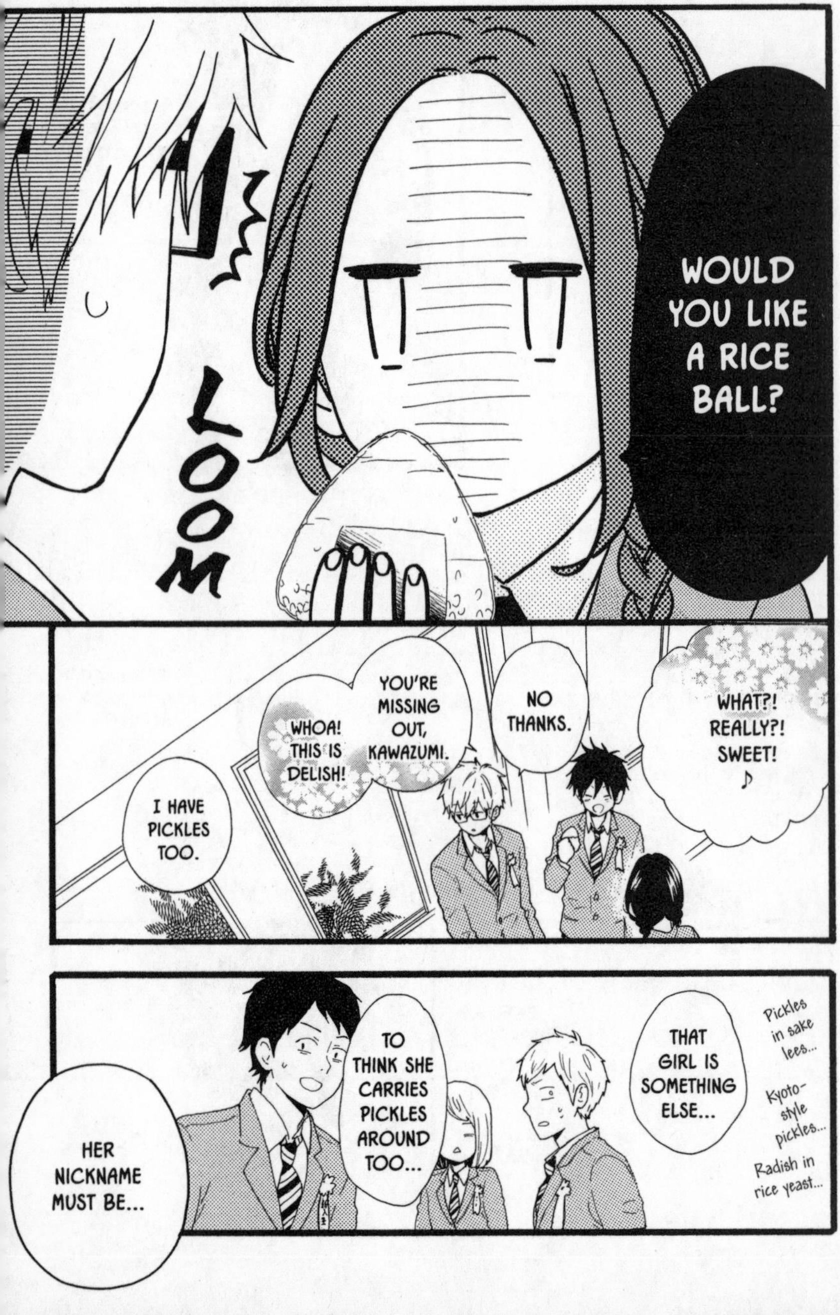
WOULD YOU LIKE A RICE BALL?
LOOM
WHAT?! REALLY?! SWEET! ♪
NO THANKS.
YOU'RE MISSING OUT, KAWAZUMI.
WHOA! THIS IS DELISH!
I HAVE PICKLES TOO.
Pickles in sake lees...
Kyoto-style pickles...
Radish in rice yeast...
THAT GIRL IS SOMETHING ELSE...
TO THINK SHE CARRIES PICKLES AROUND TOO...
HER NICKNAME MUST BE...

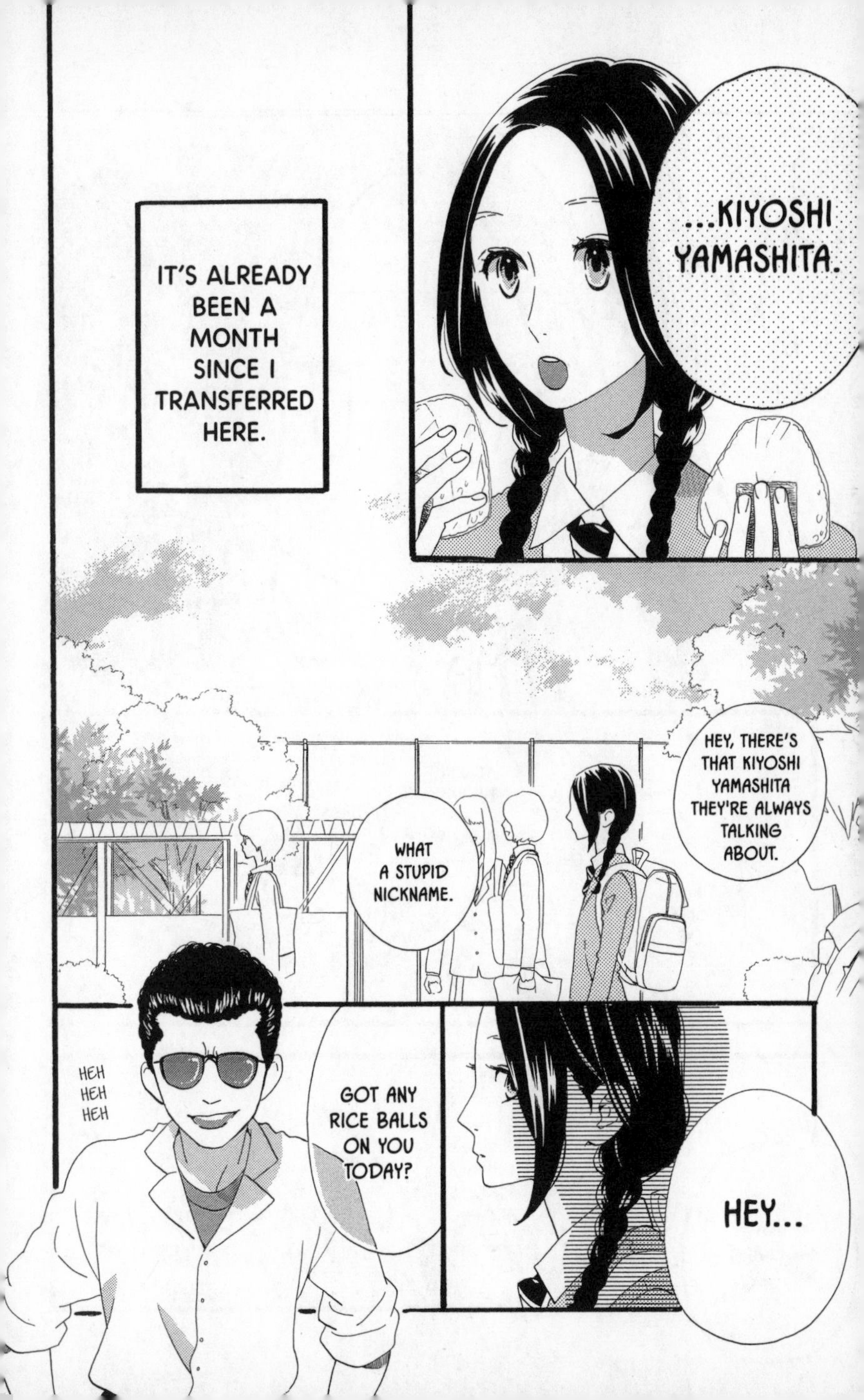
...KIYOSHI YAMASHITA.
IT'S ALREADY BEEN A MONTH SINCE I TRANSFERRED HERE.
HEY, THERE'S THAT KIYOSHI YAMASHITA THEY'RE ALWAYS TALKING ABOUT.
WHAT A STUPID NICKNAME.
HEY...
GOT ANY RICE BALLS ON YOU TODAY?
HEH HEH HEH

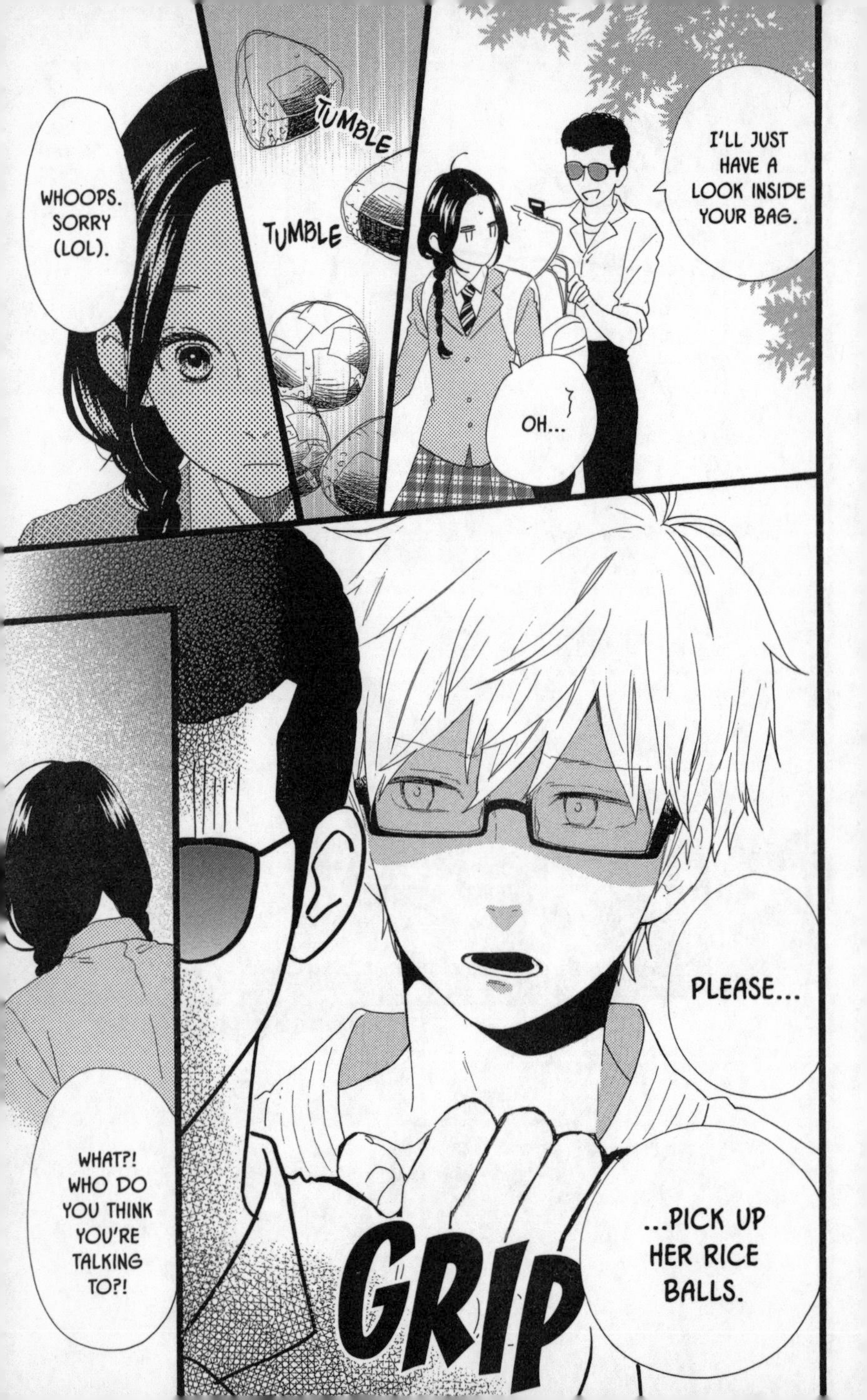
I'LL JUST HAVE A LOOK INSIDE YOUR BAG.
OH...
TUMBLE
TUMBLE
WHOOPS. SORRY (LOL).
PLEASE...
...PICK UP HER RICE BALLS.
GRIP
WHAT?! WHO DO YOU THINK YOU'RE TALKING TO?!

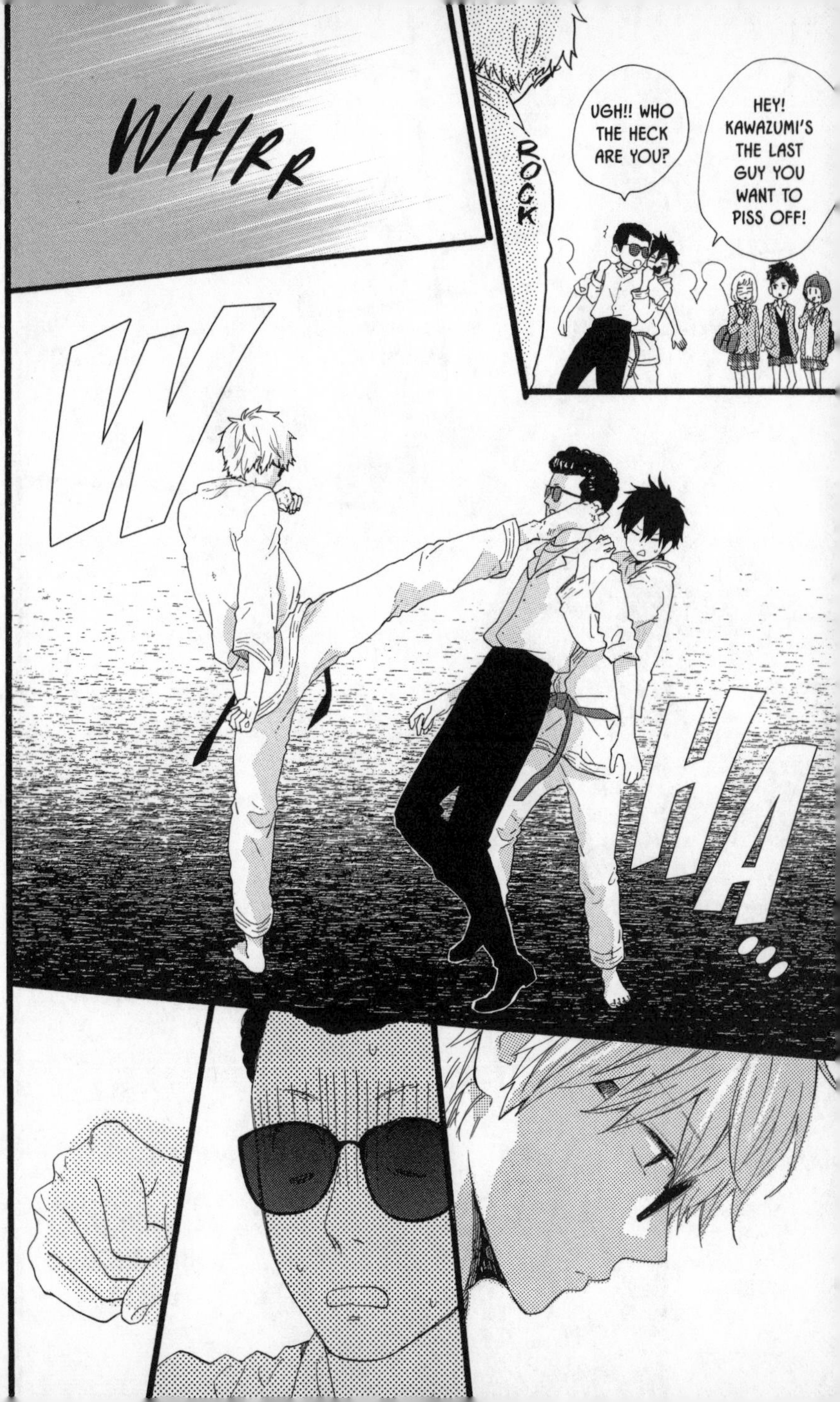
HEY! KAWAZUMI'S THE LAST GUY YOU WANT TO PISS OFF!
UGH!! WHO THE HECK ARE YOU?
ROCK
WHIRR
W HA...

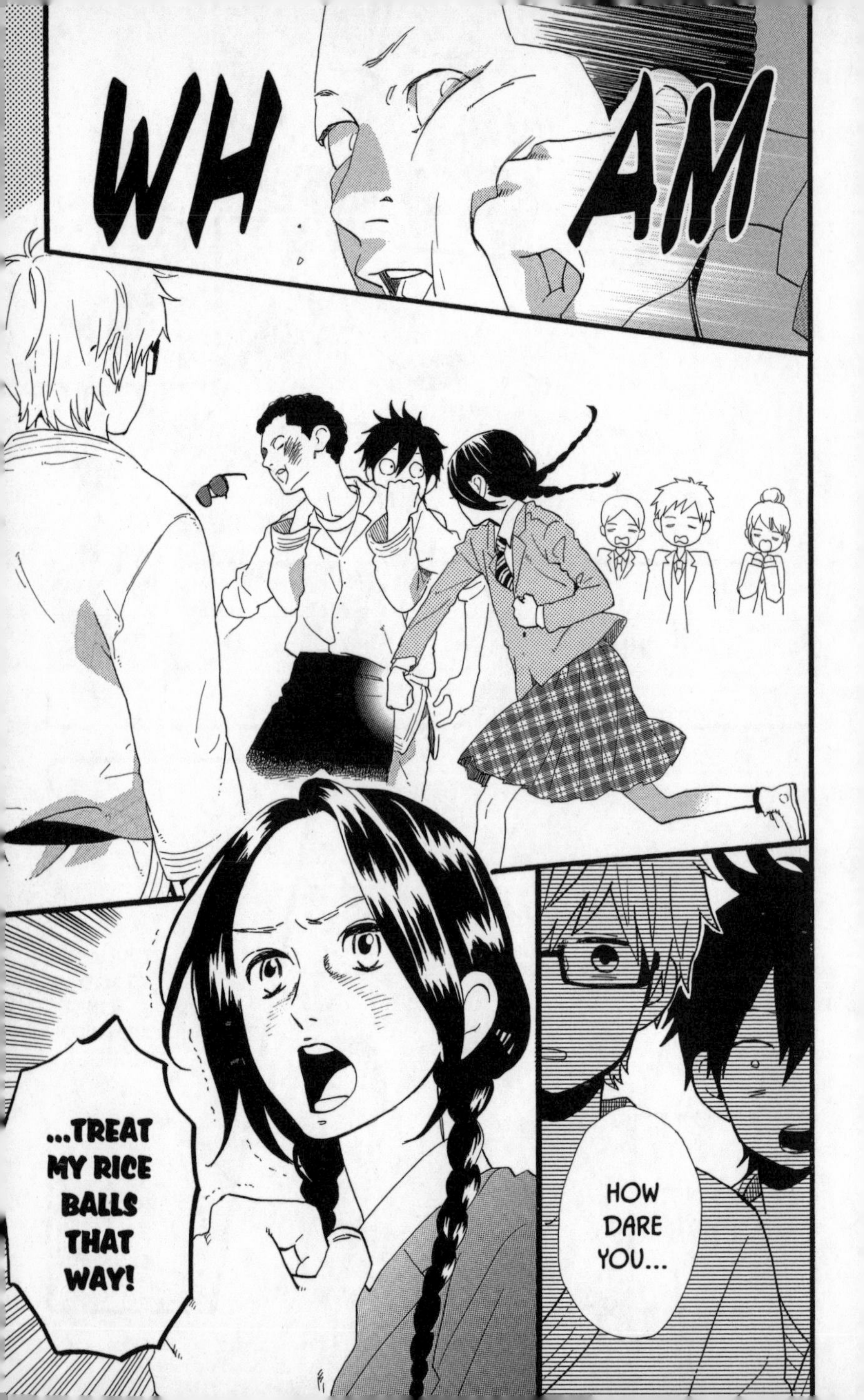
WH AM
HOW DARE YOU...
...TREAT MY RICE BALLS THAT WAY!

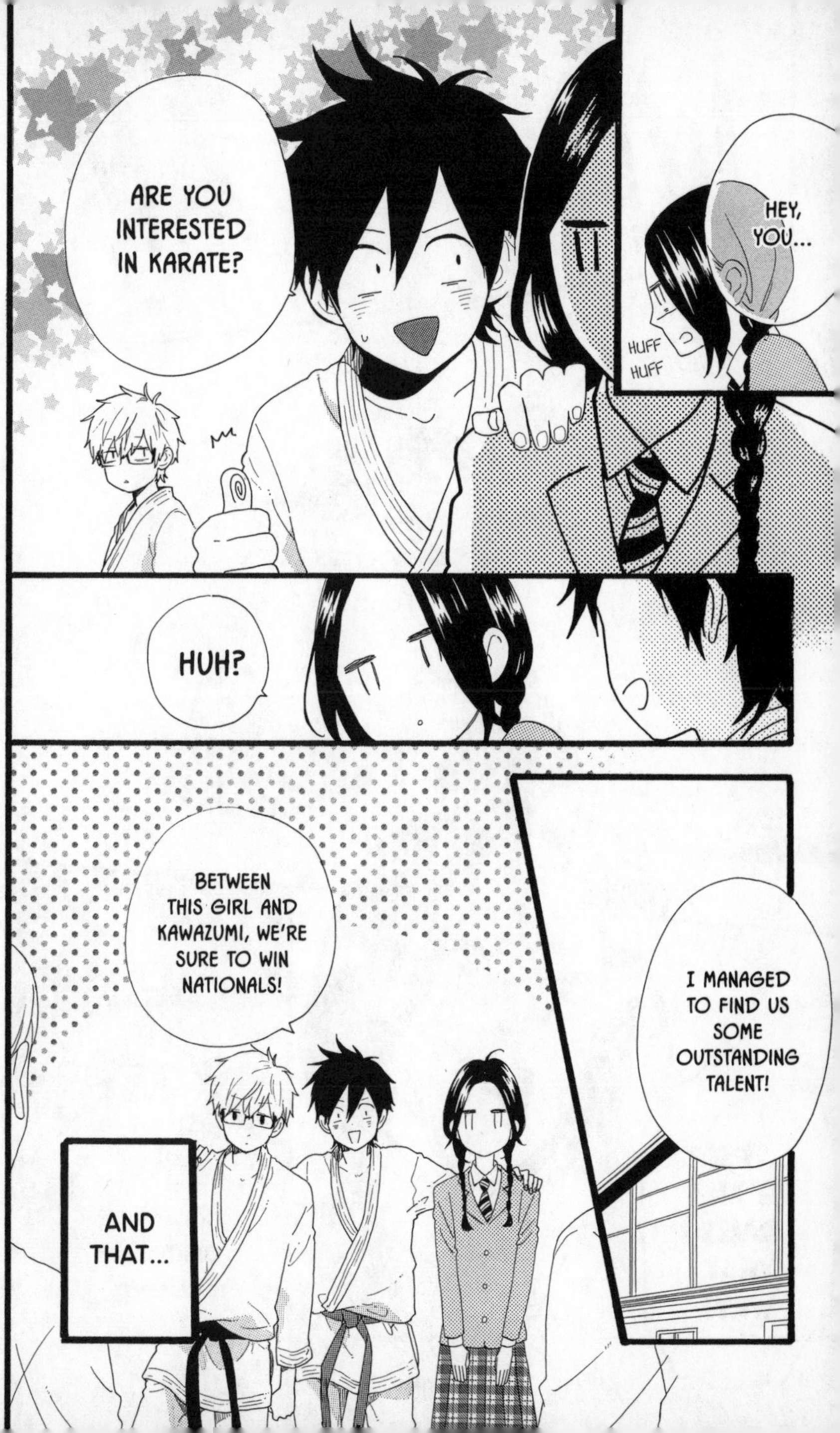
HEY, YOU...
HUFF HUFF
ARE YOU INTERESTED IN KARATE?
HUH?
I MANAGED TO FIND US SOME OUTSTANDING TALENT!
BETWEEN THIS GIRL AND KAWAZUMI, WE'RE SURE TO WIN NATIONALS!
AND THAT...

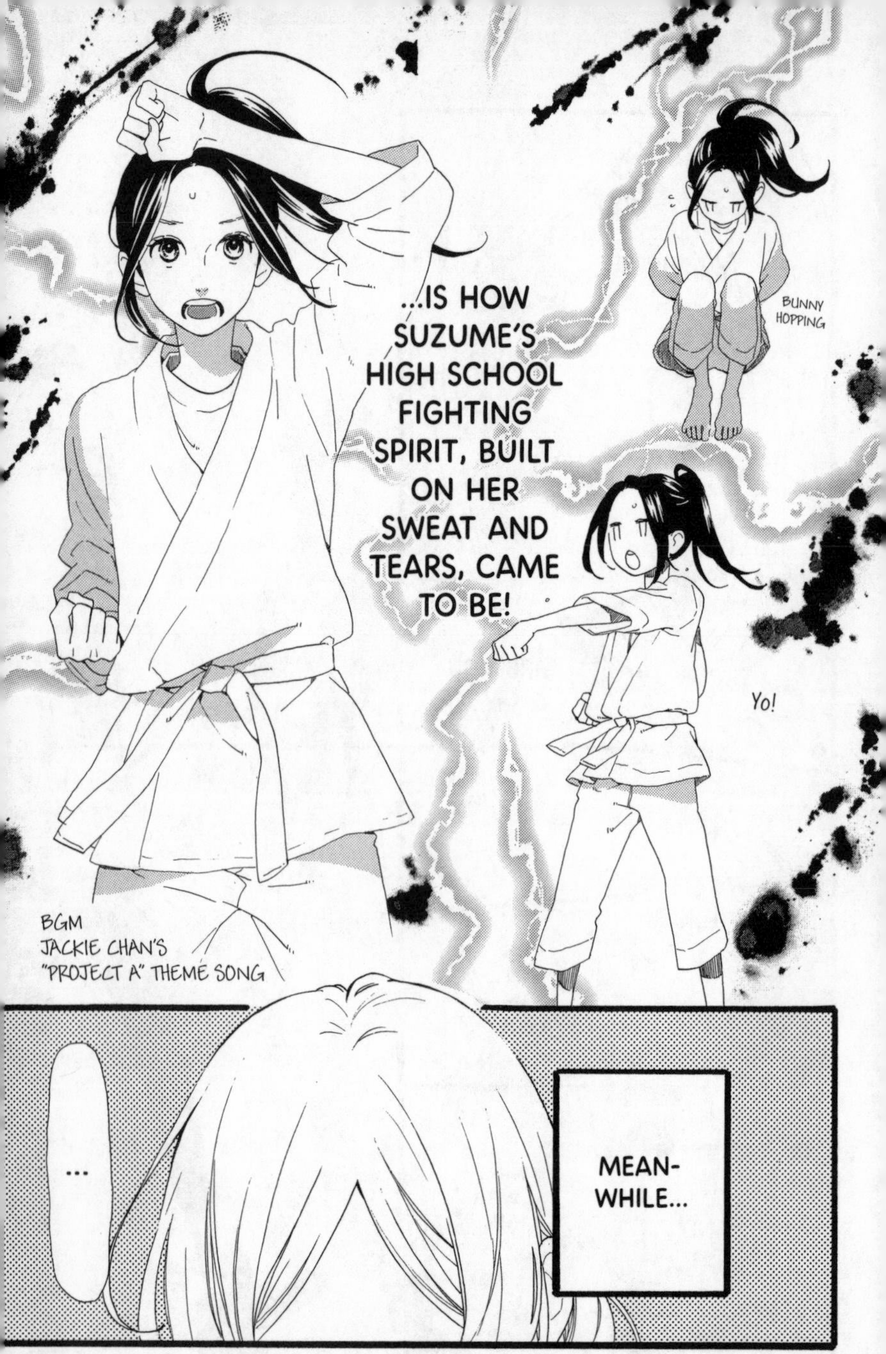
BUNNY HOPPING
...IS HOW SUZUME'S HIGH SCHOOL FIGHTING SPIRIT, BUILT ON HER SWEAT AND TEARS, CAME TO BE!
Yo!
BGM
JACKIE CHAN'S "PROJECT A" THEME SONG
MEAN-WHILE...
...

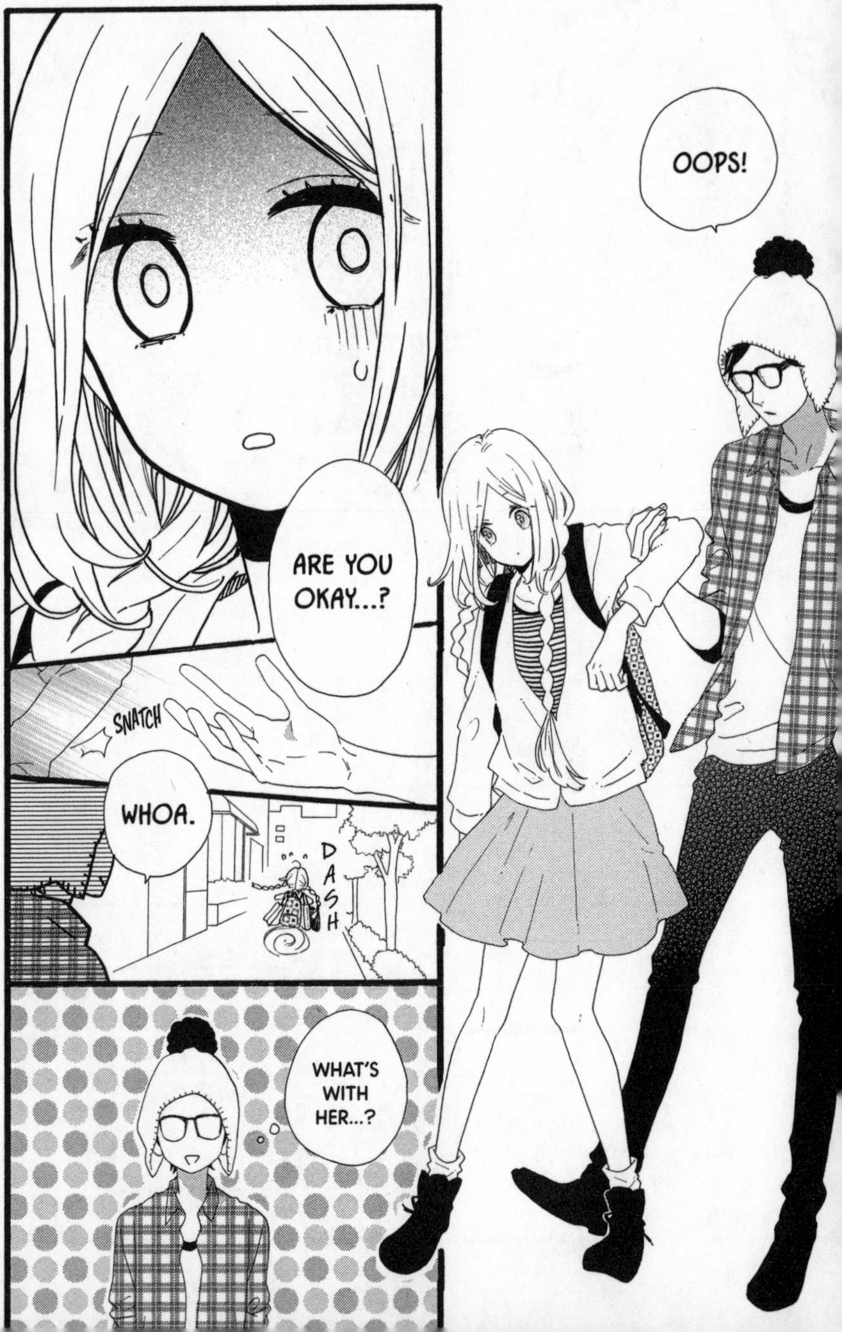
OOPS!
ARE YOU OKAY...?
SNATCH
WHOA.
DASH
WHAT'S WITH HER...?

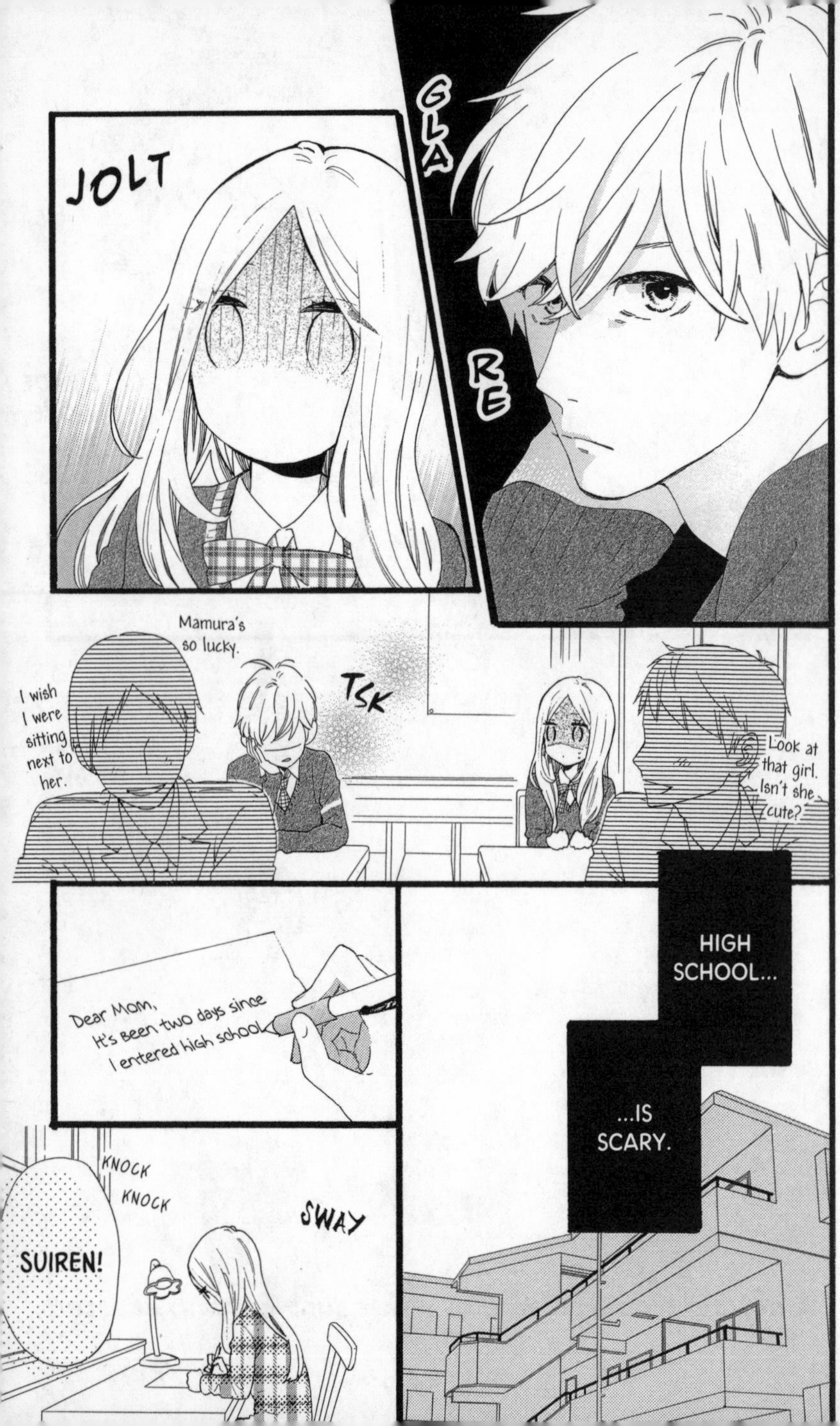
GLARE
JOLT
Look at that girl. Isn't she cute?
TSK
Mamura's so lucky.
I wish I were sitting next to her.
HIGH SCHOOL...
...IS SCARY.
Dear Mom,
It's been two days since I entered high school
SWAY
KNOCK KNOCK
SUIREN!

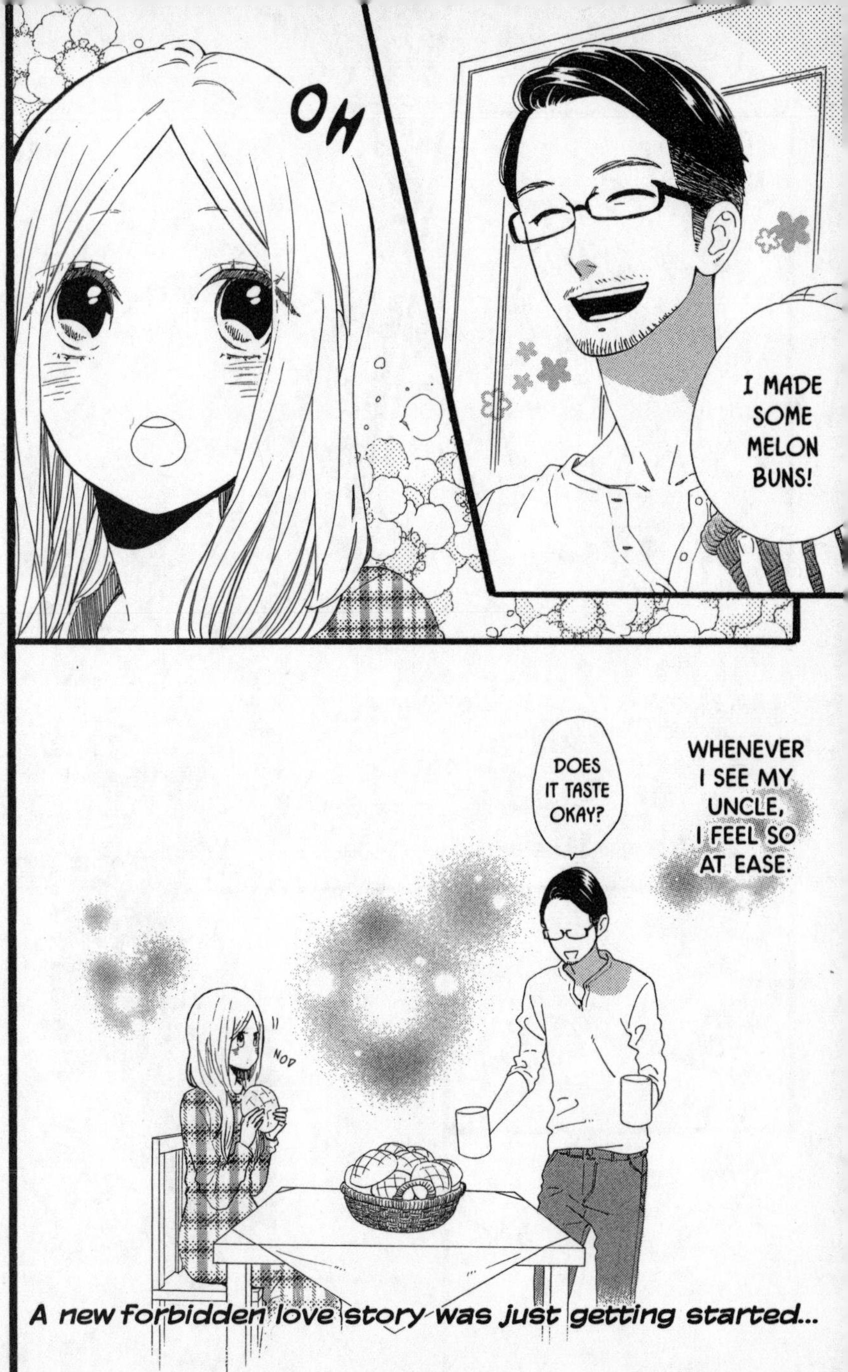
I MADE SOME MELON BUNS!
OH
WHENEVER I SEE MY UNCLE, I FEEL SO AT EASE.
DOES IT TASTE OKAY?
NOD
A new forbidden love story was just getting started...

<<The End>>

# Afterword.

And so, how did you like volume 11 of *Daytime Shooting Star*?

Huh? You say all I talked about was Suu Morishita's story?
I guess you're right! Well, let's forget about that for now.
I believe the next volume will be the last, so I hope you will stick with me to the end.

See you in the next volume!

Special Thanx
Editor U
Sachie Noborio, Nils Machimura, Sanae Kameyama
Temporary Assistants: Nachiyan (Suu Morishita), Kanon Suda
Collaborator Makiro ♡ (Morishita Team)
Designer Kawatani
The Margaret Editorial Staff
The Printer Staff
And All My Readers

See you soon.

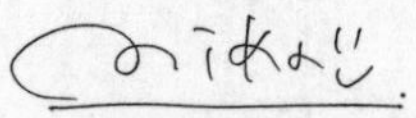

As soon as this series is done,
I plan to go to the dentist...
probably.
—Mika Yamamori

**Mika Yamamori** is from Ishikawa Prefecture in Japan. She began her professional manga career in 2006 with "Kimi no Kuchibiru kara Mahou" (The Magic from Your Lips) in *The Margaret* magazine. Her other works include *Sugars* and *Tsubaki Cho Lonely Planet*.